ITALIAN

PHRASE BOOK & DICTIONARY

CONTENTS

Hi, I'm Rick Steves.

I'm the only monolingual speaker I know who's had the nerve to design a series of European phrase books. But that's one of the things that makes them better.

You see, after more than 30 years of travel through Europe, I've learned firsthand: (1) what's essential for communication in another country; and (2) what's not. I've assembled the most important words and phrases in a logical, no-frills format, and I've worked with native Europeans and seasoned travelers to give you the simplest, clearest translation possible.

But this book is more than just a pocket translator. The words and phrases have been carefully selected to help you have a smarter, smoother trip in Italy. The key to getting more out of every travel dollar is to get closer to the local people, and to rely less on entertainment, restaurants, and hotels that cater only to foreign tourists. This book will not only help you order a meal at a locals-only Venetian restaurant—but it will also help you talk with the family who runs the place...about their kids, travel dreams, and favorite flavors of ***gelati.*** Long after your memories of museums and Roman ruins have faded, you'll still treasure the personal encounters you had with your new Italian friends.

While I've provided plenty of phrases, you'll find it as effective to use even just a word or two to convey your meaning, and rely on context, gestures, and smiles to help you out. You could walk into a post office and struggle with the Italian phrase for "I would like to buy stamps for two postcards to the United States, please." Or you can walk up to the stamp counter, smile, show the clerk your postcards, and say "America, ***per favore*** (please)." And...presto! You've got stamps. (For more advice, see the Tips for Hurdling the Language Barrier chapter on page 423.)

To get the most out of this book, take the time to internalize and put into practice my Italian pronunciation tips. But don't worry too much about memorizing grammatical rules, like the gender of a noun—forget about sex, and communicate!

This book has a nifty menu decoder and a handy dictionary. You'll also find tongue twisters, international words, telephone tips, and two handy "cheat sheets." Tear out the sheets and slip them into your pocket, so you can easily memorize key phrases during otherwise idle moments. A good phrase book should help you enjoy your travel experience—not just survive it—so I've added a healthy dose of humor. And as you prepare for your trip, you may want to read the latest edition of one of my many guidebooks on destinations in Italy.

Italians are more social and communal than most Europeans. And because they're so outgoing and their language is so fun, Italians are a pleasure to communicate with. Be melodramatic and talk with your ***mani*** (hands). Hear the melody; get into the flow. Italians want to connect, and they try harder than any other Europeans. Play with them. Even in non-touristy towns, where English is rare and Italian is the norm, showing a little warmth lets you hop right over the language barrier.

My goal is to help you become a more confident, extroverted traveler. If this phrase book helps make that happen, or if you have suggestions for making it better, I'd love to hear from you at rick@ricksteves.com.

Buon viaggio! Happy travels!

Rick Steves

GETTING STARTED

User-friendly Italian is easy to get the hang of. Some Italian words are so familiar, you'd think they were English. If you can say ***pizza, lasagna,*** and ***spaghetti,*** you can speak Italian.

Italian pronunciation differs from English in some key ways:

C usually sounds like C in cat.
  But C followed by E or I sounds like CH in chance.
CH sounds like C in cat.
G usually sounds like G in get.
  But G followed by E or I sounds like G in gentle.
GH sounds like G in spaghetti.
GLI sounds like LI (pronounced lee) in million. The G is silent.
GN sounds like GN in lasagna.
H is never pronounced.
I sounds like EE in seed.
R is rolled as in brrravo!
SC usually sounds like SK in skip.
  But SC followed by E or I sounds like SH in shape.
Z usually sounds like TS in hits, and sometimes like the sound of DZ in kids.

You can communicate a lot with only a few key Italian words: ***prego, va bene, così, questo/quello,*** and ***vorrei.***

Prego (**preh**-goh) is the all-purpose polite word. It can mean "May I help you?" or "Here you go" or "You're welcome" or "After you" (when someone's holding the door for you).

Va bene (vah **beh**-nay), meaning "It's good," is used constantly. It's the all-purpose "OK" that you'll hear a hundred times a day.

Così (koh-**zee**) basically means "like this." It can be handy, for instance, when ordering food (to show them how much of the eggplant you want on your ***antipasti*** plate).

Questo (**kweh**-stoh, "this") and ***quello*** (**kweh**-loh, "that") combine conveniently with gestures. Just point to what you want and say ***quello.***

Vorrei (voh-**reh**-ee) is an easy way to say "I would like." It's the standard and polite way to make a request in Italian. ***Vorrei un caffè, per favore*** (I would like a coffee, please).

A few language tips will help you learn some Italian and get the most out of this book. For instance, have you ever noticed that most Italian words end in a vowel? It's ***o*** if the word is masculine and ***a*** if it's feminine. So, a baby boy is a ***bambino*** and a baby girl is a ***bambina***. A man is ***generoso*** (generous), a woman is ***generosa***. In this book, we sometimes show gender-bender words like this: ***generoso[a]***.

Adjective endings agree with the noun. It's ***cara amica*** (a dear female friend) and ***caro amico*** (a dear male friend). Sometimes the adjective comes after the noun, as in ***vino rosso*** (red wine). Adjectives and nouns ending in ***e*** don't change with the gender, such as ***gentile*** (kind) or ***cantante*** (singer)—the same word applies to either sex.

Plurals are formed by changing the final letter of the noun: ***a*** becomes ***e***, and ***o*** becomes ***i***. So it's one ***pizza*** and two ***pizze***, and one ***cappuccino*** and two ***cappuccini***. If you're describing any group of people that includes at least one male, the adjective should end with ***i***. But if the group is female, the adjective ends with ***e***. A handsome man is ***bello*** and an attractive group of men (or men and women) is ***belli***. A beautiful woman is ***bella*** and a bevy of beauties is ***belle***.

The key to Italian inflection is to remember this simple rule: Most Italian words have their accent on the second-to-last syllable. To override this rule, Italians sometimes insert an accent: ***città*** (city) is pronounced chee-**tah**.

Italians are animated and even dramatic. You may think two Italians are arguing when in reality they're agreeing enthusiastically. Be confident and have fun communicating. The Italians really do want to understand you, and are forgiving of a Yankee-fied version of their language.

Here's a quick guide to the phonetics used in this book:

ah	like A in father
ay	like AY in play
eh	like E in let
ee	like EE in seed
ehr	sounds like "air"
ew	like EW in few
g	like G in go
ī	like I in light
oh	like O in note

oo	like OO in too
ow	like OW in now
s	like S in sun
ts	like TS in hits

ITALIAN BASICS

Be creative! You can combine the phrases in this chapter to say "Two, please," or "No, thank you," or "Open tomorrow?" "Please" is a magic word in any language. If you know the word for what you want, such as the bill, simply say ***Il conto, per favore*** (The bill, please).

HELLOS AND GOODBYES

Pleasantries

Hello.	Buongiorno. bwohn-**jor**-noh
Do you speak English?	Parla inglese? **par**-lah een-**gleh**-zay
Yes. / No.	Si. / No. see / noh
I don't speak Italian.	Non parlo l'italiano. nohn **par**-loh lee-tah-lee-**ah**-noh
I'm sorry.	Mi dispiace. mee dee-spee-**ah**-chay
Please.	Per favore. pehr fah-**voh**-ray
Thank you (very much).	Grazie (mille). **graht**-see-ay (**mee**-lay)
Excuse me. (to pass)	Permesso. pehr-**meh**-soh
Excuse me. (to get attention)	Mi scusi. mee **skoo**-zee
OK?	Va bene? vah **beh**-nay
OK. (Things are going well.)	Va bene. vah **beh**-nay
Good.	Bene. **beh**-nay
Great.	Benissimo. beh-**nee**-see-moh
Excellent.	Perfetto. pehr-**feh**-toh
You are very kind.	Lei è molto gentile. **leh**-ee eh **mohl**-toh jehn-**tee**-lay
It's (not) a problem.	(Non) c'è problema. (nohn) cheh proh-**bleh**-mah
It doesn't matter.	Non importa. nohn eem-**por**-tah

You're welcome.	Prego.	**preh**-goh
Goodbye!	Arrivederci!	ah-ree-veh-**dehr**-chee

Per favore is the basic "please." You might hear locals say ***per piacere*** (for my pleasure), which is used to sweetly ask for a favor. ***Per favore*** often comes at the beginning of a request, while ***per piacere*** normally goes at the end.

Grazie, an important word that means "thank you," often sounds like **graht**-see; Italians barely pronounce the final syllable: **graht**-see(ay).

Meeting and Greeting

Good morning. / Good day.	Buongiorno.	bwohn-**jor**-noh
Good afternoon.	Buon pomeriggio.	bwohn poh-meh-**ree**-joh
Good evening.	Buona sera.	**bwoh**-nah **seh**-rah
Good night.	Buona notte.	**bwoh**-nah **noh**-tay
Hi. / Bye. (informal)	Ciao.	chow
Hello. (informal)	Salve.	**sahl**-vay
Welcome.	Benvenuto.	behn-veh-**noo**-toh
Mr.	Signore	seen-**yoh**-ray
Mrs.	Signora	seen-**yoh**-rah
Miss	Signorina	seen-yoh-**ree**-nah
My name is ____.	Mi chiamo ____.	mee kee-**ah**-moh ____
What's your name?	Come si chiama?	**koh**-may see kee-**ah**-mah
Pleased to meet you.	Piacere.	pee-ah-**cheh**-ray
How are you?	Come sta?	**koh**-may stah
Very well, thank you.	Molto bene, grazie.	**mohl**-toh **beh**-nay **graht**-see-ay
Fine, thanks.	Bene, grazie.	**beh**-nay **graht**-see-ay

And you?	E Lei? ay **leh**-ee
Where are you from?	Di dove É? dee **doh**-vay eh
I am from ____.	Vengo da ____. **vehn**-goh dah ____
I am / We are...	Sono / Siamo... **soh**-noh / see-**ah**-moh
Are you...?	Lei É...? **leh**-ee eh
...on vacation	...in vacanza een vah-**kahnt**-sah
...on business	...qui per lavoro kwee pehr lah-**voh**-roh

People use the greeting ***buongiorno*** (good morning / good day) before noon. After lunch, some people shift to ***buon pomeriggio*** (good afternoon), but many stick with ***buongiorno*** until mid-afternoon, when they switch to ***buona sera*** (good afternoon / evening). Some shorten it to a very casual ***sera***. At bedtime, say ***buona notte*** (good night). Informal greetings (***ciao*** and ***salve***) are the same all day long.

In Italy, saying hello is important. When entering a shop, always offer a ***buongiorno*** or ***buona sera*** before getting down to business.

Moving On

I'm going to ____.	Vado a ____. **vah**-doh ah ____
How do I go to ____?	Come arrivo a ____? **koh**-may ah-**ree**-voh ah ____
Let's go.	Andiamo. ahn-dee-**ah**-moh
See you later.	A più tardi. ah pew **tar**-dee
See you tomorrow!	A domani! ah doh-**mah**-nee
So long! (informal)	Ci vediamo! chee veh-dee-**ah**-moh
Goodbye.	Arrivederci. ah-ree-veh-**dehr**-chee
Good luck!	Buona fortuna! **bwoh**-nah for-**too**-nah
Happy travels!	Buon viaggio! bwohn vee-**ah**-joh

STRUGGLING WITH ITALIAN

Who Speaks What?

Italian	l'italiano lee-tah-lee-**ah**-noh
English	inglese een-**gleh**-zay
Do you speak English?	Parla inglese? **par**-lah een-**gleh**-zay
A teeny weeny bit?	Nemmeno un pochino? neh-**meh**-noh oon poh-**kee**-noh
Please speak English.	Parli inglese, per favore. **par** lee een **gleh**-zay pehr fah-**voh**-ray
Speak slowly, please.	Parli lentamente, per favore. **par**-lee lehn-tah-**mehn**-tay pehr fah-**voh**-ray
Repeat?	Ripeta? ree-**peh**-tah
I understand.	Capisco. kah-**pees**-koh
I don't understand.	Non capisco. nohn kah-**pees**-koh
Do you understand?	Capisce? kah-**pee**-shay
You speak English well.	Lei parla bene l'inglese. **leh**-ee **par**-lah **beh**-nay leen-**gleh**-zay
Does somebody here speak English?	C'è qualcuno qui che parla inglese? cheh kwal-**koo**-noh kwee kay **par**-lah een-**gleh**-zay
I don't speak Italian.	Non parlo l'italiano. nohn **par**-loh lee-tah-lee-**ah**-noh
I speak a little Italian.	Parlo un po' d'italiano. **par**-loh oon poh dee-tah-lee-**ah**-noh
What does this mean?	Cosa significa? **koh**-zah seen-**yee**-fee-kah
How do you say this in Italian?	Come si dice in italiano? **koh**-may see **dee**-chay een ee-tah-lee-**ah**-noh
Write it for me?	Me lo scrive? may loh **skree**-vay

Very Italian Expressions

Prego. **preh**-goh	You're welcome. / Please. / After you. / All right. / Can I help you?
Pronto. **prohn**-toh	Hello. (answering phone) / Ready. (other situations)
Ecco. **eh**-koh	Here it is.
Certo. **chehr**-toh	Sure.
Dica. **dee**-kah	Tell me.
Allora... ah-**loh**-rah	Well... (like our "uh" before a sentence)
Senta. **sehn**-tah	Listen.
Va bene. vah **beh**-nay	OK.
Va tutto bene. vah **too**-toh **beh**-nay	Everything's fine.
Basta. **bah**-stah	That's enough.
È tutto. eh **too**-toh	That's all.
Altro? **ahl**-troh	Do you need anything else?
la dolce vita lah **dohl**-chay **vee**-tah	the sweet life
il dolce far niente eel **dohl**-chay far nee-**ehn**-tay	the sweetness of doing nothing
Mi sono cadute le braccia! mee **soh**-noh kah-**doo**-tay lay **brah**-chah	I throw my arms down!
bello **beh**-loh	beautiful / very

If Italians get frustrated, they might say ***Mi sono cadute le braccia!*** (I throw my arms down!)—sometimes literally thrusting their arms toward the floor in an "I give up" gesture.

Italians sometimes use the suffix ***issimo*** to intensify the word. If something is good, it's ***bravo,*** but if it's very good, it's ***bravissimo.***

REQUESTS

The Essentials

Can you help me?	Può aiutarmi? pwoh ah-yoo-**tar**-mee
Do you have ____?	Avete ____? ah-**veh**-tay ____
I'd like / We'd like...	Vorrei / Vorremmo... voh-**reh**-ee / voh-**reh**-moh
...this / that.	...questo / quello. **kweh**-stoh / **kweh**-loh
How much does it cost?	Quanto costa? **kwahn**-toh **koh**-stah
Is it free?	È gratis? eh **grah**-tees
Is it included?	È incluso? eh een-**kloo**-zoh
Is it possible?	È possibile? eh poh-**see**-bee-lay
Yes or no?	Si o no? see oh noh
Where is the toilet?	Dov'è la toilette? doh-**veh** lah twah-**leh**-tay
men	uomini / signori **woh**-mee-nee / seen-**yoh**-ree
women	donne / signore **doh**-nay / seen-**yoh**-ray

To prompt a simple answer, ask ***Si o no?*** (Yes or no?). To turn a word or sentence into a question, ask it in a questioning tone. An easy way to ask "Where is the toilet?" is to say ***Toilette?***

Where?

Where?	Dove? **doh**-vay
Where is...?	Dov'è...? doh-**veh**
...the tourist information office	...l'ufficio informazioni loo-**fee**-choh een-for-maht-see-**oh**-nee
...the train station	...la stazione lah staht-see-**oh**-nay
...a cash machine	...un bancomat oon **bahn**-koh-maht
Where can I buy ____?	Dove posso comprare ____? **doh**-vay **poh**-soh kohm-**prah**-ray ____
Where can I find ____?	Dove posso trovare ____? **doh**-vay **poh**-soh troh-**vah**-ray ____

Italian makes it easy if you're looking for a ***farmacia, hotel, ristorante,*** or ***supermercato.***

How Much?

How much (does it cost)?	Quanto (costa)? **kwahn**-toh (**koh**-stah)
Write it for me?	Me lo scrive? may loh **skree**-vay
I'd like...	Vorrei... voh-**reh**-ee
...a ticket.	...un biglietto. oon beel-**yeh**-toh
...the bill.	...il conto. eel **kohn**-toh
This much. (gesturing)	Così. koh-**zee**
More. / Less.	Di più. / Di meno. dee pew / dee **meh**-noh
Too much.	Troppo. **troh**-poh

When?

When?	Quando? **kwahn**-doh
What time is it?	Che ora sono? kay **oh**-rah **soh**-noh

At what time?	A che ora? ah kay **oh**-rah
open / closed	aperto / chiuso ah-**pehr**-toh / kee-**oo**-zoh
What time does this open / close?	A che ora apre / chiude? ah kay **oh**-rah **ah**-pray / kee-**oo**-day
Is this open daily?	È aperto tutti i giorni? eh ah-**pehr**-toh **too**-tee ee **jor**-nee
What day is this closed?	Che giorno chiudete? kay **jor**-noh kee-oo-**deh**-tay
On time?	In orario? een oh-**rah**-ree-oh
Late?	In ritardo? een ree-**tar**-doh
Just a moment.	Un momento. oon moh-**mehn**-toh
now / soon / later	adesso / presto / più tardi ah-**deh**-soh / **preh**-stoh / pew **tar**-dee
today / tomorrow	oggi / domani **oh**-jee / doh-**mah**-nee

For tips on telling time, see "Time and Dates" on page 31.

How Long?

How long does it take?	Quanto ci vuole? **kwahn**-toh chee **vwoh**-lay
How many minutes?	Quanti minuti? **kwahn**-tee mee-**noo**-tee
How many hours?	Quante ore? **kwahn**-tay **oh**-ray
How far?	Quanto dista? **kwahn**-toh **dee**-stah

Just Ask

Why?	Perché? pehr-**keh**
Why not?	Perché no? pehr-**keh** noh
Is it necessary?	È necessario? eh neh-cheh-**sah**-ree-oh
Can I have ____?	Posso avere ____? **poh**-soh ah-**veh**-ray

Can I / Can we...?	Posso / Possiamo...? **poh**-soh / poh-see-**ah**-moh
...borrow that for a moment	...prenderlo in prestito per un momento prehn-**dehr**-loh een **preh**-stee-toh pehr oon moh-**mehn**-toh
...use the toilet	...usare la toilette oo-**zah**-ray lah twah-**leh**-tay
Next? (in line)	Il prossimo? eel **proh**-see-moh
The last? (in line)	L'ultimo? **lool**-tee-moh
My turn?	Tocca me? **toh**-kah may
What? (didn't hear)	Che cosa? kay **koh**-zah
What is this / that?	Che cos'è questo / quello? kay koh-**zeh** **kweh**-stoh / **kweh**-loh
What's going on?	Cosa succede? **koh**-zah soo-**cheh**-day

A versatile word is ***Posso?*** (Can I?), combined with a gesture. Say it to someone when you point to a table (to mean "Can I sit here?"), or to your camera ("Can I take a picture?"), or to your combo-ticket ("Is this sight covered by this ticket?"). When ordering a menu item, you can say ***Posso avere ____?*** (Can I have ____?). At a café, you'd say ***Posso avere un caffè?*** (Can I have a coffee?)

SIMPLY IMPORTANT WORDS

Numbers

0	zero **zeh**-roh
1	uno **oo**-noh
2	due **doo**-ay
3	tre tray
4	quattro **kwah**-troh
5	cinque **cheen**-kway
6	sei **seh**-ee
7	sette **seh**-tay

8	otto **oh**-toh
9	nove **noh**-vay
10	dieci dee-**eh**-chee
11	undici **oon**-dee-chee
12	dodici **doh**-dee-chee
13	tredici **treh**-dee-chee
14	quattordici kwah-**tor**-dee-chee
15	quindici **kween**-dee-chee
16	sedici **seh**-dee-chee
17	diciassette dee-chah-**seh**-tay
18	diciotto dee-**choh**-toh
19	diciannove dee-chah-**noh**-vay
20	venti **vehn**-tee

You'll find more to count on in the "Numbers" section (page 24).

The Alphabet

If you're spelling your name over the phone, you can use the nouns in the third column to help make yourself understood. I'd say my name as: ***R…Rovigo, I…Imola, C…Como, K…Kashmir.*** (The letters *j, k, w, x,* and *y* aren't officially part of the Italian alphabet and are usually found only in words of foreign origin.)

a	ah	Ancona	ahn-**koh**-nah
b	bee	Bologna	boh-**lohn**-yah
c	chee	Como	**koh**-moh
d	dee	Domodossola	doh-moh-**doh**-soh-lah
e	ay	Empoli	**ehm**-poh-lee
f	**ehf**-ay	Firenze	fee-**rehnt**-say
g	jee	Genova	**jeh**-noh-vah
h	**ah**-kah	Hotel	oh-**tehl**
i	ee	Imola	**ee**-moh-lah

j	ee **loon**-gah	Jupiter	**joo**-pee-tehr
k	**kah**-pah	Kashmir	**kahs**-meer
l	**ehl**-ay	Livorno	lee-**vor**-noh
m	**ehm**-ay	Milano	mee-**lah**-noh
n	**ehn**-ay	Napoli	**nah**-poh-lee
o	oh	Otranto	oh-**trahn**-toh
p	pee	Palermo	pah-**lehr**-moh
q	koo	quaranta	kwah-**rahn**-tah
r	**ehr**-ay	Rovigo	roh-**vee**-goh
s	**ehs**-ay	Savona	sah-**voh**-nah
t	tee	Treviso	treh-**vee**-zoh
u	oo	Urbino	oor-**bee**-noh
v	vee	Venezia	veh-**neht**-see-ah
w	**dohp**-yoh-voo	Wi-Fi	**wee**-fee
x	eeks	xilofono	zee-**loh**-foh-noh
y	**eep**-see-lohn	yogurt	**yoh**-goort
z	**zeht**-ah	Zara	**tsah**-rah

Days and Months

Sunday	domenica doh-**meh**-nee-kah
Monday	lunedì loo-neh-**dee**
Tuesday	martedì mar-teh-**dee**
Wednesday	mercoledì mehr-koh-leh-**dee**
Thursday	giovedì joh-veh-**dee**
Friday	venerdì veh-nehr-**dee**
Saturday	sabato **sah**-bah-toh
January	gennaio jeh-**nah**-yoh
February	febbraio feh-**brah**-yoh
March	marzo **mart**-soh
April	aprile ah-**pree**-lay

May	maggio **mah**-joh
June	giugno **joon**-yoh
July	luglio **lool**-yoh
August	agosto ah-**goh**-stoh
September	settembre seh-**tehm**-bray
October	ottobre oh-**toh**-bray
November	novembre noh-**vehm**-bray
December	dicembre dee-**chehm**-bray

Big Little Words

I	io **ee**-oh
you (formal)	Lei **leh**-ee
you (informal)	tu too
we	noi **noh**-ee
he	lui **loo**-ee
she	lei **leh**-ee
it	esso / essa **eh**-soh / **eh**-sah
they	loro **loh**-roh
and	e ay
at	a ah
because	perché pehr-**keh**
but	ma mah
by (train, car, etc.)	in een
for	per pehr
from	da dah
here	qui kwee
if	se say
in	in een
not	non nohn
now	adesso ah-**deh**-soh

of	di dee
only	solo **soh**-loh
or	o oh
out	fuori foo-**oh**-ree
this	questo **kweh**-stoh
that	quello **kweh**-loh
there	lì lee
to	a ah
too	anche **ahn**-kay
very	molto **mohl**-toh

Opposites

good / bad	buono / cattivo **bwoh**-noh / kah-**tee**-voh
best / worst	il migliore / il peggiore eel meel-**yoh**-ray / eel peh-**joh**-ray
a little / a lot	poco / tanto **poh**-koh / **tahn**-toh
more / less	più / meno pew / **meh**-noh
cheap / expensive	economico / caro eh-koh-**noh**-mee-koh / **kah**-roh
big / small	grande / piccolo **grahn**-day / **pee**-koh-loh
hot / cold	caldo / freddo **kahl**-doh / **freh**-doh
warm / cool	caldo / fresco **kahl**-doh / **freh**-skoh
open / closed	aperto / chiuso ah-**pehr**-toh / kee-**oo**-zoh
entrance / exit	entrata / uscita ehn-**trah**-tah / oo-**shee**-tah
push / pull	spingere / tirare **speen**-jeh-ray / tee-**rah**-ray
arrive / depart	arrivare / partire ah-ree-**vah**-ray / par-**tee**-ray
early / late	presto / tardi **preh**-stoh / **tar**-dee

soon / later	presto / più tardi **preh**-stoh / pew **tar**-dee
fast / slow	veloce / lento veh-**loh**-chay / **lehn**-toh
here / there	qui / lì kwee / lee
near / far	vicino / lontano vee-**chee**-noh / lohn-**tah**-noh
inside / outside	dentro / fuori **dehn**-troh / foo-**oh**-ree
mine / yours	mio / suo **mee**-oh / **soo**-oh
this / that	questo / quello **kweh**-stoh / **kweh**-loh
easy / difficult	facile / difficile **fah**-chee-lay / dee-**fee**-chee-lay
left / right	sinistra / destra see-**nee**-strah / **deh**-strah
up / down	su / giù soo / joo
above / below	sopra / sotto **soh**-prah / **soh**-toh
young / old	giovane / anziano **joh**-vah-nay / ahnt-see-**ah**-noh
new / old	nuovo / vecchio **nwoh**-voh / **veh**-kee-oh
heavy / light	pesante / leggero peh-**zahn**-tay / leh-**jeh**-roh
dark / light	scuro / chiaro **skoo**-roh / kee-**ah**-roh
happy / sad	felice / triste fee-**lee**-chay / **tree**-stay
beautiful / ugly	bello[a] / brutto[a] **beh**-loh / **broo**-toh
nice / mean	carino[a] / cattivo[a] kah-**ree**-noh / kah-**tee**-voh
smart / stupid	intelligente / stupido[a] een-tehl-ee-**jehn**-tay / **stoo**-pee-doh
vacant / occupied	libero / occupato **lee**-beh-roh / oh-koo-**pah**-toh
with / without	con / senza kohn / **sehnt**-sah

SIGN LANGUAGE

Here are some signs you may see in your travels.

Acqua (non) potabile	Water (not) drinkable
Affittasi / In affitto	For rent or for hire
Allarme antincendio	Fire alarm
All'interno...	We have...
Aperto (da ____ a ____)	Open (from ____ to ____)
Apertura: ore ____	Opens at ____
Area pedonale	Pedestrian zone
Area videosorvegliata	Area under video surveillance
Arrivi	Arrivals
Attendere (qui)	Wait (here)
Attenti al gradino	Watch your step
Attenzione	Caution
Attraversamento bambini	School crossing
Azienda per turismo (A.P.T.)	Tourist information office
Bagno / Servizi / Toilette / WC	Toilet
Biglietteria	Ticket office
Cagnaccio	Mean dog
Camere libere	Vacancy
Cassa / Cassa biglietti	Cashier / Ticket desk
Centro	Town center
Chiamata d'emergenza	Emergency call
Chiuso (per ferie / per restauro)	Closed (for vacation / for restoration)
Chiusura: ore ____	Closes at ____
Completo	No vacancy
Convalidare qui	Validate here
Disponibili qui	Available here
Donne	Women
Emergenza	Emergency
Entrata	Entrance
Entrata libera	Free admission
Entrata vietata	No entry
Fuori servizio	Out of service
In caso di emergenza	In case of emergency
Ingresso	Entrance

Inizio fila	Line starts here
Noleggio	Rental shop
Non dà resto	No change given
Non disturbare	Do not disturb
Non toccare	Do not touch
Non usare in caso di emergenza	Do not use in case of emergency
Occupato	Occupied
Orario	Timetable
Orario d'apertura / Orario d'ingresso	Opening times
Parcheggio vietato	No parking
Partenze	Departures
Passo carrabile	Keep clear for traffic (no parking)
Pausa pranzo	Midday break / Lunch break
Pericolo	Danger
Piano	Floor / Level (of a building)
Premere qui / Premere il pulsante	Press here / Press the button (to change light at crosswalk)
Prendere il numero	Take a number
Prenotato	Reserved
Proibito	Prohibited
Prossima fermata	Next stop
Sciopero	Strike
Senso unico	One-way street
Servizi / Servizi igienici	Toilets
Si (non si) accettano carte di credito	We (do not) accept credit cards
Signore / Signori	Women / Men
Solo importo esatto	Exact change only
Spingere	Push
Tirare	Pull
Sportello	(Teller or cashier's) window
Ufficio informazioni turistiche	Tourist information office
Uomini	Men
Uscita	Exit
Uscita d'emergenza	Emergency exit
Vendesi / In vendita	For sale

Vietato	Forbidden
Vietato fumare	No smoking
Vietato l'accesso	No trespassing
Vietato l'ingresso ecetto personale autorizzato	Authorized personnel only
Voi siete qui	You are here (shown on map)

The ***acqua alta*** or ***alluvione*** signs you may see in riverfront or waterfront towns (such as Venice, Florence, and Rome) indicate the high-water mark of historic floods.

NUMBERS, MONEY & TIME

You can count on this chapter to cover Italian numbers, currency, credit and debit cards, time, dates, and major holidays and celebrations.

NUMBERS

0	zero **zeh**-roh
1	uno **oo**-noh
2	due **doo**-ay
3	tre tray
4	quattro **kwah**-troh
5	cinque **cheen**-kway
6	sei **seh**-ee
7	sette **seh**-tay
8	otto **oh**-toh
9	nove **noh**-vay
10	dieci dee-**eh**-chee
11	undici **oon**-dee-chee
12	dodici **doh**-dee-chee
13	tredici **treh**-dee-chee
14	quattordici kwah-**tor**-dee-chee
15	quindici **kween**-dee-chee
16	sedici **seh**-dee-chee
17	diciassette dee-chah-**seh**-tay
18	diciotto dee-**choh**-toh
19	diciannove dee-chah-**noh**-vay
20	venti **vehn**-tee
21	ventuno vehn-**too**-noh
22	ventidue vehn-tee-**doo**-ay
23	ventitre vehn-tee-**tray**
30	trenta **trehn**-tah
31	trentuno trehn-**too**-noh
40	quaranta kwah-**rahn**-tah

41	quarantuno kwah-rahn-**too**-noh
50	cinquanta cheen-**kwahn**-tah
60	sessanta seh-**sahn**-tah
70	settanta seh-**tahn**-tah
80	ottanta oh-**tahn**-tah
90	novanta noh-**vahn**-tah
100	cento **chehn**-toh
101	centouno chehn-toh-**oo**-noh
102	centodue chehn-toh-**doo**-ay
200	duecento doo-eh-**chehn**-toh
300	trecento treh-**chehn**-toh
400	quattrocento kwah-troh-**chehn**-toh
500	cinquecento cheen-kweh-**chehn**-toh
600	seicento seh-ee-**chehn**-toh
700	settecento seh-teh-**chehn**-toh
800	ottocento oh-toh-**chehn**-toh
900	novecento noh-veh-**chehn**-toh
1000	mille **mee**-lay
2000	duemila doo-eh-**mee**-lah
2019	duemiladiciannove doo-eh-mee-lah-dee chah-**noh**-vee
2020	duemilaventi doo-eh-mee-lah-**vehn**-tee
2021	duemilaventuno doo-eh-mee-lah-vehn-**too**-noh
2022	duemilaventidue doo-eh-mee-lah-vehn-tee-**doo**-ay
2023	duemilaventitré doo-eh-mee-lah-vehn-tee-**tray**
2024	duemilaventiquattro doo-eh-mee-lah-vehn-tee-**kwah**-troh
2025	duemilaventicinque doo-eh-mee-lah-vehn-tee-**cheen**-kway
2026	duemilaventisei doo-eh-mee-lah-vehn-tee-**seh**-ee
2027	duemilaventisette doo-eh-mee-lah-vehn-tee-**seh**-tay
2028	duemilaventotto doo-eh-mee-lah-vehn-**toh**-toh

2029	duemilaventinove doo-eh-mee-lah-vehn-tee-**noh**-vay
2030	duemilatrenta doo-eh-mee-lah-**trehn**-tah
million	milione mee-lee-**oh**-nay
billion	miliardo mee-lee-**ar**-doh
number one	numero uno **noo**-meh-roh **oo**-noh
first	primo **pree**-moh
second	secondo seh-**kohn**-doh
third	terzo **tehrt**-soh
once	una volta **oo**-nah **vohl**-tah
twice	due volte **doo**-ay **vohl**-tay
a quarter	un quarto oon **kwar**-toh
a third	un terzo oon **tehrt**-soh
half	mezzo **mehd**-zoh
this much	tanto così **tahn**-toh koh-**zee**
a dozen	una dozzina **oo**-nah dohd-**zee**-nah
a handful	una manciata **oo**-nah mahn-**chah**-tah
enough	basta **bah**-stah
not enough	non basta nohn **bah**-stah
too much	troppo **troh**-poh
more	di più dee pew
less	di meno dee **meh**-noh
50%	cinquanta per cento cheen-**kwahn**-tah pehr **chehn**-toh
100%	cento per cento **chehn**-toh pehr **chehn**-toh

Learning how to say your hotel-room number is a good way to practice Italian numbers. You'll likely be asked for the number frequently (at breakfast, or to claim your key when you return to your room).

MONEY

Italy uses the euro currency (€). One ***euro*** is divided into 100 cents ***(centesimi)***. Italians keep the term ***euro*** as singular, while ***centesimi*** is always plural. To say €2.50, it's ***due euro e cinquanta centesimi*** or, for short, ***due euro e cinquanta.***

Key Phrases: Money

euro (€)	euro eh-**oo**-roh
cents	centesimi chehn-**teh**-zee-mee
cash	contante kohn-**tahn**-tay
Where is...?	Dov'è...? doh-**veh**
...a cash machine	...un bancomat oon **bahn**-koh-maht
...a bank	...una banca **oo**-nah **bahn**-kah
credit card	carta di credito **kar**-tah dee **kreh**-dee-toh
debit card	carta di debito **kar**-tah dee **deh**-bee-toh
Do you accept credit cards?	Accettate carte di credito? ah-cheh-**tah**-tay **kar**-tay dee **kreh**-dee-toh

Use your common cents—***centesimi*** are like pennies, and other coins are like nickels, dimes, and half-dollars. There are also €1 and €2 coins.

Cash Machines (ATMs)

To get cash, ATMs are the way to go. All cash machines (called ***bancomats***) have multilingual instructions. However, the keys may be marked in Italian: ***esatto*** (correct), ***conferma*** (confirm), ***esegui*** (continue), and ***annullare*** (cancel).

money	soldi / denaro **sohl**-dee / deh-**nah**-roh
cash	contante kohn-**tahn**-tay
card	carta **kar**-tah
PIN code	codice segreto / codice PIN koh-**dee**-chay seh-**greh**-toh / koh-**dee**-chay peen
Where is...?	Dov'è...? doh-**veh**
...a cash machine	...un bancomat oon **bahn**-koh-maht

...a bank	...una banca **oo**-nah **bahn**-kah
My debit card has been...	La mia carta di debito è stata... lah **mee**-ah **kar**-tah dee **deh**-bee-toh eh **stah**-tah
...demagnetized.	...smagnetizzata. zmahn-yeht-eed-**zah**-tah
...stolen.	...rubata. roo-**bah**-tah
...eaten by the machine.	...trattenuta dal bancomat. trah-teh-**noo**-tah dahl **bahn**-koh-maht
My card doesn't work.	La mia carta non funziona. lah **mee**-ah **kar**-tah nohn foont-see-**oh**-nah

Credit and Debit Cards

Credit cards are widely accepted at larger businesses, though some smaller shops, restaurants, and hotels prefer cash.

credit card	carta di credito **kar**-tah dee **kreh**-dee-toh
debit card	carta di debito **kar**-tah dee **deh**-bee-toh
receipt	ricevuta ree-cheh-**voo**-tah
sign	firmare feer-**mah**-ray
pay	pagare / saldare pah-**gah**-ray / sahl-**dah**-ray
cashier	cassiere kah-see-**eh**-ray
cash advance	prelievo preh-lee-**eh**-voh
Do you accept credit cards?	Accettate carte di credito? ah-cheh-**tah**-tay **kar**-tay dee **kreh**-dee-toh
Cheaper if I pay cash?	C'è uno sconto se pago in contanti? cheh **oo**-noh **skohn**-toh say **pah**-goh een kohn-**tahn**-tee
I do not have a PIN.	Non ho un codice segreto. nohn oh oon koh-**dee**-chay seh-**greh**-toh
Can I sign a receipt instead?	Posso firmare una ricevuta invece? **poh**-soh feer-**mah**-ray **oo**-nah ree-cheh-**voo**-tah een-**veh**-chay

Print a receipt?	Stampare una ricevuta? stahm-**pah**-ray **oo**-nah ree-cheh-**voo**-tah
I have another card.	Ho un'altra carta. oh oon-**ahl**-trah **kar**-tah

Credit and debit cards have chips that authenticate and secure transactions. Some European card readers will generate a receipt for you to sign; others may prompt you to enter a PIN (make sure you know it for all cards). If your card won't work (sometimes possible at ticket machines, toll booths, gas pumps, or parking lots), look for a cashier who can process your card manually—or pay in cash.

Paying with a Credit Card

If calling to reserve tickets or a hotel room, you may need to convey your credit-card information over the phone. Prepare in advance: To fill in the blanks, use the numbers, alphabet, and months on pages 14-17 and the years on page 25.

The name on the card is ____.	Il nome sulla carta è ____. eel **noh**-may **soo**-lah **kar**-tah eh ____
The credit card number is ____.	Il numero della carta di credito è ____. eel **noo**-meh-roh **deh**-lah **kar**-tah dee **kreh**-dee-toh eh ____
The expiration date is ____.	La data di scadenza è ____. lah **dah**-tah dee skah-**dehnt**-sah eh ____
The code (on the back) is ____.	Il codice (sul retro) è ____. eel koh-**dee**-chay (sool **reh**-troh) eh ____

Exchanging Money

exchange	cambio **kahm**-bee-oh
change money	cambiare dei soldi kahm-bee-**ah**-ray **deh**-ee **sohl**-dee

exchange rate	tasso di cambio **tah**-soh dee **kahm**-bee-oh
dollars	dollari **dol**-lah-ree
buy / sell	comprare / vendere kohm-**prah**-ray / vehn-**deh**-ray
commission	commissione koh-mee-see-**oh**-nay
Any extra fee?	C'è un sovrapprezzo? cheh oon soh-vrah-**prehd**-zoh
I would like...	Vorrei... voh-**reh**-ee
...small bills.	...banconote di piccolo taglio. **bahn**-koh-**noh**-tay dee **pee**-koh-loh **tahl**-yoh
...large bills.	...banconote di grosso taglio. **bahn**-koh-**noh**-tay dee **groh**-soh **tahl**-yoh
...a mix of small and large bills.	...banconote miste di grande e piccolo taglio. **bahn**-koh-**noh**-tay **mee**-stay dee **grahn**-day eh **pee**-koh-loh **tahl**-yoh
...coins.	...monete. moh-**neh**-tay
Can you break this? (big bill into smaller bills)	Mi può cambiare questo? mee pwoh kahm-bee-**ah**-ray **kweh**-stoh
Is this a mistake?	Questo è un errore? **kweh**-stoh eh oon eh-**roh**-ray
This is incorrect.	Questo non è corretto. **kweh**-stoh nohn eh koh-**reh**-toh
Where is the nearest casino?	Dov'è il casinò più vicino? doh-**veh** eel kah-zee-**noh** pew vee-**chee**-noh

Exchange bureaus may list two rates: ***acquisito*** (we buy) and ***vendita*** (we sell). The closer together these two numbers are, the better the rate.

TIME AND DATES

Telling Time

In Italy, the 24-hour clock (military time) is used for setting formal appointments (for instance, arrival times at a hotel), for the opening and closing hours of museums and shops, and for train, bus, and ferry schedules. Informally, Italians use the same 12-hour clock we do, but they don't say "o'clock"—they instead say ***mattina*** (morning), ***pomeriggio*** (afternoon), and so on. So they might meet a friend at ***tre di pomeriggio*** (three in the afternoon) to catch a train that leaves at ***le sedici*** (16:00).

What time is it?	Che ore sono? kay **oh**-ray **soh**-noh
(in the) morning	(di) mattina (dee) mah-**tee**-nah
(in the) afternoon	(di) pomeriggio (dee) poh-meh-**ree**-joh
(in the) evening	(di) sera (dee) **seh**-rah
(at) night	(di) notte (dee) **noh**-tay
half	mezza **mehd**-zah
quarter	un quarto oon **kwar**-toh
minute	minuto mee-**noo**-toh
hour	ora **oh**-rah
It's / At...	Sono / Alle... **soh**-noh / **ah**-lay
...8:00 in the morning.	...le otto di mattina. lay **oh**-toh dee mah-**tee**-nah
...16:00.	...le sedici. lay **seh**-dee-chee
...4:00 in the afternoon.	...le quattro di pomeriggio. lay **kwah**-troh dee poh-meh-**ree**-joh
...10:30 in the evening.	...le dieci e mezza di sera. lay dee-**eh**-chee ay **mehd**-zah dee **seh**-rah
...a quarter past nine.	...le nove e un quarto. lay **noh**-vay ay oon **kwar**-toh
...a quarter to eleven.	...le undici meno un quarto. lay **oon**-dee-chee **meh**-noh oon **kwar**-toh

Key Phrases: Time and Dates

What time is it?	Che ore sono? kay **oh**-ray **soh**-noh
minute	minuto mee-**noo**-toh
hour	ora **oh**-rah
It's 1:00.	É l'una. eh **loo**-nah
It's...	Sono... **soh**-noh
...7:00 in the morning.	...le sette di mattina. lay **seh**-tay dee mah-**tee**-nah
...2:00 in the afternoon.	...le due di pomeriggio. lay **doo**-ay dee poh-meh-**ree**-joh
When does this open / close?	A che ora apre / chiude? ah kay **oh**-rah **ah**-pray / kee-**oo**-day
day	giorno **jor**-noh
today	oggi **oh**-jee
tomorrow	domani doh-**mah**-nee
(this) week	(questa) settimana (**kweh**-stah) seh-tee-**mah**-nah
August 21	il ventuno agosto eel vehn-**too**-noh ah-**goh**-stoh

at 6:00 sharp	alle sei in punto **ah**-lay **seh**-ee een **poon**-toh
from 8:00 to 10:00	dalle otto alle dieci **dah**-lay **oh**-toh **ah**-lay dee-**eh**-chee
noon	mezzogiorno mehd-zoh-**jor**-noh
midnight	mezzanotte mehd-zah-**noh**-tay
It's my bedtime.	Per me è ora di andare a dormire. pehr may eh **oh**-rah dee ahn-**dah**-ray ah dor-**mee**-ray
I will be / We will be...	Sarò / Saremo... sah-**roh** / sah-**reh**-moh

...back at 11:20.	...di ritorno alle undici e venti. dee ree-**tor**-noh **ah**-lay **oon**-dee-chee ay **vehn**-tee
...there by 18:00.	...lì per le diciotto. lee pehr lay dee-**choh**-toh

In Italy, the ***pomeriggio*** (afternoon) turns to ***sera*** (evening) generally about 4:00 or 5:00 p.m. (5:30 p.m. is ***cinque e mezza di sera***).

Timely Questions

When?	Quando? **kwahn**-doh
When is...?	Quand'è...? kwahn-**deh**
At what time?	A che ora? ah kay **oh**-rah
opening time	ora di apertura **oh**-rah dee ah-pehr-**too**-rah
When does this open / close?	Quando apre / chiude? **kwahn**-doh **ah**-pray / kee-**oo**-day
Is the train...?	È... il treno? eh... eel **treh**-noh
Is the bus...?	È... l'autobus? eh... **low**-toh-boos
...early	...in anticipo een ahn-**tee**-chee-poh
...late	...in ritardo een ree-**tar**-doh
...on time	...in orario een oh-**rah**-ree-oh
When is checkout time?	A che ora bisogna liberare la camera? ah kay **oh**-rah bee-**zohn**-yah lee-beh-**rah**-ray lah **kah**-meh-rah

It's About Time

now	adesso ah-**deh**-soh
soon	presto / tra poco **preh**-stoh / trah **poh**-koh
later	più tardi pew **tar**-dee
in one hour	tra un'ora trah oon-**oh**-rah
in half an hour	tra mezz'ora trah mehd-**zoh**-rah

in three hours	tra tre ore trah tray **oh**-ray
early	presto **preh**-stoh
late	tardi **tar**-dee
on time	puntuale poon-too-**ah**-lay
anytime	a qualsiasi ora ah kwahl-**see**-ah-zee **oh**-rah
immediately	immediatamente **ee**-meh-dee-ah-tah-**mehn**-tay
every hour	ogni ora **ohn**-yee **oh**-rah
every day	ogni giorno **ohn**-yee **jor**-noh
daily	giornaliero jor-nahl-ee-**ehr**-oh
last	scorso **skor**-soh
this	questo **kweh**-stoh
next	prossimo **proh**-see-moh
before	prima **pree**-mah
after	dopo **doh**-poh
May 15	il quindici maggio eel **kween**-dee-chee **mah**-joh
in the future	in futuro een foo-**too**-roh
in the past	nel passato nehl pah-**sah**-toh

The Day

day	giorno **jor**-noh
today	oggi **oh**-jee
sunrise	alba **ahl**-bah
this morning	stamattina stah-mah-**tee**-nah
sunset	tramonto trah-**mohn**-toh
tonight	stasera stah-**seh**-rah
last night	stanotte stah-**noh**-tay
yesterday	ieri ee-**eh**-ree
tomorrow	domani doh-**mah**-nee

tomorrow morning	domani mattina doh-**mah**-nee mah-**tee**-nah
day after tomorrow	dopodomani doh-poh-doh-**mah**-nee

The Week

Sunday	domenica doh-**meh**-nee-kah
Monday	lunedì loo-neh-**dee**
Tuesday	martedì mar-teh-**dee**
Wednesday	mercoledì mehr-koh-leh-**dee**
Thursday	giovedì joh-veh-**dee**
Friday	venerdì veh-nehr-**dee**
Saturday	sabato **sah**-bah-toh
week	settimana seh-tee-**mah**-nah
last week	la settimana scorsa lah seh-tee-**mah**-nah **skor**-sah
this week	questa settimana **kweh**-stah seh-tee-**mah**-nah
next week	la settimana prossima lah seh-tee-**mah**-nah **proh**-see-mah
weekend	weekend "weekend"
this weekend	questo weekend **kweh**-stoh "weekend"

Weekdays plus Saturday are called ***feriali*** (literally "working days"); Sundays and holidays are ***festivi***.

The Months

month	mese **meh**-zay
January	gennaio jeh-**nah**-yoh
February	febbraio feh-**brah**-yoh
March	marzo **mart**-soh
April	aprile ah-**pree**-lay

May	maggio **mah**-joh
June	giugno **joon**-yoh
July	luglio **lool**-yoh
August	agosto ah-**goh**-stoh
September	settembre seh-**tehm**-bray
October	ottobre oh-**toh**-bray
November	novembre noh-**vehm**-bray
December	dicembre dee-**chehm**-bray

For dates, say ***il*** followed by the number and month; for example, July 4 is ***il quattro luglio***.

The Year

year	anno **ahn**-noh
season	stagione stah-jee-**oh**-nay
spring	primavera pree-mah-**veh**-rah
summer	estate eh-**stah**-tay
fall	autunno ow-**too**-noh
winter	inverno een-**vehr**-noh

For a list of years, see the "Numbers" section, earlier.

Holidays and Happy Days

holiday / festival	festa **feh**-stah
Is today / tomorrow a holiday?	Oggi / Domani è festa? **oh**-jee / doh-**mah**-nee eh **feh**-stah
Is a holiday coming up soon?	Siamo vicini a una festa? see-**ah**-moh vee-**chee**-nee ah **oo**-nah **feh**-stah
When is it?	Quand'è? kwahn-**deh**
What is the holiday?	Che festa è? kay **feh**-stah eh

Mardi Gras / Carnival	Martedì Grasso / Carnevale mar-teh-**dee grah**-soh / kar-neh-**vah**-lay
Holy Week	Settimana Santa seh-tee-**mah**-nah **sahn**-tah
Easter	Pasqua **pahs**-kwah
Ascension	Ascensione ah-shehn-see-**oh**-nay
Liberation Day (April 25)	Giorno della Liberazione **jor**-noh **deh**-lah lee-beh-raht-see-**oh**-nay
May Day (May 1)	Primo Maggio **pree**-moh **mah**-joh
Pentecost	Pentecoste pehn-teh-**kohs**-tay
Corpus Christi	Corpus Domini **kor**-poos doh-**mee**-nee
Assumption (Aug 15)	Ferragosto feh-rah-**goh**-stoh
All Saints' Day (Nov 1)	Ognissanti ohn-yee-**sahn**-tee
Christmas Eve	Vigilia di Natale vee-**jeel**-yah dee nah-**tah**-lay
Christmas	Giorno di Natale **jor**-noh dee nah-**tah**-lay
Merry Christmas!	Buon Natale! bwohn nah-**tah**-lay
New Year's Eve	Capodanno kah-poh-**dahn**-noh
New Year's Day	Il primo dell'anno eel **pree**-moh dehl-**ahn**-noh
Happy New Year!	Buon Anno! bwohn **ahn**-noh
anniversary	anniversario ah-nee-vehr-**sah**-ree-oh
Happy (wedding) anniversary!	Buon anniversario (di matrimonio)! bwohn ah-nee-vehr-**sah**-ree-oh (dee mah-tree-**moh**-nee-oh)
birthday	compleanno kohm-pleh-**ahn**-noh
Happy birthday!	Buon compleanno! bwohn kohm-pleh-**ahn**-noh

Italians celebrate birthdays with the same "Happy Birthday" tune that we use. The Italian words mean "Best wishes to you": ***Tanti auguri a te, tanti auguri a te, tanti auguri, caro[a] ____, tanti auguri a te!***

TRANSPORTATION

This chapter will help you buy transit tickets, get around—by train, bus, subway, taxi, rental car, and foot—and generally find your way around.

GETTING AROUND

train	treno **treh**-noh
city bus	autobus **ow**-toh-boos
long-distance bus	pullman / autobus **pool**-mahn / **ow**-toh-boos
subway	Metropolitana / Metro meh-troh-poh-lee-**tah**-nah / **meh**-troh
taxi	taxi **tahk**-see
car	macchina **mah**-kee-nah
boat	barca **bar**-kah
ferry	traghetto trah-**geh**-toh
car ferry	autotraghetto ow-toh-trah-**geh**-toh
hydrofoil	aliscafo ah-lee-**skah**-foh
walk / by foot	camminare / a piedi kah-mee-**nah**-ray / ah pee-**eh**-dee
Where is the...?	Dov'è il / la...? doh-**veh** eel / lah
...train station	...stazione staht-see-**oh**-nay
...bus station	...stazione degli autobus staht-see-**oh**-nay **dehl**-yee **ow**-toh-boos
...bus stop	...fermata fehr-**mah**-tah
...subway station	...stazione della Metro staht-see-**oh**-nay **deh**-lah **meh**-troh
...taxi stand	...fermata dei taxi fehr-**mah**-tah **deh**-ee **tahk**-see
I'm going / We're going to ____.	Vado / Andiamo a ____. **vah**-doh / ahn-dee-**ah**-moh ah ____

Getting Tickets

When you're buying tickets for the bus, train, or subway, the following phrases will come in handy.

Where can I buy a ticket?	Dove posso comprare un biglietto? **doh**-vay **poh**-soh kohm-**prah**-ray oon beel-**yeh**-toh
How much (is a ticket to ____)?	Quant'è (il biglietto per ____)? kwahn-**teh** (eel beel-**yeh**-toh pehr ____)
I want to go to ____.	Voglio andare a ____. **vohl**-yoh ahn-**dah**-ray ah ____
One ticket / Two tickets (to ____).	Un biglietto / Due biglietti (per ____). oon beel-**yeh**-toh / **doo**-ay beel-**yeh**-tee (pehr ____)
When is the next train / bus (to ____)?	Quando è il prossimo treno / autobus (per ____)? **kwahn**-doh eh eel **proh**-see-moh **treh**-noh / **ow**-toh-boos (pehr ____)
What time does it leave?	A che ora parte? ah kay **oh**-rah **par**-tay
Is it direct?	È diretto? eh dee-**reh**-toh
Is a reservation required?	Ci vuole la prenotazione? chee **vwoh**-lay lah preh-noh-taht-see-**oh**-nay
I'd like / We'd like to reserve a seat.	Vorrei / Vorremmo prenotare un posto. voh-**reh**-ee / voh-**reh**-moh preh-noh-**tah**-ray oon **poh**-stoh
Can I buy a ticket on board?	Posso comprare un biglietto a bordo? **poh**-soh kohm-**prah**-ray oon beel-**yeh**-toh ah **bor**-doh
Exact change only?	Solo importo esatto? **soh**-loh eem-**por**-toh eh-**zah**-toh

What is the cheapest / fastest / easiest way...?	Qual'è il modo più economico / più veloce / più facile...? kwah-**leh** eel **moh**-doh pew eh-koh-**noh**-mee-koh / pew veh-**loh**-chay / pew **fah**-chee-lay
...to downtown	...al centro ahl **chehn**-troh
...to the train station	...alla stazione **ah**-lah staht-see-**oh**-nay
...to my / to our hotel	...al mio / al nostro hotel ahl **mee**-oh / ahl **noh**-stroh **oh**-tehl
...to the airport	...all'aeroporto ahl-ay-roh-**por**-toh

While you're unlikely to ride a ***motorino*** (motor scooter), you can't avoid them—they swarm around tight city streets like wasps (which is what the brand name ***Vespa*** literally means).

TRAINS

For tips and strategies about rail travel and railpasses in Italy, see www.ricksteves.com/rail. Note that many of the following train phrases work for long-distance bus travel as well.

Ticket Basics

ticket	biglietto beel-**yeh**-toh
reservation	prenotazione preh-noh-taht-see-**oh**-nay
ticket office	biglietteria beel-yeh-teh-**ree**-yah
ticket machine	biglietteria automatica beel-yeh-teh-**ree**-yah ow-toh-**mah**-tee-kah
validate	timbrare / convalidare teem-**brah**-ray / kohn-vah-lee-**dah**-ray
Where can I buy a ticket?	Dove posso comprare un biglietto? **doh**-vay **poh**-soh kohm-**prah**-ray oon beel-**yeh**-toh

Is this the line for...?	È questa la fila per...? eh **kweh**-stah lah **fee**-lah pehr
...tickets	...biglietti beel-**yeh**-tee
...reservations	...prenotazioni preh-noh-taht-see-**oh**-nee
...information	...informazioni een-for-maht-see-**oh**-nee
One ticket (to ____).	Un biglietto (per ____). oon beel-**yeh**-toh (pehr ____)
Two tickets.	Due biglietti. **doo** ay beel-**yeh**-tee
I want to go to ____.	Voglio andare a ____. **vohl**-yoh ahn-**dah**-ray ah ____
How much (is a ticket to ____)?	Quant'è (il biglietto per ____)? kwahn-**teh** (eel beel-**yeh**-toh pehr ____)
one-way	andata ahn-**dah**-tah
round-trip	andata e ritorno ahn-**dah**-tah ay ree-**tor**-noh
today / tomorrow	oggi / domani **oh**-jee / doh-**mah**-nee

Ticket Specifics

As trains and buses can sell out, it's smart to buy your tickets a day in advance even for short rides. For phrases related to discounts (such as for children, families, or seniors), see page 46.

schedule	orario oh-**rah**-ree-oh
When is the next train / bus (to ____)?	Quando è il prossimo treno / autobus (per ____)? **kwahn**-doh eh eel **proh**-see-moh **treh**-noh / **ow**-toh-boos (pehr ____)
What time does it leave?	A che ora parte? ah kay **oh**-rah **par**-tay

I'd like / We'd like to leave...	Vorrei / Vorremmo partire... voh-**reh**-ee / voh-**reh**-moh par-**tee**-ray
I'd like / We'd like to arrive...	Vorrei / Vorremmo arrivare... voh-**reh**-ee / voh-**reh**-moh ah-ree-**vah**-ray
...by ____... (name time)	...per le ____... pehr lay ____
...at ____... (name time)	...alle ____... **ah**-lay ____
...in the morning / afternoon / evening.	...di mattina / pomeriggio / sera. dee mah-**tee**-nah / poh-meh-**ree**-joh / **seh**-rah
Is there a... train / bus?	C'è un treno / autobus...? cheh oon **treh**-noh / **ow**-toh-boos
...earlier	...prima **pree**-mah
...later	...più tardi pew **tar**-dee
...overnight	...notturno noh-**toor**-noh
...cheaper	...più economico pew eh-koh-**noh**-mee-koh
...express	...espresso eh-**spreh**-soh
...direct	...diretto dee-**reh**-toh
Is it direct?	È diretto? eh dee-**reh**-toh
Is a transfer required?	Devo cambiare? **deh**-voh kahm-bee-**ah**-ray
How many transfers?	Quante volte devo cambiare treno? **kwahn**-tay **vohl**-tay **deh**-voh kahm-bee-**ah**-ray **treh**-noh
When? / Where?	Quando? / Dove? **kwahn**-doh / **doh**-vay
first / second class	prima / seconda classe **pree**-mah / seh-**kohn**-dah **klah**-say
How long is this ticket valid?	Per quanto tempo è valido questo biglietto? pehr **kwahn**-toh **tehm**-poh eh **vah**-lee-doh **kweh**-stoh beel-**yeh**-toh

Can you validate my railpass?	Può convalidare la mia tessera ferroviaria? pwoh kohn-vah-lee-**dah**-ray lah **mee**-ah **teh**-seh-rah feh-roh-vee-**ah**-ree-ah

At the train station, you can buy tickets at the windows in the ***atrio biglietteria*** or ***salone biglietti*** (ticketing hall) or at machines ***(biglietterie automatiche).*** At large stations, be sure you go to the correct window: ***biglietti*** are tickets, ***prenotazioni*** is for reservations, ***nazionali*** is for domestic trips, and ***internazionali*** is international.

Rather than wait in line, you may find it faster to use machines to buy tickets, railpass reservations, and more. Look for the big **"self service"** signs, or the even faster ***biglietto veloce*** kiosks. Some machines take credit cards, others take cash, and some take both—before using a machine, be sure it accepts your method of payment. (When the machine prompts you—"Fidelity Card?"—choose no.) For nearby destinations only, use the machines marked ***Rete regionale*** (cash only, push button for English).

For a small fee, it's also possible to book rail tickets through a travel agency ***(agenzia di viaggi).***

Ticket Types

Flessible	The most flexible (and expensive)
Base	Basic fare
Promo	Special offers
Servizi abbonati	Specials for locals with monthly passes; not available for tourists

On tickets, ***1a*** (or ***prima classe***) means first class, and ***2a*** (or ***seconda classe***) means second class.

Train Reservations

Some fast trains require a ***prenotazione*** (reservation)—often noted by an **R** in the schedule. Even if a reservation isn't required, it can be a good idea to reserve a seat on busy routes at popular times. (If you're using a railpass, you must pay an extra ***supplemento*** to reserve.)

Is a reservation required?	Ci vuole la prenotazione? chee **vwoh**-lay lah preh-noh-taht-see-**oh**-nay
I'd like / We'd like to reserve...	Vorrei / Vorremmo prenotare... voh-**reh**-ee / voh-**reh**-moh preh-noh-**tah**-ray
...a seat.	...un posto. oon **poh**-stoh
...an aisle seat.	...un posto corridoio. oon **poh**-stoh koh-ree-**doh**-yoh
...a window seat.	...un posto finestrino. oon **poh**-stoh fee-neh-**stree**-noh
...two seats.	...due posti. **doo**-ay **poh**-stee
...a couchette (sleeping berth).	...una cuccetta. **oo**-nah koo-**cheh**-tah
...an upper / middle / lower berth.	...una cuccetta di sopra / in mezzo / di sotto. **oo**-nah koo-**cheh**-tah dee **soh**-prah / een **mehd**-zoh / dee **soh**-toh
...two couchettes.	...due cuccette. **doo**-ay koo-**cheh**-tay
...a sleeper compartment. (private)	...un compartimento in vagone letto. oon kohm-par-tee-**mehn**-toh een vah-**goh**-nay **leh**-toh
...a sleeper compartment (with two beds).	...un compartimento in vagone letto (con due cuccette). oon kohm-par-tee-**mehn**-toh een vah-**goh**-nay **leh**-toh (kohn **doo**-ay koo-**cheh**-tay)
...the entire train.	...tutto il treno. **too**-toh eel **treh**-noh

Discounts

Is there a cheaper ticket?	C'è un biglietto più economico? cheh oon beel-**yeh**-toh pew eh-koh-**noh**-mee-koh
discount	sconto **skohn**-toh

reduced fare	tariffa ridotta tah-**ree**-fah ree-**doh**-tah
refund	rimborso reem-**bor**-soh
Is there a discount for...?	Fate sconti per...? **fah**-tay **skohn**-tee pehr
...children	...bambini bahm-**bee**-nee
...minors	...minorenni mee-noh-**reh**-nee
...seniors	...anziani ahnt-see-**ah**-nee
...families	...famiglie fah-**meel**-yay
...groups	...gruppi **groo**-pee
...advance purchase	...acquisto anticipato ah-**kwee**-stoh ahn-tee-chee-**pah**-toh
...weekends	...fine settimana **fee**-nay seh-tee-**mah**-nah
Are there any deals for this journey?	Ci sono delle offerte per questo viaggio? chee **soh**-noh **deh**-lay oh-**fehr**-tay pehr **kweh**-stoh vee-**ah**-joh

At the Train Station

Where is the train station?	Dov'è la stazione? doh-**veh** lah staht-see-**oh**-nay
train information	informazioni treni / informazioni e servizi een-for-maht-see-**oh**-nee **treh**-nee / een-for-maht-see-**oh**-nee ay sehr-**veet**-see
customer assistance	assistenza clienti ah-sees-**tehnt**-sah klee-**ehn**-tee
tickets	biglietti beel-**yeh**-tee
ticket hall	atrio biglietteria / salone biglietti **ah**-tree-oh beel-yeh-teh-**ree**-yah / sah-**loh**-nay beel-**yeh**-tee
ticket sales	biglietteria beel-yeh-teh-**ree**-yah

Key Phrases: Trains

train station	stazione staht-see-**oh**-nay
train	treno **treh**-noh
platform / track	binario bee-**nah**-ree-oh
What track does it leave from?	Da che binario parte? dah kay bee-**nah**-ree-oh **par**-tay
Is this the train to ____?	Questo è il treno per ____? **kweh**-stoh eh eel **treh**-noh pehr ____
Which train to ____?	Quale treno per ____? **kwah**-lay **treh**-noh pehr ____
Tell me when to get off?	Mi dice quando devo scendere? mee **dee**-chay **kwahn**-doh **deh**-voh **shehn**-deh-ray
transfer (n)	scalo **skah**-loh
Change here for ____?	Cambio qui per ____? **kahm**-bee-oh kwee pehr ____

(time of) departure / arrival	(orario di) partenza / arrivo (oh-**rah**-ree-oh dee) par-**tehnt**-sah / ah-**ree**-voh
On time?	È in orario? eh een oh-**rah**-ree-oh
Late?	In ritardo? een ree-**tar**-doh
How late?	Quanto ritardo? **kwahn**-toh ree-**tar**-doh
platform / track	binario bee-**nah**-ree-oh
What platform does it leave from?	Da che binario parte? dah kay bee-**nah**-ree-oh **par**-tay
waiting room	sala di attesa / sala d'aspetto **sah**-lah dee ah-**teh**-zah / **sah**-lah dah-**speh**-toh
lockers	armadietti ar-mah-dee-**eh**-tee

baggage check	deposito bagagli / consegna deh-**poh**-zee-toh bah-**gahl**-yee / kohn-**sehn**-yah
tourist information	informazioni per turisti een-for-maht-see-**oh**-nee pehr too-**ree**-stee
lost and found office	ufficio oggetti smarriti oo-**fee**-choh oh-**jeh**-tee smah-**ree**-tee
toilet	toilette twah-**leh**-tay

The general term for "railroad" in Italian is ***ferrovia***. Most trains in Italy are operated by the national rail company, ***Ferrovie dello Stato Italiane***—abbreviated ***FS***, and usually just called ***Trenitalia*** (trehn-ee-**tahl**-yah).

Types of Trains

Trains are classified according to how fast and how far they travel; here are the abbreviations you may see, roughly in order from slowest to fastest.

R / REG	regionali (pokey milk-run trains)
RV	regionale veloce (medium-speed)
IR	InterRegio (medium-speed)
D	diretto (medium-speed)
E	espresso (medium-speed)
IC	InterCity (fast)
EC	EuroCity (fast)
ES / AV / EAV	Eurostar Italia Alta Velocità (super-fast)

The speedy ***ES*** and ***EAV*** routes use these types of trains: ***Frecciabianca*** (White Arrow), faster ***Frecciargento*** (Silver Arrow), ***Frecciarossa*** (Red Arrow), and the newest ***Frecciarossa 1000*** or ***Freccemille.*** A private company called Italo runs fast trains between major Italian cities.

Train and Bus Schedules

European timetables use the 24-hour clock. It's like American time until noon. After that, subtract 12 and add "p.m." For example, 13:00 is 1 p.m., and 19:00 is 7 p.m.

You can check train schedules throughout Italy at the handy ticket machines. Newsstands sell up-to-date regional and all-Italy timetables *(orario ferroviaro)*.

At the station, look for the big yellow posters labeled ***Partenze*** (departures; ignore the white posters, which show arrivals). Organized in this order, each schedule has these columns:

Ora	Time of departure
Treno	Type and number of train
Classi Servizi	Services available (for example, dining car, *cuccetta* sleeping berths, etc.); if you see an [R] here, the train requires a reservation
Principali Fermate Destinazioni	Major stops and final destination
Servizi Diretti e Annotazioni	Additional notes (see bottom of poster)
Binario / Bin	Track number

On any timetable—posted or printed—you might also see some of these terms:

a	to; can mean "arrival"
anche	also
annulata	cancelled
arrive / arrivi	arrival(s)
avvisi al pubblico / al viaggiatori	advisory to the public / to travelers
categoria / cat	type of train
circa ____ minuti di ritardo	about ____ minutes late
(non) circola nei giorni festivi	does (not) run on holidays
coincidenze	connections

corsia	bus stall or platform
corse rapide	fast route (bus)
da	from
destinazione	destination
direzione e / o stazione d'arrivo	direction and / or final destination
eccetto / escluso	except
feriali	weekdays including Saturday
ferma	stops (v)
ferma anche a ____	also stops in ____
ferma in tutte le stazioni	stops at all the stations
festivi	Sundays and holidays
fino	until
G	runs even in case of strike
giornaliero	daily
giorni	days
in ritardo	late
lavori	work
minuti	minutes
NB	note
non ferma a ____	doesn't stop in ____
ogni	every
ordinaria	makes every stop (bus)
ore	hours
partenza / p	departure
per	for
più tardi (dell'orario stabilito)	later (than scheduled)
possibile prolungamento di ____ minuti dell'orario di arrivo per lavori progammati	possible delay of ____ minutes in arriving because of scheduled maintenance work
provenienza	originating from
rapida	fast route (bus)
riduzioni (delle corse)	reduced service
ritardo / rit	delay
servizio automobilistico	bus service
servizio periodico	periodic service
si effettua anche ____	also runs on ____
solo	only
tempo	time

transita da ___	stops at ___
transiti	stops
treni in arrivo	arriving trains
treni in partenza	departing trains
tutti i giorni	daily
va	goes
vacanza	holiday
via	by way of
via autostrada / superstrada	by expressway / super-expressway (bus)
1-5 / 6 / 7	Monday-Friday / Saturday / Sunday

Avvisi (advisory) is an important word: It means something is not running normally. If it appears to involve your train or bus, ask locals if there are any complications you should know about.

When perusing train schedules, it helps to know the Italian names of cities, such as ***Firenze*** (Florence), ***Venezia*** (Venice), ***Napoli*** (Naples), ***Monaco di Baviera*** (Munich), and ***Parigi*** (Paris). For tips on pronouncing Italian place names, see the end of this chapter.

Major Train Stations

Big Italian cities often have multiple stations; when arriving or departing, be clear on which station your train uses. In many cases, you'll aim for the ***Centrale*** train station. The list of major cities below tells you which train station is nearest the city-center sights.

Bolzano	Bolzano (not Bolzano Süd)
Cortona	Camucia
Florence	Firenze Santa Maria Novella (Firenze S.M.N.)
Milan	Milano Centrale
Naples	Napoli Centrale
Pisa	Pisa Centrale (Pisa San Rossore is closer to the Leaning Tower, but has fewer trains)
Rome	Roma Termini (closer to ancient Roman sites; Roma San Pietro is near Vatican City, but has fewer trains)

Venice	Venezia Santa Lucia (on the island of Venice; Venezia Mestre is on the mainland)
Verona	Verona Porta Nuova

All Aboard

To find the platforms, look for the signs ***ai treni*** (to the trains) or ***ai binari*** (to the platforms).

You'll need to validate ***(timbrare)*** most types of unreserved tickets on the platform in the machines marked ***convalida biglietti.*** If you're on the train and you forget to validate your ticket, go right away to the train conductor—before he comes to you—or you'll pay a fine.

The ***composizione principali treni*** (train-car configuration) diagram can show you where to wait for your car along the platform, though they're not always accurate.

platform / track	binario bee-**nah**-ree-oh
number	numero **noo**-meh-roh
train car	vagone vah-**goh**-nay
conductor	capotreno kah-poh-**treh**-noh
Is this the train to ____?	Questo è il treno per ____? **kweh**-stoh eh eel **treh**-noh pehr ____
Which train to ____?	Quale treno per ____? **kwah**-lay **treh**-noh pehr ____
Which train car to ____?	Quale vagone per ____? **kwah**-lay vah-**goh**-nay pehr ____
Where can I validate my ticket?	Dove posso timbrare il biglietto? **doh**-vay **poh**-soh teem-**brah**-ray eel beel-**yeh**-toh
Where is...?	Dov'è...? doh-**veh**
Is this...?	È questo...? eh **kweh**-stoh
...my seat	...il mio posto eel **mee**-oh **pohs**-toh
...first / second class	...la prima / seconda classe lah **pree**-mah / seh-**kohn**-dah **klah**-say

...the dining car	...il vagone ristorante eel vah-**goh**-nay ree-stoh-**rahn**-tay
...the sleeper car	...il vagone letto eel vah-**goh**-nay **leh**-toh
...the toilet	...la toilette lah twah-**leh**-tay
front / middle / back	in testa / in centro / in coda een **teh**-stah / een **chehn**-troh / een **koh**-dah
reserved / occupied / free	prenotato / occupato / libero preh-noh-**tah**-toh / oh-koo-**pah**-toh / **lee**-beh-roh
aisle / window	corridoio / finestrino koh-ree-**doh**-yoh / fee-neh-**stree**-noh
Is this (seat) free?	È libero? eh **lee**-beh-roh
May I / May we...?	Posso / Possiamo...? **poh**-soh / poh-see-**ah**-moh
...sit here	...sedermi / sederci qui seh-**dehr**-mee / seh-**dehr**-chee kwee
...open the window	...aprire il finestrino ah-**pree**-ray eel fee-neh-**stree**-noh
...eat here	...mangiare qui mahn-**jah**-ray kwee
...eat your food	...mangiare il suo cibo mahn-**jah**-ray eel **soo**-oh **chee**-boh
(I think) this is my seat.	(Penso che) questo è il mio posto. (**pehn**-soh kay) **kweh**-stoh eh eel **mee**-oh **poh**-stoh
These are our seats.	Sono i nostri posti. **soh**-noh ee **noh**-stree **poh**-stee
Save my place?	Mi tiene il posto? mee tee-**eh**-nay eel **poh**-stoh
Save our places?	Ci tiene i posti? chee tee-**eh**-nay ee **poh**-stee
Where are you going?	Dove va? **doh**-vay vah

I'm going / We're going to ____.	Vado / Andiamo a ____. **vah**-doh / ahn-dee-**ah**-moh ah ____
When will it arrive (in ____)?	Quando arriva (a ____)? **kwahn**-doh ah-**ree**-vah (ah ____)
Where is a (handsome) conductor?	Dov'è un (bel) capotreno? doh-**veh** oon (behl) kah-poh-**treh**-noh
Tell me when to get off?	Mi dice quando devo scendere? mee **dee**-chay **kwahn**-doh **deh**-voh **shehn**-deh-ray
I'm getting off.	Devo scendere. **deh**-voh **shehn**-deh-ray
How do I open the door?	Come si apre la porta? **koh**-may see **ah**-pray lah **por**-tah

As you approach a station on the train, you will hear an announcement such as ***Stiamo per arrivare alla Stazione di Milano Centrale*** (We are about to arrive at Milan Central Station).

Changing Trains

Change here for ____?	Cambio qui per ____? **kahm**-bee-oh kwee pehr ____
Where does one change for ____?	Dove si cambia per ____? **doh**-vay see **kahm**-bee-ah pehr ____
At what time?	A che ora? ah kay **oh**-rah
From what track does the connecting train leave?	Da che binario parte la coincidenza? dah kay bee-**nah**-ree-oh **par**-tay lah koh-een-chee-**dehnt**-sah
How many minutes in ____ (to change trains)?	Quanti minuti a ____ (per prendere la coincidenza)? **kwahn**-tee mee-**noo**-tee ah ____ (pehr **prehn**-deh-ray lah koh-een-chee-**dehnt**-sah)

Strikes

Strikes *(scioperi)* are common and generally last a day. Train employees will simply shrug and say ***Sciopero.*** But a few sporadic trains often do lumber down the tracks during most strikes. If a strike is pending, don't panic: Hoteliers and travel agencies can tell you when it will go into effect and which trains will continue to run (they're also marked "G" in train schedules.)

strike	sciopero **shoh**-peh-roh
Is there a strike?	C'è lo sciopero? cheh loh **shoh**-peh-roh
Only for today?	È solo per oggi? eh **soh**-loh pehr **oh**-jee
Tomorrow, too?	Anche domani? **ahn**-kay doh-**mah**-nee
Are there some trains today?	C'è qualche treno oggi? cheh **kwahl**-kay **treh**-noh **oh**-jee
I'm going to ____.	Vado a ____. **vah**-doh ah ____

Strikes often come with demonstrations ***(manifestazioni),*** which can close down streets and impede your progress.

LONG-DISTANCE BUSES

In Italy, buses can connect many smaller towns more efficiently and affordably than trains. In many hill towns, trains leave you at a station in the valley far below, while buses bring you right into the thick of things. If you're not sure where to buy tickets, ask ***Chi vende i biglietti dell' autobus per ____?*** (Who sells bus tickets to ____?). Some piazzas have more than one bus stop; confirm the departure point ***(Dov'è la fermata?).***

Remember that many phrases that apply to train travel can be used for bus travel as well. For ticket-buying help, see page 41.

long-distance bus	pullman / autobus **pool**-mahn / **ow**-toh-boos
bus station	stazione degli autobus staht-see-**oh**-nay **dehl**-yee **ow**-toh-boos
stall	corsia / stallo kor-**see**-ah / **stah**-loh
stop	fermata fehr-**mah**-tah

Who sells bus tickets to ____?	Chi vende i biglietti dell'autobus per ____? kee **vehn**-day ee beel-**yeh**-tee dehl-**ow**-toh-boos pehr ____
How many minutes will we be here?	Quanti minuti ci fermiamo qui? **kwahn**-tee mee-**noo**-tee chee fehr-mee-**ah**-moh kwee
Where is the bus stop?	Dov'è la fermata? doh-**veh** lah fehr-**mah**-tah
Where does the connection leave from?	Da dove parte la coincidenza? dah **doh**-vay **par**-tay lah koh-een-chee-**dehnt**-sah

Buses marked ***via autostrada*** or ***via superstrada*** on schedules take speedy expressways—they'll get you there faster than ***ordinaria*** buses, which take back roads and make every stop. On schedules, ***transiti*** are the major stops en route. (For more tips on interpreting schedules, see page 50.) Sundays and holidays are problematic; schedules are sparse, buses are jam-packed, and ticket offices are often closed. Plan ahead and buy your ticket in advance.

CITY BUSES AND SUBWAYS

Ticket Talk

Most big cities offer deals on transportation, such as one-day tickets ***(biglietto giornaliero)***, multi-day passes, cheaper fares for youths and seniors, or a discount for buying a batch of tickets. You can buy tickets and passes at some newsstands, tobacco shops (***tabacchi***, marked by a black-and-white ***T*** sign), and major Metro stations and bus stops. For more discount-related phrases, see page 46.

Where can I buy a ticket?	Dove posso comprare un biglietto? **doh**-vay **poh**-soh kohm-**prah**-ray oon beel-**yeh**-toh
I want to go to ____.	Voglio andare a ____. **vohl**-yoh ahn-**dah**-ray ah ____

How much (is a ticket to ___)?	Quant'è (il biglietto per ___)? kwahn-**teh** (eel beel-**yeh**-toh pehr ___)
single ticket	biglietto singolo beel-**yeh**-toh **seen**-goh-loh
short-ride ticket	biglietto per tragitto breve beel-**yeh**-toh pehr trah-**jee**-toh **breh**-vay
day ticket	biglietto giornaliero beel-**yeh**-toh jor-nahl-**yeh**-roh
Is there a...?	C'è un...? cheh oon
...day ticket	...biglietto giornaliero beel-**yeh**-toh jor-nahl-**yeh**-roh
...discount if I buy more tickets	...sconto se compro più biglietti **skohn**-toh say **kohm**-proh pew beel-**yeh**-tee
Can I buy a ticket on board (the bus)?	Posso comprare un biglietto a bordo (dell'autobus)? **poh**-soh kohm-**prah**-ray oon beel-**yeh**-toh ah **bor**-doh (dehl-**ow**-toh-boos)
Exact change only?	Solo importo esatto? **soh**-loh eem-**por**-toh eh-**zah**-toh
validate (here)	timbrare (qui) teem-**brah**-ray (kwee)

In many cities, you are required to ***timbrare*** (validate) your ticket by sticking it into a validation machine as you enter the subway station, bus, or tram. If you have an all-day or multi-day ticket, validate it only the first time you use it.

Transit Terms

Most big cities have the usual public-transit systems, such as the ***Metropolitana*** (subway) and ***autobus*** (city bus). Some cities have unique types of transit, like the ***elettrico*** minibuses in Rome that connect tight old neighborhoods. Venice has boats instead of buses—you'll zip around on ***vaporetti*** (motorized ferries) and ***traghetti*** (gondola ferries).

Key Phrases: City Buses and Subways

bus	autobus **ow**-toh-boos
subway	Metropolitana / Metro meh-troh-poh-lee-**tah**-nah / **meh**-troh
How do I get to ____?	Come si va a ____? **koh**-may see vah ah ____
Which stop for ____?	Qual'è la fermata per ____? kwah-**leh** lah fehr-**mah**-tah pehr ____
Tell me when to get off?	Mi dice quando devo scendere? mee **dee**-chay **kwahn**-doh **deh**-voh **shehn**-deh-ray

city bus	autobus **ow**-toh-boos
electric minibus	elettrico eh-**leh**-tree-koh
bus stop	fermata fehr-**mah**-tah
subway	Metropolitana / Metro meh-troh-poh-lee-**tah**-nah / **meh**-troh
subway station	stazione della Metro staht-see-**oh**-nay **deh**-lah **meh**-troh
public-transit map	mappa dei trasporti **mah**-pah **deh**-ee trah-**spor**-tee
entrance	entrata ehn-**trah**-tah
stop	fermata fehr-**mah**-tah
exit	uscita oo-**shee**-tah
line (subway)	linea **lee**-neh-ah
number (bus)	numero **noo**-meh-roh
direction	direzione dee-reht-see-**oh**-nay
direct	diretto dee-**reh**-toh
connection	coincidenza koh-een-chee-**dehnt**-sah
pickpocket	borseggiatore bor-seh-jah-**toh**-ray

The ***mappa dei trasporti*** is a map of the city's public transit, often accompanied by the ***orario*** (timetable) and ***tariffe*** (fares). At night, most transit stops running, except for a few ***linee notturne*** (night lines).

Public Transit

How do I get to ____?	Come si va a ____? **koh**-may see vah ah ____
How do we get to ____?	Come andiamo a ____? **koh**-may ahn-dee-**ah**-moh ah ____
Which bus to ____?	Quale autobus per ____? **kwah**-lay **ow**-toh-boos pehr ____
Does it stop at ____?	Si ferma a ____? see **fehr**-mah ah ____
Which stop for ____?	Qual'è la fermata per ____? kwah-**leh** lah fehr-**mah**-tah pehr ____
Which direction for ____?	Da che parte è ____? dah kay **par**-tay eh ____
Is a transfer required?	Devo cambiare? **deh**-voh kahm-bee-**ah**-ray
When is...?	Quando parte...? **kwahn**-doh **par**-tay
...the first / next / last...	...il primo / il prossimo / l'ultimo... eel **pree**-moh / eel **proh**-see-moh / **lool**-tee-moh
...bus / subway	...autobus / Metro **ow**-toh-boos / **meh**-troh
How often does it run (per hour / per day)?	Ogni quanto passa (all'ora / al giorno)? **ohn**-yee **kwahn**-toh **pah**-sah (ah-**loh**-rah / ahl **jor**-noh)
When does the next one leave?	Quando parte il prossimo? **kwahn**-doh **par**-tay eel **proh**-see-moh
Where does it leave from?	Da dove parte? dah **doh**-vay **par**-tay
Tell me when to get off?	Mi dice quando devo scendere? mee **dee**-chay **kwahn**-doh **deh**-voh **shehn**-deh-ray

I'm getting off.	Devo scendere. **deh**-voh **shehn**-deh-ray
How do I open the door?	Come si apre la porta? **koh**-may see **ah**-pray lah **por**-tah

If you press the button to request a stop on a bus, a sign lights up that says ***fermata richiesta*** (stop requested). Upon arrival, you might have to press a button or pull a lever to open the door—watch locals and imitate.

TAXIS

Taxis are generally affordable, efficient, and worth considering. They usually take up to four people. If you have trouble flagging down a taxi, ask for directions to a ***fermata dei taxi*** (taxi stand) or seek out a big hotel where taxis wait for guests. The simplest way to tell a cabbie where you want to go is to state your destination followed by "please" ***(Uffizi, per favore)***. Tipping isn't expected, but it's polite to round up—if the fare is €19, give €20.

Getting a Taxi

Taxi!	Taxi! **tahk**-see
Can you call a taxi?	Può chiamare un taxi? pwoh kee-ah-**mah**-ray oon **tahk**-see
Where can I get a taxi?	Dove posso prendere un taxi? **doh**-vay **poh**-soh **prehn**-deh-ray oon **tahk**-see
Where is a taxi stand?	Dov'è una fermata dei taxi? doh-**veh oo**-nah fehr-**mah**-tah **deh**-ee **tahk**-see
Are you free?	È libero? eh **lee**-beh-roh
Occupied.	Occupato. oh-koo-**pah**-toh
To ____, please.	A ____, per favore. ah ____ pehr fah-**voh**-ray
To this address.	A questo indirizzo. ah **kweh**-stoh een-dee-**reed**-zoh

Key Phrases: Taxis

Taxi!	Taxi! **tahk**-see
taxi stand	fermata dei taxi fehr-**mah**-tah **deh**-ee **tahk**-see
Are you free?	È libero? eh **lee**-beh-roh
Occupied.	Occupato. oh-koo-**pah**-toh
To ____, please.	A ____, per favore. ah ____ pehr fah-**voh**-ray
The meter, please.	Il tassametro, per favore. eel tah-sah-**meh**-troh pehr fah-**voh**-ray
Stop here.	Si fermi qui. see **fehr**-mee kwee
My change, please.	Il resto, per favore. eel **reh**-stoh pehr fah-**voh**-ray
Keep the change.	Tenga il resto. **tehn**-gah eel **reh**-stoh

I know there's a meter, but about how much is it to go...?	So che c'è il tassametro, ma più o meno quanto costa andare...? soh kay cheh eel tah-sah-**meh**-troh mah pew oh **meh**-noh **kwahn**-toh **koh**-stah ahn-**dah**-ray
...to ____	...a ____ ah ____
...to the airport	...all'aeroporto ahl-ay-roh-**por**-toh
...to the train station	...alla stazione ferroviaria **ah**-lah staht-see-**oh**-nay feh-roh-vee-**ah**-ree-ah
...to this address	...a questo indirizzo ah **kweh**-stoh een-dee-**reed**-zoh
Is there an extra supplement?	C'è qualche supplemento? cheh **kwahl**-kay soo-pleh-**mehn**-toh
Too much.	Troppo. **troh**-poh

Can you take ___ people?	Può portare ___ persone? pwoh por-**tah**-ray ___ pehr-**soh**-nay
Any extra fee?	C'è un sovrapprezzo? cheh oon soh-vrah-**prehd**-zoh
Do you have an hourly rate?	Avete una tariffa oraria? ah-**veh**-tay **oo**-nah tah-**ree**-fah oh-**rah**-ree-ah
How much for a one-hour city tour?	Quant'è per un giro della città di un'ora? kwahn-**teh** pehr oon **jee**-roh **deh**-lah chee-**tah** dee oon-**oh**-rah

Before hopping in a taxi, it's smart to ask roughly how much your trip will cost. Also, Uber works in many European cities.

Cabbie Conversation

The meter, please.	Il tassametro, per favore. eel tah-sah-**meh**-troh pehr fah-**voh**-ray
Where is the meter?	Dov'è il tassametro? doh-**veh** eel tah-sah-**meh**-troh
I'm / We're in a hurry.	Sono / Siamo di fretta. **soh**-noh / see-**ah**-moh dee **freh**-tah
Slow down.	Rallenti. rah-**lehn**-tee
If you don't slow down, I'll throw up.	Se non rallenta, vomito. say nohn rah-**lehn**-tah **voh**-mee-toh
(To the) left.	(A) sinistra. (ah) see-**nee**-strah
(To the) right.	(A) destra. (ah) **deh**-strah
Straight ahead.	Sempre dritto. **sehm**-pray **dree**-toh
Please stop here...	Per favore, si fermi qui... pehr fah-**voh**-ray see **fehr**-mee kwee
...for a moment.	...per un momento. pehr oon moh-**mehn**-toh
...for ___ minutes.	...per ___ minuti. pehr ___ mee-**noo**-tee
Can you wait?	Può aspettare? pwoh ah-speh-**tah**-ray

Crazy traffic, isn't it?	Un traffico incredibile, vero? oon **trah**-fee-koh een-kreh-**dee**-bee-lay **veh**-roh
You drive like a madman!	Guida come un pazzo! **gwee**-dah **koh**-may oon **pahd**-zoh
You drive very well.	Guida molto bene. **gwee**-dah **mohl**-toh **beh**-nay
I can see it from here.	Lo vedo da qui. loh **veh**-doh dah kwee
Point it out?	Me lo mostra? may loh **moh**-strah
Stop here.	Si fermi qui. see **fehr**-mee kwee
Here is fine.	Va bene qui. vah **beh**-nay kwee
At this corner.	A questo angolo. ah **kweh**-stoh **ahn**-goh-loh
The next corner.	Al prossimo angolo. ahl **proh**-see-moh **ahn**-goh-loh
My change, please.	Il resto, per favore. eel **reh**-stoh pehr fah-**voh**-ray
Keep the change.	Tenga il resto. **tehn**-gah eel **reh**-stoh
This ride is / was more fun than Disneyland.	Questo viaggio è / è stato più divertente di Disneyland. **kweh**-stoh vee-**ah**-joh eh / eh **stah**-toh pew dee-vehr-**tehn**-tay dee "Disneyland"

DRIVING

Renting Wheels

I'd like to rent a...	Vorrei noleggiare un / una... vor-**reh**-ee noh-leh-**jah**-ray oon / **oo**-nah
...car.	...macchina. **mah**-kee-nah
...station wagon.	...station wagon. **staht**-see-ohn **wah**-gohn
...van.	...monovolume. moh-noh-voh-**loo**-may

...convertible.	...decapottabile. dee-kah-poh-**tah**-bee-lay
...motorcycle.	...motocicletta. moh-toh-chee-**kleh**-tah
...motor scooter.	...motorino. moh-toh-**ree**-noh
How much...?	Quanto...? **kwahn**-toh
...per hour	...all'ora ah-**loh**-rah
...per half day	...per mezza giornata pehr **mehd**-zah jor-**nah**-tah
...per day	...al giorno ahl **jor**-noh
...per week	...alla settimana **ah**-lah seh-tee-**mah**-nah
car rental agency	agenzia di autonoleggio ah-**jehnt**-see-ah dee ow-toh-noh-**leh**-joh
tax / insurance	tasse / assicurazione **tah**-say / ah-see-koo-raht-see-**oh**-nay
Includes taxes and insurance?	Include tasse e assicurazione? een-**kloo**-day **tah**-say eh ah-see-koo-raht-see-**oh**-nay
Any extra fee?	Ci sono costi aggiuntivi? chee **soh**-noh **koh**-stee ah-joon-**tee**-vee
Unlimited mileage?	Chilometraggio illimitato? kee-loh-meh-**trah**-joh ee-lee-mee-**tah**-toh
manual / automatic transmission	cambio manuale / automatico **kahm**-bee-oh mahn-oo-**ah**-lay / ow-toh-**mah**-tee-koh
pick up / drop off	ritiro / riconsegna ree-**tee**-roh / ree-kohn-**sehn**-yah
Is there...?	C'è...? cheh
...a discount	...uno sconto **oo**-noh **skohn**-toh
...a deposit	...una caparra **oo**-nah kah-**pah**-rah
...a helmet	...un casco oon **kah**-skoh
When must I bring it back?	Quando devo riportarla? **kwahn**-doh **deh**-voh ree-por-**tar**-lah

Key Phrases: Driving

car	macchina **mah**-kee-nah
gas station	benzinaio behnt-see-**nah**-yoh
parking lot	parcheggio par-**keh**-joh
Where can I park?	Dove posso parcheggiare? **doh**-vay **poh**-soh par-keh-**jah**-ray
downtown	centro **chehn**-troh
straight ahead	sempre dritto **sehm**-pray **dree**-toh
left	sinistra see-**nee**-strah
right	destra **deh**-strah
I'm lost.	Mi sono perso[a]. mee **soh**-noh **pehr**-soh
How do I get to ____?	Come si va a ____? **koh**-may see vah ah ____

Can I drop it off in another city / in ____?	La posso riconsegnare in un'altra città / a ____? lah **poh**-soh ree-kohn-sehn-**yah**-ray een oon-**ahl**-trah chee-**tah** / ah ____
How do I get to the expressway / to ____?	Come arrivo alla superstrada / a ____? **koh**-may ah-**ree**-voh **ah**-lah soo-pehr-**strah**-dah / ah ____

Before leaving the car-rental office, get directions to your next destination—or at least to the expressway. For all the details on the dizzying variety of insurance options, see www.ricksteves.com/cdw. If you'd rather rent a bike, see page 243.

Getting to Know Your Rental Car

Before driving off, familiarize yourself with your rental car. Examine it to be sure that all damage is noted on the rental agreement so you won't be held responsible for it later.

It's damaged here.	Qui c'è un danno. kwee cheh oon **dah**-noh
Please add it to the rental agreement.	Lo aggiunga al contratto di noleggio per favore. loh ah-**joon**-gah ahl kohn-**trah**-toh dee noh-**leh**-joh pehr fah-**voh**-ray
That scratch / That dent was already in the car.	Quel graffio / Quella ammaccatura c'era già. kwehl **grah**-fee-oh / **kweh**-lah ah-mah-kah-**too**-rah **cheh**-rah jah
What kind of gas does it take?	Che tipo di benzina ha? kay **tee**-poh dee behnt-**see**-nah ah
gas	benzina behnt-**see**-nah
diesel	gasolio gah-**zoh**-lee-oh
How do I open the gas cap?	Come si apre il tappo della benzina? **koh**-may see **ah**-pray eel **tah**-poh **deh**-lah behnt-**see**-nah
How does this work?	Come funziona? **koh**-may foont-see-**oh**-nah
key	chiave kee-**ah**-vay
headlights	fari **fah**-ree
radio	radio **rah**-dee-oh
windshield wipers	tergicristalli tehr-jee-kree-**stah**-lee
alarm / security system	allarme / sistema di sicurezza ah-**lar**-may / see-**steh**-mah dee see-koor-**ehd**-zah
How do I turn off the security system?	Come si spegne l'allarme? **koh**-may see **spehn**-yay lah-**lar**-may
GPS	GPS jee-pee-**ehs**-ay

How do I change the language to English?	Come si cambia la lingua per avere l'inglese? **koh**-may see **kahm**-bee-ah lah **leen**-gwah pehr ah-**veh**-ray leen-**gleh**-zay

Sometimes you can rent a GPS device with your car. The language for the menus and instructions can be changed to English.

Traffic Troubles

The biggest traffic problem many visitors have in Italy is being fined for driving in restricted zones. Traffic is forbidden in many city centers (including Rome, Florence, and Milan). Don't drive or park in any area that has a sign reading ***Zona Traffico Limitato*** (***ZTL,*** often shown above a red circle). If you do, your license plate can be photographed and a hefty ticket will be mailed to your home.

traffic	traffico **trah**-fee-koh
traffic jam	ingorgo een-**gor**-goh
rush hour	ora di punta oh-rah dee **poon**-tah
delay	ritardo ree-**tar**-doh
construction	lavori stradali lah-**voh**-ree strah-**dah**-lee
accident	incidente een-chee-**dehn**-tay
detour	deviazione deh-vee-aht-see-**oh**-nay
How long is the delay?	Di quant'è il ritardo? dee kwahn-**teh** eel ree-**tar**-doh
Is there another way to go (to ____)?	C'è un'altra strada (per ____)? cheh oon-**ahl**-trah **strah**-dah (pehr ____)

For more navigational words, see "Finding Your Way," later.

Tolls

Expressways ***(autostrada)*** come with tolls but save time. Signs are sparse—stay alert so you don't miss your exit. Sometimes there's a toll-free ***superstrada*** that's just as fast for your journey—ask around.

toll road	autostrada ow-toh-**strah**-dah
tolls	pedaggio autostradale peh-**dah**-joh ow-toh-strah-**dah**-lay
tollbooth	casello kah-**zeh**-loh
toll ticket	biglietto del pedaggio beel-**yeh**-toh dehl peh-**dah**-joh
cash / card	contanti / carta kohn-**tahn**-tee / **kar**-tah
to pay	pagare pah-**gah**-ray
Is there a fast free road to ____?	C'è una superstrada per ____? cheh **oo**-nah soo-pehr-**strah**-dah pehr ____

At the Gas Station

Unleaded is ***senza piombo*** or ***benzina verde*** (which can be ***normale*** or ***super***), and diesel is ***gasolio.*** Prices are listed per liter; there are about four liters in a gallon. Small-town stations are usually cheaper than ***autostrada*** rest stops, but have shorter hours.

gas station	benzinaio behnt-see-**nah**-yoh
The nearest gas station?	Il benzinaio più vicino? eel behnt-see-**nah**-yoh pew vee-**chee**-noh
Self-service?	Self-service? sehlf-**sehr**-vees
Fill the tank.	Il pieno. eel pee-**eh**-noh
I need...	Ho bisogno di... oh bee-**zohn**-yoh dee
...gas.	...benzina. behnt-**see**-nah
...unleaded.	...benzina verde. behnt-**see**-nah **vehr**-day
...super.	...super. **soo**-pehr
...diesel.	...gasolio. gah-**zoh**-lee-oh

Parking

parking lot	parcheggio par-**keh**-joh
parking garage	garage gah-**rahj**
ticket machine / parking meter	parchimetro par-kee-**meh**-troh
parking clock (to put on dashboard)	disco **dee**-skoh
available / full	disponibile / completo dee-spoh-**nee**-bee-lay / kohm-**pleh**-toh
Where can I park?	Dove posso parcheggiare? **doh**-vay **poh**-soh par-keh-**jah**-ray
Is parking nearby?	È vicino il parcheggio? eh vee-**chee**-noh eel par-**keh**-joh
Can I park here?	Posso parcheggiare qui? **poh**-soh par-keh-**jah**-ray kwee
How long can I park here?	Per quanto tempo posso parcheggiare qui? pehr **kwahn**-toh **tehm**-poh **poh**-soh par-keh-**jah**-ray kwee
Is it safe?	È sicuro? eh see-**koo**-roh
Is it free?	È gratis? eh **grah**-tees
Where do I pay?	Dove posso pagare? **doh**-vay **poh**-soh pah-**gah**-ray
How much per hour / per day?	Quanto costa all'ora / al giorno? **kwahn**-toh **koh**-stah ahl-**loh**-rah / ahl **jor**-noh

Parking in Italian cities is expensive and hazardous. Plan to pay to use a parking garage in big cities. Leave nothing of value in your car. Take parking restrictions seriously to avoid getting fines and having your car towed away (a memorable but costly experience).

If you park on the street, white lines generally mean parking is free. Study the signs—often the free zones have a 30- or 60-minute limit. Italian cars come equipped with a ***disco*** (cardboard clock), which you can use in a ***zona disco***—set the clock to your arrival time and leave it on the dashboard. Blue lines mean you'll have to pay at the machine (then leave the time-stamped receipt on the dashboard). If there's no machine, there's probably a roving attendant who will take your money (the attendant must give you a receipt/ticket—otherwise, he's not legal). Yellow lines indicate residential permit parking.

Signs showing a street cleaner and a day of the week indicate which day the street is cleaned; there's a very high tow-fee incentive to learn the days of the week in Italian (see page 16).

Garages are more expensive than street parking but are safe, save time, and help you avoid the stress of parking tickets. You'll usually receive a ticket when you enter the garage; take it with you and pay before returning to your car.

Car Trouble and Parts

accident	incidente een-chee-**dehn**-tay
fender-bender	tamponamento tahm-poh-nah-**mehn**-toh
breakdown	guasto **gwah**-stoh
repair shop	autofficina ow-toh-fee-**chee**-nah
strange noise	rumore strano roo-**moh**-ray **strah**-noh
electrical problem	problema elettrico proh-**bleh**-mah eh-**leh**-tree-koh
warning light	luci d'emergenza **loo**-chee dee-mehr-**jehnt**-sah
smoke	fumo **foo**-moh
My car won't start.	La mia macchina non parte. lah **mee**-ah **mah**-kee-nah nohn **par**-tay
My car is broken.	La mia macchina è rotta. lah **mee**-ah **mah**-kee-nah eh **roh**-tah
This doesn't work.	Non funziona. nohn foont-see-**oh**-nah
Please check this.	Controlli questo per favore. kohn-**troh**-lee **kweh**-stoh pehr fah-**voh**-ray
oil	olio **oh**-lee-oh
(flat) tire	gomma (a terra) **goh**-mah (ah **teh**-rah)

air in the tires	aria nelle gomme **ah**-ree-ah **neh**-lay **goh**-may
radiator	radiatore rah-dee-ah-**toh**-ray
(dead) battery	batteria (scarica) bah-teh-**ree**-ah (**skah**-ree-kah)
sparkplug	candela kahn-**deh**-lah
fuse	fusibile foo-**zee**-bee-lay
headlights	fari **fah**-ree
taillights	luci posteriori **loo**-chee pos-teh-ree-**oh**-ree
turn signal	freccia **freh**-chah
brakes	freni **freh**-nee
window	finestrino fee-neh-**stree**-noh
windshield	parabrezza pah-rah-**brehd**-zah
windshield wipers	tergicristalli tehr-gee-kree-**stah**-lee
engine	motore moh-**toh**-ray
fanbelt	cinghia del ventilatore **cheen**-gee-ah (hard "g") dehl vehn-tee-lah-**toh**-ray
starter	motorino di avviamento moh-toh-**ree**-noh dee ah-vee-ah-**mehn**-toh
transmission (fluid)	(liquido della) trasmissione (**lee**-kwee-doh **deh**-lah) trahs-mee-see-**oh**-nay
key	chiave kee-**ah**-vay
alarm	allarme ah-**lar**-may
It's overheating.	Si sta surriscaldando. see stah soo-ree-skahl-**dahn**-doh
It's a lemon (a swindle).	È una fregatura. eh **oo**-nah freh-gah-**too**-rah
I need...	Ho bisogno di... oh bee-**zohn**-yoh dee
...a tow truck.	...un carro attrezzi. oon **kah**-roh ah-**trehd**-zee

...a mechanic.	...un meccanico. oon meh-**kah**-nee-koh
...a stiff drink.	...un whiskey. oon "whiskey"

For help with repair, see "Repairs" on page 299 of the Services chapter.

The Police

In any country, the flashing lights of a patrol car are a sure sign that someone's in trouble. If it's you, try this handy phrase: ***Mi dispiace, sono un turista*** (Sorry, I'm a tourist). Or, for the adventurous: ***Se non le piace come guido, si tolga dal marciapiede.*** (If you don't like how I drive, stay off the sidewalk.) If you're in serious need of assistance, turn to the Help! chapter.

police	polizia poh-leet-**see**-ah
officer	agente di polizia ah-**jehn**-tay dee poh-leet-**see**-ah
driver's license	patente di guida pah-**tehn**-tay dee **gwee**-dah
international driving permit	patente internazionale pah-**tehn**-tay een-tehr-naht-see-oh-**nah**-lay
What seems to be the problem?	Quale sarebbe il problema? **kwah**-lay sah-**reh**-bay eel proh-**bleh**-mah
restricted zone	zona a traffico limitato **zoh**-nah ah **trah**-fee-koh lee-mee-**tah**-toh
pedestrian-only	zona pedonale **zoh**-nah peh-doh-**nah**-lay
speeding	eccesso di velocità eh-**cheh**-soh dee veh-loh-chee-**tah**
I didn't know the speed limit.	Non sapevo quale fosse il limite di velocità. nohn sah-**peh**-voh **kwah**-lay **foh**-say eel **lee**-mee-tay dee veh-loh-chee-**tah**

parking ticket	multa per divieto di sosta **mool**-tah pehr dee-vee-**eh**-toh dee **soh**-stah
I didn't know where to park.	Non sapevo dove parcheggiare. nohn sah-**peh**-voh **doh**-vay par-keh-**jah**-ray
I am very sorry.	Mi dispiace molto. mee dee-spee-**ah**-chay **mohl**-toh
Can I buy your hat?	Mi vende il suo cappello? mee **vehn**-day eel **soo**-oh kah-**peh**-loh

FINDING YOUR WAY

Whether you're driving, walking, or biking, these phrases will help you get around.

Route-Finding Phrases

I'm going / We're going to ____.	Vado / Andiamo a ____. **vah**-doh / ahn-dee-**ah**-moh ah ____
Do you have a...?	Avete una...? ah-**veh**-tay **oo**-nah
...city map	...cartina della città kar-**tee**-nah **deh**-lah chee-**tah**
...road map	...cartina stradale kar-**tee**-nah strah-**dah**-lay
How many minutes...?	Quanti minuti...? **kwahn**-tee mee-**noo**-tee
How many hours...?	Quante ore...? **kwahn**-tay **oh**-ray
...on foot	...a piedi ah pee-**eh**-dee
...by bicycle	...in bicicletta een bee-chee-**kleh**-tah
...by car	...in macchina een **mah**-kee-nah
How many kilometers to ____?	Quanti chilometri per ____? **kwahn**-tee kee-**loh**-meh-tree pehr ____

What is the... route to Rome?	Qual'è la strada... per andare a Roma? kwah-**leh** lah **strah**-dah... pehr ahn-**dah**-ray ah **roh**-mah
...most scenic	...più panoramica pew pah-noh-**rah**-mee-kah
...fastest	...più veloce pew veh-**loh**-chay
...easiest	...più facile pew **fah**-chee-lay
...most interesting	...più interessante pew een-teh-reh-**sahn**-tay
Point it out?	Me lo mostra? may loh **moh**-strah
Where is this address?	Dov'è questo indirizzo? doh-**veh kweh**-stoh een-dee-**reed**-zoh

You can summit some hill towns by using a ***scala mobile*** (long escalator), ***ascensore*** (elevator), or ***funicolare*** (funicular). For terms relating to mountain lifts, see page 246.

Directions

Following signs to ***centro*** will land you in the heart of things. On a map, ***(voi) siete qui*** means "you are here."

downtown	centro **chehn**-troh
straight ahead	sempre dritto **sehm**-pray **dree**-toh
(to the) left / right	(a) sinistra / destra (ah) see-**nee**-strah / **deh**-strah
first	prima **pree**-mah
next	prossima **proh**-see-mah
intersection	incrocio een-**kroh**-choh
corner	angolo **ahn**-goh-loh
block	isolato ee-zoh-**lah**-toh
roundabout	rotonda roh-**tohn**-dah
stoplight	semaforo seh-**mah**-foh-roh
(main) square	piazza (principale) pee-**aht**-sah (preen-chee-**pah**-lay)

street	strada / via **strah**-dah / **vee**-ah
avenue	viale vee-**ah**-lay
tree-lined avenue	viale alberato vee-**ah**-lay ahl-beh-**rah**-toh
curve	curva **koor**-vah
bridge	ponte **pohn**-tay
tunnel	galleria gah-leh-**ree**-ah
road	strada **strah**-dah
highway	autostrada ow-toh-**strah**-dah
expressway	superstrada soo-pehr-**strah**-dah
north	nord nord
south	sud sood
east	est ehst
west	ovest **oh**-vehst
shortcut	scorciatoia skor-chah-**toy**-ah
traffic jam	ingorgo een-**gor**-goh

Lost Your Way

I'm lost.	Mi sono perso[a]. mee **soh**-noh **pehr**-soh
We're lost.	Ci siamo persi. chee see-**ah**-moh **pehr**-see
Excuse me, can you help me?	Scusi, mi può aiutare? **skoo**-zee mee pwoh ah-yoo-**tah**-ray
Where am I?	Dove sono? **doh**-vay **soh**-noh
Where is ____?	Dov'è ____? doh-**veh** ____
How do I get to ____?	Come si va a ____? **koh**-may see vah ah ____
Can you show me the way?	Mi può indicare la strada? mee pwoh een-dee-**kah**-ray lah **strah**-dah

Reading Road Signs

Alt / Stop	Stop
Attenzione	Caution
Carabinieri	Police
Centro / Centrocittà	Center of town
Circonvallazione	Ring road
Dare la precedenza	Yield
Deviazione	Detour
Entrata	Entrance
Lavori in corso	Road work ahead
Lavori stradali	Construction
Non si passa, c'è la manifestazione	Closed due to a demonstration
Prossima uscita	Next exit
Rallentare	Slow down
Senso unico	One-way street
Tutti le (altre) destinazioni	All (other) destinations (follow when leaving a town)
Uscita	Exit
Zona pedonale	Pedestrian zone
Zona traffico limitato (ZTL)	Cars not allowed (If you drive here, you'll get a ticket)

For a list of other signs you might see, turn to page 20.

Going Places

If you're using a Rick Steves guidebook, you're likely to see these place names. If someone doesn't understand your pronunciation, write the town name on a piece of paper.

Cinque Terre	**cheen**-kway **teh**-ray
Civita (di Bagnoregio)	chee-**vee**-tah (dee bahn-yoh-**reh**-jee-oh)
Florence (Firenze)	fee-**rehnt**-say
Italian Riviera (Riviera Ligure)	ree-vee-**yeh**-rah lee-**goo**-ray
Lake Como (Lago di Como)	**lah**-goh dee **koh**-moh

Milan (Milano)	mee-**lah**-noh
Naples (Napoli)	**nah**-poh-lee
Rome (Roma)	**roh**-mah
San Gimignano	sahn jee-meen-**yah**-noh
Vatican City (Città del Vaticano)	chee-**tah** dehl vah-tee-**kah**-noh
Venice (Venezia)	veh-**neht**-see-ah
Vernazza	vehr-**naht**-sah

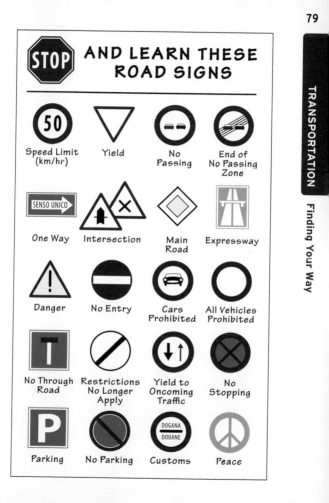

AND LEARN THESE ROAD SIGNS

Speed Limit (km/hr)

Yield

No Passing

End of No Passing Zone

One Way

Intersection

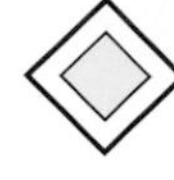

Main Road

Expressway

Danger

No Entry

Cars Prohibited

All Vehicles Prohibited

No Through Road

Restrictions No Longer Apply

Yield to Oncoming Traffic

No Stopping

Parking

No Parking

Customs

Peace

SLEEPING

This chapter covers making reservations, hotel stays (including checking in, typical hotel words, making requests, and dealing with difficulties), specific concerns (such as families and mobility issues), and hostels.

RESERVATIONS

Making a Reservation

reservation	prenotazione preh-noh-taht-see-**oh**-nay
Do you have...?	Avete...? ah-**veh**-tay
I'd like to reserve...	Vorrei prenotare... voh-**reh**-ee preh-noh-**tah**-ray
...a room for...	...una camera per... **oo**-nah **kah**-meh-rah pehr
...one person / two people	...una persona / due persone **oo**-nah pehr-**soh**-nah / **doo**-ay pehr-**soh**-nay
...today / tomorrow	...oggi / domani **oh**-jee / doh-**mah**-nee
...one night	...una notte **oo**-nah **noh**-tay
two / three nights	due / tre notti **doo**-ay / tray **noh**-tee
June 21	il ventuno giugno eel vehn-**too**-noh **joon**-yoh
How much is it?	Quanto costa? **kwahn**-toh **koh**-stah
Anything cheaper?	Niente di più economico? nee-**ehn**-tay dee pew eh-koh-**noh**-mee-koh
I'll take it.	La prendo. lah **prehn**-doh
My name is ____.	Mi chiamo ____. mee kee-**ah**-moh ____
Do you need a deposit?	Bisogna lasciare un acconto? bee-**zohn**-yah lah-**shah**-ray oon ah-**kohn**-toh

Key Phrases: Sleeping

Do you have a room?	Avete una camera? ah-**veh**-tay **oo**-nah **kah**-meh-rah
for one person / two people	per una persona / due persone pehr **oo**-nah pehr-**soh**-nah / **doo**-ay pehr-**soh**-nay
today / tomorrow	oggi / domani **oh**-jee / doh-**mah**-nee
one night / two nights	una notte / due notti **oo**-nah **noh**-tay / **doo**-ay **noh**-tee
How much is it?	Quanto costa? **kwahn**-toh **koh**-stah
hotel	hotel / albergo oh-**tehl** / ahl-**behr**-goh
small hotel	pensione / locanda pehn-see-**oh**-nay / loh-**kahn**-dah
vacancy / no vacancy	camere disponibili / completo **kah**-meh-ray dee-spoh-**nee**-bee-lee / kohm-**pleh**-toh

Do you accept credit cards?	Accettate carte di credito? ah-cheh-**tah**-tay **kar**-tay dee **kreh**-dee-toh
Can I reserve with a credit card and pay in cash?	Posso prenotare con la carta di credito e pagare in contanti? **poh**-soh preh-noh-**tah**-ray kohn lah **kar**-tah dee **kreh**-dee-toh ay pah-**gah**-ray een kohn-**tahn**-tee

Many people stay at a ***hotel*** (also called ***albergo***), but you have other choices as well. These include a small hotel (***pensione*** or ***locanda***), a country inn ***(locanda di campagna),*** or a working farm with accommodations ***(agriturismo).*** Staying at a family-run place offers double the cultural experience for half the price of a hotel. Rooms rented in a home may be called ***camere*** (rooms), ***soggiorno*** (stay), or simply ***B&B***. Other options include a hostel ***(ostello)***, a vacation apartment ***(casa vacanze)***, or accommodations in a convent (often called ***instituto***).

Getting Specific

I'd like a...	Vorrei una... voh-**reh**-ee **oo**-nah
...single room.	...camera singola. **kah**-meh-rah **seen**-goh-lah
...double room.	...camera doppia. **kah**-meh-rah **doh**-pee-ah
...triple room.	...camera tripla. **kah**-meh-rah **treep**-lah
...room for ___ people.	...camera per ___ persone. **kah**-meh-rah pehr ___ pehr-**soh**-nay
with / without / and	con / senza / e kohn / **sehnt**-sah / ay
double bed	letto matrimoniale **leh**-toh mah-tree-moh-nee-**ah**-lay
twin beds	letti singoli **leh**-tee **seen**-goh-lee
...together / separate	...uniti / separati oon-**ee**-tee / seh-pah-**rah**-tee
single bed	letto singolo **leh**-toh **seen**-goh-loh
bed without a footboard	letto senza piedi **leh**-toh **sehnt**-sah pee-**ay**-dee
private bathroom	bagno in camera **bahn**-yoh een **kah**-meh-rah
toilet	toilette / gabinetto twah-**leh**-tay / gah-bee-**neh**-toh
shower	doccia **doh**-chah
bathtub	vasca da bagno **vah**-skah dah **bahn**-yoh
with only a sink	con solo un lavandino kohn **soh**-loh oon lah-vahn-**dee**-noh
shower outside the room	doccia comune **doh**-chah koh-**moo**-nay
balcony	balcone bahl-**koh**-nay

view	vista **vee**-stah
cheap	economica eh-koh-**noh**-mee-kah
quiet	tranquilla trahn-**kwee**-lah
romantic	romantica roh-**mahn**-tee-kah
on the ground floor	al piano terra ahl pee-**ah**-noh **teh**-rah
Do you have...?	Avete...? ah-**veh**-tay
...an elevator	...l'ascensore lah-shehn-**soh**-ray
...air-conditioning	...l'aria condizionata **lah**-ree-ah kohn-deet-see-oh-**nah**-tah
...Wi-Fi (in the room)	...il Wi-Fi (in camera) eel **wee**-fee (een **kah**-meh-rah)
...parking	...un parcheggio oon par-**keh**-joh
...a garage	...un garage oon gah-**rahj**
What's your email address?	Qual'è il suo indirizzo email? kwah-**leh** eel **soo**-oh een-dee-**reed**-zoh "email"
What is your cancellation policy?	Quali sono i termini per la cancellazione della prenotazione? **kwah**-lee **soh**-noh ee **tehr**-mee-nee pehr lah kahn-cheh-laht-see-**oh**-nay **deh**-lah preh-noh-taht-see-**oh**-nay

In Italy, a true double or queen-size bed is relatively rare. Sometimes, a "double bed" is two twin beds in separate frames, pushed together.

Taller guests may want to request a ***letto senza piedi*** (bed without a footboard).

Nailing Down the Price

price	prezzo **prehd**-zoh
How much is...?	Quanto costa...? **kwahn**-toh **koh**-stah
...a room for ____ people	...una camera per ____ persone **oo**-nah **kah**-meh-rah pehr ____ pehr-**soh**-nay

What Your Hotelier Wants to Know

If you'd like to reserve by email, your hotelier needs to know the following information: number and type of rooms (i.e., single or double); number of nights; date of arrival (written day/month/year); date of departure; and any special needs (such as bathroom in the room, cheapest room, twin beds vs. one big bed, crib, air-conditioning, quiet, view, ground floor, no stairs, and so on). Here's a sample email I'd send to make a reservation.

From:	rick@ricksteves.com
Sent:	Today
To:	info@hotelcentral.com
Subject:	Reservation request for 19-22 July

Dear Hotel Central,

I would like to stay at your hotel. Please let me know if you have a room available and the price for:
- 2 people
- Double bed and en suite bathroom in a quiet room
- Arriving 19 July, departing 22 July (3 nights)

Thank you!
Rick Steves

The hotel will reply with its room availability and rates for your dates. This is not a confirmation—you must email back to say that you want the room at the given rate, and you'll likely be asked for a credit-card number for a deposit.

...your cheapest room	...la camera più economica lah **kah**-meh-rah pew eh-koh-**noh**-mee-kah
Is breakfast included?	La colazione è inclusa? lah koh-laht-see-**oh**-nay eh een-**kloo**-zah
Complete price?	Prezzo completo? **prehd**-zoh kohm-**pleh**-toh
Is it cheaper if...?	È più economico se...? eh pew eh-koh-**noh**-mee-koh say
...I stay three nights	...mi fermo tre notti mee **fehr**-moh tray **noh**-tee
...I pay cash	...pago in contanti **pah**-goh een kohn-**tahn**-tee

Many hotels are willing to lower the price if you stay for longer periods and/or pay in cash. Rates can vary by season: High season ***(alta stagione)*** is more expensive than low season ***(bassa stagione)***. At some hotels in resort towns, you're required to pay for half-pension ***(mezza pensione),*** which covers lunch or dinner at their restaurant.

Arrival and Departure

(date of) arrival	(data di) arrivo (**dah**-tah dee) ah-**ree**-voh
(date of) departure	(data di) partenza (**dah**-tah dee) par-**tent**-sah
I'll arrive / We'll arrive...	Arrivo / Arriviamo... ah-**ree**-voh / ah-ree-vee-**ah**-moh
I'll depart / We'll depart...	Parto / Partiamo... **par**-toh / par-tee-**ah**-moh
...June 16.	...il sedici giugno. eel **seh**-dee-chee **joon**-yoh

...in the morning / afternoon / evening.	...la mattina / il pomeriggio / la sera. lah mah-**tee**-nah / eel poh-meh-**ree**-joh / lah **seh**-rah
...Friday before 6 p.m.	...venerdì entro le sei di sera. veh-nehr-**dee ehn**-troh lay **seh**-ee dee **seh**-rah
I'll stay / We'll stay two nights.	Starò / Staremo due notti. stah-**roh** / stah-**reh**-moh **doo**-ay **noh**-tee
We arrive Monday, depart Wednesday.	Arriviamo lunedì, partiamo mercoledì. ah-ree-vee-**ah**-moh loo-neh-**dee** par-tee-**ah**-moh mehr-koh-leh-**dee**

For help with saying dates in Italian, see the "Time and Dates" section starting on page 31.

Confirm, Change, or Cancel

It's smart to call a day or two in advance to confirm your reservation.

I have a reservation.	Ho una prenotazione. oh **oo**-nah preh-noh-taht-see-**oh**-nay
My name is ____.	Mi chiamo ____. mee kee-**ah**-moh ____
I'd like to... my reservation.	Vorrei... una prenotazione. voh-**reh**-ee... **oo**-nah preh-noh-taht-see-**oh**-nay
...confirm	...confermare kohn-fehr-**mah**-ray
...change	...cambiare kahm-bee-**ah**-ray
...cancel	...annullare ah-noo-**lah**-ray
The reservation is for...	La prenotazione è per... lah preh-noh-taht-see-**oh**-nay eh pehr
...today / tomorrow.	...oggi / domani. **oh**-jee / doh-**mah**-nee
...August 13.	...il tredici agosto. eel **treh**-dee-chee ah-**goh**-stoh

Did you find the reservation?	Avete trovato la prenotazione? ah-**veh**-tay troh-**vah**-toh lah preh-noh-taht-see-**oh**-nay
Is everything OK?	Va bene? vah **beh**-nay
See you then.	Ci vediamo allora. chee veh-dee-**ah**-moh ah-**loh**-rah
I'm sorry that I need to cancel.	Mi dispiace ma devo cancellare la mia prenotazione. mee dee-spee-**ah**-chay mah **deh**-voh kahn-cheh-**lah**-ray lah **mee**-ah preh-noh-taht-see-**oh**-nay
Is there a penalty (for canceling the reservation)?	C'è una penalità da pagare (in caso di cancellazione)? cheh **oo**-nah peh-nah-lee-**tah** dah pah-**gah**-ray (een **kah**-zoh dee kahn-cheh-laht-see-**oh**-nay)

Depending on how far ahead you cancel a reservation—and on the hotel's cancellation policy—you might pay a penalty.

AT THE HOTEL

Checking In

My name is ____.	Mi chiamo ____. mee kee-**ah**-moh ____
I have a reservation.	Ho una prenotazione. oh **oo**-nah preh-noh-taht-see-**oh**-nay
one night	una notte **oo**-nah **noh**-tay
two / three nights	due / tre notti **doo**-ay / tray **noh**-tee
When will the room be ready?	Quando sarà pronta la camera? **kwahn**-doh sah-**rah** **prohn**-tah lah **kah**-meh-rah
Where is...?	Dov'è...? doh-**veh**
...my room	...la mia camera lah **mee**-ah **kah**-meh-rah

...the elevator	...l'ascensore lah-shehn-**soh**-ray
...the breakfast room	...la sala colazione lah **sah**-lah koh-laht-see-**oh**-nay
Is breakfast included?	La colazione è inclusa? lah koh-laht-see-**oh**-nay eh een-**kloo**-zah
When does breakfast start and end?	Quando comincia e finisce la colazione? **kwahn**-doh koh-**meen**-chah ay fee-**nee**-shay lah koh-laht-see-**oh**-nay
key	chiave kee-**ah**-vay
Two keys, please.	Due chiavi, per favore. **doo**-ay kee-**ah**-vee pehr fah-**voh**-ray

Choosing a Room

Can I see...?	Posso vedere...? **poh**-soh veh-**deh**-ray
...a room	...una camera **oo**-nah **kah**-meh-rah
...a different room	...un'altra camera oon-**ahl**-trah **kah**-meh-rah
Do you have something...?	Avete qualcosa...? ah-**veh**-tay kwahl-**koh**-zah
...larger / smaller	...di più grande / di più piccolo dee pew **grahn**-day / dee pew **pee**-koh-loh
...better / cheaper	...di più bello / di più economico dee pew **beh**-loh / dee pew eh-koh-**noh**-mee-koh
...brighter	...di più luminoso dee pew loo-mee-**noh**-zoh
...quieter	...di più tranquillo dee pew trahn-**kwee**-loh
...in the back	...sul retro sool **reh**-troh
...with a view (of the sea)	...con vista (sul mare) kohn **vee**-stah (sool **mah**-ray)

...on a lower / higher floor	...ad un piano più basso / più alto ahd oon pee-**ah**-noh pew **bah**-soh / pew **ahl**-toh
No, thank you.	No, grazie. noh **graht**-see-ay
What a charming room!	Che bella camera! kay **beh**-lah **kah**-meh-rah
I'll take it.	La prendo. lah **prehn**-doh

When selecting a room, be aware that ***con vista*** (with a view) can also come with more noise. If a ***tranquilla*** room is important to you, say so.

Hotel Words

cancellation policy	termini per la cancellazione della prenotazione **tehr**-mee-nee pehr lah kahn-cheh-laht-see-**oh**-nay **deh**-lah preh-noh-taht-see-**oh**-nay
elevator	l'ascensore lah-shehn-**soh**-ray
emergency exit	uscita d'emergenza oo-**shee**-tah deh-mehr-**jehnt**-sah
fire escape	scala anti-incendio **skah**-lah ahn-tee-een-**chehn**-dee-oh
floor...	piano... pee-**ah**-noh
...lower / higher	...più basso / più alto pew **bah**-soh / pew **ahl**-toh
ground floor	al piano terra ahl pee-**ah**-noh **teh**-rah
laundry	bucato boo-**kah**-toh
parking	parcheggio par-**keh**-joh
price	tariffe tah-**ree**-fay
reservation	prenotazione preh-noh-taht-see-**oh**-nay
room...	camera... **kah**-meh-rah
...single	...singola **seen**-goh-lah
...double	...doppia **doh**-pee-ah

...triple	...tripla **treep**-lah
...family	...per una famiglia pehr **oo**-nah fah-**meel**-yah
stairs	scale **skah**-lay
suite	suite sweet
swimming pool	la piscina lah pee-**shee**-nah
view	vista **vee**-stah
Wi-Fi	Wi-Fi **wee**-fee

In Your Room

air-conditioner	condizionatore kohn-deet-see-oh-nah-**toh**-ray
alarm clock	sveglia **svehl**-yah
balcony	balcone bahl-**koh**-nay
bathroom	bagno **bahn**-yoh
bathtub	vasca da bagno **vah**-skah dah **bahn**-yoh
bed	letto **leh**-toh
bedspread	copriletto koh-pree-**leh**-toh
blanket	coperta koh-**pehr**-tah
blinds	persiane pehr-see-**ah**-nay
city map	mappa della città **mah**-pah **deh**-lah chee-**tah**
chair	sedia **seh**-dee-ah
closet	armadio ar-**mah**-dee-oh
corkscrew	cavatappi kah-vah-**tah**-pee
crib	culla **koo**-lah
curtain	tenda **tehn**-dah
door	porta **por**-tah
double bed	letto matrimoniale **leh**-toh mah-tree-moh-nee-**ah**-lay
drain	scarico **skah**-ree-koh

electrical adapter	adattatore elettrico ah-dah-tah-**toh**-ray eh-**leh**-tree-koh
electrical outlet	presa **preh**-zah
faucet	rubinetto roo-bee-**neh**-toh
hair dryer	phon fohn
hanger	stampella stahm-**peh**-lah
key	chiave kee-**ah**-vay
kitchenette	cucina koo-**chee**-nah
lamp	lampada **lahm**-pah-dah
lightbulb	lampadina lahm-pah-**dee**-nah
lock	serratura seh-rah-**too**-rah
mirror	specchio **speh**-kee-oh
pillow	cuscino koo-**shee**-noh
radio	radio **rah**-dee-oh
remote control...	telecomando... teh-leh-koh-**mahn**-doh
...for the TV	...per la televisione pehr lah teh-leh-vee-zee-**oh**-nay
...for the air-conditioning	...per l'aria condizionata pehr **lah**-ree-ah kohn-deet-see-oh-**nah**-tah
safe	cassaforte kah-sah-**for**-tay
scissors	forbici **for**-bee-chee
shampoo	shampo **shahm**-poh
sheets	lenzuola lehnt-**swoh**-lah
shower	doccia **doh**-chah
shutters	persiane pehr-see-**ah**-nay
single bed	letto singolo **leh**-toh **seen**-goh-loh
sink	lavabo **lah**-vah-boh
sink stopper	tappo **tah**-poh
soap	sapone sah-**poh**-nay
sponge (for the shower)	spugna (per la doccia) **spoon**-yah (pehr lah **doh**-chah)
telephone	telefono teh-**leh**-foh-noh

television	televisione teh-leh-vee-zee-**oh**-nay
toilet	gabinetto gah-bee-**neh**-toh
toilet paper	carta igienica **kar**-tah ee-**jeh**-nee-kah
towel (hand)	asciugamano per il viso ah-shoo-gah-**mah**-noh pehr eel **vee**-zoh
towel (bath)	telo bagno **teh**-loh **bahn**-yoh
twin beds	letti singoli **leh**-tee **seen**-goh-lee
wake-up call	sveglia telefonica **svehl**-yah teh-leh-**foh**-nee-kah
water (hot / cold)	acqua (calda / fredda) **ahk**-wah (**kahl**-dah / **freh**-dah)
window	finestra fee-**neh**-strah
window screen	zanzariera zahn-zah-ree-**eh**-rah

If you don't see remote controls (for the TV or air-conditioner) in the room, ask for them at the front desk. A comfortable setting for the air-conditioner is about 20 degrees Celsius. On Italian faucets, a **C** stands for ***caldo*** (hot)—the opposite of cold.

Hotel Hassles

Combine these phrases with the words in the previous table to make simple and clear statements such as: ***Gabinetto non funziona*** (Toilet doesn't work).

There is a problem in my room.	C'è un problema nella mia camera. cheh oon proh-**bleh**-mah **neh**-lah **mee**-ah **kah**-meh-rah
Come with me.	Venga con me. **vehn**-gah kohn may
The room is...	La camera è... lah **kah**-meh-rah eh
...dirty.	...sporca. **spor**-kah
...noisy.	...rumorosa. roo-moh-**roh**-zah

...stinky.	...maleodorante. mah-leh-oh-doh-**rahn**-tay
...too hot / too cold.	...troppo calda / troppo fredda. **troh**-poh **kahl**-dah / **troh**-poh **freh**-dah
How can I make the room cooler / warmer?	Come devo fare per avere la camera più fresca / più calda? **koh**-may **deh**-voh **fah**-ray pehr ah-**veh**-ray lah **kah**-meh-rah pew **frehs**-kah / pew **kahl**-dah
The room is moldy / musty.	Nella camera c'è la muffa / odore di chiuso. **neh**-lah **kah**-meh-rah cheh lah **moo**-fah / oh-**doh**-ray dee kee-**oo**-zoh
It's smoky.	C'è l'odore di fumo. cheh loh-**doh**-ray dee **foo**-moh
There's no (hot) water.	Non c'è acqua (calda). nohn cheh **ahk**-wah (**kahl**-dah)
I can't open / shut / lock...	Non riesco ad aprire / a chiudere / a chiudere a chiave... nohn ree-**eh**-skoh ahd ah-**pree**-ray / ah kee-oo-**deh**-ray / ah kee-oo-**deh**-ray ah kee-**ah**-vay
...the door / the window.	...la porta / la finestra. lah **por**-tah / lah fee-**neh**-strah
How does this work?	Come funziona? **koh**-may foont-see-**oh**-nah
This doesn't work.	Non funziona. nohn foont-see-**oh**-nah
When will it be fixed?	Quando verrà riparato? **kwahn**-doh veh-**rah** ree-pah-**rah**-toh
The bed is too soft / hard.	Il letto è troppo morbido / duro. eel **leh**-toh eh **troh**-poh **mor**-bee-doh / **doo**-roh
I can't sleep.	Non riesco a dormire. nohn ree-**eh**-skoh ah dor-**mee**-ray
ants	formiche for-**mee**-kay

bedbugs	cimici **chee**-mee-chee
cockroaches	scarafaggi skah-rah-**fah**-jee
mice	topi **toh**-pee
mosquitoes	zanzare zahnt-**sah**-ray
I'm covered with bug bites.	Sono pieno[a] di punture di insetti. **soh**-noh pee-**eh**-noh dee poon-**too**-ray dee een-**seh**-tee
My... was stolen.	Mi hanno rubato... mee **ahn**-noh roo-**bah**-toh
...money	...i soldi. ee **sohl**-dee
...computer	...il computer. eel kohm-**poo**-tehr
...camera	...la macchina fotografica. lah **mah**-kee-nah foh-toh-**grah**-fee-kah
I need to speak to the manager.	Devo parlare con il direttore. **deh**-voh par-**lah**-ray kohn eel dee-reh-**toh**-ray
I want to make a complaint.	Vorrei fare un reclamo. voh-**reh**-ee **fah**-ray oon reh-**klah**-moh

Keep your valuables with you, out of sight in your room, or in a room safe (if available). For help on dealing with theft or loss, including a list of items, see page 289.

Hotel Help

Use the "In Your Room" words (on page 92) to fill in the blanks.

I'd like...	Vorrei... voh-**reh**-ee
Do you have...?	Avete...? ah-**veh**-tay
a / another	un / un altro oon / oon **ahl**-troh
extra	extra **ehk**-strah
different	altra **ahl**-trah
Please change...	Per favore può cambiare... pehr fah-**voh**-ray pwoh kahm-bee-**ah**-ray

Please don't change...	Per favore può non cambiare... pehr fah-**voh**-ray pwoh nohn kahm-bee-**ah**-ray
...the towels / sheets.	...gli asciugamani / le lenzuola. lee ah-shoo-gah-**mah**-nee / lay lent-soo-**oh**-lah
What is the charge to...?	Quanto costa...? **kwahn**-toh **koh**-stah
...use the telephone	...usare il telefono oo-**zah**-ray eel teh-**leh**-foh-noh
...use the Internet	...usare Internet oo-**zah**-ray **een**-tehr-neht
Do you have Wi-Fi...?	Avete il Wi-Fi...? ah-**veh**-tay eel **wee**-fee
...in the room / lobby	...in camera / nella reception een **kah**-meh-rah / **neh**-lah reh-sehp-see-**ohn**
What is the network name / password?	Qual'è il network name / la password? kwah-**leh** eel "network" **nah**-may / lah "password"
Is a... nearby?	C'è un / una... qui vicino? cheh oon / **oo**-nah... kwee vee-**chee**-noh
...full-service laundry	...lavanderia lah-vahn-deh-**ree**-ah
...self-service laundry	...lavanderia self-service lah-vahn-deh-**ree**-ah sehlf-**sehr**-vees
...pharmacy	...farmacia far-mah-**chee**-ah
...grocery store	...alimentari / supermercato ah-lee-mehn-**tah**-ree / soo-pehr-mehr-**kah**-toh
...restaurant	...ristorante ree-stoh-**rahn**-tay
Where do you go for lunch / dinner / coffee?	Dove si va per il pranzo / la cena / il caffè? **doh**-vay see vah pehr eel **prahnt**-soh / lah **cheh**-nah / eel kah-**feh**

Will you call a taxi for me?	Mi può chiamare un taxi? mee pwoh kee-ah-**mah**-ray oon **tahk**-see
Where can I park?	Dove posso parcheggiare? **doh**-vay **poh**-soh par-keh-**jah**-ray
What time do you lock up?	A che ora chiude? ah kay **oh**-rah kee-**oo**-day
Please wake me at 7:00.	Mi svegli alle sette, per favore. mee **svehl**-yee **ah**-lay **seh**-tay pehr fah-**voh**-ray
I'd like to stay another night.	Vorremmo fermarci un'altra notte. voh-**reh**-moh fehr-**mar**-chee oon-**ahl**-trah **noh**-tay
Will you call my next hotel...?	Può chiamare il mio prossimo hotel...? pwoh kee-ah-**mah**-ray eel **mee**-oh **proh**-see-moh oh-**tehl**
...for tonight	...per stasera pehr stah-**seh**-rah
...to make / to confirm a reservation	...per fare / confermare una prenotazione pehr **fah**-ray / kohn-fehr-**mah**-ray **oo**-nah preh-noh-taht-see-**oh**-nay
Will you please call another hotel for me? (if hotel is booked)	Chiamerebbe un altro albergo per me per favore? kee-ah-meh-**reh**-bay oon **ahl**-troh ahl-**behr**-goh pehr may pehr fah-**voh**-ray
I will pay for the call.	Pago la chiamata. **pah**-goh lah kee-ah-**mah**-tah

Checking Out

When is check-out time?	A che ora devo lasciare la camera? ah kay **oh**-rah **deh**-voh lah-**shah**-ray lah **kah**-meh-rah

Can I check out later?	Posso lasciare la camera più tardi? **poh**-soh lah-**shah**-ray lah **kah**-meh-rah pew **tar**-dee
I'll leave / We'll leave...	Parto / Partiamo... **par**-toh / par-tee-**ah**-moh
...today / tomorrow.	...oggi / domani. **oh**-jee / doh-**mah**-nee
...very early.	...molto presto. **mohl**-toh **preh**-stoh
Can I pay now?	Posso pagare subito? **poh**-soh pah-**gah**-ray **soo**-bee-toh
The bill, please.	Il conto, per favore. eel **kohn**-toh pehr fah-**voh**-ray
I think this is too high.	Credo che il conto sia troppo alto. **kreh**-doh kay eel **kohn**-toh **see**-ah **troh**-poh **ahl**-toh
Can you explain the bill?	Può spiegare il conto? pwoh spee-eh-**gah**-ray eel **kohn**-toh
Can you itemize the bill?	Posso avere il conto in dettaglio? **poh**-soh ah-**veh**-ray eel **kohn**-toh een deh-**tahl**-yoh
Do you accept credit cards?	Accettate carte di credito? ah-cheh-**tah**-tay **kar**-tay dee **kreh**-dee-toh
Is it cheaper if I pay cash?	È più economico se pago in contanti? eh pew eh-koh-**noh**-mee-koh say **pah**-goh een kohn-**tahn**-tee
Everything was great.	Tutto magnifico. **too**-toh mahn-**yee**-fee-koh
I slept like a dormouse.	Ho dormito come un ghiro. oh dor-**mee**-toh **koh**-may oon **gee**-roh (hard "g")
Can I / Can we...?	Posso / Possiamo...? **poh**-soh / poh-see-**ah**-moh
...leave baggage here until ____ o'clock	...lasciare il bagaglio qui fino a ____ lah-**shah**-ray eel bah-**gahl**-yoh kwee **fee**-noh ah ____

A tip for you.	Questo è per lei. **kweh**-stoh eh pehr **leh**-ee

SPECIAL CONCERNS

Families

Do you have...?	Avete...? ah-**veh**-tay
...a family room	...una camera per una famiglia **oo**-nah **kah**-meh-rah pehr **oo**-nah fah-**meel**-yah
...a family discount	...uno sconto per famiglie **oo**-noh **skohn**-toh pehr fah-**meel**-yay
...a discount for children	...uno sconto per bambini **oo**-noh **skohn**-toh pehr bahm-**bee**-nee
I have / We have...	Ho / Abbiamo... oh / ah-bee-**ah**-moh
...one child.	...un bambino. oon bahm-**bee**-noh
...two children.	...due bambini. **doo**-ay bahm-**bee**-nee
____ months old	di ____ mesi dee ____ **meh**-zee
____ years old	di ____ anni dee ____ **ahn**-nee
Are children allowed?	I bambini sono ammessi? ee bahm-**bee**-nee **soh**-noh ah-**meh**-see
Is there an age limit?	C'è un limite d'età? cheh oon **lee**-mee-tay deh-**tah**
I'd like / We'd like...	Vorrei / Vorremmo... voh-**reh**-ee / voh-**reh**-moh
...a crib.	...una culla. **oo**-nah **koo**-lah
...an extra bed.	...un letto in più. oon **leh**-toh een pew
...bunk beds.	...letti a castello. **leh**-tee ah kah-**steh**-loh
babysitting service	servizio di babysitter sehr-**veet**-see-oh dee bay-bee-**see**-tehr
Is... nearby?	C'è.... qui vicino? cheh... kwee vee-**chee**-noh

...a park	...un parco oon **par**-koh
...a playground	...un parco giochi oon **par**-koh **joh**-kee
...a swimming pool	...una piscina **oo**-nah pee-**shee**-nah

Mobility Issues

For related phrases, see page 326 in the Personal Care and Health chapter.

Do you have...?	Avete...? ah-**veh**-tay
...an elevator	...l'ascensore lah-shehn-**soh**-ray
...a ground-floor room	...una camera al piano terra **oo**-nah **kah**-meh-rah ahl pee-**ah**-noh **teh**-rah
...a wheelchair-accessible room	...una camera accessibile con la sedia a rotelle **oo**-nah **kah**-meh-rah ah-cheh-**see**-bee-lay kohn lah **seh**-dee-ah ah roh-**teh**-lay

AT THE HOSTEL

Europe's cheapest beds are in hostels, open to travelers of any age. Official hostels (affiliated with Hostelling International) are usually big and institutional. Independent hostels are more casual, with fewer rules.

hostel	ostello oh-**steh**-loh
dorm bed	letto in un dormitorio **leh**-toh een oon dor-mee-**toh**-ree-oh
How many beds per room?	Quanti letti per camera? **kwahn**-tee **leh**-tee pehr **kah**-meh-rah
dorm for women only	dormitorio per sole donne dor-mee-**toh**-ree-oh pehr **soh**-lay **doh**-nay

co-ed dorm	dormitorio misto dor-mee-**toh**-ree-oh **mee**-stoh
double room	camera doppia **kah**-meh-rah **doh**-pee-ah
family room	camera per una famiglia **kah**-meh-rah pehr **oo**-nah fah-**meel**-yah
Is breakfast included?	La colazione è inclusa? lah koh-laht-see-**oh**-nay eh een-**kloo**-zah
curfew	coprifuoco koh-pree-**fwoh**-koh
lockout	chiusura notturna kee-oo-**zoo**-rah noh-**toor**-nah
membership card	tessera **teh**-seh-rah

EATING

Dig into this chapter's phrases for dining at restaurants, special concerns (including dietary restrictions, children, and being in a hurry), types of food and drink, and shopping for your picnic. The next chapter is a Menu Decoder.

In general, Italians eat meals a bit later than we do. At 7:00 or 8:00 in the morning, they have a light breakfast (a roll and coffee), often while standing at a café or bar. Lunch, which is usually the main meal of the day, begins around 13:00 and can last for a couple of hours. Then they eat a late, light dinner (around 20:00-21:30, sometimes earlier in winter). To bridge the gap, people drop into a bar in the late afternoon for a ***spuntino*** (snack) and aperitif.

Most restaurant kitchens are closed between lunch and dinner. Good restaurants don't reopen for dinner before 19:00.

RESTAURANTS

Italian food is one of life's great pleasures. The Italians have an expression: ***A tavola non si invecchia*** (At the table, one does not age). To eat well in Italy, look for these key words: ***fatta in casa*** (homemade; **fah**-tah een **kah**-zah), ***per oggi*** (for today; pehr **oh**-jee), and ***stagione*** (season; stah-jee-**oh**-nay).

Types of Restaurants

Ristorante: A fine-dining establishment

Trattoria: Typically a family-owned place that serves home-cooked meals, generally at moderate prices

Osteria: An informal eatery, with large shared tables, good food, and wine

Pizzeria: A casual pizza joint that often offers pasta and more; a *pizza rustica* or *pizza al taglio* shop sells slices by weight, usually for take-out

Pizzicheria: An old-fashioned delicatessen (not to be confused with a *pizzeria*)

Rosticceria: A take-out or sit-down shop specializing in roasted meats and accompanying *antipasti* (appetizers)

Salumeria: Delicatessen specializing in *salumi* (cold cuts)

Key Phrases: Restaurants

Where's a good restaurant nearby?	Dov'è un buon ristorante qui vicino? doh-**veh** oon bwohn ree-stoh-**rahn**-tay kwee vee-**chee**-noh
I'd like...	Vorrei... voh-**reh**-ee
We'd like...	Vorremmo... voh-**reh**-moh
...a table for one / two.	...un tavolo per uno / due. oon **tah**-voh-loh pehr **oo**-noh / **doo**-ay
Is this table free?	È libero questo tavolo? eh **lee**-beh-roh **kweh**-stoh **tah**-voh-loh
How long is the wait?	Quanto c'è da aspettare? **kwahn**-toh cheh dah ah-speh-**tah**-ray
The menu (in English), please.	Il menù (in inglese), per favore. eel meh-**noo** (een een-**gleh**-zay) pehr fah-**voh**-ray
The bill, please.	Il conto, per favore. eel **kohn**-toh pehr fah-**voh**-ray
Do you accept credit cards?	Accettate carte di credito? ah-cheh-**tah**-tay **kar**-tay dee **kreh**-dee-toh

Tavola calda: Inexpensive buffet-style restaurant; a *caffetteria* is similar

Bar: The neighborhood hangout that serves coffee, soft drinks, beer, liquor, snacks, and ready-made sandwiches

Enoteca: Wine shop or wine bar that also serves snacks

Buca: Cellar restaurant

Autogrill: Cafeteria and snack bar, found at freeway rest stops and often in city centers (Ciao is a popular chain)

Locanda: A countryside restaurant serving simple local specialties

Finding a Restaurant

Where's a good... restaurant nearby?	Dov'è un buon ristorante... qui vicino? doh-**veh** oon bwohn ree-stoh-**rahn**-tay... kwee vee-**chee**-noh
...cheap	...economico eh-koh-**noh**-mee-koh
...local-style	...con cucina casereccia kohn koo-**chee**-nah kah-zeh-**reh**-chah
...untouristy	...non per turisti nohn pehr too-**ree**-stee
...romantic	...romantico roh-**mahn**-tee-koh
...vegetarian	...vegetariano veh-jeh-tah-ree-**ah**-noh
...fast	...veloce veh-**loh**-chay
...fast-food (Italian-style)	...tavola calda **tah**-voh-lah **kahl**-dah
...self-service buffet	...self-service sehlf-**sehr**-vees
...Asian	...asiatica ah-zee-**ah**-tee-kah
with terrace	con terrazza kohn teh-**rahd**-zah
with a salad bar	con un banco delle insalate kohn oon **bahn**-koh **deh**-lay een-sah-**lah**-tay
candlelit	a lume di candela ah **loo**-may dee kahn-**deh**-lah
popular with locals	che piace alla gente del posto kay pee-**ah**-chay **ah**-lah **jehn**-tay dehl **poh**-stoh
moderate price	a buon mercato ah bwohn mer-**kah**-toh
a splurge	caro **kah**-roh
Is it better than McDonald's?	È meglio di McDonald's? eh **mehl**-yoh dee "McDonald's"

Getting a Table

I'd like / We'd like...	Vorrei / Vorremmo... voh-**reh**-ee / voh-**reh**-moh
...a table...	...un tavolo... oon **tah**-voh-loh
...for one / two.	...per uno / due. pehr **oo**-noh / **doo**-ay
...inside / outside.	...dentro / fuori. **dehn**-troh / **fwoh**-ree
...by the window.	...vicino alla finestra. vee-**chee**-noh **ah**-lah fee-**neh**-strah
...with a view.	...con la vista. kohn lah **vee**-stah
quiet	tranquillo trahn-**kee**-loh
Is this table free?	È libero questo tavolo? eh **lee**-beh-roh **kweh**-stoh **tah**-voh-loh
Can I sit here?	Posso sedermi qui? **poh**-soh seh-**dehr**-mee kwee
Can we sit here?	Possiamo sederci qui? poh-see-**ah**-moh seh-**dehr**-chee kwee
How long is the wait?	Quanto c'è da aspettare? **kwahn**-toh cheh dah ah-speh-**tah**-ray
How many minutes?	Quanti minuti? **kwahn**-tee mee-**noo**-tee
Where is the toilet?	Dov'è la toilette? doh-**veh** lah twah-**leh**-tay

Reservations

reservation	prenotazione preh-noh-taht-see-**oh**-nay
Are reservations recommended?	È meglio prenotare? eh **mehl**-yoh preh-noh-**tah**-ray
I'd like to make a reservation...	Vorrei prenotare... voh-**reh**-ee preh-noh-**tah**-ray
...for myself.	...per me. pehr may
...for two people.	...per due persone. pehr **doo**-ay pehr-**soh**-nay

...for today / tomorrow.	...per oggi / domani. pehr **oh**-jee / doh-**mah**-nee
...for lunch / dinner.	...per pranzo / cena. pehr **prahnt**-soh / **cheh**-nah
...at ____. (specific time)	...alle ____. **ah**-lay ____
My name is ____.	Mi chiamo ____. mee kee-**ah**-moh ____
I have a reservation for ____ people.	Ho una prenotazione per ____ persone. oh **oo**-nah preh-noh-taht-see-**oh**-nay pehr ____ pehr-**soh**-nay

The Menu

A full Italian meal—and menu—is divided into three courses:

Antipasti: Appetizers such as *bruschetta*, grilled veggies, deep-fried tasties, or a plate of olives, cold cuts, and cheeses

Primo piatto: A "first dish," generally consisting of pasta, rice (especially *risotto*), or soup

Secondo piatto: A "second dish," equivalent to our main course, of meat and fish / seafood dishes

A side dish ***(contorno)*** may come with the ***secondo*** or cost extra. After all that food, ***dolci*** (desserts) seem gluttonous—but still very tempting.

menu	menù meh-**noo**
The menu (in English), please.	Il menù (in inglese), per favore. eel meh-**noo** (een een-**gleh**-zay) pehr fah-**voh**-ray
appetizers	antipasti ahn-tee-**pah**-stee
first course	primo piatto **pree**-moh pee-**ah**-toh
main course	secondo piatto seh-**kohn**-doh pee-**ah**-toh
side dishes	contorni kohn-**tor**-nee

specialty (of the house)	specialità (della casa) speh-chah-lee-**tah** (**deh**-lah **kah**-zah)
daily specials	piatti del giorno pee-**ah**-tee dehl **jor**-noh
menu of the day	menù del giorno meh-**noo** dehl **jor**-noh
tourist menu / fixed-price menu	menù turistico / menù fisso meh-**noo** too-**ree**-stee-koh / meh-**noo** **fee**-soh
breakfast	colazione koh-laht-see-**oh**-nay
lunch	pranzo **prahnt**-soh
dinner	cena **cheh**-nah
dishes	piatti pee-**ah**-tee
hot / cold dishes	piatti caldi / freddi pee-**ah**-tee **kahl**-dee / **freh**-dee
sandwiches	panini pah-**nee**-nee
bread	pane **pah**-nay
salad	insalata een-sah-**lah**-tah
soup	zuppa **tsoo**-pah
meat	carni **kar**-nee
poultry	pollame poh-**lah**-may
fish	pesce **peh**-shay
seafood	frutti di mare **froo**-tee dee **mah**-ray
vegetables	verdure vehr-**doo**-ray
cheese	formaggio for-**mah**-joh
dessert	dolce **dohl**-chay
bar snacks	stuzzichini stood-zee-**kee**-nee
drink menu	lista delle bevande **lee**-stah **deh**-lay beh-**vahn**-day
beverages	bevande / bibite beh-**vahn**-day / **bee**-bee-tay
beer	birra **bee**-rah
wine	vino **vee**-noh
cover charge	coperto koh-**pehr**-toh

service (not) included	servizio (non) incluso sehr-**veet**-see-oh (nohn) een-**kloo**-zoh
comes with	servito con sehr-**vee**-toh kohn
choice of	a scelta ah **shehl**-tah

For most travelers, a three-course meal is simply too much food. To avoid overeating (and to stretch your budget), share dishes. A good rule of thumb is for each person to order any two courses. For example, a couple can order and share one ***antipasto,*** one ***primo,*** one ***secondo,*** and one dessert or two ***antipasti*** and two ***primi.***

Usually a good deal, a ***menù del giorno*** (menu of the day) offers you a choice of appetizer, entrée, and dessert at a fixed price. A tourist-oriented ***menù turistico*** works the same way, but often includes less interesting or adventurous options.

Ordering

To get the waiter's attention, simply say ***Scusi*** (Excuse me) or ***Per favore*** (Please). If you have allergies or dietary restrictions, see page 119.

waiter	cameriere kah-meh-ree-**eh**-ray
waitress	cameriera kah-meh-ree-**eh**-rah
I'm ready / We're ready to order.	Sono pronto / Siamo pronti per ordinare. **soh**-noh **prohn**-toh / see-**ah**-moh **prohn**-tee pehr or-dee-**nah**-ray
I / We need a little more time.	Mi / Ci serve un altro minuto. mee / chee **sehr**-vay oon **ahl**-troh mee-**noo**-toh
I'd like / We'd like...	Vorrei / Vorremmo... voh-**reh**-ee / voh-**reh**-moh
...just a drink.	...soltanto qualcosa da bere. sohl-**tahn**-toh kwahl-**koh**-zah dah **beh**-ray
...to see the menu.	...vedere il menù. veh-**deh**-ray eel meh-**noo**

A Sample Menu of the Day

Choose a first course, second course, dessert, and beverage.

TRATTORIA DUE TORRE
STRADA FELLINI 37, ROMA

MENU TURISTICO €25

PRIMO PIATTO (FIRST COURSE)

- RISOTTO MILANESE
- SPAGHETTI CARBONARA
- PENNE AL PESTO
- ZUPPA MINESTRONE
- PROSCIUTTO E MELONE

SECONDO PIATTO (SECOND COURSE)

- PESCE AI FERRI (FISH COOKED OVER COALS)
- SALTIMBOCCA ALLA ROMANA
- GRIGLIATA DI CARNE (MIXED GRILL)
- MELANZANE ALLA PARMIGIANA (EGGPLANT)

CONTORNI (VEGETABLE SIDE DISHES)

- VERDURE DI STAGIONE (VEGETABLES OF THE SEASON) O INSALATA

DOLCI (DESSERT)

- TIRAMISU DELLA CASA
- GELATO
- FRUTTA

BEVANDE (DRINKS)

- ¼ VINO O ACQUA

BUON APPETITO!

SERVIZIO INCLUSO 10%

...to eat.	...mangiare. mahn-**jah**-ray
...only a first course.	...solo un primo piatto. **soh**-loh oon **pree**-moh pee-**ah**-toh
Do you have...?	Avete...? ah-**veh**-tay
...an English menu	...un menù in inglese oon meh-**noo** een een-**gleh**-zay
...a menu of the day	...un menù del giorno oon meh-**noo** dehl **jor**-noh
...half portions	...mezze porzioni **mehd**-zay port-see-**oh**-nee
What do you recommend?	Che cosa raccomanda? kay **koh**-zah rah-koh-**mahn**-dah
What's your favorite dish?	Qual'è il suo piatto preferito? kwah-**leh** eel **soo**-oh pee-**ah**-toh preh-feh-**ree**-toh
What is better? (point to items on menu)	Qual'è meglio? kwah-**leh mehl**-yoh
What is...?	Che cosa c'è di...? kay **koh**-zah cheh dee
Is it...?	È...? eh
...good	...buono **bwoh**-noh
...affordable	...poco caro **poh**-koh **kah**-roh
...expensive	...caro **kah**-roh
...local	...di locale dee loh-**kah**-lay
...fresh	...di fresco dee **freh**-skoh
...fast	...di veloce dee veh-**loh**-chay
...spicy (hot)	...piccante pee-**kahn**-tay
Is it filling?	Riempie molto? ree-**ehm**-pee-ay **mohl**-toh
Make me happy.	Mi faccia felice. mee **fah**-chah feh-**lee**-chay

Around ____ euros.	Intorno ai ____ euro. een-**tor**-noh ī ____ eh-**oo**-roh
What is that? (pointing)	Che cos'è quello? kay koh-**zeh kweh**-loh
How much is it?	Quanto costa? **kwahn**-toh **koh**-stah
Nothing with eyeballs.	Niente con gli occhi. nee-**ehn**-tay kohn lee **oh**-kee
Can I substitute (something) for the ____?	Posso sostituire (qualcosa d'altro) per il ____? **poh**-soh soh-stee-**twee**-ray (kwahl-**koh**-zah **dahl**-troh) pehr eel ____
Can I / Can we get it to go?	Posso / Possiamo averlo da portar via? **poh**-soh / poh-see-**ah**-moh ah-**vehr**-loh dah por-**tar vee**-ah

Many eateries post handwritten lists of the day's specials—usually based on what the chef found fresh at the market. Specials are often noted with the word ***oggi*** (today)—sometimes followed by ***lo chef consiglia*** (the chef recommends) or ***consigliamo*** (we recommend).

When going to a good restaurant with an approachable staff, I like to say ***Mi faccia felice*** (Make me happy), and set a price limit.

Here are a few things you may hear from your server: First, he'll ask what you'd like to drink ***(Da bere?).*** When ready to take your order, he'll ask ***Prego?*** He'll prompt you with ***E dopo?*** (And then?) to see what else you might want; just reply ***È tutto*** (That's all). When you're finished eating, place your utensils on your plate with the handles pointing to your right as the Italians do. This tells the waiter you're done. He'll confirm by asking ***Finito?*** He'll usually ask if you'd like dessert ***(Qualcosa di dolce?)*** and coffee ***(Un caffè?),*** and if you want anything else ***(Altro?).***

Tableware and Condiments

I'd like a...	Vorrei un / una... voh-**reh**-ee oon / **oo**-nah

We'd like a...	Vorremmo un / una... voh-**reh**-moh oon / **oo**-nah
...napkin.	...tovagliolo. toh-vahl-**yoh**-loh
...knife.	...coltello. kohl-**teh**-loh
...fork.	...forchetta. for-**keh**-tah
...spoon.	...cucchiaio. koo-kee-**ah**-yoh
...cup.	...tazza. **tahd**-zah
...glass.	...bicchiere. bee-kee-**eh**-ray
Please...	Per favore... pehr fah-**voh**-ray
...another table setting.	...un altro coperto. oon **ahl**-troh koh-**pehr**-toh
...another plate.	...un altro piatto. oon **ahl**-trah pee-**ah**-toh
silverware	posate poh-**zah**-tay
carafe	caraffa kah-**rah**-fah
water	acqua **ah**-kwah
bread	pane **pah**-nay
breadsticks	grissini gree-**see**-nee
butter	burro **boo**-roh
margarine	margarina mar-gah-**ree**-nah
salt / pepper	sale / pepe **sah**-lay / **peh**-pay
sugar	zucchero **tsoo**-keh-roh
artificial sweetener	dolcificante dohl-chee-fee-**kahn**-tay
honey	miele mee-**eh**-lay
mustard	senape **seh**-nah-pay
mayonnaise	maionese mah-yoh-**neh**-zay
toothpick	stuzzicadente stood-zee-kah-**dehn**-tay

The Food Arrives

After serving the meal, your server might wish you a cheery ***Buon appetito!***

Looks delicious!	Ha un ottimo aspetto! ah oon **oh**-tee-moh ah-**speh**-toh
Is this included with the meal?	È incluso nel pasto questo? eh een-**kloo**-zoh nehl **pah**-stoh **kweh**-stoh
I did not order this.	Io questo non l'ho ordinato. **ee**-oh **kweh**-stoh nohn loh or-dee-**nah**-toh
Can you heat it up?	Lo può scaldare? loh pwoh skahl-**dah**-ray
A little.	Un po'. oon poh
More. / Another.	Di più. / Un altro. dee pew / oon **ahl**-troh
One more, please.	Ancora un altro, per favore. ahn-**koh**-rah oon **ahl**-troh pehr fah-**voh**-ray
The same.	Lo stesso. loh **steh**-soh
Enough.	Basta. **bah**-stah
Finished.	Finito. fee-**nee**-toh
I'm full.	Sono sazio. **soh**-noh **saht**-see-oh
I'm stuffed! ("I'm as full as an egg!")	Sono pieno[a] come un uovo! **soh**-noh pee-**eh**-noh **koh**-may oon **woh**-voh
Thank you.	Grazie. **graht**-see-ay

Complaints

This is...	Questo è... **kweh**-stoh eh
...dirty.	...sporco. **spor**-koh
...greasy.	...grasso. **grah**-soh
...salty.	...salato. sah-**lah**-toh
...undercooked.	...troppo crudo. **troh**-poh **kroo**-doh
...overcooked.	...troppo cotto. **troh**-poh **koh**-toh

...cold.	...freddo. **freh**-doh
...disgusting.	...pessimo. **peh**-see-moh
Yuck!	Che schifo! kay **skee**-foh

Compliments to the Chef

If you enjoyed a good meal, it's nice to praise the chef.

Yummy!	Buono! **bwoh**-noh
Very good!	Molto buono! **mohl**-toh **bwoh**-noh
Delicious!	Delizioso! deh-leet-see-**oh**-zoh
Divinely good!	Una vera bontà! **oo**-nah **veh**-rah bohn-**tah**
I love Italian food.	Adoro la cucina italiana. ah-**doh**-roh lah koo-**chee**-nah ee-tah-lee-**ah**-nah
My compliments to the chef!	Complimenti al cuoco! kohm-plee-**mehn**-tee ahl **kwoh**-koh
A great memory!	Grande ricordo! **grahn**-day ree-**kor**-doh

Paying

bill	conto **kohn**-toh
The bill, please.	Il conto, per favore. eel **kohn**-toh pehr fah-**voh**-ray
Together.	Conto unico. **kohn**-toh **oo**-nee-koh
Separate checks.	Conto separato. **kohn**-toh seh-pah-**rah**-toh
Do you accept credit cards?	Accettate carte di credito? ah-cheh-**tah**-tay **kar**-tay dee **kreh**-dee-toh
This is not correct.	Questo non è giusto. **kweh**-stoh nohn eh **joo**-stoh

Cover and Tipping

Two extra charges are commonly found at Italian restaurants: ***coperto*** and ***servizio.*** Both charges, if assessed, by law must be listed on the menu.

The ***coperto*** (cover), sometimes called ***pane e coperto*** (bread and cover), is a minor fee (€1.50-3/person) covering the cost of the typical basket of bread, oil, salt, cutlery, and linens found on your table. It's not negotiable, and it's not a tip (it goes to the owner).

The ***servizio*** (a 10- to 15-percent service charge) is similar to the mandatory gratuity that American restaurants often add for large groups. Because the service charge is sometimes built into your bill, look carefully at your check to see if you've already paid a tip—don't leave a tip beyond this.

If there is no ***servizio*** on the bill, a common tip at a simple restaurant or pizzeria is €1 per person (or simply round up the bill). At a finer restaurant, leave a few euros per person.

Can you explain this?	Lo può spiegare? loh pwoh spee-eh-**gah**-ray
Can you itemize the bill?	Può spiegare il conto in dettaglio? pwoh spee-eh-**gah**-ray eel **kohn**-toh een deh-**tahl**-yoh
What if I wash the dishes?	E se lavassi i piatti? ay say lah-**vah**-see ee pee-**ah**-tee
Could I have a receipt, please?	Posso avere una ricevuta, per favore? **poh**-soh ah-**veh**-ray **oo**-nah ree-cheh-**voo**-tah pehr fah-**voh**-ray

Tipping

tip	mancia **mahn**-chah

service (not) included	servizio (non) incluso sehr-**veet**-see-oh (nohn) een-**kloo**-zoh
Is tipping expected?	Bisogna lasciare una mancia? bee-**zohn**-yah lah-**shah**-ray **oo**-nah **mahn**-chah
What percent?	Che percentuale? kay pehr-chehn-too-**ah**-lay
Keep the change.	Tenga il resto. **tehn**-gah eel **reh**-stoh
Change, please.	Il resto, per favore. eel **reh**-stoh pehr fah-**voh**-ray
This is for you.	Questo è per lei. **kweh**-stoh eh pehr **leh**-ee

In Italian bars and any eatery that doesn't have wait staff, there's no need to tip. See the "Cover and Tipping" sidebar (previous page) for tipping tips.

SPECIAL CONCERNS

In a Hurry

Europeans take their time at meals, so don't expect speedy service. If you're in a rush, let your server know. To hurry things up, ask for your bill when the waiter brings your food.

I'm / We're in a hurry.	Sono / Siamo di fretta. **soh**-noh / see-**ah**-moh dee **freh**-tah
I'm sorry.	Mi dispiace. mee dee-spee-**ah**-chay
I need to be served quickly.	Ho bisogno di essere servito[a] rapidamente. oh bee-**zohn**-yoh dee **eh**-seh-ray sehr-**vee**-toh rah-pee-dah-**mehn**-tay
We need to be served quickly.	Avremmo bisogno di essere serviti rapidamente. ah-**vreh**-moh bee-**zohn**-yoh dee **eh**-seh-ray sehr-**vee**-tee rah-pee-dah-**mehn**-tay

I must / We must...	Devo / Dobbiamo... **deh**-voh / doh-bee-**ah**-moh
...leave in 30 minutes / one hour.	...andarcene tra trenta minuti / un'ora. ahn-dar-**cheh**-nay trah **trehn**-tah mee-**noo**-tee / oo-**noh**-rah
When will the food be ready?	Tra quanto è pronto il cibo? trah **kwahn**-toh eh **prohn**-toh eel **chee**-boh
The bill, please.	Il conto, per favore. eel **kohn**-toh pehr fah-**voh**-ray

Allergies and Other Dietary Restrictions

If the food you're unable to eat doesn't appear in this list, look for it in the Menu Decoder. You'll find vegetarian phrases in the next section.

I'm allergic to...	Sono allergico[a] a... **soh**-noh ah-**lehr**-jee-koh ah
I cannot eat...	Non posso mangiare... nohn **poh**-soh mahn-**jah**-ray
He cannot / She cannot eat...	Lui non può / Lei non può mangiare... **loo**-ee nohn pwoh / **leh**-ee nohn pwoh mahn-**jah**-ray
He / She has a severe allergy to...	Ha un'allergia molto seria a... ah oon-ah-**lehr**-jee-ah **mohl**-toh **seh**-ree-ah ah
No...	Niente... nee-**ehn**-tay
...dairy products.	...latticini. lah-tee-**chee**-nee
...nuts.	...noci e altra frutta secca. **noh**-chee ay **ahl**-trah **froo**-tah **seh**-kah
...peanuts.	...arachidi. ah-**rah**-kee-dee
...walnuts.	...noci. **noh**-chee
...wheat / gluten.	...frumento / glutine. froo-**mehn**-toh / gloo-**tee**-nay

...seafood.	...frutti di mare.	**froo**-tee dee **mah**-ray
...shellfish.	...molluschi e crostacei.	moh-**loo**-skee ay kroh-**stah**-cheh-ee
...salt / sugar.	...sale / zucchero.	**sah**-lay / **tsoo**-keh-roh
I am diabetic.	Ho il diabete.	oh eel dee-ah-**beh**-tay
He / She is lactose intolerant.	Lui / Lei ha un'intolleranza ai latticini.	**loo**-ee / **leh**-ee ah oon-een-toh-leh-**rahnt**-sah ī lah-tee-**chee**-nee
I'd like / We'd like a...	Vorrei / Vorremmo un...	voh-**reh**-ee / voh-**reh**-moh oon
...kosher meal.	...pasto kasher.	**pah**-stoh **kah**-shehr
...halal meal.	...pasto halal.	**pah**-stoh **ah**-lahl
...light (low-fat) meal.	...pasto leggero.	**pah**-stoh leh-**jeh**-roh
Low cholesterol.	Colesterolo basso.	koh-leh-steh-**roh**-loh **bah**-soh
No caffeine.	Senza caffeina.	**sehnt**-sah kah-feh-**ee**-nah
No alcohol.	Niente alcool.	nee-**ehn**-tay **ahl**-kohl
Organic.	Biologico.	bee-oh-**loh**-jee-koh
I eat only insects.	Mangio solo insetti.	**mahn**-joh **soh**-loh een-**seh**-tee

Vegetarian Phrases

I'm a...	Sono...	**soh**-noh
...vegetarian.	...vegetariano[a].	veh-jeh-tah-ree-**ah**-noh
...strict vegetarian.	...strettamente vegetariano[a].	streh-tah-**mehn**-tay veh-jeh-tah-ree-**ah**-noh
...vegan.	...vegano[a].	veh-**gah**-noh

Is any meat or animal fat used in this?	Contiene carne o grassi animali? kohn-tee-**eh**-nay **kar**-nay oh **grah**-see ah-nee-**mah**-lee
What is vegetarian? (pointing to menu)	Quali piatti sono vegetariani? **kwah**-lee pee-**ah**-tee **soh**-noh veh-jeh-tah-ree-**ah**-nee
I don't eat...	Io non mangio... **ee**-oh nohn **mahn**-joh
I'd like this without...	Vorrei questo ma senza... voh-**reh**-ee **kweh**-stoh mah **sehnt**-sah
...meat.	...carne. **kar**-nay
...eggs.	...uova. **woh**-vah
...animal products.	...prodotti animali. proh-**doh**-tee ah-nee-**mah**-lee
I eat...	Io mangio... **ee**-oh **mahn**-joh
Do you have...?	Avete...? **ah**-veh-tay
...anything with tofu	...qualcosa con il tofu kwahl-**koh**-zah kohn eel **toh**-foo
...veggie burgers	...hamburger vegetariani ahm-**boor**-gehr veh-jeh-tah-ree-**ah**-nee

Children

Children's menus and special dishes for ***bambini*** are rare in Italy. Most Italian parents request a ***mezza porzione*** (half portion, not always available), or simply order from the regular menu and customize it for their kids.

Do you have a children's menu?	Avete un menù per bambini? ah-**veh**-tay oon meh-**noo** pehr bahm-**bee**-nee
children's portions	delle porzioni per bambini **deh**-lay port-see-**oh**-nee pehr bahm-**bee**-nee

half portions	mezze porzioni **mehd**-zay port-see-**oh**-nee
high chair	un seggiolone oon seh-joh-**loh**-nay
booster seat	un seggiolino oon seh-joh-**lee**-noh
noodles	pasta **pah**-stah
rice	del riso dehl **ree**-zoh
with butter	con il burro kohn eel **boo**-roh
without sauce	senza sugo **sehnt**-sah **soo**-goh
sauce / dressing on the side	il sugo / il condimento a parte eel **soo**-goh / eel kohn-dee-**mehn**-toh ah **par**-tay
pizza	pizza "pizza"
...cheese only	...Margherita mar-geh-**ree**-tah
...pepperoni	...con salame piccante kohn sah-**lah**-may pee-**kahn**-tay
cheese sandwich...	un panino... al formaggio oon pah-**nee**-noh... ahl for-**mah**-joh
...toasted	...scaldato skahl-**dah**-toh
hot dog	wurstel **voor**-stehl
hamburger	hamburger ahm-**boor**-gehr
french fries	patate fritte pah-**tah**-tay **free**-tay
ketchup	ketchup "ketchup"
small milk	un po' di latte oon poh dee **lah**-tay
straw	cannuccia kah-**noo**-chah
More napkins, please.	Degli altri tovaglioli, per favore. **dehl**-yee **ahl**-tree toh-vahl-**yoh**-lee pehr fah-**voh**-ray

Don't expect to find peanut butter sandwiches in Italy. Italian kids would rather have a sandwich with Nutella ***(un panino con la Nutella),*** the popular chocolate-hazelnut spread.

WHAT'S COOKING?

Breakfast

Italian breakfasts, like Italian bath towels, are small: coffee and a roll with butter and marmalade. Some hotels, accustomed to American travelers, may serve hard-boiled eggs and cereal—but don't count on it. The strong coffee is often mixed about half-and-half with heated milk. The delicious red orange juice *(succo di arance rosse)* is made from Sicilian blood oranges.

I'd like / We'd like...	Vorrei / Vorremmo... voh-**reh**-ee / voh-**reh**-moh
breakfast	colazione koh-laht-see-**oh**-nay
bread	pane **pah**-nay

Key Phrases: What's Cooking?

food	cibo **chee**-boh
breakfast	colazione koh-laht-see-**oh**-nay
lunch	pranzo **prahnt**-soh
dinner	cena **cheh**-nah
bread	pane **pah**-nay
cheese	formaggio for-**mah**-joh
soup	minestra / zuppa mee-**neh**-strah / **tsoo**-pah
salad	insalata een-sah-**lah**-tah
fish	pesce **peh**-shay
chicken	pollo **poh**-loh
meat	carni **kar**-nee
vegetables	verdure vehr-**doo**-ray
fruit	frutta **froo**-tah
dessert	dolci **dohl**-chee

baguette	baguette bah-**geh**-tay
roll	pane / panino **pah**-nay / pah-**nee**-noh
sweet roll	brioche **bree**-ohsh
croissant	cornetto kor-**neh**-toh
toast	toast "toast"
butter	burro **boo**-roh
jam	marmellata mar-meh-**lah**-tah
honey	miele mee-**eh**-lay
fruit cup	macedonia mah-cheh-**doh**-nee-ah
milk	latte **lah**-tay
coffee / tea	caffè / tè kah-**feh** / teh
fruit juice	succo di frutta **soo**-koh dee **froo**-tah
fresh orange juice	spremuta di arancia spreh-**moo**-tah dee ah-**rahn**-chah
blood orange juice	succo di arance rosse **soo**-koh dee ah-**rahn**-chay **roh**-say
hot chocolate	cioccolata calda choh-koh-**lah**-tah **kahl**-dah

If you want to skip your hotel breakfast, consider browsing for a morning picnic at a local open-air market. Or do as the Italians do: Stop into a bar or café to drink a cappuccino and munch a ***cornetto*** (croissant) while standing at the bar.

Pastries

Pastries go by the generic name ***pasticcini*** or simply ***dolci*** (sweets; sometimes called ***brioche*** in the north, ***cornetti*** in the south, and ***paste*** in Florence).

pastries	pasticcini / dolci pah-stee-**chee**-nee / **dohl**-chee
cream puff	bignè alla crema been-**yeh ah**-lah **kreh**-mah

filled with...	ripieno di / alla... ree-pee-**eh**-noh dee / **ah**-lah
...jam...	...marmellata di... mar-meh-**lah**-tah dee
...strawberry	...fragola **frah**-goh-lah
...apricot	...albicocca ahl-bee-**koh**-kah
...cherry	...ciliegia chee-lee-**eh**-jah
...blackberry	...more **moh**-ray
...apple	...mela **meh**-lah
...chocolate	...cioccolato choh-koh-**lah**-toh
...custard / crème	...crema **kreh**-mah
...nuts / almonds	...noci / mandorle **noh**-chee / mahn-**dor**-lay
...raisins	...uvetta oo-**veh**-tah
What is fresh now?	Cosa c'è di fresco in questo periodo? **koh**-zah cheh dee **freh**-skoh een **kweh**-stoh pehr-ee-**oh**-doh

While most bars serve basic pastries for breakfast, you'll find a wider selection at a ***pasticceria*** (pastry shop).

What's Probably Not For Breakfast

These items are not typical on a traditional Italian breakfast table, but you may find them at international hotels or cafés catering to foreigners.

omelet	omelette / frittata oh-meh-**leh**-tay / free-**tah**-tah
eggs...	uova... **woh**-vah
...fried	...fritte **free**-tay
...scrambled	...strapazzate strah-pahd-**zah**-tay
...poached	...in camicia een kah-**mee**-chah
...hard-boiled	...sode **soh**-day
...soft-boiled	...alla coque **ah**-lah kohk

ham	prosciutto cotto proh-**shoo**-toh **koh**-toh
cheese	formaggio for-**mah**-joh
yogurt	yogurt **yoh**-goort
cereal	cereali cheh-reh-**ah**-lee

Sandwiches

sandwich (on a baguette)	panino pah-**nee**-noh
I'd like a sandwich.	Vorrei un panino. voh-**reh**-ee oon pah-**nee**-noh
white bread	pane bianco **pah**-nay bee-**ahn**-koh
whole-grain bread	pane integrale **pah**-nay een-teh-**grah**-lay
toasted ham and cheese	toast con prosciutto cotto e formaggio "toast" kohn proh-**shoo**-toh **koh**-toh ay for-**mah**-joh
cheese	formaggio for-**mah**-joh
tuna	tonno **toh**-noh
fish	pesce **peh**-shay
chicken	pollo **poh**-loh
turkey	tacchino tah-**kee**-noh
ham	prosciutto proh-**shoo**-toh
air-cured beef	bresaola breh-zah-**oh**-lah
salami	salame sah-**lah**-may
lettuce	lattuga lah-**too**-gah
tomato	pomodoro poh-moh-**doh**-roh
onion	cipolla chee-**poh**-lah
mustard	senape **seh**-nah-pay
mayonnaise	maionese mah-yoh-**neh**-zay

on sandwich bread / on a roll	con pane in cassetta / panino kohn **pah**-nay een kah-**seh**-tah / pah-**nee**-noh
toasted / grilled / heated	scaldato / alla griglia / caldo skahl-**dah**-toh / **ah**-lah **greel**-yah / **kahl**-doh
Does this come cold or hot?	Si mangia freddo o caldo? see **mahn**-jah **freh**-doh oh **kahl**-doh
That. (pointing)	Quello. **kway**-loh
What is that?	Che cos'è? kay **koh**-zeh
What is good with that?	Cosa è buono con questo? **koh**-zah eh **bwoh**-noh kohn **kweh**-stoh
What do you suggest?	Cosa mi consiglia? **koh**-zah mee kohn-**seel**-yah
very filling (big sandwich)	molto pieno **mohl**-toh pee-**eh**-noh
just a taste (small sandwich)	solo un assaggino **soh**-loh oon ah-sah-**jee**-noh
well heated / cooked	molto caldo / cotto **mohl**-toh **kahl**-doh / **koh**-toh
not overcooked	non troppo caldo nohn **troh**-poh **kahl**-doh

To grab a sandwich, stop by a ***panificio*** (bakery)—or, better yet, a ***paninoteca*** or ***foccaceria,*** where they can custom-make you a sandwich. Beyond the basic ingredients, you may see ***pomodoro gratinato*** (tomatoes grilled and dusted with breadcrumbs) or ***alla toscana*** (with chicken liver paste). You can also look for ***panini farciti*** (premade sandwiches) at ***enoteche*** (wine bars), other bars, and cafés.

Types of Sandwiches

The generic Italian sandwich comes on a baguette—it's called a ***panino***. Another common sandwich—especially in central Italy—is the ***foccacia***, made on the puffy bread of the same name.

panino pah-**nee**-noh
baguette sandwich

foccacia foh-**kah**-chah
rustic, pillowy bread "stuffed" to make sandwiches

foccacina foh-kah-**chee**-nah
small foccacia sandwich

schiacciata skee-ah-**chah**-tah
thin, "squashed" bread sprinkled with sea salt and olive oil; used to make a foccacia-type sandwich (Tuscany)

piadina pee-ah-**dee**-nah
soft, thin, pita-like bread, often served with fillings

panini farciti pah-**nee**-nee far-**chee**-tee
prepared sandwiches—just grab and go

tramezzini trah-mehd-**zee**-nee
sandwiches served cold and stuffed with mayo and a variety of fillings (such as egg, tuna, or shrimp)

crostini kroh-**stee**-nee
small toasted bread rounds topped with meat or vegetable pastes

In central Italy, ***porchetta*** stands serve tasty rolls stuffed with slices of roasted suckling pig.

If You Knead Bread

bread	pane **pah**-nay
whole-grain bread	pane integrale **pah**-nay een-teh-**grah**-lay
olive bread	pane alle olive **pah**-nay **ah**-lay oh-**lee**-vay
rye bread	pane di segale **pah**-nay dee seh-**gah**-lay

brown bread	pane scuro **pah**-nay **skoo**-roh
Tuscan bread (unsalted)	pane toscano **pah**-nay toh-**skah**-noh
loaf of bread	filone fee-**loh**-nay
breadsticks	grissini gree-**see**-nee

Every region of Italy has its own bread, highly prized by the locals. We have the saying "good as gold," but the Italians say "good as bread."

Say Cheese

cheese	formaggio for-**mah**-joh
cheese shop	formaggeria for-mah-jeh-**ree**-ah
Do you have a cheese that is...?	Avete un formaggio...? ah-**veh**-tay oon for-**mah**-joh
...mild / sharp	...dolce / saporito **dohl**-chay / sah-poh-**ree**-toh
...fresh / aged	...fresco / stagionato **freh**-skoh / stah-joh-**nah**-toh
...soft / hard	...morbido / duro **mor**-bee-doh / **doo**-roh
...from a cow / sheep / goat	...di mucca / di pecora / di capra dee **moo**-kah / dee **peh**-koh-rah / dee **kah**-prah
...sliced	...affettato ah-feh-**tah**-toh
...smoked	...affumicato ah-foo-mee-**kah**-toh
May I taste it?	Posso avere un assagio? **poh**-soh ah-**veh**-ray oon ah-**sah**-joh
What is your favorite cheese?	Qual'è il suo formaggio preferito? kwah-**leh** eel **soo**-oh for-**mah**-joh preh-feh-**ree**-toh
I would like three or four types of cheese for a picnic.	Vorrei tre o quattro tipi di formaggi per un picnic. voh-**reh**-ee tray oh **kwah**-troh **tee**-pee dee for-**mah**-jee pehr oon **peek**-neek

Choose for me, please.	Scelga lei, per favore. **shehl**-gah **leh**-ee pehr fah-**voh**-ray
This much. (showing size)	Tanto così. **tahn**-toh koh-**zee**
More. / Less.	Di più. / Di meno. dee pew / dee **meh**-noh
Can you please slice it?	Lo può affettare, per favore? loh pwoh ah-feh-**tah**-ray pehr fah-**voh**-ray

Italian Cheeses

Italian cheeses ***(formaggi)*** come in various types: ***a pasta molle*** (soft, like ricotta or mozzarella); ***a pasta semidura*** (semi-hard, like provolone); or ***a pasta dura*** or ***grana*** (hard, crumbly, and granular, like ***parmigiano-reggiano***).

asiago (mezzano / stravecchio)
ah-zee-**ah**-goh (mehd-**zah**-noh / strah-**veh**-kee-oh)
hard, mild cow cheese (young, firm, and creamy / aged, pungent, and granular)

bel paese behl pah-**eh**-zay
mild, white, creamy cow cheese

bocconcini boh-kohn-**chee**-nee
small balls of mozzarella

burrata boo-**rah**-tah
mozzarella with cream added, extremely soft

caciocavallo / ragusano kah-choh-kah-**vah**-loh / rah-goo-**zah**-noh
semi-hard cow cheeses (Southern Italy and Sicily)

formaggio di capra / caprino
for-**mah**-joh dee **kah**-prah / kah-**pree**-noh
goat cheese

formaggio fresco for-**mah**-joh **freh**-skoh
cream cheese

fontina (Val d'Aosta) fohn-**tee**-nah (vahl **doh**-stah)
semi-hard, nutty, Gruyère-style cheese—best from Val d'Aosta

formaggio di fossa for-**mah**-joh dee **foh**-sah
sheep or cow cheese aged in an underground "pit" (*fossa*)

gorgonzola gor-gohnt-**soh**-lah
pungent, blue-veined cheese, either creamy (*dolce*) or aged and hard (*stagionato*)

grana padano **grah**-nah pah-**dah**-noh
grainy grating cheese from cows, similar to *parmigiano-reggiano* but lower quality

mascarpone mah-skar-**poh**-nay
sweet, buttery, spreadable dessert cheese

mozzarella (di bufala) mohd-zah-**reh**-lah (dee **boo**-fah-lah)
mozzarella (from water buffalo)

parmigiano-reggiano par-mee-**jah**-noh reh-gee-**ah**-noh
hard, crumbly, sharp, aged cow cheese

pecorino (fresco / stagionato)
peh-koh-**ree**-noh (**freh**-skoh / stah-joh-**nah**-toh)
ewe cheese (fresh, soft, and mild / aged and sharp)

pecorino romano peh-koh-**ree**-noh roh-**mah**-noh
variation on *pecorino* that's hard, aged, and often grated over food

piacentino di enna pee-ah-chehn-**tee**-noh dee **eh**-nah
hard, spicy sheep cheese with saffron and pepper (Sicily)

provolone / provola proh-voh-**loh**-nay / **proh**-voh-lah
rich, firm, aged cow cheese

ricotta ree-**koh**-tah
soft, airy cheese made by "recooking" leftover whey

scamorza skah-**mort**-sah
cow cheese similar to mozzarella, often smoked

stracchino strah-**kee**-noh
spreadable, soft cow cheese

taleggio tah-**leh**-joh
rich, creamy, cow cheese

Certain cheeses—including ***gorgonzola*** and ***pecorino***—taste very different depending on how long they're aged; specify ***fresco*** (soft and mild) or ***stagionato*** (hard and sharp).

Antipasti and Cured Meats

Antipasti (starters) are typically an assortment of local cheeses, meats, and vegetables. An Italian specialty is ***salumi*** (cured meats).

Antipasti

antipasto misto ahn-tee-**pah**-stoh **mee**-stoh
mix of cold cuts, marinated vegetables, and sometimes cheeses

antipasto (frutti) di mare
ahn-tee-**pah**-stoh (**froo**-tee) dee **mah**-ray
marinated mix of fish and shellfish, served chilled

bruschetta broo-**skeh**-tah
toast brushed with olive oil and garlic or chopped tomatoes

carciofi alla giudia / romana
kar-**choh**-fee **ah**-lah **joo**-dee-ah / roh-**mah**-nah
artichokes flattened and deep-fried ("Jewish-style") /
artichokes simmered with garlic and mint ("Roman-style")

carpaccio kar-**pah**-choh
thinly sliced raw beef served with olive oil, lemon juice, and shaved *parmigiano-reggiano*

cipolloti chee-poh-**loh**-tee
mini-onions marinated in oil

crocchette kroh-**keh**-tay
croquettes (deep-fried mashed potato balls)

crostini kroh-**stee**-nee
toast topped with liver pâtés or other meat or veggie pastes

fagioli all'uccelletto fah-**joh**-lee ah-loo-cheh-**leh**-toh
beans slow-cooked with tomato and sage (Tuscany)

farro **fah**-roh
spelt (grain often used in salads and soups)

fave al guanciale **fah**-vay ahl gwahn-**chah**-lay
fava beans simmered with *guanciale* (cured pork cheek) and onion

filetti di baccalà fee-**leh**-tee dee bah-kah-**lah**
batter-fried salted cod

fiori di zucca fee-**oh**-ree dee **tsoo**-kah
lightly fried squash blossoms, filled with mozzarella and anchovies

frittata con le erbe free-**tah**-tah kohn lay **ehr**-bay
an unfolded omelet with fresh herbs

fritti **free**-tee
little deep-fried snacks (often croquettes, mozzarella, or olives stuffed with meat)

gattafin gah-**tah**-feen
greens stuffed in pastry and deep-fried (Riviera)

inzimino eent-see-**mee**-noh
anything—often cuttlefish—marinated in tomatoes and greens

involtini een-vohl-**tee**-nee
stuffed rolls of meat or vegetables

olive con peperoni oh-**lee**-vay kohn peh-peh-**roh**-nee
green olives stuffed with red hot peppers

olive nere / verdi oh-**lee**-vay **neh**-ray / **vehr**-dee
black olives / green olives

orzo **ord**-zoh
tiny, rice-shaped pasta

prosciutto e melone / fichi proh-**shoo**-toh ay meh-**loh**-nay / **fee**-kee
air-cured ham wrapped around cantaloupe / fresh figs

salumi misti sah-**loo**-mee **mee**-stee
assortment of sliced, cured meats

sarde in saor **sar**-day een **sah**-or
sardines marinated with onions

supplì / arancini soo-**plee** / ah-rahn-**chee**-nee
deep-fried balls of rice, tomato sauce, and mozzarella

tagliere tahl-**yeh**-ray
sampling of meats and cheeses on a wooden board (Tuscany)

vitello tonnato vee-**teh**-loh toh-**nah**-toh
thin-sliced roasted veal with tuna-caper mayonnaise

Salumi

Salumi (literally "salted meats")—also called ***affettati*** (sliced)—are an Italian staple. The Italians have invented innumerable ways to encase, cook, and cure meat (usually pork).

bresaola breh-zah-**oh**-lah
air-cured beef; "della Valtellina" is low-fat and top quality

capocollo / coppa kah-poh-**koh**-loh / **koh**-pah
peppery, air-cured pork shoulder

cotechino / zampone koh-teh-**kee**-noh / zahm-**poh**-nay
pork sausage traditionally stuffed into a pig's leg (*zampone* still is; *cotechino* is just in a casing)

finocchiona fee-noh-kee-**oh**-nah
salami with fennel seeds

guanciale gwahn-**chah**-lay
tender, flavorful, air-cured pork cheek

lampredotto lahm-preh-**doh**-toh
cow stomach that resembles a lamprey (eel)—a Florentine favorite

lardo **lar**-doh
strips of seasoned lard, often served on toast

lonzino lohn-**zee**-noh
air-cured pork loin

mortadella mor-tah-**deh**-lah
pink, finely ground, baloney-like pork loaf

'nduja **doo**-yah
spicy, spreadable salami

pancetta pahn-**cheh**-tah
salt-cured, peppery pork belly meat

pancetta arrotolata pahn-**cheh**-tah ah-roh-toh-**lah**-tah
pancetta rolled into a tight, sausage-like bundle and sliced

salame sah-**lah**-may
air-dried sausage, sometimes spicy

salamino sah-lah-**mee**-noh
small salami

salsiccia sahl-**see**-chah
link sausage

sbriciolona zbree-choh-**loh**-nah
less aged, "crumbly" *finocchiona*

sopressata soh-preh-**sah**-tah
in the south, a coarsely ground, spicy salami; in Tuscany (*sopressata toscana*), a headcheese-like gelatinous brick of pork trimmings

speck spehk
smoked, juniper-flavored, thinly sliced pork shoulder

For a sampler plate, look for ***affettato misto*** (mixed cold cuts) or—in Tuscany—***tagliere*** (a "board" that often includes cheeses).

Prosciutto

Produced mainly in the north of Italy, ***prosciutto*** is thinly sliced ham that can be sweet or salty.

prosciutto (crudo) proh-**shoo**-toh (**kroo**-doh)
air-cured ham hock, thinly sliced

prosciutto dolce proh-**shoo**-toh **dohl**-chay
sweet prosciutto

prosciutto salato / stagionato
proh-**shoo**-toh sah-**lah**-toh / stah-joh-**nah**-toh
salty prosciutto

prosciutto di Parma proh-**shoo**-toh dee **par**-mah
premium, super-lean, sweet prosciutto

prosciutto toscano proh-**shoo**-toh toh-**skah**-noh
Tuscan prosciutto, generally dark and salty

culatello koo-lah-**teh**-loh
made with the finest pork and sometimes wine-cured

Purists claim that the best ***prosciutto*** comes from ***cinta senese*** (Sienese-branded) pigs, with black hooves.

Pasta

Italy is the land of pasta, with more than 600 varieties. Each variation has a purpose, usually as the perfect platform for highlighting the sauce, meat, or regional ingredients of a particular dish. While ***pasta secca*** (dry-stored pasta) can be delicious, nothing can match ***pasta fresca*** (fresh-made pasta). Italians prefer their pasta cooked ***al dente*** ("to the tooth"—still quite firm compared to American tastes).

Long Noodles

Pasta lunga are long enough to twist around a fork. Here are some favorites:

spaghetti "spaghetti"
the classic Italian pasta

capellini / capelli d'angelo
kah-peh-**lee**-nee / kah-**peh**-lee **dahn**-jeh-loh
extremely thin spaghetti ("little hairs" / "angel hair")

vermicelli vehr-mee-**cheh**-lee
slightly thinner than spaghetti ("little worms")

bucatini boo-kah-**tee**-nee
long, thick, hollow tubes

fusilli bucati foo-**zee**-lee boo-**kah**-tee
long, tightly coiled hollow tubes

pici / bigoli **pee**-chee / **bee**-goh-lee
hand-rolled thick strands (Tuscany / Veneto)

barbina bar-**bee**-nah
very skinny spaghetti often coiled into nest-like "beards"

spaghetti alla chitarra "spaghetti" **ah**-lah kee-**tah**-rah
square spaghetti cut on a "guitar"-shaped stringed device

Pasta lunga can also be flattened and/or ribbon-shaped; the first four are listed in order of width:

linguine leen-**gwee**-nay
narrow, flat spaghetti ("little tongues")

fettuccine feh-too-**chee**-nay
slightly wider, flat egg noodles cut into "small ribbons"

tagliatelle tahl-yah-**teh**-lay
even wider, flat noodles

pappardelle pah-par-**deh**-lay
very wide, flat noodles, best with meat sauces

trenette treh-**neh**-tay
long, flat, thin noodles similar to linguine

tripoline tree-poh-**lee**-nay
long, flat, thick noodles ruffled on one side ("tripe"-shaped)

mafalde mah-**fahl**-day
wide, flat, rectangular noodles ruffled on both sides

If a pasta is a bit thicker, ***one*** is added to the end; if it's a bit thinner, ***ine, ette,*** or ***elle*** is added. For example, ***spaghettini*** is skinnier than ***spaghetti,*** while ***spaghettoni*** is thicker. ***Vermicelloni*** is thicker ***vermicelli.*** You may also see variations that are ***mezzi*** (half the length).

Short Noodles

Pasta corta are scooped or speared with a fork. Most are tube-shaped and come in different lengths and thicknesses. Some are ***lisce*** (smooth) and others are ***rigate*** (grooved—better for clinging to sauce).

penne **pehn**-nay
angle-cut tubes ("quills"); draw out the *nn* sound to avoid saying *pene* (penis)

rigatoni ree-gah-**toh**-nee
"ridged," square-cut, hollow tubes

ziti **zee**-tee
long, hollow tubes (wider than penne); these "grooms" are traditionally served at weddings

mostaccioli moh-stah-**choh**-lee
"moustache"-like smooth penne (Southern Italy)

Short Noodles *(cont.)*

fusilli foo-**zee**-lee
spiral shapes ideal for cream or cheese sauces

rotini roh-**tee**-nee
like fusilli, but shorter

garganelli gar-gah-**neh**-lee
flat egg pasta rolled into a tube

Other types of ***pasta corta*** are named for their distinctive shapes:

conchiglie / cocciole kohn-**keel**-yay / koh-**choh**-lay
hollow, "seashell" shape

farfalle far-**fah**-lay
"butterfly" or bowtie shape

orecchiette oh-reh-kee-**eh**-tay
"ear" or bowl shape

orzo **ord**-zoh
tiny "barley" shape (looks like rice)

rotelle roh-**teh**-lay
"wagon wheel" shape

strozzapreti strohd-zah-**preh**-tee
"priest-stranglers"—shaped like a priest's collar

trofie / trofiette **troh**-fee-ay / troh-fee-**eh**-tay
twisted noodle, ideal for pesto

umbricelli oom-bree-**cheh**-lee
thick, chewy, rolled pasta (Umbria)

There are many, many other shapes, including ***alfabeto*** (letter), ***fiori*** (flower), ***galletti*** (rooster's comb, ruffled on one side), ***lumache*** (snail), and ***marziani*** (spirals resembling "martian" antennae)...to name but a few.

Stuffed Pasta

Some pasta is almost always made fresh and often designed to be filled ***(ripieni).*** Aside from the familiar ***ravioli*** and ***tortellini,*** you'll find:

manicotti mah-nee-**koh**-tee
large tubes ("sleeves"); usually stuffed (often with ricotta) and baked

cannelloni kah-neh-**loh**-nee
wide tube similar to manicotti; often used in baked dishes

cappelletti kah-peh-**leh**-tee
meat-filled dumplings, usually cooked in chicken broth

gnocchi **nyoh**-kee
shell-shaped, hand-rolled dumplings made from potatoes

tortelli / tordelli tor-**teh**-lee / tor-**deh**-lee
small, C-shaped pasta filled with meat or cheese

agnolotti / mezzelune ahn-yoh-**loh**-tee / mehd-zeh-**loo**-nay
stuffed pasta shaped like a "priest's hat" or "half-moon"

girasoli jee-rah-**zoh**-lee
"sunflower"-shaped ravioli

pansotti pahn-**soh**-tee
ravioli with ricotta, greens, and often walnut sauce (Riviera)

Pasta and Rice Dishes

Words describing a pasta sauce or preparation are usually preceded by ***in*** or ***alla*** (in the style of).

aglio e olio **ahl**-yoh ay **oh**-lee-oh
garlic and olive oil

alfredo ahl-**freh**-doh
butter, cream, and *parmigiano*

amatriciana ah-mah-tree-chee-**ah**-nah
sauce of pork cheek, pecorino cheese, and tomato

arrabbiata ah-rah-bee-**ah**-tah
"angry," spicy tomato sauce with chili peppers

Pasta and Rice Dishes *(cont.)*

bigoli in salsa **bee**-goh-lee een **sahl**-sah
thick, whole-wheat noodles with anchovy sauce (Venice)

bolognese boh-lohn-**yeh**-zay
meat and tomato sauce

boscaiola boh-skah-**yoh**-lah
with mushrooms and sausage

brodo **broh**-doh
in broth

burro e salvia **boo**-roh ay **sahl**-vee-ah
butter and sage

cacio e pepe **kah**-choh ay **peh**-pay
cheese and pepper

carbonara kar-boh-**nah**-rah
bacon, egg, cheese, and pepper

carrettiera kah-reh-tee-**eh**-rah
spicy, with garlic, lots of olive oil, and little tomatoes

contadina kohn-tah-**dee**-nah
"peasant's wife-style," rustic and hearty—can be with beans, pancetta, or tomatoes

diavola dee-**ah**-voh-lah
"devil-style," spicy hot

forno **for**-noh
oven-baked

ai funghi ī **foon**-gee (hard "g")
with mushrooms

frutti di mare **froo**-tee dee **mah**-ray
seafood sauce

genovese jeh-noh-**veh**-zay
with pesto

gricia **gree**-chah
with cured pork and *pecorino romano* cheese

marinara mah-ree-**nah**-rah
usually a tomato sauce, often with garlic and onions; can also refer to a dish with seafood

noci **noh**-chee
with walnuts

norma **nor**-mah
tomato, eggplant, and ricotta-cheese sauce

dell'ortolano deh-lor-tah-**lah**-noh
"greengrocer-style," with vegetables

pajata / pagliata pah-**yah**-tah / pahl-**yah**-tah
with calf intestines (Rome)

panna **pah**-nah
cream

pescatore peh-skah-**toh**-ray
seafood ("fishermen's"-style)

pesto **peh**-stoh
basil ground with *parmigiano*, garlic, pine nuts, and olive oil

pomodoro poh-moh-**doh**-roh
tomato only

puttanesca poo-tah-**neh**-skah
"harlot"-style tomato sauce with anchovies, olives, and capers

quattro formaggi **kwah**-troh for-**mah**-jee
four cheeses

ragù rah-**goo**
meaty tomato sauce

risi e bisi **ree**-zee ay **bee**-zee
rice and peas (Venice)

risotto (al nero di seppia / ai porcini / alla milanese)
ree-**zoh**-toh (ahl **neh**-roh dee **sehp**-yah / ī por-**chee**-nee / **ah**-lah mee-lah-**neh**-zay)
short-grain rice, slowly simmered in broth (made with cuttlefish ink / with porcini mushrooms / with saffron)

scoglio **skohl**-yoh
with mussels, clams, and tomatoes

Pasta and Rice Dishes *(cont.)*

sorrentina soh-rehn-**tee**-nah
"Sorrento-style"—tomatoes, basil, and mozzarella (usually over gnocchi)

spezzatino spehd-zah-**tee**-noh
with diced meat in a rich sauce

strascicata alla fiorentina
strah-shee-**kah**-tah **ah**-lah fee-oh-rehn-**tee**-nah
sautéed with meat sauce ("dragged" in a skillet)

sugo **soo**-goh
sauce, usually tomato

sugo di lepre **soo**-goh dee **leh**-pray
rich sauce made of wild hare

tartufo / tartufata tar-**too**-foh / tar-too-**fah**-tah
with truffles

umbra **oom**-brah
sauce of anchovies, garlic, tomatoes, and truffles

vongole **vohn**-goh-lay
with clams and spices

Soups

soup...	zuppa... **tsoo**-pah
...of the day	...del giorno dehl **jor**-noh
...chicken	...di pollo dee **poh**-loh
...beef	...di carne dee **kar**-nay
...fish	...di pesce dee **peh**-shay
...vegetable	...di verdure dee vehr-**doo**-ray
...with noodles	...con pastina kohn pah-**stee**-nah
...with rice	...con riso kohn **ree**-zoh
vegetable soup	minestrone mee-neh-**stroh**-nay
stew	stufato stoo-**fah**-toh
broth	brodo **broh**-doh

Soup Specialties

carabaccia kah-rah-**bah**-chah
onion soup (Tuscany)

impepata di cozze eem-peh-**pah**-tah dee **kohd**-zay
soup with mussels in the shell

minestrone mee-neh-**stroh**-nay
classic Italian vegetable soup

pappa al pomodoro **pah**-pah ahl poh-moh-**doh**-roh
thick soup of tomatoes, olive oil, and bread (Tuscany)

pasta e fagioli **pah**-stah ay fah-**joh**-lee
bean and pasta soup

peposo peh-**poh**-zoh
highly peppered beef stew (Florence)

ribollita / zuppa alla volterrana
ree-boh-**lee**-tah / **tsoo**-pah **ah**-lah vohl-teh-**rah**-nah
"reboiled" stew of white beans, veggies, and olive oil, layered with bread (Tuscany)

stracciatella alla romana strah-chah-**teh**-lah **ah**-lah roh-**mah**-nah
egg-drop meat broth topped with *parmigiano-reggiano* (Rome)

zuppa di pesce **tsoo**-pah dee **peh**-shay
seafood stew

zuppa lombarda **tsoo**-pah lohm-**bar**-dah
Tuscan bean soup

Salad

Insalate (salads) are usually served as a side dish with the main course (if you don't order a ***secondo,*** the waiter will ask when you'd like the salad served). Salad dressing is normally just the oil and vinegar at the table; if it's missing, ask for the ***oliera***.

salad...	insalata... een-sah-**lah**-tah
...green	...verde **vehr**-day
...mixed	...mista **mee**-stah

...niçoise	...nizzarda need-**zar**-dah
...with ham and cheese	...con prosciutto e formaggio kohn proh-**shoo**-toh ay for-**mah**-joh
...with egg	...con uova kohn **woh**-vah
lettuce	lattuga lah-**too**-gah
tomato	pomodoro poh-moh-**doh**-roh
onion	cipolla chee-**poh**-lah
cucumber	cetriolo cheh-tree-**oh**-loh
carrot	carota kah-**roh**-tah
oil / vinegar	olio / aceto **oh**-lee-oh / ah-**cheh**-toh
oil and vinegar	oliera oh-lee-**eh**-rah
dressing (on the side)	condimento (a parte) kohn-dee-**mehn**-toh (ah **par**-tay)
What is in this salad?	Che cosa c'è in questa insalata? kay **koh**-zah cheh een **kweh**-stah een-sah-**lah**-tah

Salad bars at fast-food restaurants and ***autostrada*** rest stops can be a good budget bet.

Salad Specialties

insalata caprese een-sah-**lah**-tah kah-**preh**-zay
sliced tomato topped with fresh mozzarella, basil leaves, and olive oil

insalata di mare een-sah-**lah**-tah dee **mah**-ray
chilled, cooked seafood tossed with parsley, lemon, and olive oil

insalata russa een-sah-**lah**-tah **roo**-sah
vegetable salad with mayonnaise

misticanza mee-stee-**kahnt**-sah
mixed green salad of arugula, curly endive, and anchovies

panzanella pahnt-sah-**neh**-lah
bread, chopped tomatoes, onions, and basil tossed in a light vinaigrette

Pizza

For a fresh, fast, and frugal meal, drop by a ***pizzeria***. Get it to go (***da portar via***—for the road), or eat it on the spot. To get cold pizza warmed up, say ***Caldo, per favore*** (Hot, please). Listed below are some types and toppings to look for, as well as other tasty snacks sold at ***pizzerias.***

Types of Pizza

acciughe ah-**choo**-gay
anchovies

bianca / ciaccina bee-**ahn**-kah / chah-**chee**-nah
"white" pizza (no tomatoes)

capricciosa kah-pree-**choh**-zah
"chef's choice"—usually ham, mushrooms, olives, and artichokes

carciofi kar-**choh**-fee
artichokes

(alla) diavola (**ah**-lah) dee-**ah**-voh-lah
spicy (usually spicy salami)

funghi **foon**-gee (hard "g")
mushrooms

genovese jeh-noh-**veh**-zay
with a thick, foccacia-like crust

margherita mar-geh-**ree**-tah
tomato sauce, mozzarella, and basil

marinara mah-ree-**nah**-rah
tomato sauce, oregano, and garlic, but no cheese

melanzane meh-lahnt-**sah**-nay
eggplant

napoletana / napoli nah-poh-leh-**tah**-nah / **nah**-poh-lee
mozzarella, anchovies, and tomato sauce

peperoni peh-peh-**roh**-nee
green or red peppers (not spicy salami!)

Types of Pizza *(cont.)*

porcini por-**chee**-nee
porcini mushrooms

prosciutto proh-**shoo**-toh
ham

quattro formaggi / stagioni
kwah-troh for-**mah**-jee / stah-**joh**-nee
pizza divided into quarters with four different cheeses / toppings

ripiena ree-pee-**eh**-nah
stuffed

salame piccante / salamino
sah-**lah**-may pee-**kahn**-tay / sah-lah-**mee**-noh
spicy salami (similar to American "pepperoni")

salsa di pomodoro **sahl**-sah dee poh-moh-**doh**-roh
just tomato sauce (no cheese)

salsiccia sahl-**see**-chah
sausage

siciliana see-chee-lee-**ah**-nah
capers, olives, and often anchovies

tonno e cipolla **toh**-noh ay chee-**poh**-lah
tuna and onions

vegetariana / ortolana veh-jeh-tah-ree-**ah**-nah / or-toh-**lah**-nah
veggie

viennese vee-eh-**nay**-zay
tomato, mozzarella, and German-style sausage

calzone kahlt-**soh**-nay
folded pizza turnover with various fillings

farinata / cecina / torta di ceci
fah-ree-**nah**-tah / cheh-**chee**-nah / **tor**-tah dee **cheh**-chee
savory chickpea crêpe

For take-out ***(pizza al taglio),*** you'll most likely find ***pizza rustica:*** pizza baked in a big rectangular pan and sold by weight. Order 100 grams ***(un etto)*** for a snack-size piece; 200 grams ***(due etti)*** makes a light meal. Or show the size you want with your hands and say ***Tanto così*** (**tahn**-toh koh-**zee;** This much).

If you want a pepperoni pizza, don't order ***peperoni*** (which means peppers)—instead, go for ***diavola*** or ***salame piccante***.

Meat

For terms relating to ***prosciutto, salumi,*** and other cold cuts, see page 134.

meat	carne **kar**-nay
cold cuts / cured meats	salumi / affettati sah-**loo**-mee / ah-feh-**tah**-tee
cutlet	cotoletta koh-toh-**leh**-tah
ribs	costolette koh-stoh-**leh**-tay
shoulder	spalla **spah**-lah
shank (leg meat)	stinco **steen**-koh
beef	manzo **mahnt**-soh
beef steak	bistecca di manzo bee-**steh**-kah dee **mahnt**-soh
sirloin steak	entrecote ehn-treh-**koh**-tay
rib-eye steak	costata koh-**stah**-tah
roast beef	roast beef "roast beef"
air-cured beef	bresaola breh-zah-**oh**-lah
goat (kid)	capretto kah-**preh**-toh
ham...	prosciutto... proh-**shoo**-toh
...dried, air-cured	...crudo **kroo**-doh
...smoked	...affumicato ah-foo-mee-**kah**-toh
...cooked	...cotto **koh**-toh
...roasted	...arrosto ah-**roh**-stoh
bacon, salt-cured	pancetta pahn-**cheh**-tah
lamb	agnello ahn-**yeh**-loh
mutton	montone mohn-**toh**-nay

oxtail	coda di bue **koh**-dah dee **boo**-ay
pork	maiale mī-**yah**-lay
suckling pig	porchetta / maialino por-**keh**-tah / mī-yah-**lee**-noh
boar	cinghiale cheen-gee-**ah**-lay
sausage	salsiccia sahl-**see**-chah
blood sausage	sanguinaccio sahn-gwee-**nah**-choh
rabbit	coniglio koh-**neel**-yoh
veal	vitello vee-**teh**-loh
veal, thin-sliced	scaloppine skah-loh-**pee**-nay
venison	selvaggina sehl-vah-**jee**-nah
Is this cooked?	È cotto questo? eh **koh**-toh **kweh**-stoh

On a menu, the price of steak is often listed per ***etto*** (100 grams, about a quarter-pound); the letters ***s.q.*** (for ***secondo quantità***) mean "according to quantity." It is most common to order four or five ***etti*** of steak to share. There's often a minimum-weight order—ask.

Meat, but...

brains	cervella chehr-**veh**-lah
kidney	rognone rohn-**yoh**-nay
liver	fegato **feh**-gah-toh
neck	collo **koh**-loh
organs (entrails)	frattaglie frah-**tahl**-yay
tongue	lingua **leen**-gwah
horse meat	carne equina **kar**-nay eh-**kwee**-nah
sweetbreads (veal)	animelle (di vitello) ah-nee-**meh**-lay (dee vee-**teh**-loh)
tripe	trippa **tree**-pah
cow's stomach	lampredotto lahm-preh-**doh**-toh
calf intestines (Rome)	pajata / pagliata pah-**yah**-tah / pahl-**yah**-tah

Avoiding Mis-Steaks

alive	vivo **vee**-voh
raw	crudo **kroo**-doh
very rare	molto al sangue **mohl**-toh ahl **sahn**-gway
rare	al sangue ahl **sahn**-gway
medium	cotto **koh**-toh
well-done	ben cotto behn **koh**-toh
very well-done	completamente cotto kohm-pleh-tah-**mehn**-tay **koh**-toh
almost burnt	quasi bruciato **kwah**-zee broo-**chah**-toh
loin	lombo **lohm**-boh
tenderloin	filetto fee-**leh**-toh
sirloin	entrecote / lombatina ehn-treh-**koh**-tay / lohm-bah-**tee**-nah
rib-eye steak	costata koh-**stah**-tah
T-bone	bistecca (alla fiorentina) bee-**steh**-kah (**ah**-lah fee-oh-rehn-**tee**-nah)
rib	costoletta koh-stoh-**leh**-tah
chop	cotoletta / braciola koh-toh-**leh**-tah / brah-**choh**-lah
fillet	filetto fee-**leh**-toh
huge chunk of meat	trancio **trahn**-choh

In Tuscany, the best beef comes from the white ***Chianina*** cow. It's cooked seven minutes on one side, seven on the other, and 15 minutes later, you get steak. There's no asking how you'd like it done; *this* is the way it's done.

Look out—especially in Rome—for the phrase ***quinto quarto:*** The so-called "fifth quarter" includes tripe, tail, brains, and pigs' feet.

Italians have many variations on headcheese—unwanted cuts of meat (often organs) preserved in meat gelatin. If you're not a fan of organs, avoid anything with the word ***testa*** (head), including ***testa in cassetta, coppa di testa,*** or ***formaggio di testa.*** Also be careful with ***sopressata***—in the south, this word means a spicy salami, but in Tuscany, it could be headcheese.

Poultry

poultry	pollame poh-**lah**-may
chicken	pollo **poh**-loh
duck	anatra **ah**-nah-trah
goose	oca **oh**-kah
turkey	tacchino tah-**kee**-noh
partridge	pernice pehr-**nee**-chay
breast	petto **peh**-toh
thigh	sovracoscia soh-vrah-**koh**-shah
drumstick	coscia **koh**-shah
white / dark meat	carne bianca / scura **kar**-nay bee-**ahn**-kah / **skoo**-rah
liver (pâté)	fegato (patè) **feh**-gah-toh (pah-**teh**)
eggs	uova **woh**-vah
free-range eggs	uova di galline allevate a terra **woh**-vah dee gah-**lee**-nay ah-leh-**vah**-tay ah **teh**-rah
How long has this been dead?	Da quanto tempo è morto questo? dah **kwahn**-toh **tehm**-poh eh **mor**-toh **kweh**-stoh

Meat and Poultry Specialties

abbacchio alla romana ah-**bah**-kee-oh **ah**-lah roh-**mah**-nah
grilled baby lamb chops

arrosto misto ah-**roh**-stoh **mee**-stoh
assortment of roasted meats, usually veal, pork, and lamb

bistecca alla fiorentina bee-**steh**-kah **ah**-lah fee-oh-rehn-**tee**-nah
thick T-bone steak, grilled very rare (Florence)

bollito misto boh-**lee**-toh **mee**-stoh
various meats boiled and served with a selection of sauces

canederli kah-**neh**-dehr-lee
large dumplings with ham, liver, spinach, or cheese, served in broth or with butter (Dolomites)

carrè affumicato kah-**reh** ah-foo-mee-**kah**-toh
pork shank that's smoked, then boiled (Dolomites)

Chianina kee-ah-**nee**-nah
top-quality Tuscan beef, from white cows

cinghiale cheen-gee-**ah**-lay (hard "g")
boar, served grilled or in soups, stews, and pasta (Tuscany)

coda alla vaccinara **koh**-dah **ah**-lah vah-chee-**nah**-rah
oxtail braised with garlic, wine, tomato, and celery

cotoletta alla milanese koh-toh-**leh**-tah **ah**-lah mee-lah-**neh**-zay
breaded veal chop (like wiener schnitzel)

crauti rossi **krow**-tee **roh**-see ("krow" rhymes with "cow")
red-cabbage sauerkraut (Dolomites)

fegatelli feh-gah-**teh**-lee
liver meatballs (Tuscany)

fegato alla veneziana **feh**-gah-toh **ah**-lah veh-neht-see-**ah**-nah
liver and onions (Venice)

involtini di vitello (al sugo)
een-vohl-**tee**-nee dee vee-**teh**-loh (ahl **soo**-goh)
thinly sliced veal rolled with prosciutto, celery, and cheese (in a tomato sauce)

Meat and Poultry Specialties *(cont.)*

ossobuco (alla genovese)
oh-soh-**boo**-koh (**ah**-lah jeh-noh-**veh**-zay)
veal shank (braised in broth with carrots, onions, and tomatoes)

pollo alla cacciatora **poh**-loh **ah**-lah kah-chah-**toh**-rah
"hunter-style" chicken with red wine, rosemary, garlic, tomato, and often mushrooms

saltimbocca alla romana sahl-teem-**boh**-kah **ah**-lah roh-**mah**-nah
thinly sliced veal layered with prosciutto and sage, then lightly fried

stinco di maiale **steen**-koh dee mī-**yah**-lay
roasted pork shank (Dolomites)

straccetti strah-**cheh**-tee
meat sliced very thinly, sautéed, and served with arugula and cherry tomatoes or mushrooms

tagliata tahl-**yah**-tah
thin slices of grilled tenderloin, typically on a bed of arugula

trippa alla fiorentina **tree**-pah **ah**-lah fee-oh-rehn-**tee**-nah
tripe and vegetables sautéed in a tomato sauce, sometimes baked with *parmigiano-reggiano* (Florence)

trippa alla romana **tree**-pah **ah**-lah roh-**mah**-nah
tripe braised with onions, carrots, and mint (Rome)

Fish and Seafood

seafood	frutti di mare **froo**-tee dee **mah**-ray
assorted seafood	misto di frutti di mare **mee**-stoh dee **froo**-tee dee **mah**-ray
fish	pesce **peh**-shay
shellfish	crostacei kroh-**stah**-cheh-ee
anchovies	acciughe ah-**choo**-gay
bream (fish)	orata oh-**rah**-tah
clams	vongole **vohn**-goh-lay
cod	merluzzo mehr-**lood**-zoh

crab / spider crab	granchio / granseola **grahn**-kee-oh / grahn-seh-**oh**-lah
crayfish	gambero di fiume gahm-**beh**-roh dee fee-**oo**-may
cuttlefish	seppia **sehp**-yah
dogfish	palombo pah-**lohm**-boh
eel	anguilla ahn-**gwee**-lah
hake	nasello nah-**zeh**-loh
halibut	ippoglosso / halibut ee-poh-**gloh**-soh / **ah**-lee-boot
herring	aringa ah-**reen**-gah
lobster	aragosta ah-rah-**goh**-stah
monkfish	rana pescatrice **rah**-nah peh-skah-**tree**-chay
mussels	cozze **kohd**-zay
octopus	polpo **pohl**-poh
oysters	ostriche **oh**-stree-kay
prawns	scampi / gamberi **skahm**-pee / gahm-**beh**-ree
jumbo prawns	gamberoni gahm-beh-**roh**-nee
salmon	salmone sahl-**moh**-nay
salt cod	baccalà bah-kah-**lah**
sardines	sardine sar-**dee**-nay
scad (like mackerel)	sgombro **zgohm**-broh
scallops	capesante kah-peh-**zahn**-tay
sea bass	branzino brahnt-**see**-noh
shrimp / small shrimp...	gamberi / gamberetti... gahm-**beh**-ree / gahm-beh-**reh**-tee
...in the shell	...interi een-**teh**-ree
...peeled	...sgusciati zgoo-**shah**-tee
sole	sogliola sohl-**yoh**-lah
squid	calamari kah-lah-**mah**-ree

swordfish	pesce spada **peh**-shay **spah**-dah
trout	trota **troh**-tah
tuna	tonno **toh**-noh
turbot (like flounder)	rombo **rohm**-boh
How much for a portion?	Quanto per una porzione? **kwahn**-toh pehr **oo**-nah port-see-**oh**-nay
What's fresh today?	Cosa c'è di fresco oggi? **koh**-zah cheh dee **freh**-skoh **oh**-jee
How do you eat this?	Come si mangia? **koh**-may see **mahn**-jah
Do you eat this part?	Si mangia anche questa parte? see **mahn**-jah **ahn**-kay **kweh**-stah **par**-tay
Just the head, please.	Solo la testa, per favore. **soh**-loh lah **teh**-stah pehr fah-**voh**-ray

Italians like to stuff seafood—be it mussels, sardines, or anchovies—with delicious herbs, bread crumbs, and cheese. Like steak, seafood is often served by the *etto* (100 grams). Fish is usually served whole with the head and tail, but it's also prepared as just a fillet ***(filetto)***. To find out how much a typical portion costs, ask ***Quanto per una porzione?***

Fish and Seafood Specialties

anguillette in umido ahn-gwee-**leh**-tay een **oo**-mee-doh
stewed baby eels (Rome)

baccalà alla livornese bah-kah-**lah ah**-lah lee-vor-**neh**-zay
salt cod with tomato and herbs

branzino al cartoccio brahnt-**see**-noh ahl kar-**toh**-choh
sea bass steamed in parchment

cozze ripiene **kohd**-zay ree-pee-**eh**-nay
mussels stuffed with herbs, cheese, and bread crumbs

fritto misto **free**-toh **mee**-stoh
deep-fried calamari, prawns, and assorted small fish

missoltino mee-sohl-**tee**-noh
shad-like lake fish that's salted and air-dried (Lakes)

moleche col pien **moh**-leh-kay kohl **pee**-ehn
fried soft-shell crabs (Venice)

pesce spade alla ghiotta
peh-shay **spah**-day **ah**-lah gee-**oh**-tah (hard "g")
swordfish with tomatoes, olives, and capers

seppie al nero **sehp**-yay ahl **neh**-roh
cuttlefish (like squid) served in its own ink, often over spaghetti or with polenta

spiedini alla griglia spee-eh-**dee**-nee **ah**-lah **greel**-yah
fish or shellfish grilled on a skewer, often with vegetables

tegame alla Vernazza teh-**gah**-may **ah**-lah vehr-**naht**-sah
fresh anchovies, potatoes, tomatoes, white wine, oil, and herbs (Cinque Terre)

zuppa di pesce **tsoo**-pah dee **peh**-shay
fish soup or stew

How Food Is Prepared

aged	stagionato stah-joh-**nah**-toh
assorted	assortiti ah-sor-**tee**-tee
baked	al forno ahl **for**-noh
barbecued	alla griglia **ah**-lah **greel**-yah
boiled	bollito / lesso boh-**lee**-toh / **leh**-soh
braised	brasato brah-**zah**-toh
breaded	impanato eem-pah-**nah**-toh
broiled	alla brace **ah**-lah **brah**-chay
browned	rosolato roh-zoh-**lah**-toh
cold	freddo **freh**-doh
cooked	cotto **koh**-toh
chopped	tritato tree-**tah**-toh
crispy	croccante kroh-**kahn**-tay
cured	stagionato stah-joh-**nah**-toh
fresh	fresco **freh**-skoh

fried / pan-fried	fritto / in padella **free**-toh / een pah-**deh**-lah
pan-fried with bread crumbs	alla milanese **ah**-lah mee-lah-**neh**-zay
garnished	guarnizione gwar-neet-see-**oh**-nay
glazed	glassato glah-**sah**-toh
grated	grattuggiato grah-too-**jah**-toh
grilled	alla griglia **ah**-lah **greel**-yah
homemade	fatto in casa **fah**-toh een **kah**-zah
hot	caldo **kahl**-doh
in cream sauce	con panna kohn **pah**-nah
juicy	succoso soo-**koh**-zoh
marinated	marinato mah-ree-**nah**-toh
melted	fuso **foo**-zoh
minced	macinato mah-chee-**nah**-toh
mixed	misto **mee**-stoh
pickled	sott'aceto soh-tah-**cheh**-toh
poached	affogato ah-foh-**gah**-toh
rare	al sangue ahl **sahn**-gway
raw	crudo **kroo**-doh
roasted	arrosto ah-**roh**-stoh
sautéed	saltato in padella sahl-**tah**-toh een pah-**deh**-lah
skewer(ed)	spiedino spee-eh-**dee**-noh
smoked	affumicato ah-foo-mee-**kah**-toh
steamed	al vapore ahl vah-**poh**-ray
steamed in parchment	al cartoccio ahl kar-**toh**-choh
stuffed	ripieno ree-pee-**eh**-noh
with tomato, cheese, and bread crumbs	alla parmigiana **ah**-lah par-mee-**jah**-nah

Flavors and Spices

spicy (flavorful)	speziato speht-see-**ah**-toh
spicy (hot)	piccante pee-**kahn**-tay
(too) salty	(troppo) salato (**troh**-poh) sah-**lah**-toh
sour	agro **ah**-groh
sweet	dolce **dohl**-chay
bitter	amaro ah-**mah**-roh
cayenne	pepe di caienna **peh**-peh dee kī-**yeh**-nah
cilantro (coriander)	coriandolo koh-ree-**ahn**-doh-loh
cinnamon	cannella kah-**neh**-lah
citrus	agrumi ah-**groo**-mee
garlic	aglio **ahl**-yoh
ginger	zenzero **tsehnt**-seh-roh
horseradish	rafano rah-**fah**-noh
mint	menta **mehn**-tah
oregano	origano oh-**ree**-gah-noh
paprika	paprika pah-**pree**-kah
parsley	prezzemolo prehd-zeh-**moh**-loh
pepper	pepe **peh**-peh
rosemary	rosmarino roh-smah-**ree**-noh
salt	sale **sah**-lay
sugar	zucchero **tsoo**-keh-roh

You can look up more herbs and spices in the Menu Decoder (next chapter).

Veggies and Sides

Expect main dishes to be served without vegetables or other side dishes. That's why ***contorni*** (sides) appear separately on the menu.

vegetables	verdure vehr-**doo**-ray
mixed vegetables	misto di verdure **mee**-stoh dee vehr-**doo**-ray

artichoke	carciofo kar-**choh**-foh
giant artichoke	carciofo romanesco kar-**choh**-foh roh-mah-**neh**-skoh
arugula (rocket)	rucola **roo**-koh-lah
asparagus	asparagi ah-spah-**rah**-jee
avocado	avocado ah-voh-**kah**-doh
bean	fagiolo fah-**joh**-loh
beet	barbabietola bar-bah-bee-**eh**-toh-lah
broccoli	broccoli **broh**-koh-lee
cabbage	verza **vehrt**-sah
capers	capperi **kah**-peh-ree
carrot	carota kah-**roh**-tah
cauliflower	cavolfiore kah-vohl-fee-**oh**-ray
chickpea (garbanzo)	cece **cheh**-cheh
corn	granoturco / mais grah-noh-**toor**-koh / "mice"
cucumber	cetriolo cheh-tree-**oh**-loh
eggplant	melanzana meh-lahnt-**sah**-nah
endive	indivia een-**dee**-vee-ah
fennel	finocchio fee-**noh**-kee-oh
French fries	patate fritte pah-**tah**-tay **free**-tay
garlic	aglio **ahl**-yoh
green bean	fagiolino fah-joh-**lee**-noh
lentil	lenticchia lehn-**tee**-kee-ah
mushroom	fungo **foon**-goh
olive	oliva oh-**lee**-vah
onion	cipolla chee-**poh**-lah
peas	piselli pee-**zeh**-lee
pepper (green / red)	peperone (verde / rosso) peh-peh-**roh**-nay (**vehr**-day / **roh**-soh)
pepper (hot)	peperoncino peh-peh-rohn-**chee**-noh
pickle	cetriolino cheh-tree-oh-**lee**-noh

polenta	polenta poh-**lehn**-tah
potato / roasted potatoes	patata / patate arrosto pah-**tah**-tah / pah-**tah**-tay ah-**roh**-stoh
rice	riso **ree**-zoh
spinach	spinaci spee-**nah**-chee
tomato	pomodoro poh-moh-**doh**-roh
turnip	rapa **rah**-pah
truffle	tartufo tar-**too**-foh
zucchini	zucchine tsoo-**kee**-nay

Polenta (cornmeal) is a popular side dish in the north, either served warm and soft, or cut into firm slabs and grilled. ***Polenta*** is a standard accompaniment with salt cod ***(baccalà)*** or Venetian calf liver and onions ***(fegato alla veneziana).***

Fruits

fruit	frutta **froo**-tah
fruit salad	macedonia mah-cheh-**doh**-nee-ah
fruit smoothie	frullato di frutta froo-**lah**-toh dee **froo**-tah
apple	mela **meh**-lah
apricot	albicocca ahl-bee-**koh**-kah
banana	banana bah-**nah**-nah
berries	frutti di bosco **froo**-tee dee **boh**-skoh
blackberry	mora **moh**-rah
blueberry	mirtillo meer-**tee**-loh
cantaloupe	melone meh-**loh**-nay
cherry	ciliegia chee-lee-**eh**-jah
...sour cherry	...amarena / visciola ah-mah-**reh**-nah / vee-**shoh**-lah
date	dattero **dah**-teh-roh
fig	fico **fee**-koh

grapefruit	pompelmo pohm-**pehl**-moh
grapes	uva **oo**-vah
honeydew melon	melone d'inverno meh-**loh**-nay deen-**vehr**-noh
lemon	limone lee-**moh**-nay
mango	mango **mahn**-goh
orange	arancia ah-**rahn**-chah
peach	pesca **peh**-skah
pear	pera **peh**-rah
persimmon	caco **kah**-koh
pineapple	ananas **ah**-nah-nahs
plum	susina soo-**zee**-nah
pomegranate	melograno meh-loh-**grah**-noh
prune	prugna **proon**-yah
raisin	uvetta oo-**veh**-tah
raspberry	lampone lahm-**poh**-nay
strawberry	fragola **frah**-goh-lah
tangerine	mandarino mahn-dah-**ree**-noh
watermelon	cocomero / anguria koh-koh-**meh**-roh / ahn-**goo**-ree-ah

On a menu, you might see ***frutta fresca di stagione*** (fresh fruit of the season). Mixed berries are called ***frutti di bosco*** (forest fruits). If you ask for ***sottobosco*** (under the forest), you'll get a bowl of mixed berries with lemon and sugar.

Nuts to You

nuts	noci **noh**-chee
almond	mandorla mahn-**dor**-lah
cashew	anacardo ah-nah-**kar**-doh
chestnut	castagna kah-**stahn**-yah
coconut	cocco **koh**-koh

hazelnut	nocciola noh-**choh**-lah
peanut	arachide / nocciolina ah-**rah**-kee-day / noh-choh-**lee**-nah
pine nut	pinolo pee-**noh**-loh
pistachio	pistacchio pee-**stah**-kee-oh
seed	seme **seh**-may
sunflower	girasole jee-rah-**zoh**-lay
walnut	noce **noh**-chay

Just Desserts

I'd like / We'd like...	Vorrei / Vorremmo... voh-**reh**-ee / voh-**reh**-moh
dessert	dolce **dohl**-chay
cake	torta **tor**-tah
cookies	biscotti bee-**skoh**-tee
ice cream	gelato jeh-**lah**-toh
sorbet	sorbetto sor-**beh**-toh
fruit salad	macedonia mah-cheh-**doh**-nee-ah
tart	crostata kroh-**stah**-tah
pie	torta **tor**-tah
whipped cream	panna **pah**-nah
chocolate mousse	mousse di cioccolato moos dee choh-koh-**lah**-toh
pudding	budino boo-**dee**-noh
candy	caramella kah-rah-**meh**-lah
chocolates	cioccolatini choh-koh-lah-**tee**-nee
low calorie	poche calorie **poh**-kay kah-loh-**ree**-ay
homemade	fatto in casa **fah**-toh een **kah**-zah
We'll split one.	Ne dividiamo uno. nay dee-vee-dee-**ah**-moh **oo**-noh

Two forks / spoons, please.	Due forchette / cucchiai, per favore. **doo**-ay for-**keh**-tay / koo-kee-ī-ee pehr fah-**voh**-ray
I shouldn't, but...	Non dovrei, ma... nohn doh-**vreh**-ee mah
Super tasty!	Super gustoso! **soo**-pehr goo-**stoh**-zoh
Exquisite!	Squisito! skwee-**zee**-toh
Sinfully good ("A sin of the throat").	Un peccato di gola. oon peh-**kah**-toh dee **goh**-lah

Dessert Specialties

buccellato boo-cheh-**lah**-toh
wreath-shaped anise-and-raisin bread (Lucca)

cannoli kah-**noh**-lee
fried pastry tubes filled with whipped ricotta, candied fruit, and chocolate

cannoncini kah-nohn-**chee**-nee
baked pastry tubes filled with cream

cantucci / cantuccini kahn-**too**-chee / kahn-too-**chee**-nee
crunchy almond biscotti, often dipped in Vin Santo (sweet dessert wine)

cassata kah-**sah**-tah
ice cream, sponge cake, ricotta cheese, fruit, and pistachios (Sicily)

crespella kreh-**speh**-lah
baked crêpe, often stuffed with ricotta

crostata di ricotta kroh-**stah**-tah dee ree-**koh**-tah
cheesecake-like dessert with ricotta, Marsala wine, cinnamon, and chocolate

delizia al limone deh-**leet**-see-ah ahl lee-**moh**-nay
cake with lemon-flavored whipped cream (Amalfi Coast)

Kaiserschmarrn **kī**-zehr-shmarn
eggy crêpe with raisins, jam, and powdered sugar (Dolomites)

ossi di morto **oh**-see dee **mor**-toh
"bones of the dead" Tuscan cookies

panettone pah-neh-**toh**-nay
Milanese yeast cake with raisins and candied fruit

panforte pahn-**for**-tay
dense fruit and nut cake (Siena)

panna cotta **pah**-nah **koh**-tah
custard-like dessert, served with berries or other toppings

pignolo peen-**yoh**-loh
almond cookie with pine nuts

pizzelle peet-**seh**-lay
thin, delicate waffle cookie

profiterole proh-fee-teh-**roh**-lay
cream-filled pastry with warm chocolate sauce

ricciarelli ree-chah-**reh**-lee
white macaroon-and-almond cookie (Tuscany)

rocciata roh-**chah**-tah
apple strudel with raisins (Umbria)

semifreddo seh-mee-**freh**-doh
"semi-frozen" dessert (like a frozen mousse)

tartufo (con panna) tar-**too**-foh (kohn **pah**-nah)
dark-chocolate gelato ball with a cherry inside (and whipped cream on top)

tiramisù tee-rah-mee-**soo**
espresso-soaked cake with chocolate, cream, and sweet Marsala wine

torta della nonna **tor**-tah **deh**-lah **noh**-nah
"grandma-style" custard tart with pine nuts

torta di mele **tor**-tah dee **meh**-lay
apple cake

zabaglione tsah-bahl-**yoh**-nay
custard of egg yolks, sugar, and sweet wine

zeppola **tseh**-poh-lah
deep-fried doughnut filled with custard

zuppa inglese **tsoo**-pah een-**gleh**-zay
rum-soaked cake layered with whipped cream and fruit (like trifle)

There are hundreds of different desserts and cookies made in Italy. Even Romeo and Juliet have their own special sweets named for them: ***baci di Giulietta*** (vanilla meringues, literally "Juliet's kisses") and ***sospiri di Romeo*** (hazelnut and chocolate cookies, literally "Romeo's sighs").

Gelato

Gelato is an edible art form. To find the best ***gelateria***, look for the words ***artiginale, nostra produzione,*** and ***produzione propia,*** meaning it's made on the premises. Gelato displayed in covered metal tins (rather than white plastic) is more likely to be homemade. Seasonal flavors and pastel hues (not garish colors) are also good signs.

cone	cono **koh**-noh
cup	coppa / copetta **koh**-pah / koh-**peh**-tah
one scoop	una pallina **oo**-nah pah-**lee**-nah
two scoops	due palline **doo**-ay pah-**lee**-nay
one flavor / two flavors	un gusto / due gusti oon **goo**-stoh / **doo**-ay **goo**-stee
with whipped cream	con panna kohn **pah**-nah
sorbet	sorbetto sor-**beh**-toh
slushy ice with sweet syrup	granita / grattachecca grah-**nee**-tah / grah-tah-**keh**-kah
mix of slushy ice and gelato	cremolata kreh-moh-**lah**-tah
What is that?	Che cos'è? kay koh-**zeh**
A little taste?	Un assaggio? oon ah-**sah**-joh
How many flavors can I have?	Quanti gusti posso avere? **kwahn**-tee **goo**-stee **poh**-soh ah-**veh**-ray
Which flavors go well together?	Quali gusti stanno bene insieme? **kwah**-lee **goo**-stee **stah**-noh **beh**-nay een-see-**eh**-may
a cone / a cup for ____ euros (fill in amount)	un cono / una coppa da ____ euro oon **koh**-noh / **oo**-nah **koh**-pah dah ____ eh-**oo**-roh

To avoid having your request for a cone turn into a €10 "tourist special," survey the size options and be very clear in your order: for example, ***un cono da due euro*** (a €2 cone).

Gelato Flavors

If you're debating flavors, ask the vendor ***Quali gusti stanno bene insieme?*** (Which flavors go well together?). To order fruit flavors, see "Fruits" on page 159.

After Eight "After Eight"
chocolate and mint

bacio **bah**-choh
chocolate hazelnut

caffè kah-**feh**
coffee

cassata kah-**sah**-tah
mixed with dried fruits

cioccolato choh-koh-**lah**-toh
chocolate

cocco **koh**-koh
coconut

crema **kreh**-mah
cream

crème caramel krehm **kah**-rah-mehl
flan

croccantino kroh-kahn-**tee**-noh
"crunchy," with toasted peanut bits

fior di latte fee-**or** dee **lah**-tay
milk

liquirizia lee-kwee-**reet**-see-ah
licorice

macedonia mah-cheh-**doh**-nee-ah
mixed fruit

Gelato Flavors *(cont.)*

malaga **mah**-lah-gah
rum raisin (more or less)

menta **mehn**-tah
mint

meringa meh-**reen**-gah
meringue

nocciola noh-**choh**-lah
hazelnut

noce **noh**-chay
nut

riso **ree**-zoh
rice

rosa **roh**-zah
rose

stracciatella strah-chah-**teh**-lah
vanilla with shreds of chocolate

tartufo tar-**too**-foh
super chocolate

torrone toh-**roh**-nay
nougat

vaniglia vah-**neel**-yah
vanilla

yogurt **yoh**-goort
yogurt

zuppa inglese **tsoo**-pah een-**gleh**-zay
trifle

DRINKING

Water

mineral water...	acqua minerale... **ah**-kwah mee-neh-**rah**-lay
...with carbonation / sparkling	...con gas / frizzante kohn gahs / freed-**zahn**-tay
...without carbonation / natural	...senza gas / naturale **sehnt**-sah gahs / nah-too-**rah**-lay
lightly carbonated water	acqua leggermente effervescente **ah**-kwah leh-jehr-**mehn**-tay eh-fehr-veh-**shehn**-tay
(half) liter	(mezzo) litro (**mehd**-zoh) **lee**-troh
tap water	acqua del rubinetto **ah**-kwah dehl roo-bee-**neh**-toh
(not) drinkable	(non) potabile (nohn) poh-**tah**-bee-lay
Is this water safe to drink?	È potabile quest'acqua? eh poh-**tah**-bee-lay kweh-**stah**-kwah

You can ask for ***acqua del rubinetto*** (tap water) in restaurants, but your server may give you a funny look. Italians are notorious water snobs; your server just can't understand why you wouldn't want good water to go with your good food. It's customary and never expensive to order a ***litro*** (liter) or ***mezzo litro*** (half liter) of bottled water. ***Acqua leggermente effervescente*** (lightly carbonated water) is a meal-time favorite. To pare down to the simplest form, ask for ***con gas*** if you want fizzy water and ***senza gas*** if you prefer still water.

Milk

whole milk	latte intero **lah**-tay een-**teh**-roh
skim milk	latte magro **lah**-tay **mah**-groh
fresh milk	latte fresco **lah**-tay **freh**-skoh
milk shake	frullato / frappè froo-**lah**-toh / frah-**peh**
cold / hot	freddo / caldo **freh**-doh / **kahl**-doh

Key Phrases: Drinking

drink	bibita **bee**-bee-tah
(mineral) water	acqua (minerale) **ah**-kwah (mee-neh-**rah**-lay)
tap water	acqua del rubinetto **ah**-kwah dehl roo-bee-**neh**-toh
milk	latte **lah**-tay
juice	succo **soo**-koh
coffee	caffè kah-**feh**
tea	tè teh
wine	vino **vee**-noh
beer	birra **bee**-rah
Cheers!	Cin cin! cheen cheen

straw	cannuccia kah-**noo**-chah
hot chocolate (with whipped cream)	cioccolata calda (con panna) choh-koh-**lah**-tah **kahl**-dah (kohn **pah**-nah)

Juice and Other Drinks

(fruit) juice	succo (di frutta) **soo**-koh (dee **froo**-tah)
freshly squeezed juice	spremuta spreh-**moo**-tah
100% juice	100% succo di frutta **chehn**-toh pehr **chehn**-toh **soo**-koh dee **froo**-tah
orange juice	succo di arancia **soo**-koh dee ah-**rahn**-chah

freshly squeezed orange juice	spremuta di arancia spreh-**moo**-tah dee ah-**rahn**-chah
blood orange juice	succo di arance rosse **soo**-koh dee ah-**rahn**-chay **roh**-say
apple juice	succo di mela **soo**-koh dee **meh**-lah
grape juice	succo d'uva **soo**-koh **doo**-vah
pineapple juice	succo d'ananas **soo**-koh **dah**-nah-nahs
fruit smoothie	frullato di frutta froo-**lah**-toh dee **froo**-tah
lemonade	limonata lee-moh-**nah**-tah
(diet) soda	bibita gassata ("light") **bee**-bee-tah gah-**sah**-tah ("light")
energy drink	bibita energetica **bee**-bee-tah eh-nehr-**jeh**-tee-kah
with / without...	con / senza... kohn / **sehnt**-sah
...sugar	...zucchero **tsoo**-keh-roh
...ice	...ghiaccio gee-**ah**-choh (hard "g")

Coffee

When you're ordering coffee in bars in bigger cities, you'll notice that the price board ***(lista dei prezzi)*** clearly lists two price levels: the cheaper level for the stand-up ***bar*** and the more expensive for the ***tavolo*** (table) or ***terrazza*** (out on the terrace or sidewalk). If standing at the bar, don't order from the bartender—instead, order and pay first at the ***cassa*** (cash register), then take your receipt to the person who makes the coffee. Refills are never free (except at hotel breakfasts).

espresso...	caffè... kah-**feh**
...with milk	...latte **lah**-tay
...with foamed milk	...cappuccino kah-poo-**chee**-noh
...American-style (with hot water)	...americano ah-meh-ree-**kah**-noh

...with sugar	...con zucchero kohn **tsoo**-keh-roh
...iced and sweetened	...freddo **freh**-doh
...double shot	...doppio **dohp**-yoh
instant	solubile soh-**loo**-bee-lay
decaffeinated	decaffeinato / Hag deh-kah-feh-**nah**-toh / ahg
price list...	lista dei prezzi... **lee**-stah **deh**-ee **preht**-see
...at the bar / at a table / on the terrace	...al bar / al tavolo / in terrazza ahl bar / ahl **tah**-voh-loh / een teh-**raht**-sah
Same price if I sit or stand?	Costa uguale al tavolo o al banco? **koh**-stah oo-**gwah**-lay ahl **tah**-voh-loh oh ahl **bahn**-koh
Very hot, please.	Molto caldo, per favore. **mohl**-toh **kahl**-doh pehr fah-**voh**-ray
Hotter, please.	Più caldo, per favore. pew **kahl**-doh pehr fah-**voh**-ray

In Italian, ***caffè*** means espresso. If you ask for ***un latte,*** you'll get a glass of hot milk; instead, order ***un caffè latte***. For the closest thing to a cup of drip coffee, request ***un caffè americano***.

Italians like their coffee only warm—to get it hot, request ***molto caldo*** (very hot) or ***più caldo, per favore*** (hotter, please).

Coffee Specialties

Italians use precise terminology to get just the right combination of espresso with hot water and/or milk. While coffee is popular any time of day, Italians drink the kinds with lots of milk only in the morning. After lunchtime, Italians add just a splash of milk to their coffee (for example, ***caffè macchiato***). But ***baristas*** are willing—perhaps with a raised eyebrow—to serve milky drinks to tourists in the afternoon.

These coffee drinks are listed in order of containing increasing amounts of hot water:

caffè kah-**feh**
a shot of espresso in a little cup

caffè corto kah-**feh kor**-toh
extra-strong espresso with only a bit of hot water, in a small cup

caffè lungo kah-**feh loon**-goh
espresso diluted with a bit more ("long") hot water, in a small cup

caffè americano kah-**feh** ah-meh-ree-**kah**-noh
espresso diluted with more hot water, in a larger cup (closest to American-style drip coffee)

These coffee drinks are listed in order of containing increasing amounts of milk:

caffè macchiato kah-**feh** mah-kee-**ah**-toh
espresso "marked" with just a splash of milk, served in a small cup

caffè schiumato kah-**feh** skoo-**mah**-toh
caffè macchiato with extra foam

cappuccino kah-poo-**chee**-noh
espresso with foamed milk on top

caffè latte kah-**feh lah**-tay
espresso mixed with hot milk, no foam, in a tall glass

latte macchiato **lah**-tay mah-kee-**ah**-toh
layers of hot milk and foam, "marked" by an espresso shot, in a tall glass

When ordering a ***macchiato*** in Italy, specify either ***caffè macchiato*** (espresso with a tiny bit of milk) or ***latte macchiato*** (lots of milk and foam with a shot of espresso).

Here are some other popular coffee drinks:

caffè corretto kah-**feh** koh-**reh**-toh
espresso "corrected" with a shot of liqueur (typically grappa, amaro, or Sambuca)

Coffee Specialties *(cont.)*

marocchino mah-roh-**kee**-noh
"Moroccan" coffee with espresso, foamed milk, and cocoa powder

mocaccino moh-kah-**chee**-noh
similar to *marocchino*, but with chocolate instead of cocoa

caffè freddo kah-**feh freh**-doh
sweet, iced espresso

cappuccino freddo kah-poo-**chee**-noh **freh**-doh
iced cappuccino

While the frappuccino is an American invention, a ***cappuccino freddo*** comes close.

Tea

hot water	acqua calda **ah**-kwah **kahl**-dah
tea	tè teh
lemon	limone lee-**moh**-nay
tea bag	bustina di tè boo-**stee**-nah dee teh
herbal tea	tisana tee-**zah**-nah
chamomile	camomilla kah-moh-**mee**-lah
black tea	tè nero teh **neh**-roh
green tea	tè verde teh **vehr**-day
lemon tea	tè al limone teh ahl lee-**moh**-nay
citrus tea	tè agli agrumi teh **ahl**-yee ah-**groo**-mee
fruit tea	tè alla frutta teh **ah**-lah **froo**-tah
mint tea	tè alla menta teh **ah**-lah **mehn**-tah
iced tea	tè freddo teh **freh**-doh

Tè freddo (iced tea) is usually from a can—sweetened and flavored with lemon or peach.

Wine Lingo

The ancient Greeks who colonized Italy more than 2,000 years ago called it ***Oenotria*** (land of the grape). Italian wines are named by grape, place, descriptive term, or a combination of these.

wine	vino **vee**-noh
table wine	vino da tavola **vee**-noh dah **tah**-voh-lah
house wine	vino della casa **vee**-noh **deh**-lah **kah**-zah
red	rosso **roh**-soh
white	bianco bee-**ahn**-koh
rosé	rosato roh-**zah**-toh
sparkling	frizzante / spumante freed-**zahn**-tay / spoo-**mahn**-tay
sparkling white wine	prosecco proh-**seh**-koh
local	locale loh-**kah**-lay
of the region	della regione **deh**-lah reh-**joh**-nay
chilled	ghiacciato gee-ah-**chah**-toh (hard "g")
at room temperature	a temperatura ambiente ah tehm-peh-rah-**too**-rah ahm-bee-**ehn**-tay
cork	tappo **tah**-poh
corkscrew	cavatappi kah-vah-**tah**-pee
vineyard	vigneto veen-**yeh**-toh
harvest	vendemmia vehn-**deh**-mee-ah
wine-tasting	degustazione deh-goo-staht-see-**oh**-nay

Ordering Wine

I'd like / We'd like...	Vorrei / Vorremo... voh-**reh**-ee / voh-**reh**-moh
...the wine list.	...la lista dei vini. lah **lee**-stah **deh**-ee **vee**-nee
...a glass...	...un bicchiere... oon bee-kee-**eh**-ray

...a small glass...	...un bicchiere piccolo... oon bee-kee-**eh**-ray **pee**-koh-loh
...a quarter liter...	...un quartino... oon kwar-**tee**-noh
...a half liter...	...un mezzo... oon **mehd**-zoh
...a liter...	...un litro... oon **lee**-troh
...a carafe...	...una caraffa... **oo**-nah kah-**rah**-fah
...a bottle...	...una bottiglia... **oo**-nah boh-**teel**-yah
...of red wine.	...di rosso. dee **roh**-soh
...of white wine.	...di bianco. dee bee-**ahn**-koh
...of house wine / table wine.	...di vino della casa / vino da tavola. dee **vee**-noh **deh**-lah **kah**-zah / **vee**-noh dah **tah**-voh-lah

For a good, light, affordable, straightforward wine at a meal, order ***Una caraffa di vino della casa*** (A carafe of the house wine).

Finding the Right Wine

Visit an ***enoteca*** (wine shop or bar) to sample a variety of regional wines.

I'd like to sample a typical local wine.	Vorrei provare un vino locale tipico. voh-**reh**-ee proh-**vah**-ray oon **vee**-noh loh-**kah**-lay **tee**-pee-koh
What do you recommend?	Cosa raccomanda? **koh**-zah rah-koh-**mahn**-dah
Choose for me, please.	Scelga lei, per favore. **shehl**-gah **leh**-ee pehr fah-**voh**-ray
Around ____ euros.	Intorno ai ____ euro. een-**tor**-noh ī ____ eh-**oo**-roh
I like ____. (fill in type of wine)	Mi piace il ____. mee pee-**ah**-chay eel ____
I like something that is ____ and ____.	Preferisco qualcosa di ____ e ____. preh-feh-**ree**-skoh kwahl-**koh**-zah dee ____ ay ____

sweet	dolce / abboccato / amabile **dohl**-chay / ah-boh-**kah**-toh / ah-**mah**-bee-lay
semi-dry	semi-secco seh-mee-**seh**-koh
(very) dry	(molto) secco (**mohl**-toh) **seh**-koh
light / heavy	leggero / gustoso leh-**jeh**-roh / goo-**stoh**-zoh
full-bodied	corposo / pieno kor-**poh**-zoh / pee-**eh**-noh
young	giovane **joh**-vah-nay
mature	maturo mah-**too**-roh
fruity	fruttato froo-**tah**-toh
earthy	terroso teh-**roh**-zoh
tannic	tannico **tah**-nee-koh
elegant	elegante eh-leh-**gahn**-tay
smooth	morbido **mor**-bee-doh
sharp	spigoloso spee-goh-**loh**-zoh
easy to drink	facile da bere **fah**-chee-lay dah **beh**-ray
Another, please.	Un altro, per favore. oon **ahl**-troh pehr fah-**voh**-ray

Wine Labels

The information on an Italian wine label can help you choose something decent. In general, Italy designates its wines by one of four official categories.

VDT (Vino da Tavola): Table wine, the lowest grade—made anywhere in Italy, but often still quite good

IGT (Indicazione Geografica Tipica): From a more specific region within Italy; this broad category includes higher-quality wines (such as Super Tuscans) that don't meet strict DOC or DOCG rules

Regional Wines

Tuscany: Many Tuscan wines are made with sangiovese ("blood of Jupiter") grapes, including the well-known Chiantis, which range from cheap, acidic basket-bottles of table wine (called *fiaschi*) to the hearty Chianti Classico. Vino Nobile di Montepulciano is a high-quality dry ruby red that pairs well with meat, especially chicken. One of Italy's top reds is Brunello di Montalcino (smooth, dry, aged at least four years in wood); a cheaper, younger "baby Brunello" is Rosso di Montalcino. Pricey Super Tuscans blend traditional grapes with locally grown non-Italian grapes (such as cabernet or merlot). Your only decent white choice is Vernaccia di San Gimignano (medium-dry, pairs well with pasta and salad). Trebbiano and Vermentino are two other local white grapes. Vin Santo is a sweet, syrupy, "holy" dessert wine, often served with biscotti for dipping.

Veneto (near Venice): Valpolicella grapes are used to make a light, fruity, dry, red table wine (also called Valpolicella), as well as Amarone (full-bodied red aged for at least four years in oak) and Recioto (sweet dessert wine made with high-sugar grapes). Bardolino is a light, fruity, Beaujolais-like picnic wine. Whites include Soave (crisp, dry white that pairs well with seafood; the best is Soave Classico), Pinot Grigio, and Bianco di Custoza. If you like bubbles, try Fragolino (sweet, slightly fizzy dessert wine made from a strawberry-flavored grape) or Prosecco (connoisseurs say the best hails from Valdobbiadene).

Umbria: Trebbiano is this region's main white grape. Look for Orvieto Classico (a golden, dry white). For reds, consider Sagrantino de Montefalco (dark, tannic) or Torgiano Rosso Riserva (elegant, smooth). Wines from the quality producer Lungarotti are worth trying.

Cinque Terre (Liguria): This coastal region produces light, delicate whites (using mostly bosco grapes) that go well with seafood. Dolce acqua is a medium-bodied red. After dinner, try Sciacchetrà (shah-keh-**trah**; a silky sweet, potent, amber-colored wine made with raisins).

Rome (Lazio): Wines to try include Frascati (inexpensive dry white); Castelli Romani, Marino, Colli Albani, and Velletri (all light and fairly dry); and Torre Ercolana (balanced, medium-bodied, best-quality red).

Dolomites: While beer is king here, look for reds such as St. Magdalaner (light, dry, made from Schiava grapes), Lagrein Scuro (full-bodied, dry and fruity, similar to a cabernet sauvignon or merlot), or whites like Pinot Grigio, Gewürztraminer, and Pinot Blanc. Nosiola is an aromatic local grape used for dessert and sparkling wine.

Piedmont: This region specializes in bold, dry reds. Nebbiolo is the main red grape. Wine lovers drool over Barolo (big, tannic, aged three years or more) or its little brother Barbaresco (elegant, aged two years). For lighter, less tannic reds, try Barbera or Dolcetto (soft, fruity). Whites include Gavi (light, fruity) and Arneis (flowery, medium-bodied). For bubbly wines, try Brachetto (crimson, sweet, berry notes, excellent aperitif), Moscato d'Asti (semi-sweet, slightly fizzy), and Asti Spumante (dry).

Campania: Plentiful sun and Mt. Vesuvius' volcanic soils provide great wine-growing conditions. Taurasi is an excellent ruby-colored, tannic, aged, full-bodied red from the Aglianico grape. Lacryma Christi ("tears of Christ") comes in both red (medium body) and white (dry and fruity, great with seafood). Other whites are Greco di Tufo (dry, pale-yellow) and Fiano di Avellino (soft, flavorful, dry).

Sicily: The main red is Nero d'Avola (jammy, full-bodied, tannic). Corvo, Regaleali, and Planeta are some established producers. White wines use indigenous grapes like Grillo, Inzolio, and Catarrato. Try Bianco d'Alcamo (dry, fresh, fruity) and Etna Bianco (dry, lemon flavors, pairs well with shellfish). Marsala is a (usually) sweet, fortified dessert wine.

DOC (Denominazione di Origine Controllata): High-quality wine—usually quite affordable—made from specific grapes grown in a delimited area

DOCG (Denominazione di Origine Controllata e Garantita): Highest-quality wine made with grapes from a defined area whose quality is guaranteed; these wines, with a pink or green label on the neck, are a good bet if you want a quality wine

You may also see these terms on wine labels:

Riserva: DOCG or DOC wine matured for a longer, specified time
Classico: From a defined, select area
Annata: Year of harvest
Vendemmia: Harvest
Imbottigliato dal produttore all'origine: Bottled by producers

Red wine dominates in Italy. Many small-town Italians in the hotel business have a cellar or ***cantina*** that they are proud to show off. They'll often jump at any excuse to descend and drink.

Beer

I'd like / We'd like...	Vorrei / Vorremo... voh-**reh**-ee / voh-**reh**-moh
beer...	birra... **bee**-rah
...from the tap	...alla spina **ah**-lah **spee**-nah
bottle	bottiglia boh-**teel**-yah
can	lattina lah-**tee**-nah
light / dark	chiara / scura kee-**ah**-rah / **skoo**-rah
local / imported	locale / importata loh-**kah**-lay / eem-por-**tah**-tah
small / large	piccola / grande **pee**-koh-lah / **grahn**-day
wheat	birra di frumento **bee**-rah dee froo-**mehn**-toh
microbrew	birra artigianale **bee**-rah ar-tee-jah-**nah**-lay

a glass of draft beer	una birra alla spina **oo**-nah **bee**-rah **ah**-lah **spee**-nah
small (11 oz) beer	birra piccola **bee**-rah **pee**-koh-lah
medium (1 pint) beer	birra media **bee**-rah **meh**-dee-ah
large (1 liter) beer	birra grande **bee**-rah **grahn**-day
half-liter bottle	bottiglia da mezzo litro boh-**teel**-yah dah **mehd**-zoh **lee**-troh
shandy (beer with lemon soda)	birra con limonata **bee**-rah kohn lee-moh-**nah**-tah
low-calorie ("light")	leggera leh-**jeh**-rah
non-alcoholic beer	analcolica ahn-ahl-**koh**-lee-kah

Italians drink mainly lager beers. You'll find local brews (Peroni or Moretti) and imports such as Heineken. Italians never drink beer with meat.

Remember, bars often have a tiered price system; you'll pay more to sit than to stand. (For details, see page 169.)

Bar Talk

bar	bar bar
Shall we go for a drink?	Andiamo a prendere qualcosa da bere? ahn-dee-**ah**-moh ah **prehn**-deh-ray kwahl-**koh**-zah dah **beh**-ray
I'll buy you a drink.	Ti offro qualcosa da bere. tee **oh**-froh kwahl-**koh**-zah dah **beh**-ray
It's on me.	Pago io. **pah**-goh **ee**-oh
The next one's on me.	Offro io la prossima. **oh**-froh **ee**-oh lah **proh**-see-mah
What would you like?	Che cosa prendi? kay **koh**-zah **prehn**-dee
I'll have ____.	Prendo ____. **prehn**-doh ____
I don't drink.	Non bevo. nohn **beh**-voh

What is the local specialty?	Qual'è la specialità locale? kwah-**leh** lah speh-chah-lee-**tah** loh-**kah**-lay
Straight.	Liscio. **lee**-shoh
With / Without ice.	Con / Senza ghiaccio. kohn / **sehnt**-sah gee-**ah**-choh (hard "g")
One more.	Un altro. oon **ahl**-troh
I'm a little drunk.	Mi sento un po' ubriaco[a]. mee **sehn**-toh oon poh oo-bree-**ah**-koh
Cheers!	Cin cin! cheen cheen
To your health!	Salute! sah-**loo**-tay
Long live Italy!	Viva l'Italia! **vee**-vah lee-**tahl**-yah
I'm hung over.	Ho i postumi della sbronza. oh ee poh-**stoo**-mee **deh**-lah **zbrohnt**-sah

Aperitivo Specialties

Before dinner, try an ***aperitivo*** to stimulate your palate.

Americano ah-meh-ree-**kah**-noh
vermouth with bitters, brandy, and lemon peel

Bellini beh-**lee**-nee
Prosecco and white peach juice (Venice)

Campari kahm-**pah**-ree
dark-colored bitters with herbs and orange peel

Cinzano cheent-**sah**-noh
popular brand of vermouth (red and white)

Cynar **chee**-nar
flavored with artichoke

Martini mar-**tee**-nee
popular brand of vermouth (red and white)

Punt e Mes poont ay mehs
sweet red vermouth and red wine

spremuta di frutta spreh-**moo**-tah dee **froo**-tah
freshly squeezed fruit juice

spritz con Campari / con Aperol
spreetz kohn kahm-**pah**-ree / kohn **ah**-peh-rohl
white wine, soda, and ice with Campari (bitter) or Aperol (sweet), garnished with an olive or skewer of fruit (Venice)

Tiziano teet-see-**ah**-noh
grape juice and Prosecco

Digestivo Specialties

After dinner, try a ***digestivo,*** a liqueur thought to aid in digestion. Many restaurants make their own brew, using a secret combination of herbs.

amaretto ah-mah-**reh**-toh
almond-flavored liqueur

amaro ah-**mah**-roh
sweet, strong bitters (well-known brands are Montenegro and Fernet Branca)

Frangelico frahn-**jeh**-lee-koh
hazelnut liqueur

grappa **grah**-pah
brandy distilled from grape skins (*vinacce*) and stems

limoncello lee-mohn-**cheh**-loh
lemon liqueur

nocino noh-**chee**-noh
dark, sweet walnut liqueur—similar to Jägermeister

sambuca (con mosca) sahm-**boo**-kah (kohn **moh**-skah)
syrupy, anise-flavored liqueur (with "flies"—three coffee beans)

Sgroppino zgroh-**pee**-noh
squeezed lemon juice, lemon gelato, and vodka

stravecchio strah-**veh**-kee-oh
aged (mellower) grappa

PICNICKING

While you can opt for the one-stop ***supermercato,*** it's more fun to assemble your picnic and practice your Italian visiting an ***alimentari*** (small grocery), individual shops, or a ***mercato*** (open-air market).

Tasty Picnic Words

picnic	picnic **peek**-neek
sandwich or roll	panino pah-**nee**-noh
bread	pane **pah**-nay
whole-wheat bread	pane integrale **pah**-nay een-teh-**grah**-lay
cured ham	prosciutto crudo proh-**shoo**-toh **kroo**-doh
cooked ham	prosciutto cotto proh-**shoo**-toh **koh**-toh
sausage	salsiccia sahl-**see**-chah
cheese	formaggio for-**mah**-joh
mustard...	senape... **seh**-nah-pay
mayonnaise...	maionese... mah-yoh-**neh**-zay
...in a tube	...in tubetto een too-**beh**-toh
olives...	olive... oh-**lee**-vay
pickles...	cetriolini... cheh-tree-oh-**lee**-nee
...in a jar	...in vasetto een vah-**zeh**-toh
yogurt	yogurt **yoh**-goort
fruit	frutta **froo**-tah
box of juice	cartone di succo di frutta kar-**toh**-nay dee **soo**-koh dee **froo**-tah
cold drinks	bibite ghiacciate **bee**-bee-tay gee-ah-**chah**-tay (hard "g")
spoon / fork...	cucchiaio / forchetta... koo-kee-**ī**-yoh / for-**keh**-tah
...made of plastic	...di plastica dee **plah**-stee-kah

cup / plate...	bicchiere / piatto... bee-kee-**eh**-ray / pee-**ah**-toh
...made of paper	...di carta dee **kar**-tah

To get real juice, look for ***100% succo*** on the label. Don't forget the wine for your picnic. Public consumption may be forbidden back home, but Europeans see no problem with sipping a glass of wine outside—in parks, on benches, or along the riverbank.

At the Grocery

Meat and cheese are sold by the gram. One hundred grams ***(un etto)*** is enough for two sandwiches.

Is it self-service?	È self-service? eh sehlf-**sehr**-vees
Fifty grams.	Cinquanta grammi. cheeng-**kwahn**-tah **grah**-mee
One hundred grams.	Un etto. oon **eh**-toh
More. / Less.	Di più. / Di meno. dee pew / dee **meh**-noh
A piece.	Un pezzo. oon **pehd**-zoh
Half.	Metà. meh-**tah**
A slice.	Una fetta. **oo**-nah **feh**-tah
Four slices.	Quattro fette. **kwah**-troh **feh**-tay
A thin slice.	Una fettina. **oo**-nah feh-**tee**-nah
Cut into slices (fine).	Affettato (sottile). ah-feh-**tah**-toh (soh-**tee**-lay)
Can you please slice it?	Lo può affettare, per favore? loh pwoh ah-feh-**tah**-ray pehr fah-**voh**-ray
Does it need to be cooked?	Bisogna cucinarlo prima di mangiarlo? bee-**zohn**-yah koo-chee-**nar**-loh **pree**-mah dee mahn-**jar**-loh
Ripe for today?	Da mangiare oggi? dah mahn-**jah**-ray **oh**-jee

May I taste it?	Posso assaggiarlo? **poh**-soh ah-sah-**jar**-loh
Will you make... for me / us?	Mi / Ci può fare...? mee / chee pwoh **fah**-ray
...a sandwich	...un panino oon pah-**nee**-noh
...two sandwiches	...due panini **doo**-ay pah-**nee**-nee
To take out.	Da portar via. dah por-**tar vee**-ah
A container.	Un contenitore. oon kohn-teh-nee-**toh**-ray
A small bag.	Un sacchettino. oon sah-keh-**tee**-noh
A bag, please.	Un sacchetto, per favore. oon sah-**keh**-toh pehr fah-**voh**-ray
Can I use the microwave?	Posso usare il forno a microonde? **poh**-soh oo-**zah**-ray eel **for**-noh ah mee-kroh-**ohn**-day
May I borrow a...?	Posso prendere in prestito...? **poh**-soh **prehn**-deh-ray een **preh**-stee-toh
Do you have a...?	Avete un...? ah-**veh**-tay oon
Where can I buy / find a...?	Dove posso comprare / trovare un...? **doh**-vay **poh**-soh kohm-**prah**-ray / troh-**vah**-ray oon
...corkscrew	...cavatappi kah-vah-**tah**-pee
...can opener	...apriscatole ah-pree-skah-**toh**-lay
...bottle opener	...apribottiglie ah-pree-boh-**teel**-yay
Is there a park nearby?	C'è un parco qui vicino? cheh oon **par**-koh kwee vee-**chee**-noh
Where is a good place to picnic?	Dov'è un bel posto per fare un picnic? doh-**veh** oon behl **poh**-stoh pehr **fah**-ray oon **peek**-neek
Is picnicking allowed here?	Va bene fare un picnic qui? vah **beh**-nay **fah**-ray oon **peek**-neek kwee

When buying cold cuts for a picnic, you can order by the ***fettina*** (thin slice). For two people, I might get ***cinque fettine*** (five slices) of prosciutto.

When selecting ***antipasti,*** you can also ask for ***una porzione*** (a portion) in a take-out container ***(contenitore)***. Use gestures to show exactly how much you want. The word ***basta*** (enough) works as a question or as a statement.

Produce Markets

It's customary to let the merchant choose produce for you. Say ***per oggi*** (pehr **oh**-jee; for today), and he or she will grab you something ready to eat. Pointing and gesturing go a long way.

Pay careful attention, as the unit of measure can differ from item to item. It could be ***al kg*** (per kilogram—1,000 grams), ***al kilo, per ½ kg*** (500 grams or ***per 500 gr***), ***per ¼ kg*** (250 grams), ***per etto*** (100 grams or ***per 100 gr***), and so on. If a price is listed without a unit, then it's usually per kilo, but confirm just in case by asking ***Il prezzo è al kilo?*** (In Italian, the words kilogram and kilo can also be written as ***chilogram*** and ***chilo.***) Some items may be priced by the ***etto,*** by the piece (***pezzo*** or ***l'uno***), or by the bunch (***manciata*** or ***mazzo***).

Is it priced by the kilo?	Il prezzo è al kilo? eel **prehd**-zoh eh ahl **kee**-loh
kilo	kilo **kee**-loh
½ kilo	mezzo kilo **mehd**-zoh **kee**-loh
200 grams	due etti **doo**-ay **eh**-tee
100 grams	un etto oon **eh**-toh (**chehn**-toh **grah**-mee)
that	quello **kweh**-loh
this much	tanto così **tahn**-toh koh-**zee**
more / less	di più / di meno dee pew / dee **meh**-noh
too much	troppo **troh**-poh
enough	basta così **bah**-stah koh-**zee**

in one piece	un unico pezzo oon **oo**-nee-koh **pehd**-zoh
one / two	l'uno / due **loo**-noh / **doo**-ay
bunch of produce / stemmed things	manciata / mazzo mahn-**chah**-tah / **mahd**-zoh
bunch (a lot)	un bel pò oon behl poh

MENU DECODER

This handy Italian–English decoder (followed by an English–Italian decoder) won't list every word on the menu, but it will help you get ***trota*** (trout) instead of ***tripa*** (tripe). Note that this list includes only the most common beverages. For a rundown of Italian regional wines, turn to page 176; for aperitifs and digestifs, see page 180.

Menu Categories

When you pick up a menu, you'll likely see these categories of offerings.

Colazione	Breakfast
Pranzo	Lunch
Cena	Dinner
Antipasti	Appetizers
Piatti Caldi	Hot Dishes
Piatti Freddi	Cold Dishes
Panini	Sandwiches
Insalate	Salads
Minestre / Zuppe	Soups
Menù a Prezzo Fisso	Fixed-Price Meal(s)
Specialità	Specialties
Piatti	Dishes
Primo Piatto (Primi)	First Course(s)
Secondo Piatto (Secondi)	Main Course(s)
Carne	Meat
Pollame	Poultry
Pesce	Fish
Frutti di Mare	Seafood
Contorni	Side Dishes
Riso	Rice Dishes
Verdure	Vegetables
Pane	Bread
(Lista delle) Bevande	Drinks (Menu)
(Lista dei) Vini	Wine (List)
Dolci	Dessert
La Nostra	"Our"
Selezione di...	Selection of...

And for the fine print:

cover charge	coperto
service (not) included	servizio (non) incluso
tax included	I.V.A. inclusa

Small Words

alla / alle / della / delle	in the style of
con / senza	with / without
di	of
e	and
l'etto	price per 100 grams
in	in
-ine, -ette, -elle	small
-one	big
oppure	or
s.q. (secondo quantità)	price according to quantity
su	served over

If you see a phrase that begins with ***alla*** or ***della,*** the next word might not appear in this decoder. That's because these phrases mean "in the style of," and are often flowery, artsy, or obscure descriptions. Even if you knew the exact meaning, it might not make things much clearer.

ITALIAN / ENGLISH

abbacchio alla romana grilled spring lamb chops
abboccato sweet (wine)
acciuga anchovy
acero maple
aceto vinegar
acqua water
acqua del rubinetto tap water
acqua minerale (naturale / con gas) mineral water (still / carbonated)
affettati cold cuts; cured meats
affettato sliced
affogato poached
affogato al caffè ice cream with coffee
affumicato smoked (often refers to salty smoked fish)
aglio garlic
aglio e olio with garlic and olive oil (pasta)
aglio fresco garlic shoot
agnello lamb
agnolotti stuffed pasta shaped like a "priest's hat"
agrodolce sweet and sour
agrumi citrus
albicocca apricot
albume egg white
alcool alcohol
alfabeto letter-shaped pasta
alfredo butter, cream, and *parmigiano* sauce (pasta)
amabile sweet (wine)
amarena sour cherry
amaro bitter; also a type of digestif
amatriciana sauce of pork cheek, pecorino cheese, and tomato (pasta)
anacardo cashew
analcolica alcohol-free
ananas pineapple
anatra duck
aneto dill
anguilla eel
anguillette in umido stewed baby eels
anguria watermelon
anice anise
animelle (di vitello) sweetbreads (of veal)
annata vintage (wine)
antipasti appetizers
antipasto (frutti) di mare assortment of fish and shellfish
antipasto misto assortment of meats and veggies
arachide peanut
aragosta lobster
arancia orange
arancia rossa blood orange
aranciata orange soda
arancini deep-fried balls of rice, tomato sauce, and mozzarella
aringa / aringhe herring
arista pork loin
arrabbiata "angry," spicy pasta sauce with tomatoes and hot peppers

arrosto roasted
arrosto misto assortment of roasted meats
asiago hard, mild cow cheese
asiago mezzano young, firm, and creamy asiago
asiago stravecchio aged, pungent, and granular asiago
asparagi asparagus
assortiti assorted
astice lobster
babà (al rhum) mushroom-shaped, rum-soaked cake
baccalà rehydrated Atlantic salt cod
baccalà alla livornese salt cod with tomato and herbs
baccalà mantecato whipped spread of cod and mayonnaise
bacio chocolate hazelnut candy
barbabietola beet
barbina very skinny spaghetti often coiled into nest-like "beards"
basilico basil
bavette flank steak
bavette / bavettine skinnier tagliatelle
bel paese mild, white, creamy cow cheese
ben cotto / molto ben cotto well-done / very well-done (meat)
bevande beverages
bianco white
bibite beverages
bicchiere glass
bietola chard
bignè (alla crema) (cream) puff
bignole cream puff
bigoli (in salsa) thick pasta strands made of whole wheat or buckwheat (with anchovy sauce)
biologico organic
birra beer
birra alla spina beer on tap
bis split course
biscotto cookie
bistecca (di manzo) (beef) steak
bistecca alla fiorentina Florence-style, very rare T-bone steak
bistecca di fesa di manzo rump steak
bocconcini small balls of mozzarella; also refers to bite-size stew meat
bollente boiling hot
bollito boiled
bollito misto various boiled meats with sauces
bolognese meat and tomato sauce (pasta)
bombolone / bomba filled doughnut
boscaiola mushroom and sausage sauce (pasta and pizza)
(di) bosco wild ("of the forest")
bottarga cured fish roe
bottiglia bottle
(alla) brace broiled
braciola chop
branzino sea bass

brasato braised
bresaola air-cured beef, thinly sliced
brioche sweet roll
broccolo romanesco a cross between broccoli and cauliflower
brodo broth
bruciatini cured pork, similar to pancetta
bruciato burned
bruschetta toast brushed with olive oil and garlic or chopped tomatoes
bucatini long, thick, hollow pasta tubes
buccellato wreath-shaped anise-and-raisin bread
budino pudding
burrata soft, creamy mozzarella
burro butter
burro d'arachidi peanut butter
burro e salvia butter and sage (pasta)
bussoli Easter cookies
bustina di tè tea bag
buzzara seafood (often shrimp) and tomato pasta sauce
cacciatora "hunter-style" chicken or rabbit, with red wine, rosemary, garlic, tomato, and often mushrooms
cacio e pepe cheese and pepper (pasta)
caciocavallo semi-hard cow cheese
caciucco Tuscan fish soup
caco persimmon
caffè espresso (a shot in a little cup)
caffè americano espresso diluted with hot water (closest to American-style drip coffee)
caffè con panna espresso with a dollop of whipped cream
caffè corretto espresso "corrected" with a shot of liqueur
caffè corto extra-strong espresso
caffè freddo sweet, iced espresso
caffè latte espresso with hot milk
caffè lungo espresso diluted with some hot water
caffè macchiato espresso with just a splash of milk
caffè schiumato caffè macchiato with extra foam
caffè solubile instant coffee
caffeina caffeine
calamarata "squid"-shaped pasta with spicy tomato sauce and squid
calamari squid
caldo hot
calzone pizza turnover
camomilla chamomile
campanelle "bell"-shaped pasta
canederli large dumplings with ham, liver, spinach, or cheese
cannella cinnamon

cannelloni big, stuffed pasta tube
cannoli fried pastry tubes filled with whipped ricotta, candied fruit, and chocolate
cannoncini baked pastry tubes filled with cream
cantucci / cantuccini Tuscan almond cookies
capellini / capelli d'angelo extremely thin spaghetti
capesante scallops
capocollo peppery, air-cured pork shoulder
caponata eggplant and vegetable salad
cappelletti meat-filled dumplings
cappero caper
cappuccino espresso with foamed milk
capra goat
capretto kid (goat)
capricciosa chef's choice; combo
caprino goat cheese
capriolo roe deer
carabaccia Tuscan onion soup
caraffa carafe
caramelle candy
carbonara sauce with bacon, egg, cheese, and pepper (pasta)
carbonella charcoal
carciofi alla giudia artichokes flattened and deep-fried
carciofi alla romana artichokes stuffed with garlic, mint, and parsley
carciofo artichoke
carciofo romanesco giant artichoke
cardamomo cardamom
carne meat
carne bianca white meat
carne di cervo venison
carne equina horse meat
carne in umido meat stew
carne scura dark meat
carota carrot
carpaccio thinly sliced air-cured meat
carrè affumicato pork shank that's smoked then boiled
carrè di rack of
carrettiera spicy sauce with garlic, olive oil, and little tomatoes (pasta)
(al) cartoccio steamed in parchment
(della) casa of the house
casarecce short pasta with S-shaped cross-section
casereccio home-style
cassata ice cream, sponge cake, ricotta, fruit, and pistachios; also a gelato flavor with dried fruits (Sicily)
castagne chestnut
castellane pasta shaped like a castle tower
cavatappi corkscrew; "corkscrew"-shaped pasta
cavatelli croissant-shaped pasta
cavolfiore cauliflower
cavolini di bruxelles Brussels sprouts

cavolo cabbage
cavolo nero Tuscan kale
cavolo riccio kale
cazzotto calzone-like folded pizza
cece chickpea (garbanzo bean)
cecina savory chickpea crêpe
cedro citron (lemon-like citrus fruit)
cellentani corkscrew-shaped pasta
cena dinner
cereali cereal
cereali misti multigrain
cervella brains
cervo deer
cetriolino pickle
cetriolo cucumber
(lo) chef consiglia "the chef recommends"
chiacchiere fritters with powdered sugar
Chianina top-quality Tuscan beef
chiantigiana Chianti-style
chicche small potato dumplings; sometimes describes sweets
chiodo di garofano clove (spice)
ciabatta crusty, flat, rustic bread
ciambella filled doughnut
ciambellone pound cake
cibo food
ciccheti small appetizers (Venice)
ciccioli (frolli) compressed dried pork belly; crispy pork belly
ciliegia cherry
cinese Chinese
cinghiale boar
cioccolata chocolate
cipolla onion
cipollina chive
cipolloti mini-onions marinated in oil
ciuffi tufts
classico wine from a defined, select area
cocciole hollow, "seashell"-shaped pasta
cocomero watermelon
coda alla vaccinara oxtail braised with garlic, wine, tomato, and celery
coda di bue oxtail
collo neck
(di) Colonnata best-quality lardo (seasoned lard)
(al) coltello hand-sliced to order
con panna with whipped cream
conchiglie hollow, "seashell"-shaped pasta
condito seasoned
congelato frozen
coniglio rabbit
cono cone
conserva preserves
consigliamo "we recommend"
contadina "peasant-style"; rustic
coppa small bowl; also peppery, air-cured pork shoulder
coppa di testa headcheese (organs in aspic)
coriandolo cilantro; coriander
cornetti generic term for pastries

cornetto croissant
corposo full-bodied (wine)
corretto, caffè espresso with a shot of liqueur
corto, caffè extra-strong espresso
corzetti pasta that resembles stamped coins
coscia drumstick
cosciotto di agnello leg of lamb
costata rib-eye steak
costoletta rib
cotechino pork sausage
cotoletta chop or cutlet; often a breaded veal chop
cotto cooked; medium (meat)
cotto al forno oven-baked
cotto sul momento cooked on request (à la minute)
cozza mussel
cozze ripiene mussels stuffed with herbs, cheese, and bread crumbs
crauti rossi red-cabbage sauerkraut
crema custard
crème caramel custard with carmelized topping
cremolata mix of slushy ice and gelato
crescenza mild, soft cheese
crescione watercress
crespella baked crêpe, often stuffed with ricotta
croccante crisp; crispy
croccantino "crunchy" gelato flavor with toasted peanut bits
crocchetta croquette (deep-fried mashed potato ball)
crosta crust (bread); rind (cheese)
crostacei shellfish
crostata (di marmellata) tart (with jam)
crostata di ricotta cheesecake-like dessert
crostino toast with pâté
crudo raw; air-cured (prosciutto)
cucina kitchen
culatello air-cured, high-quality prosciutto
cumino cumin
cuoco cook; chef
da portar via to go
daterini sweet cherry tomatoes
dattero date
decaffeinato decaffeinated
deglassato deglazed
delicato mild (cheese)
delizia al limone cake with lemon-flavored whipped cream
dello chef chef's choice
(al) dente cooked firm, "to the tooth" (pasta)
diavola "devil-style," spicy hot; with pepperoni-like salami (pizza)
digestivo digestif (after-dinner drink)
disossato boneless
ditali / ditalini "thimble"-shaped pasta
dolce sweet; dessert
dolci sweets (often sweet rolls)

dolci dal carrello dessert cart
dolcificante artificial sweetener
dozzina dozen
dragoncello tarragon
effervescente carbonated
eliche "propeller"-shaped pasta
emmenthal Swiss cheese
entrecote sirloin steak
erba cipollina chive
erbe herbs
espresso espresso coffee
etto 100 grams
extravergine extra virgin (top-quality olive oil)
facile da bere easy to drink (wine)
fagiano pheasant
fagioli all'uccelletto "bird-style" beans with tomato and sage
fagiolino green bean; also a green bean-shaped pasta
fagiolo bean
fagiolo lima lima bean
fagottino puff pastry turnover
faraona guinea hen
farcito stuffed
farfalle "butterfly"- or bowtie-shaped pasta
farinata savory chickpea crêpe (Liguria); also a porridge
farro spelt (nutty-tasting grain)
fatto in casa homemade
fava fava bean
fave al guanciale fava beans simmered with cured pork cheek and onion
fedelini thin, long pasta noodle
fegatelli liver meatballs
fegato (patè) liver (pâté)
fegato alla veneziana liver and onions
fettina slice
fettuccine flat egg noodles cut into "small ribbons"
fettuce wider fettucine noodle
fettucelle skinnier fettucine noodle
fico fig
filetto tenderloin; fillet
filetto di baccalà salt cod fried in batter
filone loaf of bread
finocchio fennel
finocchiona salami with fennel seeds
fiorentina "Florence-style"
fiori "flower"-shaped pasta
fiori di zucca fried squash blossoms filled with mozzarella and anchovies
foccacia rustic, flat bread (or a sandwich made with that bread)
foccacina small foccacia sandwich
foglia di vite grape leaf
foglia / verdura a foglia leaf / leafy vegetable
fontina (Val d'Aosta) semi-hard, nutty, Gruyère-style cheese
formaggi, quattro four cheeses (pizza or pasta)
formaggio cheese
formaggio di capra / formaggio di caprino goat cheese

formaggio di fossa cheese aged underground
formaggio di testa headcheese (organs in aspic)
formaggio fresco cream cheese
(al) forno oven-baked
fragola strawberry
frangelico hazelnut liqueur
frappè milkshake
frattaglie offal (organs)
freddo cold; iced (coffee drinks)
fresco fresh
fricassea fricassee
frittata omelet
frittata con le erbe eggs pan-cooked with fresh herbs
frittella fritter
fritti little deep-fried snacks
fritto fried
fritto misto deep-fried calamari, prawns, and assorted small fish
frittole small doughnuts eaten during Carnevale
frittura deep-fried food
frizzante sparkling
frullato di frutta fruit smoothie
frumento wheat
frutta fruit
fruttato fruity (young wine)
frutti di bosco berries
frutti di mare seafood
(ai) funghi (with) mushrooms
fungo mushroom
fungo porcino porcini mushroom
fusilli spiral-shaped pasta
fusilli bucati long, tightly coiled hollow pasta
fuso melted
galletti pasta shaped like a rooster's comb; chanterelle mushrooms
galletto cockerel (rooster)
gamberetto small shrimp
gambero shrimp
gambero di fiume crayfish
gamberone big shrimp
garganelli flat egg pasta rolled into a tube
gassata carbonated
gattafin deep-fried pastry filled with greens
gelatina jelly
gelato ice cream
gemelli pasta shaped like a double helix ("twins")
genovese with pesto sauce; with a thick crust (pizza)
ghiacciato chilled
ghiaccio ice
gigli conical "lily"-shaped pasta
(del) giorno (of the) day
giovane young (wine)
girasole sunflower; also a ravioli shape
glassato glazed
glutine gluten
gnocchi little potato dumplings
gomiti "elbow" macaroni
gorgonzola blue cheese
grana padano grainy, hard cheese, similar to *parmigiano-reggiano* but a cheaper version
granchio crab
grande large

granita flavored shaved ice
granoturco corn
grappa brandy distilled from fermented grapes
grasso cooking fat
(al) gratin topped with browned cheese
gratinate au gratin (with melted cheese)
grattachecca slushy ice with sweet syrup
grattuggiato grated
gricia with cured pork and *pecorino romano* cheese (pasta)
griglia grilled
grissini breadsticks
groviera Swiss cheese
guanciale tender, air-cured pork cheek
guarnizione garnish
guscio shell; peel; rind
gusto flavor (gelato)
gustoso flavorful; heavy (wine)
Hag decaffeinated coffee
impanato breaded
impepata (di cozze) mussel soup (with mussels in the shell)
importato imported
incluso included
indivia endive
insalata salad
insalata caprese salad of sliced tomato, mozzarella, and basil
insalata di mare seafood salad
insalata mista mixed salad
insalata russa vegetable salad with mayonnaise
insalata verde green salad
integrale whole-grain
involtini stuffed; rolls, wraps; meat or fish fillets with fillings
involtini al sugo veal cutlets rolled with prosciutto and cheese in tomato sauce
inzimino marinated in tomatoes and greens
ippoglosso halibut
kaiserschmarrn eggy crêpe with raisins, jam, and powdered sugar
kasher kosher
lampone raspberry
lampredotto cow's stomach
lardellato larded
lardo (di Colonnata) strips of seasoned lard (top-quality)
latte milk
latte fresco fresh milk
latte intero whole milk
latte macchiato hot milk and foam, layered in a tall glass, "marked" by an espresso shot
latte magro skim milk
latticini dairy products
lattuga lettuce
lattuga romana Romaine lettuce
leggermente mild; mildly
leggero light (not heavy)
legume pulses
lenticchia lentil
lepre / sugo di lepre hare / rich sauce with hare
(su) letto on a bed of
lieviti breakfast pastries

lievito yeast
limonata lemon soda
limoncello lemon liqueur
limone lemon
lingua tongue
linguettine skinny linguine
linguine narrow, flat spaghetti
liquirizia licorice
locale local
lombarda, zuppa Tuscan bean soup
lombatina sirloin
lombo / lombata loin
lonzino air-cured pork loin
luccio pike
lumaca snail
lungo, caffè espresso diluted with water
maccheroni tube-shaped pasta
macchiato, caffè espresso "marked" with a splash of milk
macchiato, latte hot milk and foam, layered in a tall glass, "marked" by an espresso shot
macedonia fruit salad
macinato minced
mafalde / mafaldine wide, flat, rectangular noodles ruffled on both sides
maggiorana marjoram
maiale pork
maiale sotto sale salt pork
maionese mayonnaise
mais sweet corn
malaga gelato flavor resembling rum raisin
maltagliati "roughly cut" pasta
mandarino tangerine
mandorla almond
mango mango
manicotti big, stuffed pasta tube
manzo beef
margarina margarine
margherita with tomato sauce, mozzarella, and basil (pizza)
marinara tomato sauce—on pasta, sometimes with seafood; on pizza, without cheese
marinato marinated
marmellata jam
marocchino "Moroccan" coffee with espresso, foamed milk, and cocoa powder
(al) Marsala sweet Marsala wine sauce
marziani pasta spirals resembling "Martian" antennae
mascarpone sweet, buttery dessert cheese
maturo mature (wine)
mela apple
mela cotogna quince
melanzana eggplant
melograno pomegranate
melone cantaloupe; melon
melone d'inverno honeydew melon
menta mint
menù del giorno menu of the day
menù fisso fixed-price meal
meridionale southern Italian
meringa meringue
merluzzo cod

mezzani hollow, tubular pasta
mezzano young, firm, creamy asiago cheese
mezzelune stuffed pasta shaped like "half-moons"
mezzo half
midollo marrow; marrowbone
miele honey
millefoglie layers of sweet, buttery pastry
minestra soup
minestrone classic Italian vegetable soup
mirtillo blueberry
missoltino salted, air-dried shad-like lake fish
misticanza mixed green salad of arugula, curly endive, and anchovies
misto mixed; assorted
mocaccino espresso with foamed milk and chocolate
moleche col pien fried soft-shell crabs
mollusco shellfish
montone mutton
mora blackberry
morbido soft (cheese); smooth (wine)
mortadella baloney-like pork loaf
moscardino (bianco) octopus
mostaccioli "moustache"-like penne pasta
mozzarella (di bufala) mozzarella cheese (from water-buffalo milk)
napoletana / napoli with mozzarella, anchovies, and tomato sauce (pizza)
nasello hake (whitefish)
naturale still (bottled water)
'nduja spicy, spreadable salami
nero black
nero di seppia cuttlefish ink
nocciola hazelnut
nocciolina peanut
noce walnut
noce di cocco coconut
noce moscata nutmeg
nocino walnut liqueur
nodino knuckle
norma tomato, eggplant, and ricotta cheese sauce (pasta)
oca goose
oggi today
olio oil
oliva olive
olive con peperoni olives stuffed with red hot peppers
olive nero black olives
olive verde very green olives
omelette omelet
orata bream (fish)
orecchiette "ear"-shaped pasta
origano oregano
(dell') ortolano "greengrocer-style," with vegetables
orzo tiny, barley-shaped pasta; barley
ossi di morto "bones of the dead" Tuscan cookies

ossobuco (alla genovese) veal shank (braised in broth with vegetables)
ostricha oyster
otto "8"-shaped pastry
paccheri short, very wide pasta tubes
pagliata / pajata calf intestines
pallina scoop (ice cream)
palombo dogfish
pan di spagna sponge cake
pancetta salt-cured pork belly meat
pancetta arrotolata pancetta rolled into a tight, sausage-like bundle and sliced
pane bread; rolls
pane alle olive olive bread
pane aromatico herb or vegetable bread
pane bianco white bread
pane casereccio home-style bread
pane di segale rye bread
pane integrale whole-grain bread
pane scuro brown bread
pane toscano rustic bread made without salt
panettone Milanese yeast cake with raisins and candied fruit (Christmas)
panforte dense fruit and nut cake
panificio bakery
panini farciti premade sandwiches
panino roll; baguette sandwich
panna cream; whipped cream
panna cotta custard-like dessert, served with berries or other toppings
pansotti ravioli with ricotta and greens
panzanella bread salad with tomatoes
panzerotto calzone-like folded pizza
papaia papaya
pappa al pomodoro soup of tomatoes, olive oil, and bread
pappardelle very wide, flat noodles
paprika paprika
parmigiana with tomato, cheese, and bread crumbs
parmigiano-reggiano hard, sharp, aged cow cheese
passito sweet dessert wine
pasta e fagioli bean and pasta soup
pasta fresca fresh-made pasta
pasta secca dry-stored pasta
pasta sfoglia puff pastry
paste sweet rolls (Florence); plural of "pasta"
pasticcino pastry
pasticcio di carne hash
pasticciotto small custard pie
pastina small soup noodle
patata potato
patate arrosto roasted potatoes
patate fritte French fries

patate sabbiose deep-fried potato chunks
patè di fegato chicken liver paste
pecora sheep
pecorino ewe cheese
pecorino fresco fresh, soft, mild ewe cheese
pecorino romano hard, aged ewe cheese
pecorino stagionato aged, sharp ewe cheese
pellizzoni thicker spaghetti
penne angle-cut pasta tubes
pennette smaller penne
pennoni larger penne
pepato with pepper
pepe pepper (spice)
pepe di caienna cayenne pepper
peperonata peppers with tomato sauce
peperoncino hot chili pepper
peperone bell pepper
peposo highly peppered beef stew
pera pear
perciatelli hollow, tubular pasta noodles
pernice partridge
pesante heavy (rich, hard to digest)
pesca peach
pescatore seafood sauce ("fisherman-style")
pesce fish
pesce lupo catfish
pesce spada swordfish
pesce spada alla ghiotta swordfish with tomatoes, olives, and capers
pesto basil and pine nut sauce
petto (di ____) breast (of ____)
pezzo piece
piacentino di enna hard, spicy sheep cheese with saffron and pepper
(a) piacere to order (as you like)
piadina stuffed, soft, flat bread
piatto plate
piatto di formaggi misti cheese plate
piccante spicy hot
piccione / piccioncino squab (young pigeon)
piccolo small
pici hand-rolled thick pasta strands
pieno full-bodied (wine)
pignolo macaroon
pinolo pine nut
pisello pea
pistacchio pistachio
pizza al taglio pizza by the slice
pizza bianca "white" pizza (no tomato sauce)
pizza ciaccina Tuscan "white" pizza (no tomato sauce)
pizza rustica "rustic" pizza, sold by weight
pizzelle thin, delicate waffle cookie
pizzoccheri short, thick buckwheat tagliatelle
platessa plaice (whitefish)

poche calorie low calorie
polenta slow-cooked cornmeal
pollame poultry
pollastrella game hen
pollo chicken
pollo alla cacciatora "hunter-style" chicken with red wine, rosemary, garlic, tomato, and often mushrooms
polpa di riccio sea urchin
polpo octopus
pomodorino vesuvio very sweet cherry tomatoes
pomodoro tomato
pomodoro gratinato tomatoes grilled and dusted with breadcrumbs
pompelmo grapefruit
pompelmo rosa pink grapefuit
porchetta roast suckling pig
porcini porcini mushroom
porro leek
prezzemolo parsley
prezzo al peso priced by the weight
prezzo di mercato market price
profiterole cream-filled pastry with warm chocolate sauce
prosciutto cured ham
prosciutto cotto cooked ham
prosciutto crudo air-cured ham
prosciutto di Parma top-quality prosciutto
prosciutto dolce "sweet" (less salty) air-cured ham
prosciutto e melone / fichi air-cured ham wrapped around melon / fresh figs
prosciutto salato "salty" air-cured ham
prosciutto toscano dark and salty air-cured ham
provolone / provola rich, firm, aged cow cheese
prugna prune
puntarella curly endive served with anchovy dressing
purè di patate mashed potatoes
puro pure
puttanesca "harlot"-style tomato sauce with anchovies, olives, and capers (pasta)
quaglia quail
quattro formaggi four cheeses (pizza or pasta)
quattro stagioni with four separate toppings (pizza)
quinto quarto offal ("fifth quarter")
radiatore radiator-shaped pasta
radicchio bitter, deep-purple lettuce
radice root
rafano horseradish
ragù meaty tomato sauce (pasta)
ragusano semi-hard cow cheese
rana pescatrice monkfish
rapa turnip
ravanello radish
ribes nero black currant
ribes rosso red currant

ribollita "reboiled" stew of white beans, veggies, bread, and olive oil
ricciarelli white macaroon-and-almond cookie
riccio di mare sea urchin ("sea hedgehog")
ricoperto coated
ricotta white cheese resembling cottage cheese
rigatino croccante crispy bacon (Tuscany)
rigatoncini shorter rigatoni
rigatoni "ridged," square-cut pasta tubes
ripassate sautéed with garlic and olive oil (usually a green vegetable)
ripieno stuffed; filled
risi e bisi rice and peas (Venice)
riso rice
riso basmati basmati rice
riso condito seasoned rice
riso integrale brown rice
riso jasmine jasmine rice
risotto short-grain rice, simmered in broth
risotto ai porcini simmered rice with porcini mushrooms
risotto al nero di seppia rice simmered in cuttlefish ink
risotto alla milanese simmered rice with saffron
rocciata apple strudel with raisins
rognone kidney
romana "Roman style"
rombo turbot (flounder-like fish)
rosa rose
rosato rosé (wine)
rosmarino rosemary
rosolato browned
rospo frogfish (small marine fish)
rosso red
rotelli "wagon wheel"-shaped pasta
rotini short, spiral-shaped pasta
rubinetto, acqua del tap water
russa, insalata vegetable salad with mayonnaise
sagnarelli thick, flat, short noodles with wavy edges
salame cured sausage, sometimes spicy
salame di Sant'Olcese Genoa salami
salame piccante spicy salami (similar to American pepperoni)
salamino small salami
salato salty
sale salt
salmone salmon
salmone in bellavista braised salmon, usually elegantly presented
salsa bruna gravy
salsa di pomodoro tomato and garlic sauce
salsiccia link sausage
saltato sautéed ("skipped")
saltimbocca alla romana thinly sliced sautéed veal layered with prosciutto and sage
salumi cold cuts

salumi misti assortment of sliced, cured meats
salvia sage
sambuca anise liqueur
(al) sangue / molto al sangue rare / very rare (meat)
sanguinaccio blood sausage
saporito sharp (cheese)
sarda / sardina sardine
sarde in saor sardines marinated with onions
sbrisolona / sbriciolona crumbly; can refer to crumble cake and / or a less-aged, "crumbly" fennel salami
scaldato toasted
scalogno shallot
scaloppine thin-sliced veal
scamerita (di maiale) pork shoulder
scamorza mozzarella-like cow cheese, often smoked
scampi prawns
scarola escarole
schiacciata thin, "squashed" bread sprinkled with sea salt and olive oil
schiuma milky foam on espresso
sciachetrà sweet dessert wine
scialatelli like linguine, but squared instead of rounded
scoglio pasta sauce with mussels, clams, and tomatoes
scottadito "scorch your fingers" (can't wait to eat them)
scottato blanched
scremato skimmed
secco dry (wine)
selvaggina game
selvatico wild-grown
seme seed
semifreddo frozen mousse-like dessert
semola semolina
senape mustard
senza glutine gluten-free
seppia cuttlefish, sometimes squid
seppie al nero cuttlefish served in its own ink
sfoglia puff pastry, often filled with fruit
sfogliatella crispy pastry filled with sweet ricotta
sformato / sformatino casserole
sfornato baked
sfusato juicy lemon (Amalfi Coast)
sgombro scad (like mackerel)
sgroppino after-dinner drink of vodka and lemon gelato
sgusciato peeled (shellfish)
siciliana with capers, olives, and often anchovies (pizza)
sogliola sole (fish)
sopressata in the south, a coarsely ground, spicy salami; in Tuscany (*sopressata toscana*), headcheese
sorbetto sherbet
sorrentina "Sorrento-style," pasta sauce with tomatoes, basil, and mozzarella
sott'aceto pickled

sott'oli pickled
sovracoscia thigh (poultry)
spaghetti alla chitarra spaghetti cut with a stringed ("guitar") device
spaghettini skinny spaghetti
spaghettoni thicker spaghetti
spagnolo Spanish-style (spicy) salami
spalla shoulder (of beef, pork, lamb)
spalla di manzo beef chuck
specialità specialty
speck smoked, thinly sliced pork shoulder
sperlano smelt
spezia spice
speziato spicy (flavorful)
spezzatino stew
spiedini alla griglia grilled on a skewer
spiedino skewer
spigola bass
spigoloso sharp (wine)
(alla) spina from the tap (beer)
spinaci spinach
spirali / spiralini "spiral"-shaped tube of pasta
spremuta freshly squeezed juice
spritz white wine and liquor spritzer
spuntino snack
stagionato aged, sharp, and hard (cheese)
(di) stagione seasonal
stinco shank (leg meat)
straccetti sautéed slices of meat with arugula and tomatoes or mushrooms
stracchino spreadable, soft cow cheese
stracciatella vanilla gelato with shreds of chocolate
stracciatella alla romana egg-drop meat broth topped with *parmigiano-reggiano* cheese
strangolapreti twisted pasta
strapazzate scrambled
strascicate sautéed (with meat sauce); scrambled
stravecchio well-aged (cheese)
stringozzi "shoestring"-shaped pasta noodles
stricchetti bow-tie pasta
strozzapreti pasta shaped like a priest's collar ("priest-strangler")
stufato (di agnello) (lamb) stew
stuzzicadente toothpick
su letto on a bed of
succo juice
succoso juicy
sughetto gravy; sauce
(al) sugo with sauce (usually tomato)
supplì deep-fried balls of rice, tomato sauce, and mozzarella
suprema (di pollo) (chicken) breast with cream sauce
susina plum
tacchino turkey

tagliata thin slices of grilled tenderloin, typically on bed of arugula
tagliatelle wide, flat noodles
tagliere wooden platter with meats and cheeses
taglierini thinner tagliatelle noodles
(al) taglio by the slice
taleggio rich, creamy, cow cheese
tannico tannic (wine)
tartina canapé
tartine farcite finger sandwiches
tartufata with truffles
tartufo truffle
tartufo (con panna) dark-chocolate gelato ball with a cherry inside (and whipped cream on top)
tavola calda buffet-style eatery
tazza cup
tazzina small coffee cup
tè tea
tè agli agrumi citrus tea
tè al limone lemon tea
tè alla frutta fruit tea
tè alla menta mint tea
tè freddo iced tea
tè nero black tea
tè verde green tea
tegame alla Vernazza anchovies served with potatoes, tomatoes, white wine, oil, and herbs
temperatura ambiente room temperature
terroso earthy
testa head
testa in cassetta / coppa di testa / formaggio di testa headcheese (organs in aspic)
testicolo testicle
tiepido lukewarm
timo thyme
tiramisù espresso-soaked cake with chocolate, cream, and Marsala
tisana herbal tea
tomino goat cheese
tonno tuna
torchietti "torch"-shaped pasta
torello bullock (young bull)
torrefazione roasted
torrone nougat and almond sweet
torta cake; pie
torta de ceci savory chickpea crêpe
torta della nonna custard tart with pine nuts
torta di mele apple cake
torta di ricotta ricotta cake with chocolate chips
torta salata quiche
tortelli / tordelli small, C-shaped pasta filled with meat or cheese
tortellini smaller tortelli
tortelloni larger tortelli
tortiglioni narrow rigatoni pasta
toscana "Tuscan style"; also chicken-liver paste
totani squid
tovagliolo napkin

tramezzini small, crustless sandwiches
trancia slice
trenette long, flat, thin noodle similar to linguine
triglia red mullet (fish)
tripoline long, flat, thick noodle ruffled on one side
trippa tripe
trippa alla fiorentina tripe and vegetables sautéed in a tomato sauce, sometimes baked with *parmigiano-reggiano* cheese
trippa alla romana tripe braised with onions, carrots, and mint
tritato / trito chopped
trofie / trofiette twisted noodle
trota trout
tuorlo egg yolk
umbria pasta sauce of anchovies, garlic, tomatoes, and truffles
umbricelli thick, chewy, rolled pasta
(in) umido stewed
ungherese Hungarian-style (smoky) salami
uova di galline allevate a terra free-range eggs
uova di pesce fish roe
uova di riccio di mare sea urchin roe
uova fritte fried eggs
uova strapazzate scrambled eggs
uovo egg
uovo alla coque (molle / sodo) boiled egg (soft / hard)
uovo in camicia poached egg
uva grape
uvetta raisin
Valtellina, bresaola della best-quality air-cured beef
vaniglia vanilla
(al) vapore steamed
vegetariano vegetarian
veloce fast
vendemmia harvest (wine)
ventriglio gizzard
verace authentic; fresh
verde green
verdura vegetable
vermicelli long noodles slightly thicker than spaghetti
vermicelloni thicker vermicelli
verza cabbage
viennese with tomato, mozzarella, and German-style sausage (pizza)
vigneto vineyard
Vin Santo sweet dessert wine
vino wine
vino da tavola table wine
vino della casa house wine
vino riserva high-quality, aged wine
vino selezionato select wine (good year)
vino sfuso house wine in a jug
visciola sour cherry
vitello veal
vitello di mare porbeagle shark ("sea veal"), similar to swordfish

vitello milanese breaded and pan-fried veal cutlet
vitello tonnato thin-sliced roasted veal with tuna-caper mayonnaise
vongola clam
wurstel hot dog; German-style sausage
zabaglione custard dessert of egg yolks, sugar, and sweet wine
zafferano saffron
zampone sausage-stuffed pig's leg
zenzero ginger
zeppola deep-fried doughnut filled with oozing custard
ziti long, hollow pasta tubes
zucca summer squash
zucca gialla yellow pumpkin
zucca invernale winter squash
zucchero sugar
zucchero di canna brown sugar
zucchina zucchini
zuppa soup
zuppa alla volterrana stew of white beans, veggies, bread, and olive oil
zuppa di pesce fish soup or stew
zuppa inglese trifle (rum-soaked cake layered with whipped cream and fruit)
zuppa lombarda Tuscan bean soup

ENGLISH / ITALIAN

A

aged (cheese) stagionato; stravecchio
alcohol alcool
alcohol-free analcolico; senza alcool
almond mandorla
anchovy acciuga
anise anice
appetizer antipasto
apple mela
apple cake torta di mele
apple strudel rocciata; strudel di mele
apricot albicocca
artichoke carciofo
artificial sweetener dolcificante
arugula (rocket) rucola
asparagus asparagi
assorted assortiti
au gratin (with melted cheese) gratinate
avocado avocado
bacon (salt-cured) pancetta
baked al forno
baloney mortadella
banana banana
basil basilico
basmati rice riso basmati
bass spigola
bean and pasta soup pasta e fagioli
bean / green bean fagiolo / fagiolino
beef manzo
beef steak bistecca
beef, air-cured bresaola
beer (on tap) birra (alla spina)
beet barbabietola
bell pepper peperone
belly (pork) pancetta di maiale
berries frutti di bosco
beverages bevande; bibite
bitter amaro
black currant ribes nero
black olives olive nero
blackberry mora
blanched scottato
blood orange arancia rossa
blood sausage sanguinaccio
blue cheese gorgonzola
blueberry mirtillo
boar cinghiale
boiled bollito
boneless disossato
bottle bottiglia
brains cervella
braised brasato
bread pane...
- **brown** ...scuro; ...integrale
- **herb or vegetable** ...aromatico
- **olive** ...alle olive
- **rye** ...di segale
- **white** ...bianco
- **whole grain** ...integrale

breaded impanato
breadsticks grissini
breakfast colazione; prima colazione
bream (fish) orata

breast (of chicken) petto (di pollo)
broiled alla brace
broth brodo
browned rosolato
Brussels sprouts cavolini di bruxelles
burned bruciato
butter burro
cabbage cavolo; verza
cake torta
candy caramelle
cantaloupe melone
caper cappero
carafe caraffa
carbonated gassata; con gas; effervescente; frizzante
cardamom cardamomo
carrot carota
cashew anacardo
casserole sformato
catfish pesce lupo
cauliflower cavolfiore
cayenne pepper pepe di caienna
cereal cereali
chamomile camomilla
charcoal carbonella
chard bietola
cheese formaggio
cheese plate piatto di formaggi misti
cherry ciliegia
cherry, sour visciola; amarena
chestnut castagna
chicken pollo
chicken liver paste patè di fegato
chickpea cece
chilled ghiacciato
chive cipollina
chocolate cioccolata
choice of a scelta
chop (meat) cotoletta; braciola
chopped tritato; trito
chuck (beef) spalla di manzo
cilantro / coriander coriandolo
cinnamon cannella
citrus agrumi
clam vongola
clove chiodo di garofano
coated ricoperto
coconut noce di cocco
cod / salt cod merluzzo / baccalà
coffee (espresso) caffè...
  iced and sweetened ...freddo
  instant ...solubile
  with a shot of liqueur ...corretto
  with a splash of milk ...macchiato
  with foamed milk ...cappuccino
  with lots of milk ...latte
  with very little / more / lots of hot water ...corto / lungo / americano
  with whipped cream ...con panna
cold freddo
cold cuts affettati; salumi
cone cono
cooked cotto
cookie biscotto

corkscrew cavatappi
corn mais; granoturco
crab granchio
crayfish gambero di fiume
cream panna
cream cheese formaggio fresco
cream puff bignè (alla crema)
cream, whipped panna montata
crêpe crespella
crisp / crispy croccante
croissant cornetto
croquette crocchetta
cucumber cetriolo
cumin cumino
cup tazza
cured meats affettati
custard crema
cutlet cotoletta
cuttlefish (in its own ink) seppia (al nero)
date dattero
decaffeinated decaffeinato; Hag
deep-fried fritto
deer / roe deer cervo / capriolo
deglazed deglassato
dessert dolce
dill aneto
dinner cena
dogfish palombo
doughnut ciambella
dozen dozzina
drumstick coscia
dry (wine) secco
duck anatra
dumpling (potato) gnocchi
eel anguilla
egg uovo...
boiled (soft / hard) ...alla coque (molle / sodo)
fried ...fritte
poached ...in camicia
scrambled ...strapazzate
egg white albume
egg yolk tuorlo
eggplant melanzana
endive indivia
escarole scarola
espresso caffè
fava bean fava
fennel finocchio
fig fico
filled / filling ripieno
fillet filetto
first course primo piatto
fish pesce
fish soup zuppa di pesce
fixed-price meal menù fisso
flank steak bavette
flatbread schiacciata
flesh carne (meat); polpa (fruit)
free-range eggs uova di galline allevate a terra
French fries patate fritte
fresh fresco
fresh-squeezed juice spremuta
fricassee fricassea
fried fritto
fritter frittella
frozen congelato
fruit frutta
fruit salad macedonia
fruit smoothie frullato di frutta
fruitcake panforte
fruity fruttato

full-bodied (wine) corposo; pieno
game (wild) selvaggina
game hen pollastrella
garbanzo bean (chickpea) cece
garlic aglio
garlic shoot aglio fresco
garnish guarnizione
Genoa salami salame di Sant'Olcese
ginger zenzero
gizzard ventriglio
glass bicchiere
glazed glassato
gluten(-free) (senza) glutine
goat capra
goat cheese formaggio di capra / caprino
goose oca
grape uva
grape leaf foglia di vite
grapefruit pompelmo
grated grattuggiato
gravy sughetto; salsa bruna
green verde
green bean fagiolino
grilled griglia
guinea fowl faraona
hake (whitefish) nasello
half mezzo
halibut ippoglosso
ham (air-cured / cooked) prosciutto (crudo / cotto)
hare lepre
harvest (wine) vendemmia
hash pasticcio di carne
hazelnut nocciola
head testa
headcheese testa in cassetta
heavy (wine) gustoso
herb erbe
herring aringa
homemade fatto in casa
honey miele
honeydew melon melone d'inverno
horse meat carne equina
horseradish rafano
hot caldo
hot dog hot dog; würstel
(of the) house (della) casa
house wine vino della casa; vino sfuso
ice ghiaccio
ice cream gelato
imported importato
instant coffee caffè solubile
jam marmellata
jelly gelatina
juice succo
juice, freshly squeezed spremuta
juicy succoso
kale cavolo riccio; cavolo nero
kid (goat) capretto
kidney rognone
knuckle nodino
kosher kasher
lamb agnello; abbacchio
lamb stew stufato di agnello
lamb, leg of cosciotto di agnello
large grande
leaf / leafy foglia
leek porro
lemon limone

lemon soda limonata
lentil lenticchia
lettuce lattuga
licorice liquirizia
light (not hearty) leggero
lima bean fagiolo lima
liver (pâté) fegato (patè)
liver and onions fegato alla veneziana
liver meatballs fegatelli
loaf (of bread) filone
lobster aragosta; astice
local locale
loin (beef) lombo
loin (pork) arista
low calorie poche calorie; ipocalorico
lukewarm tiepido
lunch pranzo
mackerel sgombro
mango mango
maple acero
margarine margarina
marinated marinato
marjoram maggiorana
market price prezzo di mercato
marrow / marrowbone midollo
mature (wine) maturo
mayonnaise maionese
meat carne
meat, dark (poultry) carne scura
meat, white (poultry) carne bianca
medium (meat) cotto
melon / honeydew melone / melone d'inverno
melted fuso
mild delicato
milk latte...
  fresh ...fresco
  skim ...magro
  whole ...intero
milkshake frappè
minced macinato
mineral water acqua minerale
mint menta
mixed misto
monkfish rana pescatrice
mozzarella (from water buffalo) mozzarella (di bufala)
mullet (fish) triglia
multigrain cereali misti
mushroom fungo
mussel cozza
mustard senape
mutton montone
neck collo
noodles pasta
nutmeg noce moscata
octopus polpo; moscardino
offal (butchering by-products) frattaglie
oil olio
olive oliva
olive oil olio di oliva
olives, black olive nere
olives, green olive verdi
omelet frittata; omelette
onion cipolla
orange soda aranciata
orange / blood orange arancia / arancia rossa
oregano origano

organic biologico
oven-baked al forno
oxtail coda di bue
oyster ostrica
papaya papaia
paprika paprika
parsley prezzemolo
partridge pernice
passionfruit passion fruit
pasta (noodle) pasta
pasta sauce sugo
  bacon, egg, cheese, and pepper carbonara
  butter, cream, and parmigiano cheese alfredo
  clams and spices vongole
  meat and tomato sauce bolognese; ragù
  seafood frutti di mare; sometimes marinara
  tomato sauce with anchovies, olives, and capers puttanesca
  tomato sauce with chili peppers arrabbiata
pastries pasticcini
pea pisello
peach pesca
peanut arachide; nocciolina
peanut butter burro d'arachidi
pear pera
peeled (seafood) sgusciato
pepper (bell) peperone
pepper (spice) pepe
pepperoni (pizza) salame piccante; alla diavola
persimmon caco
pheasant fagiano
pickle cetriolino
pickled sott'aceto; sott'oli
pie torta
piece pezzo
pig maiale
pig, roast suckling porchetta; maialino
pike luccio
pine nut pinolo
pineapple ananas
pistachio pistacchio
pizza pizza...
  by the slice ...al taglio
  "rustic" pizza sold by weight ...rustica
  vegetarian ...all'ortolana
  with capers, olives, and often anchovies ...alla siciliana
  with cheese, basil, and tomato sauce ...margherita
  with cheese, anchovies, and tomato sauce ...alla napoletana
  with four different cheeses / toppings ...quattro formaggi / stagioni
  with spicy salami similar to pepperoni ...alla diavola; salame piccante
  with tomato sauce, oregano, and garlic, but no cheese ...marinara
plaice (whitefish) platessa
plate piatto
platter tagliere
plum susina
poached affogato

pomegranate melograno
porcini (mushroom) porcini
pork maiale
pork belly, salt-cured pancetta
pork cheek, air-cured guanciale
pork sausage (cured) salame
pork shoulder scamerita (di maiale)
pork shoulder, smoked and thinly sliced speck
porridge farinata
potato patata
potatoes, mashed purè di patate
potatoes, roasted patate arrosto
poultry pollame
pound cake ciambellone
prawns scampi
preserves conserva
prune prugna
pudding budino
puff pastry pasta sfoglia
pure puro
quail quaglia
quiche quiche; torta salata
quince mela cotogna
rabbit coniglio
rack of carré di
radicchio radicchio
radish ravanello
raisin uvetta
rare / very rare (meat) al sangue / molto al sangue
raspberry lampone
raw crudo
red rosso
red currant ribes rosso
red mullet (fish) triglia
rib (meat) costoletta
rib-eye steak costata
rice riso...
  basmati ...basmati
  brown ...integrale
  jasmine ...jasmine
roast beef roast beef
roasted arrosto; torrefazione
roe (fish eggs) uova di pesce
roll pane; panino
Romaine lettuce lattuga romana
room temperature temperatura ambiente
root radice
rosé (wine) rosato
rosemary rosmarino
rump (steak) bistecca di fesa di manzo
saffron zafferano
sage salvia
salad insalata...
  bread and tomato ...panzanella
  green ...verde
  mixed ...mista
  mozzarella, tomato, and basil ...caprese
  seafood ...di mare
  with veggies and mayo ...russa
salami salame
salmon salmone
salt sale
salt pork maiale sotto sale
salty salato
sandwich panino
sardine sarda; sardina

sauce sugo; see "pasta sauce"
sausage salsiccia
sausage (German-style) wurstel
sautéed saltato (in padella)
scad sgombro
scallops capesante
scoop (ice cream) pallina
scrambled (eggs) (uova) strapazzate
sea bass branzino
sea urchin polpa di riccio; riccio di mare
seafood frutti di mare
seafood salad insalata di mare
seafood sauce pescatore
seafood stew zuppa di pesce
seasonal di stagione
second course secondo piatto
seed seme
semolina (grain) semola
shallot scalogno
shank (leg meat) stinco
sharp (cheese) saporito
sheep pecora
sheep cheese pecorino
shell guscio
shellfish mollusco
sherbet sorbetto
shoulder (meat) spalla
shrimp (big / small) gambero (gamberone / gamberetto)
sirloin steak entrecote
skewer(ed) spiedino
skimmed scremato
small piccolo
smelt sperlano
smoked affumicato
smooth (wine) morbido
snack spuntino
snail lumaca
soft (cheese) morbido
sole (fish) sogliola
sorbet sorbetto
soup zuppa...
bean ...lombarda
fish ...di pesce
soup, bean and pasta pasta e fagioli
soup, vegetable minestrone
sour agro
sparkling (wine) frizzante
specialty specialità
spice spezia
spicy (flavorful) speziato
spicy (hot) piccante; alla diavola
spinach spinaci
sponge cake pan di spagna
squab piccione
squash blossoms fiori di zucca
squash, summer zucca
squash, winter zucca invernale
squid calamari; totani
steak bistecca
steak, sirloin entrecote
steak, T-bone (Florence-style) bistecca (alla fiorentina)
steamed al vapore
stew stufato; in umido; spezzatino
still (water) naturale
strawberry fragola
stuffed ripieno; farcito
sugar zucchero
sugar, brown zucchero di canna

sunflower girasole
sweet dolce
sweet (wine) abbocato
sweet roll brioche
sweetbreads (veal) animelle (di vitello)
sweetener, artificial dolcificante
sweets dolci
Swiss chard bietola
Swiss cheese emmenthal; groviera
swordfish pesce spada
table tavola
tangerine mandarino
tannic (wine) tannico
tarragon dragoncello
tart crostata
tea tè...
  black ...nero
  citrus ...agli agrumi
  fruit ...alla frutta
  green ...verde
  iced ...freddo
  lemon ...al limone
  mint ...alla menta
tea bag bustina di tè
tea, herbal tisana
tenderloin filetto
testicle testicolo
thigh (poultry) sovracoscia
thyme timo
to go da portar via
toasted scaldato
tomato pomodoro
tongue lingua
toothpick stuzzicadente
trifle zuppa inglese
tripe trippa
trout trota
truffles tartufi
tuna tonno
turbot rombo
turkey tacchino
turnip rapa
vanilla vaniglia
veal vitello
veal shank ossobuco
vegetable verdura
vegetable soup minestrone
vegetarian vegetariano
venison carne di cervo
vinaigrette vinaigrette
vinegar aceto
vineyard vigneto
vintage (wine) annata
walnut noce
water acqua...
  carbonated / uncarbonated ...con gas / ...senza gas
  mineral ...minerale
  tap ...rubinetto
watercress crescione
watermelon anguria; cocomero
well-done / very well-done (meat) ben cotto / molto ben cotto
wheat frumento
whipped cream panna montata
white bianco
whole-grain integrale
wild game selvaggine
wild-grown selvatico

wine vino...
house ...della casa
red ...rosso
rosé ...rosato
sparkling ...frizzante
table ...da tavola
white ...bianco

yeast lievito
yogurt yogurt
yolk (egg) tuorlo
young (wine) giovane
zucchini zucchina

SIGHTSEEING

Whether you're touring a museum, going on a city walking tour, visiting a church, or conquering a castle, these phrases will help you make the most of your sightseeing time.

WHERE?

Where is the...?	Dov'è...? doh-**veh**
Where are the...?	Dove sono...? **doh**-vay **soh**-noh
tourist information office	l'ufficio informazioni loo-**fee**-choh een-for-maht-see-**oh**-nee
toilet	la toilette lah twah-**leh**-tay
main square	la piazza principale lah pee-**aht**-sah preen-chee-**pah**-lay
old town center	il centro storico eel **chehn**-troh **stoh**-ree-koh
entrance	l'entrata lehn-**trah**-tah
exit	l'uscita loo-**shee**-tah
town hall	il municipio eel moo-nee-**chee**-pee-oh
museum	il museo eel moo-**zeh**-oh
cathedral	il duomo / la cattedrale eel **dwoh**-moh / lah kah-teh-**drah**-lay

Key Phrases: Sightseeing

ticket	biglietto beel-**yeh**-toh
How much is it?	Quanto costa? **kwahn**-toh **koh**-stah
Is there a guided tour in English?	Avete una visita guidata in inglese? ah-**veh**-tay **oo**-nah vee-**zee**-tah gwee-**dah**-tah een een-**gleh**-zay
When?	Quando? **kwahn**-doh
What time does this open / close?	A che ora apre / chiude? ah kay **oh**-rah **ah**-pray / kee-**oo**-day

church	la chiesa lah kee-**eh**-zah
castle	il castello eel kah-**steh**-loh
palace	il palazzo eel pah-**lahd**-zoh
ruins	le rovine lay roh-**vee**-nay
amusement park	un parco dei divertimenti oon **par**-koh **deh**-ee dee-vehr-tee-**mehn**-tee
aquarium	l'acquario lah-**kwah**-ree-oh
zoo	lo zoo loh zoh
best view	la vista più bella lah **vee**-stah pew **beh**-lah
viewpoint	il punto panoramico eel **poon**-toh pah-noh-**rah**-mee-koh
Is there a fair / local festival nearby?	Qui vicino c'è un fiera / sagra? kwee vee-**chee**-noh cheh oon fee-**eh**-rah / **sah**-grah

A major town square can be called a ***piazza*** or ***campo,*** while a smaller square might be a ***piazzetta*** or ***campiello***.

AT SIGHTS

Tickets and Discounts

ticket office	biglietteria beel-yeh-teh-**ree**-yah
ticket	biglietto beel-**yeh**-toh
combo-ticket	biglietto cumulativo beel-**yeh**-toh koo-moo-lah-**tee**-voh
reduced ticket	biglietto ridotto beel-**yeh**-toh ree-**doh**-toh
reservation	prenotazione preh-noh-taht-see-**oh**-nay
museum pass	pass per più musei pahs pehr pew moo-**zeh**-ee
price	prezzo **prehd**-zoh

discount	sconti **skohn**-tee
Is there a discount for...?	Fate sconti per...? **fah**-tay **skohn**-tee pehr
...children	...bambini bahm-**bee**-nee
...youths	...giovani **joh**-vah-nee
...students	...studenti stoo-**dehn**-tee
...families	...famiglie fah-**meel**-yay
...seniors	...anziani ahnt-see-**ah**-nee
...groups	...comitive koh-mee-**tee**-vay
I am...	Io ho... **ee**-oh oh
He / She is...	Lui / Lei ha... **loo**-ee / **leh**-ee ah
... ____ years old.	... ____ anni. ____ **ahn**-nee
...extremely old.	...vecchissimo[a]. veh-**kee**-see-moh
reservation	prenotazione preh-noh-taht-see-**oh**-nay
Is it possible to make a reservation?	Si può prenotare? see pwoh preh-noh-**tah**-ray
How do I make a reservation?	Come si prenota? **koh**-may see preh-**noh**-tah
What time?	A che ora? ah kay **oh**-rah
Where?	Dove? **doh**-vay
Is the ticket good all day?	È valido per tutto il giorno? eh **vah**-lee-doh pehr **too**-toh eel **jor**-noh
Can I get back in?	Posso rientrare? **poh**-soh ree-ehn-**trah**-ray

For some very crowded museums (such as Florence's Uffizi Gallery or Rome's Vatican Museums), it's wise to book tickets in advance. Ask locals or check your guidebook for details—it could save you hours in line.

Some cities sell admission passes that let you skip ticket-buying lines at multiple museums. At some popular places (such as Venice's Doge's Palace), you can get in more quickly by buying your ticket or pass at a less-crowded sight.

Information and Tours

information	informazioni een-for-maht-see-**oh**-nee
tour	tour toor
tour guide	guida turistica **gwee**-dah too-**ree**-stee-kah
in English	in inglese een een-**gleh**-zay
Is there a...?	C'è una...? cheh **oo**-nah
...city walking tour	...visita guidata della città **vee**-zee-tah gwee-**dah**-tah **deh**-lah chee-**tah**
...guided tour	...visita guidata **vee**-zee-tah gwee-**dah**-tah
...audioguide	...audioguida ow-dee-oh-**gwee**-dah
...city guidebook	...guida della città **gwee**-dah **deh**-lah chee-**tah**
...museum guidebook	...guida del museo **gwee**-dah dehl moo-**zeh**-oh
Is it free?	È gratis? eh **grah**-tees
How much is it?	Quanto costa? **kwahn**-toh **koh**-stah
How long does it last?	Quanto dura? **kwahn**-toh **doo**-rah
When is the next tour in English?	Quando è il prossimo tour in inglese? **kwahn**-doh eh eel **proh**-see-moh toor een een-**gleh**-zay

Some sights are tourable only by groups with a guide ***(guida turistica)***. At other sights, booking a guided tour can help you avoid lines. Individuals usually end up on the next Italian tour. To get an English tour, call in advance or check online to see if one's scheduled. You may be able to tag along with a large tour group.

Visiting Sights

opening times	orario d'apertura oh-**rah**-ree-oh dah-pehr-**too**-rah
last entry	ultimo ingresso **ool**-tee-moh een-**greh**-soh

What time does this open / close?	A che ora apre / chiude? ah kay **oh**-rah **ah**-pray / kee-**oo**-day
When is the last entry?	Quando è l'ultimo ingresso? **kwahn**-doh eh **lool**-tee-moh een-**greh**-soh
Do I have to check this / this bag?	Devo lasciare questo / questa borsa? **deh**-voh lah-**shah**-ray **kweh**-stoh / **kweh**-stah **bor**-sah
bag check	deposito per le borse deh-**poh**-zee-toh pehr lay **bor**-say
floor plan	pianta pee-**ahn**-tah
floor	piano pee-**ah**-noh
room / large room	sala / salone **sah**-lah / sah-**loh**-nay
collection	collezione koh-leht-see-**oh**-nay
exhibit / exhibition...	esposizione / mostra... eh-spoh-zeet-see-**oh**-nay / **moh**-strah
...temporary / special	...temporanea / speciale tehm-poh-**rah**-neh-ah / speh-**chah**-lay
...permanent	...permanente pehr-mah-**nehn**-tay
café	bar bar
elevator	ascensore ah-shehn-**soh**-ray
toilet	toilette twah-**leh**-tay
Where is ____?	Dov'è ____? doh-**veh** ____
I'd like to see ____.	Mi piacerebbe vedere ____. mee pee-ah-cheh-**reh**-bay veh-**deh**-ray ____
Photo / Video OK?	Foto / Video è OK? **foh**-toh / **vee**-deh-oh eh "OK"
flash / tripod	flash / treppiede "flash" / treh-pee-**eh**-day
Will you take my / our photo?	Mi / Ci fa una foto? mee / chee fah **oo**-nah **foh**-toh

Please let me / us in. (if room or sight is closing)	Per favore, mi / ci faccia entrare. pehr fah-**voh**-ray mee / chee **fah**-chah ehn-**trah**-ray
I promise I'll be fast.	Prometto che sarò veloce. proh-**meh**-toh kay sah-**roh** veh-**loh**-chay
It was my mother's dying wish that I see this.	Ho promesso a mia madre sul letto di morte che avrei visto questo. oh proh-**meh**-soh ah **mee**-ah **mah**-dray sool **leh**-toh dee **mor**-tay kay ah-**vreh**-ee **vee**-stoh **kweh**-stoh

Once at the sight, get your bearings by viewing the ***pianta*** (floor plan). ***Voi siete qui*** means "You are here." Many museums have an official, one-way route that all visitors take—just follow signs for ***percorso della visita*** (direction of visit).

Signs at Sights

First figure out which line is for buying tickets ***(biglietteria / biglietti)*** and which is for the entrance ***(entrata).*** Larger museums might have separate entrances for individuals ***(singoli),*** for groups ***(gruppi),*** and for people who already have tickets reserved ***(prenotati).***

Adulti	Adults
Alle sale	To the exhibit
Anziani	Seniors
Armadietti	Lockers
Ascensori	Elevators
Audioguida	Audioguide
Bambini	Children
Biglietteria	Ticket office
Biglietti	Tickets
Biglietto cumulativo	Combo-ticket
Chiuso per restauro	Closed for restoration
Classe	Classroom
Collezione	Collection
Deposito per le borse	Bag check

Entrata	Entrance
Esposizione	Exhibition
Giornaliero	Daily
Giovani	Youths
Giro guidato	Guided tour
Guardaroba	Cloakroom
Ingresso	Entrance
Ingresso per disabili	Disabled entrance
Non è permesso	Not allowed
Non è permesso fotografare	No photography
Non è permesso il consumo di bevande	No drinking
Non è permesso l'uso del flash	No flash
Non è permesso l'uso del treppiede	No tripod
Non è permesso mangiare	No eating
Non toccare	Do not touch
Obbligatorio	Required
Opera in prestito	Work on loan
Opera in restauro	Work undergoing restoration
Orario d'ingresso	Opening times
Pass	Museum pass
(Per) gruppi	(For) groups
(Per) singoli	(For) individuals
Percorso della visita	Direction of visit ("this way")
Piano	Floor
Piano Terra / Primo / Secondo	Ground / First / Second Floor
Prenotazioni	Reservations
Punto vendita	Museum shop
Riservato al personale	Staff only
Sconti	Discount
Voi siete qui / Siete qui	You are here (on map)
Silenzio	Silence
Studenti	Students
Uscita	Exit
Uscita di emergenza	Emergency exit

(È) vietato	(It is) forbidden
Vietato uscire	Not an exit
Visita guidata	Guided tour

Toilets can be marked ***toilette*** or ***bagni***.

MUSEUMS

Types of Museums

museum	museo moo-**zeh**-oh
gallery	galleria gah-leh-**ree**-ah
art gallery	galleria d'arte gah-leh-**ree**-ah **dar**-tay
painting gallery	pinacoteca pee-nah-koh-**teh**-kah
modern art	arte moderna **ar**-tay moh-**dehr**-nah
contemporary art	arte contemporanea **ar**-tay kohn-tehm-poh-**rah**-neh-ah
folk	folclore fohl-**kloh**-ray
history	storia **stoh**-ree-ah
town / city	paese / città pah-**eh**-zay / chee-**tah**
children's	per bambini pehr bahm-**bee**-nee
Jewish	ebreo eh-**breh**-oh
memorial	monumento alla memoria moh-noo-**mehn**-toh **ah**-lah meh-**moh**-ree-ah

Art Appreciation

I like it.	Mi piace. mee pee-**ah**-chay
It's so...	È così... eh koh-**zee**
...beautiful.	...bello. **beh**-loh
...ugly.	...brutto. **broo**-toh
...strange.	...strano. **strah**-noh

...boring.	...noioso. noh-**yoh**-zoh
...interesting.	...interessante. een-teh-reh-**sahn**-tay
It's thought-provoking.	Fa pensare. fah pehn-**sah**-ray
It's B.S.	È una stronzata. eh **oo**-nah strohnt-**sah**-tah
I don't get it.	Non capisco. nohn kah-**pees**-koh
Is it upside down?	È rovesciato? eh roh-veh-**shah**-toh
Who did this?	Chi l'ha fatto? kee lah **fah**-toh
How old is this?	Quando è stato fatto? **kwahn**-doh eh **stah**-toh **fah**-toh
Wow!	Wow! wow
My feet hurt!	Mi fanno male i piedi! mee **fah**-noh **mah**-lay ee pee-**eh**-dee

Art and Architecture

art	arte **ar**-tay
artist	artista ar-**tee**-stah
painting	quadro **kwah**-droh
sculptor	scultore skool-**toh**-ray
sculpture	scultura skool-**too**-rah
architect	architetto ar-kee-**teh**-toh
architecture	architettura ar-kee-teht-**too**-rah
original	originale oh-ree-jee-**nah**-lay
restored	restaurato reh-stow-**rah**-toh
B.C. / A.D.	A.C. / D.C. ah chee / dee chee
century	secolo **seh**-koh-loh
style	stile **stee**-lay
prehistoric	preistorico preh-ee-**stoh**-ree-koh
ancient	antico ahn-**tee**-koh
Etruscan	etrusco eh-**troo**-skoh

classical	classico **klah**-see-koh
Greek	greco **greh**-koh
Roman	romano roh-**mah**-noh
Byzantine	bizantino bee-zahn-**tee**-noh
Islamic	islamico ees-**lah**-mee-koh
medieval	Medievale meh-dee-eh-**vah**-lay
Romanesque	Romanico roh-**mah**-nee-koh
Gothic	gotico **goh**-tee-koh
1300s	Trecento treh-**chehn**-toh
1400s	Quattrocento kwah-troh-**chehn**-toh
1500s	Cinquecento cheen-kweh-**chehn**-toh
Renaissance	Rinascimento ree-nah-shee-**mehn**-toh
Baroque	barocco bah-**roh**-koh
Rococo	rococò roh-koh-**koh**
Neoclassical	Neoclassico nee-oh-**klah**-see-koh
Romantic	Romantico roh-**mahn**-tee-koh
Impressionist	Impressionista eem-preh-see-oh-**nee**-stah
Art Nouveau	Art Nouveau **ar**-tay **noo**-voh
Modern	Moderno moh-**dehr**-noh
abstract	astratta ah-**strah**-tah
contemporary	contemporaneo kohn-tehm-poh-**rah**-neh-oh

The Italians refer to their three greatest centuries of art in an unusual way. They call the 1300s the ***Trecento*** (literally "300"). The 1400s (early Renaissance) are the ***Quattrocento*** (400), and the 1500s (High Renaissance) are the ***Cinquecento*** (500).

Italian Art

Some of these terms, which originated in Italy, have become widely used in English as well.

chiaroscuro kee-ah-roh-**skoo**-roh
strong visual contrast between light (*chiaro*) and dark (*scuro*)

contrapposto kohn-trah-**poh**-stoh
a classical pose in sculpture, with the figure's weight on one leg

pietà pee-eh-**tah**
the dead Christ and sorrowful Virgin Mary

putti **poo**-tee
chubby cherubs that populate many religious scenes

sacra conversazione **sah**-krah kohn-vehr-saht-see-**oh**-nay
the Virgin Mary and Baby Jesus surrounded by saints

sprezzatura sprehd-zah-**too**-rah
the appearance of artistic effortlessness

terribilità teh-ree-bee-lee-**tah**
ability to command respect and inspire awe

tondo **tohn**-doh
circular painting

uomo universale **woh**-moh oo-nee-vehr-**sah**-lay
Renaissance Man—a person with a wide array of interests

Historical Terms

Ancient Greece	greco antico **greh**-koh ahn-**tee**-koh
Roman	romano roh-**mah**-noh
republic / empire	repubblica / impero reh-**poo**-blee-kah / eem-**peh**-roh
Caesar	cesare cheh-**zah**-ray
"Roman Peace"	"pax romana" pahks roh-**mah**-nah
barbarians	barbari **bar**-bah-ree
fall of Rome	caduta dell'impero romano kah-**doo**-tah deh-leem-**peh**-roh roh-**mah**-noh

Charlemagne	Carlomagno kar-loh-**mahn**-yoh
Holy Roman Emperor	Sacro Romano Impero **sah**-kroh roh-**mah**-noh eem-**peh**-roh
Golden Age	età d'oro eh-**tah doh**-roh
Middle Ages	medioevo meh-dee-oh-**eh**-voh
Crusades	crociate kroh-**chah**-tay
Renaissance	Rinascimento ree-nah-shee-**mehn**-toh
Reformation	Riforma ree-**for**-mah
Counter-Reformation	Controriforma kohn-troh-ree-**for**-mah
Enlightenment	Illuminismo ee-loo-mee-**nees**-moh
Industrial Revolution	Rivoluzione Industriale ree-voh-loot-see-**oh**-nay een-doo-stree-**ah**-lay
Italian Unification	Risorgimento ree-sor-jee-**mehn**-toh
Romanticism	Romanticismo roh-mahn-tee-**cheez**-moh
World War I	prima guerra mondiale **pree**-mah **gweh**-rah mohn-dee-**ah**-lay
fascism	fascismo fah-**sheez**-moh
"The Leader" (Mussolini's title)	Il Duce eel **doo**-chay
World War II	seconda guerra mondiale seh-**kohn**-dah **gweh**-rah mohn-dee-**ah**-lay
postwar	dopoguerra doh-poh-**gweh**-rah
"Bribe City" (postwar corruption)	Tangentopoli tahn-jehn-**toh**-poh-lee
European Union (EU)	Unione Europea (UE) oo-nee-**oh**-nay eh-oo-roh-**peh**-ah (oo ay)

All around Rome, you'll see the letters ***SPQR*** (for instance, stamped on manhole covers in the street). Representing both ancient Rome and today's municipality, they stand for the Latin phrase ***Senatus Populusque Romanus***—the Senate and People of Rome.

CHURCHES

Church Words

cathedral	il duomo / la cattedrale eel **dwoh**-moh / lah kah-teh-**drah**-lay
church	chiesa kee-**eh**-zah
chapel	cappella kah-**peh**-lah
prayer hall	oratorio oh-rah-**toh**-ree-oh
baptistery	battistero bah-tee-**steh**-roh
altar	altare ahl-**tah**-ray
bells	campane kahm-**pah**-nay
choir	coro **koh**-roh
cloister	chiostro kee-**oh**-stroh
cross	croce **kroh**-chay
crypt	cripta **kreep**-tah
dome	cupola **koo**-poh-lah
organ	organo **or**-gah-noh
pulpit	pulpito pool-**pee**-toh
relic	reliquie reh-**lee**-kwee-ay
sacristy	sacrestia sah-kreh-**stee**-ah
stained glass	vetrata veh-**trah**-tah
steeple / bell tower	campanile kahm-pah-**nee**-lay
treasury	tesoro teh-**zoh**-roh
pope	papa **pah**-pah
priest	prete **preh**-teh
nun / monk	suora / frate soo-**oh**-rah / **frah**-tay
(holy) Mass	(santa) messa (**sahn**-tah) **meh**-sah
When is the Mass?	A che ora è la messa? ah kay **oh**-rah eh lah **meh**-sah
Are there church concerts?	Ci sono concerti in chiesa? chee **soh**-noh kohn-**chehr**-tee een kee-**eh**-zah

Can I climb the tower?	Posso salire nel campanile? **poh**-soh sah-**lee**-ray nehl kahm-pah-**nee**-lay

A fancy canopy over the altar (like the famous Bernini-designed one at St. Peter's Basilica) is called a ***baldacchino***.

Confusingly, ***opera*** is Italian for "work"—so a ***museo dell'opera del duomo*** is a "museum of the cathedral's workshop."

Signs at Churches

You might see some of these signs around the church (also check "Signs at Sights," on page 227).

Confessione	Confession
Confessione prima e dopo le sante messe	Confession before and after Mass
È vietato l'ingresso in pantaloni corti	No entry if wearing shorts
Non sono ammesse visite turistiche durante la messa	No sightseeing during Mass
Offerte	Offerings
Orario feriale	Schedule of services on weekdays (Mon-Sat)
Orario festivo	Schedule of services on Sundays and holidays
Orario sante messe	Mass schedule
Orario visite turistiche	Opening times for tourist visits
Questo è un luogo sacro	This is a place of worship
Si prega di entrare in chiesa con un abbigliamento adeguato	Please dress respectfully to enter the church
Si prega di spegnere i cellulari	Please turn off cell phones
Silenzio	Silence
Vespri	Vespers service

At many churches, including Venice's St. Mark's and the Vatican's St. Peter's, you will not be allowed to enter with shorts or bare shoulders.

Look for little votive plaques posted inside churches, often marked ***per grazia ricevuta*** (for answered prayers).

MORE SIGHTS

Castles and Palaces

castle	castello kah-**steh**-loh
palace	palazzo pah-**lahd**-zoh
royal residence	palazzo reale pah-**lahd**-zoh reh-**ah**-lay
fortress	fortezza for-**tehd**-zah
hall	sala **sah**-lah
kitchen	cucina koo-**chee**-nah
dungeon	segrete seh-**greh**-tay
moat	fossato foh-**sah**-toh
fortified walls	mura fortificate **moo**-rah for-tee-fee-**kah**-tay
tower	torre **toh**-ray
fountain	fontana fohn-**tah**-nah
garden	giardino jar-**dee**-noh
king	re ray
queen	regina ray-**jee**-nah
knight	cavaliere kah-vah-lee-**eh**-ray
fair maiden	damigella dah-mee-**jeh**-lah
dragon	drago **drah**-goh

Most Venetian palaces are called simply ***Ca'*** (house), as in ***Ca' d'Oro*** (House of Gold). The ground floor of a palace is often referred to as the ***piano nobile***—the "noble floor" where aristocrats lived and hosted friends.

Ancient Sites

ancient sites	siti archeologici **see**-tee ar-keh-oh-**loh**-jee-chee
Roman	romano roh-**mah**-noh
walls	mura **moo**-rah
forum (main square)	foro **foh**-roh
temple	tempio **tehm**-pee-oh
column	colonna koh-**loh**-nah
mosaic	mosaico moh-**zah**-ee-koh
theater	teatro tee-**ah**-troh
arena	arena ah-**reh**-nah
aqueduct	acquedotto ah-kweh-**doh**-toh
mill	mulino moo-**lee**-noh
lighthouse	faro **fah**-roh
catacombs	catacombe kah-tah-**kohm**-bay

RECREATION AND ENTERTAINMENT

This chapter offers phrases for your recreational pleasure, whether you're going to the park or beach, swimming, biking, hiking, or enjoying other sports. It also covers your options for nightlife and entertainment.

RECREATION

Outdoor Fun

Where is the best place for...?	Dov'è il posto migliore per...? doh-**veh** eel **poh**-stoh meel-**yoh**-ray pehr
...biking	...andare in bicicletta ahn-**dah**-ray een bee-chee-**kleh**-tah
...walking	...passeggiare pah-seh-**jah**-ray
...hiking	...fare trekking / fare escursioni **fah**-ray **treh**-keeng / **fah**-ray eh-skoor-see-**oh**-nee
...running	...correre koh-**reh**-ray
...picnicking	...fare un picnic **fah**-ray oon **peek**-neek
...sunbathing	...prendere il sole **prehn**-deh-ray eel **soh**-lay
Where is...?	Dov'è...? doh-**veh**
...a park	...un parco oon **par**-koh
...playground equipment	...parco giochi **par**-koh **joh**-kee
...a snack shop	...un bar oon bar
...the toilet	...la toilette lah twah-**leh**-tay
Where can I rent...?	Dove posso noleggiare...? **doh**-vay **poh**-soh noh-leh-**jah**-ray
...a bike	...una bici / bicicletta **oo**-nah **bee**-chee / bee-chee-**kleh**-tah
...that	...quello **kweh**-loh

What's a fun activity...?	Qual'è un'attività divertente...? kwah-**leh** oon-ah-tee-vee-**tah** dee-vehr-**tehn**-tay
...for a boy / a girl...	...per un bambino / una bambina... pehr oon bahm-**bee**-noh / **oo**-nah bahm-**bee**-nah
... ____ years old	...di ____ anni dee ____ **ahn**-nee

At most parks, people—usually men—play ***bocce*** (**boh**-chay): Players take turns tossing croquet-size balls into a dirt playing area, with the object of getting them close to the target, a small wooden ball ***(pallino)***.

Swimming and Water Sports

swimming	fare un bagno **fah**-ray oon **bahn**-yoh
Where is a...?	Dov'è un / una...? doh-**veh** oon / **oo**-nah
...swimming pool	...piscina pee-**shee**-nah
...water park	...parco acquatico **par**-koh ah-**kwah**-tee-koh
...(good) beach	...(bella) spiaggia (**beh**-lah) spee-**ah**-jah
...nude beach	...spiaggia nudista spee-**ah**-jah noo-**dee**-stah
Is it safe for swimming?	È sicuro fare un bagno? eh see-**koo**-roh **fah**-ray oon **bahn**-yoh
Where can I rent a...?	Dove posso noleggiare un / una...? **doh**-vay **poh**-soh noh-leh-**jah**-ray oon / **oo**-nah
Where can I buy a...?	Dove posso comprare un / una...? **doh**-vay **poh**-soh kohm-**prah**-ray oon / **oo**-nah
swimsuit	costume da bagno koh-**stoo**-may dah **bahn**-yoh
towel	asciugamano ah-shoo-gah-**mah**-noh

sunscreen	protezione solare	proh-teht-see-**oh**-nay soh-**lah**-ray
sunglasses	occhiali da sole	oh-kee-**ah**-lee dah **soh**-lay
flip-flops	ciabatte da piscina	chah-**bah**-tay dah pee-**shee**-nah
water shoes	dei calzari da surf	**deh**-ee kahlt-**sah**-ree dah soorf
umbrella	ombrellone	ohm-breh-**loh**-nay
lounge chair	lettino	leh-**tee**-noh
inner tube	ciambella	chahm-**beh**-lah
goggles	occhialini	oh-kee-ah-**lee**-nee
snorkel and mask	boccaglio e maschera	boh-**kahl**-yoh ay **mah**-skeh-rah
surfing	surfing	**soor**-feeng
surfboard	tavola da surf	**tah**-voh-lah dah soorf
windsurfing	windsurf	**weend**-soorf
waterskiing	sci acquatico	shee ah-**kwah**-tee-koh
jet ski	jet ski	"jet ski"
paddleboard	stand-up paddle	"stand-up paddle"
boat	barca	**bar**-kah
rowboat	barca a remi	**bar**-kah ah **reh**-mee
paddleboat	pedalò	peh-dah-**loh**
canoe / kayak	canoa / kayak	kah-**noh**-ah / "kayak"
sailboat	barca a vela	**bar**-kah ah **veh**-lah

A beach can also be called a ***lido***. Sometimes you'll have to pay for a seat; look for ***libere*** signs to find a free area. A pier or breakwater (another fine place to catch some rays) is called a ***molo***.

In Italy, nearly any beach is topless, but if you want to go to (or avoid) a nude beach, keep your eyes peeled for a ***spiaggia nudista.***

Renting

Whether you're renting a bike or a boat, here's what to ask.

Where can I rent a...?	Dove posso noleggiare una...? **doh**-vay **poh**-soh noh-leh-**jah**-ray **oo**-nah
Can I rent a...?	Posso noleggiare una...? **poh**-soh noh-leh-**jah**-ray **oo**-nah
...bike	...bicicletta bee-chee-**kleh**-tah
...boat	...barca **bar**-kah
How much per...?	Quanto costa...? **kwahn**-toh **koh**-stah
...hour	...all'ora ah-**loh**-rah
...half-day	...per mezza giornata pehr **mehd**-zah jor-**nah**-tah
...day	...al giorno ahl **jor**-noh
Is a deposit required?	Ci vuole un deposito? chee **vwoh**-lay oon deh-**poh**-zee-toh

Bicycling

bicycle / bike	bicicletta / bici bee-chee-**kleh**-tah / **bee**-chee
I'd like to rent a bicycle.	Vorrei noleggiare una bicicletta. voh-**reh**-ee noh-leh-**jah**-ray **oo**-nah bee-chee-**kleh**-tah
two bicycles	due biciclette **doo**-ay bee-chee-**kleh**-tay
kid's bike	bicicletta da bambino[a] bee-chee-**kleh**-tah dah bahm-**bee**-noh
mountain bike	mountain bike "mountain bike"
helmet	casco **kah**-skoh
map	cartina kar-**tee**-nah
lock	lucchetto loo-**keh**-toh
chain	catena kah-**teh**-nah

Way to Go!

Whether you're biking or hiking, you'll want to know the best way to go.

Can you recommend a route / hike that is...?	Può raccomandare un'itinerario / un'escursione...? pwoh rah-koh-mahn-**dah**-ray oon-ee-tee-neh-**rah**-ree-oh / oon-eh-skoor-see-**oh**-nay
...easy	...facile **fah**-chee-lay
...moderate	...moderato moh-deh-**rah**-toh
...strenuous	...faticoso fah-tee-**koh**-zoh
...safe	...sicuro see-**koo**-roh
...scenic	...panoramico pah-noh-**rah**-mee-koh
...about ____ kilometers	...circa ____ chilometri **cheer**-kah ____ kee-**loh**-meh-tree
How many minutes / hours?	Quante minuti / ore? **kwahn**-tay mee-**noo**-tee / **oh**-ray
uphill / level / downhill	salita / in pianura / discesa sah-**lee**-tah / een pee-ah-**noo**-rah / dee-**sheh**-zah

pedal	pedale peh-**dah**-lay
wheel	ruota roo-**oh**-tah
tire	gomma **goh**-mah
air / no air	aria / senza aria **ah**-ree-ah / **sehnt**-sah **ah**-ree-ah
pump	pompa **pohm**-pah
brakes	freni **freh**-nee
How does this work?	Come funziona? **koh**-may foont-see-**oh**-nah

How many gears?	Quante marce? **kwahn**-tay **mar**-chay
Is there a bike path?	C'è una pista ciclabile? cheh **oo**-nah **pee**-stah chee-**klah**-bee-lay
I don't like hills or traffic.	Non mi piacciono le salite nè il traffico. nohn mee pee-ah-**choh**-noh lay sah-**lee**-tay neh eel **trah**-fee-koh
I brake for bakeries.	Mi fermo ad ogni pasticceria. mee **fehr**-moh ahd **ohn**-yee pah-stee-cheh-**ree**-ah

Hiking

hiking	escursione / trekking eh-skoor-see-**oh**-nay / **treh**-keeng
a hike	un'escursione oon-eh-skoor-see-**oh**-nay
trail	sentiero sehn-tee-**eh**-roh
Where can I buy a...?	Dove posso comprare una...? **doh**-vay **poh**-soh kohm-**prah**-ray **oo**-nah
...hiking map	...cartina dei sentieri kar-**tee**-nah **deh**-ee sehn-tee-**eh**-ree
...compass	...bussola **boo**-soh-lah
Where's the trailhead?	Dov'è il punto di partenza del sentiero? doh-**veh** eel **poon**-toh dee par-**tehnt**-sah dehl sehn-tee-**eh**-roh
How do I get there?	Come ci arrivo? **koh**-may chee ah-**ree**-voh
Show me?	Me lo mostra? may loh **moh**-strah
How is the trail marked?	Com'è segnato il sentiero? koh-**meh** sehn-**yah**-toh eel sehn-tee-**eh**-roh

Most hiking trails are well-marked with signs listing the destination and duration (***ore di cammino***, literally "hours of walking") or length of the trail ***(lunghezza del percorso).*** Some signs have abbreviations for the degree of difficulty:

T = tourist trail, easy
E = longer, more varied, marked along the way
EE = for experts
EEA = for experts with equipment

To reach the best views, consider taking advantage of the network of ***ferrovie di montagna*** (mountain railways). There are various types: ***ferrovia a cremagliera*** (cogwheel train), ***funicolare*** (funicular), ***funivia*** (cable car), and ***telecabine*** (gondola).

Sports Talk

sports	gli sport lee sport
game	partita par-**tee**-tah
team	squadra **skwah**-drah
championship	campionato kahm-pee-oh-**nah**-toh
field / court	campo **kahm**-poh
fitness club	palestra pah-**leh**-strah
I like to play...	Mi piace giocare... mee pee-**ah**-chay joh-**kah**-ray
I like to watch...	Mi piace guardare... mee pee-**ah**-chay gwar-**dah**-ray
American football	football Americano **foot**-bahl ah-meh-ree-**kah**-noh
baseball	baseball **bays**-bahl
basketball	basket **bah**-skeht
golf	golf gohlf
miniature golf	minigolf **mee**-nee-gohlf
soccer	calcio / football **kahl**-choh / **foot**-bahl
tennis	tennis **teh**-nees
volleyball	pallavolo pah-lah-**voh**-loh
skiing	sci shee
snowboarding	snowboarding "snowboarding"

ice skating	pattinaggio su ghiaccio pah-tee-**nah**-joh soo gee-**ah**-choh (hard "g")
Where can I play ___?	Dove posso giocare a ___? **doh**-vay **poh**-soh joh-**kah**-ray ah ___
Where can I rent / buy sports equipment?	Dove posso noleggiare / comprare l'attrezzatura sportiva? **doh**-vay **poh**-soh noh-leh-**jah**-ray / kohm-**prah**-ray lah-trehd-zah-**too**-rah spor-**tee**-vah
Where can I see a game?	Dove posso vedere una partita? **doh**-vay **poh**-soh veh-**deh**-ray **oo**-nah par-**tee**-tah

Like most Europeans, Italians take ***il calcio*** (soccer) very seriously. Rome has two teams: ***Roma*** (representing the city) and ***Lazio*** (the region). When Romans are introduced, they ask each other ***Laziale o romanista?*** The answer can compromise a relationship.

ENTERTAINMENT

What's Happening

event guide	guida agli eventi **gwee**-dah **ahl**-yee eh-**vehn**-tee
What's happening tonight?	Che cosa succede stasera? kay **koh**-zah soo-**cheh**-day stah-**seh**-rah
What do you recommend?	Che cosa raccomanda? kay **koh**-zah rah-koh-**mahn**-dah
Where is it?	Dov'è? doh-**veh**
How do I get there?	Come ci arriva? **koh**-may chee ah-**ree**-vah
Is it free?	È gratis? eh **grah**-tees
Are there seats available?	Ci sono ancora dei posti? chee **soh**-noh ahn-**koh**-rah **deh**-ee **poh**-stee

Where can I buy a ticket?	Dove si comprano i biglietti? **doh**-vay see kohm-**prah**-noh ee beel-**yeh**-tee
Do you have tickets for today / tonight?	Avete dei biglietti per oggi / stasera? ah-**veh**-tay **deh**-ee beel-**yeh**-tee pehr **oh**-jee / stah-**seh**-rah
When does it start?	A che ora comincia? ah kay **oh**-rah koh-**meen**-chah
When does it end?	A che ora finisce? ah kay **oh**-rah fee-**nee**-shay
Where is the best place to stroll?	Dov'è il posto migliore per una passeggiata? doh-**veh** eel **poh**-stoh meel-**yoh**-ray pehr **oo**-nah pah-seh-**jah**-tah

For cheap entertainment, join the locals and ***fare una passeggiata*** (take a stroll) through town. People gather at the town's ***piazza d'incontro*** (meeting place). As you do laps ***(vasche)*** and bump shoulders in the crowd, you'll know why it's also called ***struscio*** (rubbing). On workdays, Italians stroll between work and dinner. On Sundays and holidays, they hit the streets after lunch. People are strutting. This is Italy on parade.

Music and Dance

Where's a good place for...?	Dov'è un buon posto per...? doh-**veh** oon bwohn **poh**-stoh pehr
...dancing	...ballare bah-**lah**-ray
...(live) music	...musica (dal vivo) **moo**-zee-kah (dahl **vee**-voh)
rock	rock rohk
jazz	jazz jahz
blues	blues "blues"
classical	classica **klah**-see-kah

choir	corale koh-**rah**-lay
folk	folk fohlk
folk dancing	danze popolari **dahnt**-say poh-poh-**lah**-ree
disco	discoteca dee-skoh-**teh**-kah
karaoke	karaoke kah-rah-**oh**-kay
singer	cantante kahn-**tahn**-tay
band	gruppo musicale **groo**-poh moo-zee-**kah**-lay
bar with live music	locale con musica dal vivo loh-**kah**-lay kohn **moo**-zee-kah dahl **vee**-voh
nightclub	locale notturno loh-**kah**-lay noh-**toor**-noh
cover charge	coperto koh-**pehr**-toh
free entry	ingresso libero een-**greh**-soh **lee**-beh-roh
concert	concerto kohn-**chehr**-toh
opera	lirica **lee**-ree-kah
symphony	sinfonica seen-**foh**-nee-kah
show	spettacolo speh-**tah**-koh-loh
theater	teatro tee-**ah**-troh
best / cheap seats	posti migliori / economici **poh**-stee meel-**yoh**-ree / eh-koh-**noh**-mee-chee
sold out	tutto esaurito **too**-toh eh-zow-**ree**-toh

The piano was invented in Italy. Unlike a harpsichord, it could be played soft and loud, so it was called just that: ***piano-forte*** (soft-loud). Here are other Italian musical words: ***subito*** (suddenly), ***crescendo*** (growing louder), ***come sopra*** (as above—meaning like the previous tempo), ***sotto voce*** (very softly), ***ritardando*** (slowing down), and ***fine*** (end).

Movies

movie	film feelm
Is there a movie theater nearby?	C'è un cinema qui vicino? cheh oon **chee**-neh-mah kwee vee-**chee**-noh
Is this movie in English?	Questo film è in inglese? **kweh**-stoh feelm eh een een-**gleh**-zay
original version	versione originale vehr-see-**oh**-nay oh-ree-jee-**nah**-lay
with subtitles	con sottotitoli kohn soh-toh-**tee**-toh-lee
dubbed	doppiato doh-pee-**ah**-toh
3D	3D **tray**-dee
show times	orario degli spettacoli oh-**rah**-ree-oh **dehl**-yee speh-**tah**-koh-lee
matinee	spettacolo pomeridiano speh-**tah**-koh-loh poh-meh-ree-dee-**ah**-noh
ticket	biglietto beel-**yeh**-toh
discount	sconto **skohn**-toh
popcorn	popcorn "popcorn"
I liked it.	Mi è piaciuto. mee eh pee-ah-**choo**-toh
The book is better.	Il libro è meglio. eel **lee**-broh eh **mehl**-yoh

In Italy, most American movies are dubbed in Italian, but you can sometimes find them screened in the original version (English with Italian subtitles)—look for ***V.O.***

SHOPPING

These phrases will give you the basics on browsing and bargaining; help you shop for various items, including souvenirs, clothes, and jewelry; and assist you in shipping items home.

SHOP TILL YOU DROP

Shop Talk

opening hours	orario d'apertura oh-**rah**-ree-oh dah-pehr-**too**-rah
sale	saldi **sahl**-dee
special offer	offerta speciale oh-**fehr**-tah speh-**chah**-lay
cheap	economico eh-koh-**noh**-mee-koh
affordable	accessibile ah-cheh-**see**-bee-lay
(too) expensive	(troppo) costoso (**troh**-poh) koh-**stoh**-zoh
a good value	un buon prezzo oon bwohn **prehd**-zoh
Excuse me.	Scusi. **skoo**-zee
Where can I buy ____?	Dove posso comprare ____? **doh**-vay **poh**-soh kohm-**prah**-ray ____
How much is it?	Quanto costa? **kwahn**-toh **koh**-stah
Can I take a look?	Posso guardare? **poh**-soh gwar-**dah**-ray
I'm just browsing.	Sto solo guardando. stoh **soh**-loh gwar-**dahn**-doh
I'd like...	Vorrei... voh-**reh**-ee
Do you have...?	Avete...? ah-**veh**-tay
...more (m / f)	...altri / altre **ahl**-tree / **ahl**-tray
...something cheaper	...qualcosa di meno caro kwahl-**koh**-zah dee **meh**-noh **kah**-roh
...something nicer	...qualcosa di più elegante kwahl-**koh**-zah dee pew eh-leh-**gahn**-tay
Can I see more?	Posso vederne di più? **poh**-soh veh-**dehr**-nay dee pew

Key Phrases: Shopping

How much is it?	Quanto costa? **kwahn**-toh **koh**-stah
I'm just browsing.	Sto solo guardando. stoh **soh**-loh gwar-**dahn**-doh
Can I see more?	Posso vederne di più? **poh**-soh veh-**dehr**-nay dee pew
I'll think about it.	Ci penserò. chee pehn-seh-**roh**
I'll take it.	Lo prendo. loh **prehn**-doh
Do you accept credit cards?	Accettate carte di credito? ah-cheh-**tah**-tay **kar**-tay dee **kreh**-dee-toh
Can I try it on?	Lo posso provare? loh **poh**-soh proh-**vah**-ray
It's too expensive / big / small.	È troppo costoso / grande / piccolo. eh **troh**-poh koh-**stoh**-zoh / **grahn**-day / **pee**-koh-loh

This one.	Questo qui. **kweh**-stoh kwee
I'll think about it.	Ci penserò. chee pehn-seh-**roh**
I'll take it.	Lo prendo. loh **prehn**-doh
What time do you close?	A che ora chiudete? ah kay **oh**-rah kee-oo-**deh**-tay
What time do you open tomorrow?	A che ora aprite domani? ah kay **oh**-rah ah-**pree**-tay doh-**mah**-nee

Bargain hunters keep an eye out for ***saldi*** (sales) and ***sconti*** (discounts).

Pay Up

Where do I pay?	Dove si paga? **doh**-vay see **pah**-gah
cashier	cassa **kah**-sah

Do you accept credit cards?	Accettate carte di credito? ah-cheh-**tah**-tay **kar**-tay dee **kreh**-dee-toh
VAT (Value-Added Tax)	IVA (imposta sul valore aggiunto) ee vee ah (eem-**poh**-stah sool vah-**loh**-ray ah-**joon**-toh)
Can I get...?	Posso avere...? **poh**-soh ah-**veh**-ray
I need the paperwork for...	Mi serve il modulo per... mee **sehr**-vay eel **moh**-doo-loh pehr
...a VAT refund	...un rimborso IVA oon reem-**bor**-soh ee vee ah
Can you ship this?	Può spedirmelo? pwoh speh-deer-**meh**-loh

When you're ready to pay, look for a ***cassa*** (cashier). The cashier might ask you something like ***Ha quindici centesimi?*** (Do you have 15 cents?), ***Ce l'ha spicci?*** (Do you have exact change?), or ***Vuole una busta?*** (Do you want a bag?).

If you make a major purchase from a single store, you may be eligible for a VAT refund; for details, see www.ricksteves.com/vat.

WHERE TO SHOP

Types of Shops

Where is a...?	Dov'è un / una...? doh-**veh** oon / **oo**-nah
antique shop	negozio di antiquariato neh-**goht**-see-oh dee ahn-tee-kwah-ree-**ah**-toh
art gallery	galleria d'arte gah-leh-**ree**-ah **dar**-tay
bakery	panificio pah-nee-**fee**-choh
barber shop	barbiere bar-bee-**eh**-ray
beauty salon	parrucchiere pah-roo-kee-**eh**-ray
bookstore...	libreria... lee-breh-**ree**-ah

used bookstore...	negozio di libri usati... neh-**goht**-see-oh dee **lee**-bree oo-**zah**-tee
...with books in English	...che vende libri in inglese kay **vehn**-day **lee**-bree een een-**gleh**-zay
clothing boutique	boutique di abbigliamento boo-**teek** dee ah-beel-yah-**mehn**-toh
coffee shop	bar bar
crafts shop	negozio di artigianato locale neh-**goht**-see-oh dee ar-tee-jah-**nah**-toh loh-**kah**-lay
delicatessen	salumeria sah-loo-meh-**ree**-ah
department store	grande magazzino **grahn**-day mah-gahd-**zee**-noh
electronics store	negozio di elettronica neh-**goht**-see-oh dee eh-leh-**troh**-nee-kah
fabric store	negozio di tessuti neh-**goht**-see-oh dee teh-**soo**-tee
flea market	mercato delle pulci mehr-**kah**-toh **deh**-lay **pool**-chee
flower market	mercato dei fiori mehr-**kah**-toh **deh**-ee fee-**oh**-ree
grocery store	alimentari ah-lee-mehn-**tah**-ree
hardware store	ferramenta feh-rah-**mehn**-tah
jewelry store	gioielleria joh-yeh-leh-**ree**-ah
launderette	lavanderia lah-vahn-deh-**ree**-ah
leather shop	pelletteria peh-leh-teh-**ree**-ah
liquor store	enoteca eh-noh-**teh**-kah
mobile-phone shop	negozio di cellulari neh-**goht**-see-oh dee cheh-loo-**lah**-ree
newsstand	edicola / giornalaio eh-**dee**-koh-lah / jor-nah-**lah**-yoh
office supply shop	cartoleria kar-toh-leh-**ree**-ah
open-air market	mercato mehr-**kah**-toh

optician	ottico **oh**-tee-koh
pastry shop	pasticceria pah-stee-cheh-**ree**-ah
pharmacy	farmacia far-mah-**chee**-ah
photocopy shop	copisteria koh-pee-steh-**ree**-ah
pottery shop	negozio di ceramica neh-**goht**-see-oh dee cheh-**rah**-mee-kah
shoe store	negozio di calzature neh-**goht**-see-oh dee kahlt-sah-**too**-ray
shopping mall	centro commerciale **chehn**-troh koh-mehr-**chah**-lay
souvenir shop	negozio di souvenir neh-**goht**-see-oh dee **soo**-veh-neer
supermarket	supermercato soo-pehr-mehr-**kah**-toh
sweets shop	negozio di dolciumi / pasticceria neh-**goht**-see-oh dee dohl-**choo**-mee / pah-stee-cheh-**ree**-ah
tobacco stand	tabacchi tah-**bah**-kee
toy store	negozio di giocattoli neh-**goht**-see-oh dee joh-**kah**-toh-lee
travel agency	agenzia di viaggi ah-**jehnt**-see-ah dee vee-**ah**-jee
wine shop	negozio di vini neh-**goht**-see-oh dee **vee**-nee

In Italy, shops are often closed for a long lunch (generally daily between 1:00 p.m. and 3:00 or 4:00 p.m.). While most people are familiar with the Spanish term ***siesta*** to describe this relaxed lifestyle, Italians call it ***pausa pranzo*** (lunch break). Many stores in the larger cities close for all or part of August—not a good time to plan a shopping spree.

At tobacco shops (known as ***tabacchi,*** often indicated with a big **T** sign), you can pay for street parking, buy stamps, and get tickets for buses and subways.

For tips and phrases on shopping for a picnic—at grocery stores or open-air markets—see page 182 in the Eating chapter.

Department Stores

department store	grande magazzino **grahn**-day mah-gahd-**zee**-noh
floor	piano pee-**ah**-noh
Excuse me.	Scusi. **skoo**-zee
Where is / Where are...?	Dov'è / Dove sono...? doh-**veh** / **doh**-vay **soh**-noh
men's / women's department	reparto uomo / donna reh-**par**-toh **woh**-moh / **doh**-nah
children's department	reparto bambino reh-**par**-toh bahm-**bee**-noh
accessories	accessori ah-cheh-**soh**-ree
books	libri **lee**-bree
electronics	elettronica eh-leh-**troh**-nee-kah
fashion	moda **moh**-dah
footwear	calzature kahlt-sah-**too**-ray
groceries	alimentari ah-lee-mehn-**tah**-ree
housewares / kitchenware	casalinghi / articoli per la cucina kah-zah-**leen**-gee (hard "g") / ar-**tee**-koh-lee pehr lah koo-**chee**-nah
intimates	intimo **een**-tee-moh
jewelry	gioielli joh-**yeh**-lee
maternity wear	abiti premaman **ah**-bee-tee preh-**mah**-mahn
mobile phones	telefoni cellulari teh-**leh**-foh-nee cheh-loo-**lah**-ree
stationery (office supplies / cards)	cartoleria car-toh-leh-**ree**-ah

Department stores—like the popular Oviesse, Coin, and La Rinascente—sell nearly everything and are a good place to get cheap souvenirs and postcards. Most have a directory (often with English) by the escalator or elevator.

Street Markets

Did you make this?	L'avete fatto voi questo? lah-**veh**-tay **fah**-toh **voh**-ee **kweh**-stoh
Is this made in Italy?	Questo è made in Italy? **kweh**-stoh eh "made in Italy"
How much is it?	Quanto costa? **kwahn**-toh **koh**-stah
Cheaper?	Me lo dà a meno? may loh dah ah **meh**-noh
And if I give you ____? (name price)	E se le do ____? ay say lay doh ____
Cheaper if I buy two or three?	Costa meno se ne compro due o tre? **koh**-stah **meh**-noh say nay **kohm**-proh **doo**-ay oh tray
Good price.	Buon prezzo. bwohn **prehd**-zoh
My last offer.	La mia ultima offerta. lah **mee**-ah **ool**-tee-mah oh-**fehr**-tah
I'll take it.	Lo prendo. loh **prehn**-doh
We'll take it.	Lo prendiamo. loh prehn-dee-**ah**-moh
I'm / We're nearly broke.	Sono / Siamo quasi al verde. **soh**-noh / see-**ah**-moh **kwah**-zee ahl **vehr**-day
My male friend / My female friend...	Il mio amico / La mia amica... eel **mee**-oh ah-**mee**-koh / lah **mee**-ah ah-**mee**-kah
My husband / My wife...	Mio marito / Mia moglie... **mee**-oh mah-**ree**-toh / **mee**-ah **mohl**-yay
...has the money.	...ha i soldi. ah ee **sohl**-dee

It's OK to bargain at street markets, though not every vendor will drop prices. Expect to pay cash and be wary of pickpockets. For help with numbers and prices, see page 24.

WHAT TO BUY

Here are some of the items you might buy, ranging from souvenirs to clothing to jewelry. For personal care items, see page 306. For electronics, see page 272.

Souvenirs

Do you have a...?	Avete un / una...? ah-**veh**-tay oon / **oo**-nah
I'm looking for a...	Sto cercando un / una... stoh chehr-**kahn**-doh oon / **oo**-nah
book	libro **lee**-broh
guidebook	guida turistica **gwee**-dah too-**ree**-stee-kah
children's book	libro per bambini **lee**-broh pehr bahm-**bee**-nee
bookmark	segnalibro sehn-yah-**lee**-broh
calendar	calendario kah-lehn-**dah**-ree-oh
candle	candela kahn-**deh**-lah
doll	bambola **bahm**-boh-lah
journal	diario dee-**ah**-ree-oh
magnet	magnete mahn-**yeh**-tay
notecards	biglietti d'auguri beel-**yeh**-tee dow-**goo**-ree
ornament	decorazione deh-koh-raht-see-**oh**-nay
pen / pencil	penna / matita **peh**-nah / mah-**tee**-tah
postcard	cartolina kar-toh-**lee**-nah
poster	poster **poh**-stehr
print	stampa **stahm**-pah
toy	giocattolo joh-**kah**-toh-loh
umbrella	ombrello ohm-**breh**-loh

Specifically Italian Souvenirs

cameo (Amalfi Coast)	cammeo kah-**meh**-oh
carnival mask (Venice)	maschera di carnevale **mah**-skeh-rah dee kar-neh-**vah**-lay
Christmas crèche (Naples)	presepe preh-**seh**-pay
hand-painted ceramics	ceramiche dipinte a mano cheh-**rah**-mee-kay dee-**peen**-tay ah **mah**-noh
gold jewelry (Florence)	gioielli in oro joh-**yeh**-lee een **oh**-roh
leather gloves / handbag (Florence)	guanti / borsa in pelle **gwahn**-tee / **bor**-sah een **peh**-lay
marbled paper (Florence)	carta marmorizzata **kar**-tah mar-mor-eed-**zah**-tah
soccer-team jersey	maglia da calcio **mahl**-yah dah **kahl**-choh
Venetian glass	vetro veneziano **veh**-troh veh-nehl-see-**ah**-noh

Clothing

clothing	vestiti veh-**stee**-tee
This one.	Questo qui. **kweh**-stoh kwee
Can I try it on?	Lo posso provare? loh **poh**-soh proh-**vah**-ray
Do you have a...?	Avete...? ah-**veh**-tay
...mirror	...uno specchio **oo**-noh **speh**-kee-oh
...fitting room	...un camerino oon kah-meh-**ree**-noh
(It's) too...	(È) troppo... (eh) **troh**-poh
...expensive.	...costoso. koh-**stoh**-zoh
...big / small.	...grande / piccolo. **grahn**-day / **pee**-koh-loh

...short / long.	...corto / lungo.	**kor**-toh / **loon**-goh
...tight / loose.	...stretto / largo.	**streh**-toh / **lar**-goh
...dark / light.	...scuro / chiaro.	**skoo**-roh / kee-**ah**-roh
Do you have a different color / a different pattern?	Avete un colore diverso / una fantasia diversa?	ah-**veh**-tay oon koh-**loh**-ray dee-**vehr**-soh / **oo**-nah fahn-tah-**zee**-ah dee-**vehr**-sah
What's it made of?	Di che cosa è fatto?	dee kay **koh**-zah eh **fah**-toh
Is it machine washable?	Si può lavare in lavatrice?	see pwoh lah-**vah**-ray een lah-vah-**tree**-chay
Will it shrink?	Si ritira?	see ree-**tee**-rah
Will it fade in the wash?	Scolora quando si lava?	skoh-**loh**-rah **kwahn**-doh see **lah**-vah
Dry clean only?	Solo lavasecco?	**soh**-loh lah-vah-**seh**-koh

For a list of colors, see page 265, and for fabrics, see page 266.

Types of Clothes and Accessories

For a...	Per un / una...	pehr oon / **oo**-nah
...man.	...uomo.	**woh**-moh
...woman.	...donna.	**doh**-nah
...teenager. (m / f)	...ragazzo / ragazza.	rah-**gahd**-zoh / rah-**gahd**-zah
...child. (m / f)	...bambino / bambina.	bahm-**bee**-noh / bahm-**bee**-nah
...baby. (m / f)	...neonato / neonata.	neh-oh-**nah**-toh / neh-oh-**nah**-tah
I'm looking for a...	Sto cercando un / una...	stoh chehr-**kahn**-doh oon / **oo**-nah

SHOPPING
What to Buy

I want to buy a...	Vorrei comprare un / una... voh-**reh**-ee kohm-**prah**-ray oon / **oo**-nah
bathrobe	accappatoio ah-kah-pah-**toh**-yoh
bib	bavaglino bah-vahl-**yee**-noh
belt	cintura cheen-**too**-rah
bra	reggiseno reh-jee-**zeh**-noh
dress	vestito da donna veh-**stee**-toh dah **doh**-nah
flip-flops	ciabatte da piscina chah-**bah**-tay dah pee-**shee**-nah
gloves	guanti **gwahn**-tee
handbag	borsa **bor**-sah
hat	cappello kah-**peh**-loh
jacket	giacca **jah**-kah
jeans	jeans "jeans"
leggings	dei leggings **deh**-ee "leggings"
nightgown	camicia da notte kah-**mee**-chah dah **noh**-tay
nylons	collant **koh**-lahnt
pajamas	pigiama pee-**jah**-mah
pants	pantaloni pahn-tah-**loh**-nee
raincoat	impermeabile eem-pehr-meh-**ah**-bee-lay
sandals	sandali **sahn**-dah-lee
scarf	sciarpa / foulard **shar**-pah / foo-**lard**
shirt...	camicia... kah-**mee**-chah
...long-sleeved	...a maniche lunghe ah **mah**-nee-kay **loon**-gay
...short-sleeved	...a maniche corte ah **mah**-nee-kay **kor**-tay
...sleeveless	...senza maniche **sehnt**-sah **mah**-nee-kay
shoes	scarpe **skar**-pay

shoelaces	lacci da scarpe **lah**-chee dah **skar**-pay
shorts	pantaloni corti pahn-tah-**loh**-nee **kor**-tee
skirt	gonna **goh**-nah
sleeper (for baby)	tutina (da neonato) too-**tee**-nah (dah neh-oh-**nah**-toh)
slip	sottoveste soh-toh-**veh**-stay
slippers	ciabatte / pantofole chah-**bah**-tay / pahn-**toh**-foh-lay
socks	calzini kahlt-**see**-nee
sweater	maglione mahl-**yoh**-nay
swimsuit	costume da bagno koh-**stoo**-may dah **bahn**-yoh
tank top	canottiera kah-noh-tee-**eh**-rah
tennis shoes	scarpe da ginnastica **skar**-pay dah jee-**nah**-stee-kah
tie	cravatta krah-**vah**-tah
tights	dei collant **deh**-ee **koh**-lahnt
T-shirt	maglietta mahl-**yeh**-tah
underwear	intimo **een**-tee-moh
vest	gilè jee-**lay**
wallet	portafoglio por-tah-**fohl**-yoh

Clothing Sizes

extra-small	extra-small "extra-small"
small	small "small"
medium	media **meh**-dee-ah
large	large "large"
extra-large	extra-large "extra-large"

I need a bigger / smaller size.	Mi serve una misura più grande / più piccola. mee **sehr**-vay **oo**-nah mee-**zoo**-rah pew **grahn**-day / pew **pee**-koh-lah
What's my size?	Qual'è la mia misura? kwah-**leh** lah **mee**-ah mee-**zoo**-rah

US-to-European Comparisons

When shopping for clothing, use these US-to-European comparisons as a guideline (but note that no conversion is perfect).

Women's pants and dresses: Add 36 (US 10 = European 46)
Women's blouses and sweaters: Add 8 (US 32 = European 40)
Men's suits and jackets: Add 10 (US 40 regular = European 50)
Men's shirts: Multiply by 2 and add about 8 (US 15 collar = European 38)
Women's shoes: Add 30-31 (US 7 = European 37/38)
Men's shoes: Add 32-34 (US 9 = European 41; US 11 = European 45)
Children's clothing: Clothing is sized by height—in centimeters (2.5 cm = 1 inch). A US size 8 roughly equates to 132-140. Juniors, subtract 4 (US 14 = European 10)
Children's shoes: For shoes up to size 13, add 16-18. For sizes 1 and up, add 30-32

Sew What?

Traveling is hard on clothes.

I need...	Mi serve... mee **sehr**-vay
...a button.	...un bottone. oon boh-**toh**-nay
...a needle.	...un ago per cucire. oon **ah**-goh pehr koo-**chee**-ray
...thread.	...del filo. dehl **fee**-loh
...scissors.	...delle forbici. **deh**-lay **for**-bee-chee
...stain remover.	...uno smacchiatore. **oo**-noh zmah-kee-ah-**toh**-ray
...a new zipper.	...una zip nuova. **oo**-nah tseep noo-**oh**-vah
Can you fix it?	Lo può riparare? loh pwoh ree-pah-**rah**-ray

Colors

black	nero **neh**-roh
blue	azzurro ahd-**zoo**-roh
brown	marrone mah-**roh**-nay
gray	grigio **gree**-joh
green	verde **vehr**-day
orange	arancio ah-**rahn**-choh
pink	rosa **roh**-zah
purple	viola vee-**oh**-lah
red	rosso **roh**-soh
white	bianco bee-**ahn**-koh
yellow	giallo **jah**-loh
dark(er)	(più) scuro (pew) **skoo**-roh
light(er)	(più) chiaro (pew) kee-**ah**-roh
bright(er)	(più) brillante (pew) bree-**lahn**-tay

Fabrics

What's this made of?	Di che cosa è fatto? dee kay **koh**-zah eh **fah**-toh
A mix of...	Un misto di... oon **mee**-stoh dee
cashmere	cashmere kahs-**meh**-ray
cotton	cotone koh-**toh**-nay
denim	jeans "jeans"
flannel	flanella flah-**neh**-lah
fleece	pile **pee**-lay
lace	pizzo **peed**-zoh
leather	cuoio / pelle **kwoh**-yoh / **peh**-lay
linen	lino **lee**-noh
nylon	nylon **nee**-lohn
polyester	poliestere poh-lee-**eh**-steh-ray
silk	seta **seh**-tah
velvet	velluto veh-**loo**-toh
wool	lana **lah**-nah

Jewelry

jewelry	gioielli joh-**yeh**-lee
jewelry store	gioielleria joh-yeh-leh-**ree**-ah
bracelet	bracciale brah-**chah**-lay
brooch	spilla **spee**-lah
cuff links	gemelli jeh-**meh**-lee
earrings	orecchini oh-reh-**kee**-nee
necklace	collana koh-**lah**-nah
ring	anello ah-**neh**-loh
watch	orologio oh-roh-**loh**-joh
watch battery	batteria per orologio bah-teh-**ree**-ah pehr oh-roh-**loh**-joh
silver / gold	argento / oro ar-**jehn**-toh / **oh**-roh

Is this...?	Questo è...? **kweh**-stoh eh
...sterling silver	...argento sterling ar-**jehn**-toh **stehr**-leeng
...real gold	...oro zecchino **oh**-roh tseh-**kee**-noh
...made in Italy	...made in Italy "made in Italy"
...handmade	...fatto a mano **fah**-toh ah **mah**-noh
...stolen	...rubato roo-**bah**-toh

SHIPPING AND MAIL

Though you can ship home goods from ***la posta*** (the post office), it may be more reliable to send packages (especially expensive or fragile objects) using DHL, UPS, or FedEx, which can provide tracking numbers. If you just need stamps, you can often get them at the corner ***tabacchi*** (tobacco shop).

At the Post Office

post office	posta **poh**-stah
Where is the post office?	Dov'è l'ufficio postale? doh-**veh** loo-**fee**-choh poh-**stah**-lay
stamps	francobolli frahn-koh-**boh**-lee
postcard	cartolina kar-toh-**lee**-nah
letter	lettera **leh**-teh-rah
package	pacco **pah**-koh
window	sportello spor-**teh**-loh
line	fila **fee**-lah
Which window?	Qual'è lo sportello? kwah-**leh** loh spor-**teh**-loh
Is this the line?	È questa la fila? eh **kweh**-stah lah **fee**-lah
I need some stamps.	Mi servono dei francobolli. mee sehr-**voh**-noh **deh**-ee frahn-koh-**boh**-lee

I need to mail a package...	Ho bisogno di spedire un pacco... oh bee-**zohn**-yoh dee speh-**dee**-ray oon **pah**-koh
...to the United States.	...per Stati Uniti. pehr **stah**-tee oo-**nee**-tee
by air mail	per via aerea pehr **vee**-ah ah-**eh**-reh-ah
by express mail	posta espressa **poh**-stah eh-**spreh**-sah
by surface mail	via terra **vee**-ah **teh**-rah
slow and cheap	lento e economico **lehn**-toh ay eh-koh-**noh**-mee-koh
How much is it?	Quanto costa? **kwahn**-toh **koh**-stah
How much to send a letter / postcard to ____?	Quanto costa mandare una lettera / una cartolina a ____? **kwahn**-toh **koh**-stah mahn-**dah**-ray **oo**-nah **leh**-teh-rah / **oo**-nah kar-toh-**lee**-nah ah ____
Pretty stamps, please.	Dei bei francobolli, per favore. **deh**-ee **beh**-ee frahn-koh-**boh**-lee pehr fah-**voh**-ray
Can I buy a box?	Posso comprare una scatola? **poh**-soh kohm-**prah**-ray **oo**-nah **skah**-toh-lah
This big.	Grande così. **grahn**-day koh-**zee**
Do you have tape?	Avete dello scotch? ah-**veh**-tay **deh**-loh "scotch"
How many days will it take?	Quanti giorni ci vogliono? **kwahn**-tee **jor**-nee chee vohl-**yoh**-noh
I always choose the slowest line.	Scelgo sempre la fila più lenta. **shehl**-goh **sehm**-pray lah **fee**-lah pew **lehn**-tah

You might have to take a number ***(prenotazione)***, then wait to report to the window ***(sportello)***. Since the post office also operates a bank, and locals come here to take care of other business, you'll want to choose the correct window. The window for stamps is usually labeled ***filatelia*** (or ***lo sportello filatelico***), and ***spedizione lettere e pacchi*** means sending letters and packages.

When putting a stamped letter into a mailbox ***(impostazione),*** be sure to use the right slot: ***per la città*** is for letters being mailed within the city, while ***per tutte le altre destinazioni*** is for all other destinations.

Licking the Postal Code

to / from	da / a dah / ah
address	indirizzo een-dee-**reed**-zoh
zip code	codice postale koh-**dee**-chay poh-**stah**-lay
envelope	busta **boo**-stah
package	pacco **pah**-koh
box	scatola **skah**-toh-lah
packing material	materiale per pacchi mah-teh-ree-**ah**-lay pehr **pah**-kee
tape	scotch "scotch"
string	filo **fee**-loh
mailbox	cassetta postale kah-**seh**-tah poh-**stah**-lay
book rate	prezzo di listino **prehd**-zoh dee lee-**stee**-noh
weight limit	limite di peso **lee**-mee-tay dee **peh**-zoh
registered	raccomandata rah-koh-mahn-**dah**-tah
insured	assicurato ah-see-koo-**rah**-toh
fragile	fragile **frah**-jee-lay
contents	contenuto kohn-teh-**noo**-toh
customs	dogana doh-**gah**-nah
tracking number	codice per il tracking koh-**dee**-chay pehr eel "tracking"

Post offices sell sturdy boxes, which you can assemble, fill with souvenirs, and mail home...so you can keep packing light.

TECHNOLOGY

This chapter covers phrases for your tech needs—from buying headphones to taking photos, from making phone calls to getting online.

TECH TERMS

Portable Devices and Accessories

I need a...	Mi serve un / una... mee **sehr**-vay oon / **oo**-nah
Do you have a...?	Avete un / una...? ah-**veh**-tay oon / **oo**-nah
Where can I buy a...?	Dove posso comprare un / una...? **doh**-vay **poh**-soh kohm-**prah**-ray oon / **oo**-nah
battery (for my ___)	batteria (per il mio ___) bah-teh-**ree**-ah (pehr eel **mee**-oh ___)
battery charger	carica batterie **kah**-ree-kah bah-teh-**ree**-ay
computer	computer kohm-**poo**-tehr
convertor	convertitore elettrico kohn-vehr-tee-**toh**-ray eh-**leh**-tree-koh
ebook reader	libro elettronico **lee**-broh eh-leh-**troh**-nee-koh
electrical adapter	adattatore elettrico ah-dah-tah-**toh**-ray eh-**leh**-tree-koh
flash drive	flash drive "flash drive"
headphones / earbuds	cuffie / auricolari **koo**-fee-ay / ow-ree-koh-**lah**-ree
laptop	portatile por-**tah**-tee-lay
memory card	memory card "memory card"
mobile phone	cellulare cheh-loo-**lah**-ray
SIM card	carta SIM **kar**-tah seem
speakers (for my ___)	casse (per il mio ___) **kah**-say (pehr eel **mee**-oh ___)

tablet	tablet "tablet"
USB cable / mini-cable	cavo / cavetto USB **kah**-voh / kah-**veh**-toh oo-**ehs**-ay-bee
video game	videogioco vee-deh-oh-**joh**-koh
Wi-Fi	Wi-Fi **wee**-fee

Familiar brands (like iPad, Facebook, YouTube, Instagram, or whatever the latest craze) are just as popular in Europe as they are back home. Invariably, these go by their English names, sometimes with an Italian accent.

Cameras

camera	macchina fotografica **mah**-kee-nah foh-toh-**grah**-fee-kah
digital camera	macchina fotografica digitale **mah**-kee-nah foh-toh-**grah**-fee-kah dee-jee-**tah**-lay
video camera	videocamera vee-deh-oh-**kah**-meh-rah
lens cap	tappo obiettivo **tah**-poh oh-bee-**eh**-tee-voh
Will you take my / our photo?	Mi / Ci fa una foto? mee / chee fah **oo**-nah **foh**-toh
Can I take a photo of you?	Posso farle una foto? **poh**-soh **far**-lay **oo**-nah **foh**-toh
Smile! (sing / pl)	Sorrida! / Sorridete! soh-**ree**-dah / soh-ree-**deh**-tay

You'll find words for batteries, chargers, and more in the previous list.

TELEPHONES

Travelers have several phoning options. The simplest solution is to bring your own mobile phone and use it just as you would at home (such as getting an international plan or connecting to free Wi-Fi whenever possible). Another option is to buy a European SIM card for your US mobile phone. As this is a fast-changing scene, check my latest tips at www.ricksteves.com/phoning. Public pay phones are rare (and often require buying an insertable phone card).

Telephone Terms

telephone	telefono teh-**leh**-foh-noh
phone call...	chiamata... kee-ah-**mah**-tah
...local (within the city)	...urbana oor-**bah**-nah
...domestic (elsewhere in Italy)	...nazionale naht-see-oh-**nah**-lay
...international	...internazionale een-tehr-naht-see-oh-**nah**-lay
...toll-free	...numero verde / freephone **noo**-meh-roh **vehr**-day / "freephone"
...with credit card	...con la carta di credito kohn lah **kar**-tah dee **kreh**-dee-toh
...collect	...a carico del destinatario ah **kah**-ree-koh dehl deh-stee-nah-**tah**-ree-oh
mobile phone	cellulare cheh-loo-**lah**-ray
mobile number	numero di cellulare **noo**-meh-roh dee cheh-loo-**lah**-ray
landline	numero fisso **noo**-meh-roh **fee**-soh
country code	prefisso per il paese preh-**fee**-soh pehr eel pah-**eh**-zay
area code	prefisso preh-**fee**-soh
phone number	numero di telefono **noo**-meh-roh dee teh-**leh**-foh-noh

Key Phrases: Telephones

telephone	telefono teh-**leh**-foh-noh
phone call	chiamata kee-ah-**mah**-tah
mobile phone	cellulare cheh-loo-**lah**-ray
What is the phone number?	Qual è il numero di telefono? kwahl eh eel **noo**-meh-roh dee teh-**leh**-foh-noh
May I use your phone?	Posso usare il telefono? **poh**-soh oo-**zah**-ray eel teh-**leh**-foh-noh
Where is a mobile-phone shop?	Dov'è un negozio di cellulari? doh-**veh** oon neh-**goht**-see-oh dee cheh-loo-**lah**-ree

extension	numero interno **noo**-meh-roh een-**tehr**-noh

For tips on calling in Italy, see page 434.

Making Calls

Where is the nearest phone?	Dov'è il telefono più vicino? doh-**veh** eel teh-**leh**-foh-noh pew vee-**chee**-noh
What is the phone number?	Qual è il numero di telefono? kwahl eh eel **noo**-meh-roh dee teh-**leh**-foh-noh
May I use your phone?	Posso usare il telefono? **poh**-soh oo-**zah**-ray eel teh-**leh**-foh-noh
Can you talk for me?	Può parlare per me? pwoh par-**lah**-ray pehr may
It's busy.	È occupato. eh oh-koo-**pah**-toh
It doesn't work.	Non funziona. nohn foont-see-**oh**-nah

out of service	guasto **gwah**-stoh
Try again?	Può riprovare? pwoh ree-proh-**vah**-ray

On the Phone

Hello, this is ____.	Pronto, sono ____. **prohn**-toh **soh**-noh ____
My name is ____.	Mi chiamo ____. mee kee-**ah**-moh ____
My phone number is ____.	Il mio numero di telefono è ____. eel **mee**-oh **noo**-meh-roh dee teh-**leh**-foh-noh eh ____
Do you speak English?	Parla inglese? **par**-lah een-**gleh**-zay
Sorry, I speak only a little Italian.	Mi dispiace, parlo solo un po' d'italiano. mee dee-spee-**ah**-chay **par**-loh **soh**-loh oon poh dee-tah-lee-**ah**-noh
Speak slowly, please.	Parli lentamente, per favore. **par**-lee lehn-tah-**mehn**-tay pehr fah-**voh**-ray
Wait a moment.	Un momento. oon moh-**mehn**-toh

Italians answer a call by saying ***Pronto*** (Hello). They may ask ***Chi parla?*** (Who is speaking?)

In this book, you'll find the phrases you need to reserve a hotel room (page 82) or a table at a restaurant (page 107). To spell your name over the phone, refer to the code alphabet on page 15. To provide your phone number, see the numbers on page 24.

Mobile Phones

It's easy and convenient to use your US mobile phone in Europe. Alternatively, you can buy a phone when you get there.

mobile phone	cellulare cheh-loo-**lah**-ray
roaming	roaming **roh**-meen

text message	SMS **ehs**-ay-**ehm**-ay-**ehs**-ay
Where is a mobile-phone shop?	Dov'è un negozio di cellulari? doh-**veh** oon neh-**goht**-see-oh dee cheh-loo-**lah**-ree
I'd like to buy...	Vorrei comprare... voh-**reh**-ee kohm-**prah**-ray
...a (cheap) mobile phone.	...un cellulare (economico). oon cheh-loo-**lah**-ray (eh-koh-**noh**-mee-koh)
...a SIM card.	...una carta SIM. **oo**-nah **kar**-tah seem
(prepaid) credit	credito (prepagato) **kreh**-dee-toh (preh-pah-**gah**-toh)
calling time	durata della chiamata doo-**rah**-tah **deh**-lah kee-ah-**mah**-tah
contract	contratto kohn-**trah**-toh
locked / unlocked	bloccato / sbloccato bloh-**kah**-toh / zbloh-**kah**-toh
Is this phone unlocked?	Questo telefono è sbloccato? **kweh**-stoh teh-**leh**-foh-noh eh zbloh-**kah**-toh
Can you unlock this phone?	Può sbloccare questo telefono? pwoh zbloh-**kah**-ray **kweh**-stoh teh-**leh**-foh-noh
How do I...?	Come faccio a...? **koh**-may **fah**-choh ah
...make calls	...fare una chiamata **fah**-ray **oo**-nah kee-ah-**mah**-tah
...receive calls	...ricevere una chiamata ree-**cheh**-veh-ray **oo**-nah kee-ah-**mah**-tah
...send a text message	...mandare un SMS mahn-**dah**-ray oon **ehs**-ay-**ehm**-ay-**ehs**-ay

...check voicemail	...controllare i messaggi vocali kohn-troh-**lah**-ray ee meh-**sah**-jee voh-**kah**-lee
...set the language to English	...impostare in lingua inglese eem-poh-**stah**-ray een **leen**-gwah een-**gleh**-zay
...mute the ringer	...silenziare la suoneria see-lehnt-see-**ah**-ray lah swoh-neh-**ree**-ah
...change the ringer	...cambiare la suoneria kahm-bee-**ah**-ray lah swoh-neh-**ree**-ah
...turn it on	...accenderlo ah-chehn-**dehr**-loh
...turn it off	...spegnerlo spehn-**yehr**-loh

Buying a Mobile Phone SIM Card

The simplest solution is to roam with your US phone in Europe. If your phone is unlocked ***(sbloccato),*** you can save money by buying a cheap European SIM card at a mobile-phone shop or a newsstand.

Where can I buy...?	Dove posso comprare...? **doh**-vay **poh**-soh kohm-**prah**-ray
I'd like to buy...	Vorrei comprare... voh-**reh**-ee kohm-**prah**-ray
...a SIM card	...una carta SIM **oo**-nah **kar**-tah seem
...more calling time	...una ricarica **oo**-nah ree-**kah**-ree-kah
Will this SIM card work in my phone?	Questa carta SIM funziona per il mio telefono? **kweh**-stah **kar**-tah seem foont-see-**oh**-nah pehr eel **mee**-oh teh-**leh**-foh-noh
Which SIM card is best for my phone?	Qual'è la carta SIM migliore per il mio telefono? kwah-**leh** lah **kar**-tah seem meel-**yoh**-ray pehr eel **mee**-oh teh-**leh**-foh-noh

How much per minute for...?	Quanto costa al minuto per....? **kwahn**-toh **koh**-stah ahl mee-**noo**-toh pehr
...making...	...chiamare... kee-ah-**mah**-ray
...receiving...	...ricevere... ree-**cheh**-veh-ray
...domestic calls	...chiamate nazionali kee-ah-**mah**-tay naht-see-oh-**nah**-lee
...international calls	...chiamate internazionali kee-ah-**mah**-tay een-tehr-naht-see-oh-**nah**-lee
...calls to the US	...chiamare a gli Stati Uniti kee-ah-**mah**-ray ah lee **stah**-tee oo-**nee**-tee
How much to send a text message?	Quanto costa mandare un SMS? **kwahn**-toh **koh**-stah mahn-**dah**-ray oon **ehs**-ay-**ehm**-ay-**ehs**-ay
How much credit is included?	Quanto credito è incluso? **kwahn**-toh **kreh**-dee-toh eh een-**kloo**-zoh
Can I roam with this card in another country?	Con questa carta posso fare roaming in un altro paese? kohn **kweh**-stah **kar**-tah **poh**-soh **fah**-ray **roh**-meen een oon **ahl**-troh pah-**eh**-zay
Do you have a list of rates?	Avete una lista delle tariffe? ah-**veh**-tay **oo**-nah **lee**-stah **deh**-lay tah-**ree**-fay
How do I...?	Come si fa a...? **koh**-may see fah ah
...insert this into the phone	...inserire questo nel telefono een-seh-**ree**-ray **kweh**-stoh nehl teh-**leh**-foh-noh
...check my credit balance	...controllare il credito residuo kohn-troh-**lah**-ray eel **kreh**-dee-toh reh-**zee**-doo-oh
...buy more time	...comprare una ricarica kohm-**prah**-ray **oo**-nah ree-**kah**-ree-kah

...change the language to English	...impostare in lingua inglese eem-poh-**stah**-ray een **leen**-gwah een-**gleh**-zay

Ask the clerk to change the prompts and messages to English. When you run out of credit, you can top it up at newsstands, tobacco shops, mobile-phone stores, or many other businesses (look for your SIM card's logo in the window).

Hotel-Room Phones

prepaid international phone card	carta telefonica prepagata internazionale **kar**-tah teh-leh-**foh**-nee-kah preh-pah-**gah**-tah een-tehr-naht-see-oh-**nah**-lay
Can I call from my room?	Posso chiamare dalla mia camera? **poh**-soh kee-ah-**mah**-ray **dah**-lah **mee**-ah **kah**-meh-rah
How do I dial out?	Che numero faccio per chiamare fuori? kay **noo**-meh-roh **fah**-choh pehr kee-ah-**mah**-ray foo-**oh**-ree
How much per minute for...?	Quanto costa al minuto per...? **kwahn**-toh **koh**-stah ahl mee-**noo**-toh pehr
...local calls (in the city)	...chiamate urbane kee-ah-**mah**-tay oor-**bah**-nay
...domestic calls (elsewhere in Italy)	...chiamate interurbane kee-ah-**mah**-tay een-tehr-oor-**bah**-nay
...international calls	...chiamate internazionali kee-ah-**mah**-tay een-tehr-naht-see-oh-**nah**-lee
Can I dial this number for free?	Posso fare questo numero gratis? **poh**-soh **fah**-ray **kweh**-stoh **noo**-meh-roh **grah**-tees

Most hotels charge a fee for placing calls—ask for rates before you dial. You can use a prepaid international phone card—usually available at newsstands, tobacco shops, and train stations—to call out from your hotel. Dial the toll-free access number, enter the card's PIN code, then dial the number.

GETTING ONLINE

To get online in Europe, you can bring your own mobile device or use public computers (such as at a library or your hotel).

Internet Terms

Internet access	accesso all'Internet ah-**cheh**-soh ahl-**een**-tehr-neht
Wi-Fi	Wi-Fi **wee**-fee
email	email / posta elettronica "email" / **poh**-stah eh-leh-**troh**-nee-kah
computer	computer kohm-**poo**-tehr
username	username oo-zehr-**nah**-may
password	password "password"
network key	chiave di sicurezza kee-**ah**-vay dee see-koo-**rehd**-zah
secure network	rete sicura **reh**-tay see-**koo**-rah
website	sito Internet **see**-toh **een**-tehr-neht
download	scaricare skah-ree-**kah**-ray
print	stampare stahm-**pah**-ray
My email address is ___.	Il mio indirizzo email è ___. eel **mee**-oh een-dee-**reed**-zoh "email" eh ___
What's your email address?	Qual'è il suo indirizzo email? kwah-**leh** eel **soo**-oh een-dee-**reed**-zoh "email"

The ***www*** found at the beginning of most URLs is pronounced ***voo-voo-voo,*** and the dot is ***punto.***

Key Phrases: Getting Online

Where is a Wi-Fi hotspot?	Dov'è un hot spot Wi-Fi? doh-**veh** oon "hot spot" **wee**-fee
Where can I get online?	Dove posso connettermi all'Internet? **doh**-vay **poh**-soh koh-neh-**tehr**-mee ahl-**een**-tehr-neht
Can I check my email?	Posso controllare la mia email? **poh**-soh kohn-troh-**lah**-ray lah **mee**-ah "email"

Tech Support

Help me, please.	Mi aiuti, per favore. mee ah-**yoo**-tee pehr fah-**voh**-ray
How do I...?	Come faccio a...? **koh**-may **fah**-choh ah
...start this	...accendere questo ah-**chehn**-deh-ray **kweh**-stoh
...get online	...connettermi all'Internet koh-neh-**tehr**-mee ahl-**een**-tehr-neht
...get this to work	...farlo funzionare **far**-loh foont-see-oh-**nah**-ray
...stop this	...fermarlo fehr-**mar**-loh
...send this	...inviare questo een-vee-**ah**-ray **kweh**-stoh
...print this	...stampare questo stahm-**pah**-ray **kweh**-stoh
...make this symbol	...fare questo simbolo **fah**-ray **kweh**-stoh **seem**-boh-loh
...copy and paste	...fare copia e incolla **fah**-ray **koh**-pee-ah ay een-**koh**-lah
...type @	...fare la chiocciola **fah**-ray lah kee-**oh**-choh-lah

This isn't working.	Non funziona. nohn foont-see-**oh**-nah

For do-it-yourself tips, see "Italian Keyboards" on page 285.

Using Your Own Mobile Device

You can get online at hotels, cafés, train stations, TIs, and many other places. While Wi-Fi is often free, sometimes you'll have to pay.

laptop	portatile por-**tah**-tee-lay
tablet	tablet "tablet"
mobile phone	cellulare "cheh-loo-**lah**-ray"
Where is a Wi-Fi hotspot?	Dov'è un hot spot Wi-Fi? doh-**veh** oon "hot spot" **wee**-fee
Do you have Wi-Fi?	Avete la rete Wi-Fi? ah-**veh**-tay lah **reh**-tay **wee**-fee
What is the...?	Qual'è...? kwah-**leh**
...network name	...il network name eel "network" **nah**-may
...username	...lo username loh oo-zehr-**nah**-may
...password	...la password lah "password"
Do you have a...?	Avete un...? ah-**veh**-tay oon
Can I borrow a...?	Posso prendere in prestito un...? **poh**-soh **prehn**-deh-ray een **preh**-stee-toh oon
...charging cable	...cavo per la carica **kah**-voh pehr lah **kah**-ree-kah
...USB cable	...cavo USB **kah**-voh oo-**ehs**-ay-bee
Free?	Gratis? **grah**-tees
How much?	Quanto costa? **kwahn**-toh **koh**-stah
Do I have to buy something to use the Internet?	Devo comprare qualcosa per usare l'Internet? **deh**-voh kohm-**prah**-ray kwahl-**koh**-zah pehr oo-**zah**-ray **leen**-tehr-neht

Using a Public Computer

Some hotels have a computer in the lobby for guests to get online. Otherwise you may find a public computer at a library or TI.

Where can I get online?	Dove posso connettermi all'Internet? **doh**-vay **poh**-soh koh-**neh**-tehr-mee ahl-**een**-tehr-neht
May I use this computer to...?	Posso usare questo computer per...? **poh**-soh oo-**zah**-ray **kweh**-stoh kohm-**poo**-tehr pehr
...get online	...connettermi all'Internet koh-**neh**-tehr-mee ahl-**een**-tehr-neht
...check my email	...controllare la mia email kohn-troh-**lah**-ray lah **mee**-ah "email"
...download my photos	...scaricare le mie foto skah-ree-**kah**-ray lay **mee**-ay **foh**-toh
...print (something)	...stampare (qualcosa) stahm-**pah**-ray (kwahl-**koh**-zah)
boarding passes	carte d'imbarco **kar**-tay deem-**bar**-koh
tickets	biglietti beel-**yeh**-tee
reservation confirmation	conferma della prenotazione kohn-**fehr**-mah **deh**-lah preh-noh-taht-see-**oh**-nay
Free?	Gratis? **grah**-tees
How much (for... minutes)?	Quanto costa (per... minuti)? **kwahn**-toh **koh**-stah (pehr... mee-**noo**-tee)
...10	...dieci dee-**eh**-chee
...15	...quindici **kween**-dee-chee
...30	...trenta **trehn**-tah
...60	...sessanta seh-**sahn**-tah
I have a...	Ho un / una... oh oon / **oo**-nah
Do you have a...?	Avete un / una...? ah-**veh**-tay oon / **oo**-nah
...webcam	...webcam **web**-kahm
...headset	...cuffie **koo**-fee-ay

...USB cable	...cavo USB	**kah**-voh oo-**ehs**-ay-bee
...memory card	...memory card	"memory card"
...flash drive	...flash drive	"flash drive"
Can you switch the keyboard to English?	Può impostare la tastiera in inglese?	pwoh eem-poh-**stah**-ray lah tah-stee-**eh**-rah een een-**gleh**-zay

If you're using a public computer, the keyboard, menus, and on-screen commands will likely be designed for Italian speakers. Some computers allow you to make the Italian keyboard work as if it were an American one (look for the box in the lower right-hand corner of the screen to switch to English, or ask if it's possible).

Italian Keyboards

Italian keyboards differ from American ones. Here's a rundown of how major commands are labeled on an Italian keyboard:

YOU'LL SEE...	IT MEANS...	YOU'LL SEE...	IT MEANS...
Invio	Enter	**Fine**	End
↑	Shift	**Pag ↑**	Page Up
Canc.	Delete	**Pag ↓**	Page Down
←	Backspace	**Alt Gr**	Alternate Graphics
Ins	Insert		

The **Alt** key to the right of the space bar is actually a different key, called **Alt Gr** (for Alternate Graphics). Press this key to insert the extra symbol that appears on some keys (such as the # in the lower-right corner of the **à** key).

A few often-used keys look the same, but have different names in Italian:

@ symbol ("snail")	chiocciola	kee-**oh**-choh-lah
dot (.)	punto	**poon**-toh
hyphen (-)	trattino	trah-**tee**-noh
underscore (_)	linea bassa	**lee**-neh-ah **bah**-sah
slash (/)	barra	**bah**-rah

Italian speakers call the @ symbol ***chiocciola*** (snail). When saying an email address, you say ***chiocciola*** in the middle. You'll find the @ symbol next to the letter **L,** sharing space with **ç** and **ò.**

To type @, press **Alt Gr** and **ò** at the same time. If that doesn't work, try copy-and-pasting the @ sign from elsewhere on the page.

On Screen

YOU'LL SEE...	IT MEANS...	YOU'LL SEE...	IT MEANS...
Rete	Network	**Inserisci**	Insert
Tasto	Key	**Formato**	Format
Cartella	Folder	**Strumenti**	Tools
Documento	File	**Aiuto**	Help
Nuovo	New	**Opzioni**	Options
Aprire	Open	**Posta**	Mail
Chiudi	Close	**Messaggio**	Message
Salvare	Save	**Rispondere a tutti**	Reply to All
Stampare	Print	**CC**	CC
Cancellare	Delete	**Inoltra**	Forward
Cerca	Search	**Inviare**	Send
Modifica	Edit	**Ricevi**	Receive
Taglia	Cut	**Posta in arrivo**	Inbox
Copia	Copy	**Allega**	Attach
Incolla	Paste	**Caricare**	Upload
Visualizza	View	**Scaricare**	Download

HELP!

These phrases will help you in case of medical emergency, theft, loss, fire, or—if you're a woman—harassment. For any emergency service—ambulance, police, or fire—call **112** from a mobile phone or landline. Operators, who in most countries speak English, will deal with your request or route you to the right emergency service. If you're lost, see the phrases on page 76.

EMERGENCIES

Medical Help

Help!	Aiuto! ah-**yoo**-toh
Help me, please.	Mi aiuti, per favore. mee ah-**yoo**-tee pehr fah-**voh**-ray
emergency	emergenza eh-mehr-**jehnt**-sah
accident	incidente een-chee-**dehn**-tay
clinic / hospital	clinica / ospedale **klee**-nee-kah / oh-speh-**dah**-lay
Call...	Chiamate... kee-ah-**mah**-tay

Key Phrases: Help!

Help!	Aiuto! ah-**yoo**-toh
emergency	emergenza eh-mehr-**jehnt**-sah
clinic / hospital	clinica / ospedale **klee**-nee-kah / oh-speh-**dah**-lay
Call a doctor.	Chiamate un dottore. kee-ah-**mah**-tay oon doh-**toh**-ray
police	polizia poh-leet-**see**-ah
ambulance	ambulanza ahm-boo-**lahnt**-sah
thief	ladro **lah**-droh
Stop, thief!	Fermatelo! Ladro! fehr-**mah**-teh-loh **lah**-droh

...a doctor.	...un dottore. oon doh-**toh**-ray
...the police.	...la polizia. lah poh-leet-**see**-ah
...an ambulance.	...un'ambulanza. oon-ahm-boo-**lahnt**-sah
I / We need...	Ho / Abbiamo bisogno di... oh / ah-bee-**ah**-moh bee-**zohn**-yoh dee
...a doctor.	...un dottore. oon doh-**toh**-ray
...to go to the hospital.	...andare in ospedale. ahn-**dah**-ray een oh-speh-**dah**-lay
It's urgent.	È urgente. eh oor-**jehn**-tay
injured	ferito feh-**ree**-toh
bleeding	sanguinare sahn-gwee-**nah**-ray
choking	soffocare soh-foh-**kah**-ray
unconscious	svenuto zfeh-**noo**-toh
not breathing	non respira nohn reh-**spee**-rah
Thank you for your help.	Grazie dell'aiuto. **graht**-see-ay dehl-ah-**yoo**-toh
You are very kind.	Lei è molto gentile. **leh**-ee eh **mohl**-toh jehn-**tee**-lay

For other health-related words, see the Personal Care and Health chapter on page 305.

Theft and Loss

thief	ladro **lah**-droh
pickpocket	borseggiatore bor-seh-jah-**toh**-ray
police	polizia poh-leet-**see**-ah
embassy	ambasciata ahm-bah-**shah**-tah
Stop, thief!	Fermatelo! Ladro! fehr-**mah**-teh-loh **lah**-droh
Call the police!	Chiamate la polizia! kee-ah-**mah**-tay lah poh-leet-**see**-ah

I've been robbed.	Sono stato[a] derubato[a]. **soh**-noh **stah**-toh deh-roo-**bah**-toh
We've been robbed.	Siamo stati derubati. see-**ah**-moh **stah**-tee deh-roo-**bah**-tee
We've been robbed. (said by females)	Siamo state derubate. see-**ah**-moh **stah**-tay deh-roo-**bah**-tay
A thief took...	Un ladro ha preso... oon **lah**-droh ah **preh**-zoh
Thieves took...	I ladri hanno preso... ee **lah**-dree **ahn**-noh **preh**-zoh
I've lost my...	Ho perso il mio / la mia... oh **pehr**-soh eel **mee**-oh / lah **mee**-ah
We've lost our...	Abbiamo perso i nostri... ah-bee-**ah**-moh **pehr**-soh ee **noh**-stree
money	soldi **sohl**-dee
credit / debit card	carta di credito / debito **kar**-tah dee **kreh**-dee-toh / **deh**-bee-toh
passport	passaporto pah-sah-**por**-toh
ticket	biglietto beel-**yeh**-toh
railpass	tessera ferroviaria **teh**-seh-rah feh-roh-vee-**ah**-ree-ah
baggage	bagaglio bah-**gahl**-yoh
purse	borsa **bor**-sah
wallet	portafoglio por-tah-**fohl**-yoh
watch	orologio oh-roh-**loh**-joh
jewelry	gioielli joh-**yeh**-lee
camera	macchina fotografica **mah**-kee-nah foh-toh-**grah**-fee-kah
mobile phone	cellulare cheh-loo-**lah**-ray
iPod / iPad	iPod / iPad "iPod" / "iPad"
tablet	tablet "tablet"
computer	computer kohm-**poo**-tehr
laptop	portatile por-**tah**-tee-lay

faith in humankind	fiducia nel prossimo fee-**doo**-chah nehl **proh**-see-moh
I want to contact my embassy.	Vorrei contattare la mia ambasciata. voh-**reh**-ee kohn-tah-**tah**-ray lah **mee**-ah ahm-bah-**shah**-tah
I need to file a police report (for my insurance).	Devo fare una denuncia (per la mia assicurazione). **deh**-voh **fah**-ray **oo**-nah deh-**noon**-chah (pehr lah **mee**-ah ah-see-koo-raht-see-**oh**-nay)
Where is the police station?	Dov'è la questura? doh-**veh** lah kweh-**stoo**-rah

In addition to civilian cops, you may also see police clad in dark blue. They are members of Italy's military police, the ***Carabinieri***.

To replace a passport, you'll need to go in person to your embassy (see page 436). Cancel and replace your credit and debit cards by calling your credit-card company (as of this printing, these are the 24-hour US numbers that you can call collect: Visa—tel. 303/967-1096, MasterCard—tel. 636/722-7111, American Express—tel. 336/393-1111). If you'll want to submit an insurance claim for lost or stolen gear, be sure to file a police report, either on the spot or within a day or two. For more info, see www.ricksteves.com/help. Precautionary measures can minimize the effects of loss—back up your digital photos and other files frequently.

Fire!

fire	fuoco **fwoh**-koh
smoke	fumo **foo**-moh
exit	uscita oo-**shee**-tah
emergency exit	uscita d'emergenza oo-**shee**-tah deh-mehr-**jehnt**-sah
fire extinguisher	estintore eh-steen-**toh**-ray

Call the fire department.	Chiamate i vigili del fuoco. kee-ah-**mah**-tay ee **vee**-jee-lee dehl **fwoh**-koh

HELP FOR WOMEN

Whenever macho males threaten to make leering a contact sport, local women stroll arm-in-arm or holding hands. Wearing conservative clothes and avoiding smiley eye contact can help convey an "I'm not interested" message.

Generally the best way to react to unwanted attention is loudly and quickly.

No!	No! noh
Stop it!	La smetta! lah **zmeh**-tah
Enough!	Basta! **bah**-stah
Don't touch me.	Non mi tocchi. nohn mee **toh**-kee
Leave me alone.	Mi lasci in pace. mee **lah**-shee een **pah**-chay
Go away.	Se ne vada. say nay **vah**-dah
Get lost!	Sparisca! spah-**ree**-skah
Drop dead!	Crepi! **kreh**-pee
Police!	Polizia! poh-leet-**see**-ah

Safety in Numbers

If a guy is bugging you, approach a friendly-looking couple, family, or business for a place to stay safe.

A man is bothering me.	Un uomo mi sta importunando. oon **woh**-moh mee stah eem-por-too-**nahn**-doh
May I...?	Posso...? **poh**-soh
...join you	...unirmi a voi oo-**neer**-mee ah voy

...sit here	...sedermi qui seh-**dehr**-mee kwee
...wait here until he's gone	...aspettare qui finchè va via ah-speh-**tah**-ray kwee feen-**keh** vah **vee**-ah

You Want to Be Alone

I want to be alone.	Voglio stare sola. **vohl**-yoh **stah**-ray **soh**-lah
I'm not interested.	Non sono interessata. nohn **soh**-noh een-teh-reh-**sah**-tah
I'm married.	Sono sposata. **soh**-noh spoh-**zah**-tah
I'm waiting for my husband.	Sto aspettando mio marito. stoh ah-speh-**tahn**-doh **mee**-oh mah-**ree**-toh
I'm a lesbian.	Sono lesbica. **soh**-noh **lehz**-bee-kah
I have a contagious disease.	Ho una malattia contagiosa. oh **oo**-nah mah-lah-**tee**-ah kohn-tah-**joh**-zah

RENZACCI
RENZACCI
IMPORTANTE
IN QUESTA LAVANDERIA PER L'IGIENE DEI VOSTRI CAPI
AD OGNI LAVAGGIO VIENE USATO IL DISINFETTANTE
ANTIBATTERICO OZONIT ANCHE ALLE BASSE
TEMPERATURE REGISTRATO COME PRESIDIO
MEDICO CHIRURGICO PRESSO IL MINISTERO DELLA SANIT
(REG. N° 14160)
SEGUENDO LE ISTRUZIONI AVRETE IL VOSTRO BUCATO
IGIENICAMENTE LAVATO E ASCIUGATO IN 1 ORA CIRC

SERVICES

Whether you're getting a haircut, going to a spa, getting something fixed, or doing laundry, you'll find the phrases you need in this chapter.

HAIR AND BODY

At the Hair Salon

haircut	taglio di capelli **tahl**-yoh dee kah-**peh**-lee
Where is...?	Dov'è...? doh-**veh**
...a hair salon	...un parrucchiere oon pah-roo-kee-**eh**-ray
...a barber	...un barbiere oon bar-bee-**eh**-ray
...the price list	...il listino prezzi eel lee-**stee**-noh **prehd**-zee
I'd like...	Vorrei... voh-**reh**-ee
...a haircut.	...un taglio. oon **tahl**-yoh
...a shampoo.	...uno shampoo. **oo**-noh **shahm**-poo
...highlights.	...colpi di sole. **kohl**-pee dee **soh**-lay
...my hair colored.	...tingermi i capelli. teen-**jehr**-mee ee kah-**peh**-lee
...a permanent.	...una permanente. **oo**-nah pehr-mah-**nehn**-tay
...just a trim.	...solo una spuntatina. **soh**-loh **oo**-nah spoon-tah-**tee**-nah
How much?	Quanto costa? **kwahn**-toh **koh**-stah
Cut about this much off.	Tagli tanto cosi. **tahl**-yee **tahn**-toh **koh**-zee
Here. (gesturing)	Qui. kwee
Short.	Corti. **kor**-tee
Shorter.	Più corti. pew **kor**-tee
Shave it all off.	Rasati. rah-**zah**-tee
As long as possible.	Più lunghi possibile. pew **loon**-gee (hard "g") poh-**see**-bee-lay

Longer.	Più lunghi. pew **loon**-gee (hard "g")
long layers	lunghi e scalati **loon**-gee ay skah-**lah**-tee
bangs	frangia **frahn**-jah
Cut my bangs here.	Mi tagli la frangia qui. mee **tahl**-yee lah **frahn**-jah kwee
front	davanti dah-**vahn**-tee
top	sopra **soh**-prah
back	dietro dee-**eh**-troh
sides	lati **lah**-tee
sideburns	basette bah-**zeh**-tay
beard / moustache	barba / baffi **bar**-bah / **bah**-fee
hair color	colore koh-**loh**-ray
blonde / brown / black / red	biondo / bruno / nero / rosso bee-**ohn**-doh / **broo**-noh / **neh**-roh / **roh**-soh
Please touch up my roots.	Mi può ritoccare le radici. mee pwoh ree-toh-**kah**-ray lay rah-**dee**-chee
I'd like my hair...	Vorrei... voh-**reh**-ee
...blow-dried.	...una piega con il phon. **oo**-nah pee-**eh**-gah kohn eel fohn
...styled.	...piega. pee-**eh**-gah
...straightened (with a flat iron).	...lisci (con la piastra). **lee**-shee (kohn lah pee-**ah**-strah)
...wavy.	...ondulati. ohn-doo-**lah**-tee
I want to look like I just got out of bed.	Voglio un look da appena sveglia[o]. **vohl**-yoh oon look dah ah-**peh**-nah **svehl**-yah
hair gel	gel (per capelli) jehl (pehr kah-**peh**-lee)
hairspray	lacca (per capelli) **lah**-kah (pehr kah-**peh**-lee)
It looks good.	Sta bene. stah **beh**-nay
A tip for you.	Questo è per lei. **kweh**-stoh eh pehr **leh**-ee

At the Spa

spa	centro estetico **chehn**-troh eh-**steh**-tee-koh
spa treatment	trattamento estetico trah-tah-**mehn**-toh eh-**steh**-tee-koh
Where can I get a...?	Dove posso andare per un / una...? **doh**-vay **poh**-soh ahn-**dah**-ray pehr oon / **oo**-nah
I'd like a...	Vorrei un / una... voh-**reh**-ee oon / **oo**-nah
...massage	...massaggio mah-**sah**-joh
...manicure	...manicure mah-nee-**koo**-ray
...pedicure	...pedicure peh-dee-**koo**-ray
...facial	...trattamento viso trah-tah-**mehn**-toh **vee**-zoh
...wax	...ceretta cheh-**reh**-tah
eyebrows	delle sopracciglia **deh**-lay soh-prah-**cheel**-yah
upper lip	del labbro superiore dehl **lah**-broh soo-peh-ree-**oh**-ray
legs	delle gambe **deh**-lay **gahm**-bay
bikini	dell'inguine deh-**leen**-gwee-nay
Brazilian	brasiliana brah-zee-lee-**ah**-nah

Massage

massage	massaggio mah-**sah**-joh
Where can I get a massage?	Dove posso andare per un massaggio? **doh**-vay **poh**-soh ahn-**dah**-ray pehr oon mah-**sah**-joh
30 minutes / 1 hour / 90 minutes	trenti minuti / un'ora / novanti minuti **trehn**-tee mee-**noo**-tee / oon-**oh**-rah / noh-**vahn**-tee mee-**noo**-tee

How much?	Quanto costa? **kwahn**-toh **koh**-stah
More / less time on my...	Più / meno tempo... pew / **meh**-noh **tehm**-poh
...back.	...sulla schiena. **soo**-lah skee-**eh**-nah
...neck.	...sul collo. sool **koh**-loh
...shoulders.	...sulle spalle. **soo**-lay **spah**-lay
...head.	...sulla testa. **soo**-lah **teh**-stah
...arms.	...sulle braccia. **soo**-lay **brah**-chah
...hands.	...sulle mani. **soo**-lay **mah**-nee
...legs.	...sulle gambe. **soo**-lay **gahm**-bay
...feet.	...sui piedi. swee pee-**eh**-dee
It hurts.	Fa male. fah **mah**-lay
Ouch!	Ahi! **ah**-ee
Light / Medium / Firm pressure.	Pressione leggera / media / intensa. preh-see-**oh**-nay leh-**jeh**-rah / **meh**-dee-ah / een-**tehn**-sah
Less / More pressure.	Meno / Più pressione. **meh**-noh / pew preh-see-**oh**-nay
(Don't) stop.	(Non) si fermi. (nohn) see **fehr**-mee
That feels good.	È piacevole. eh pee-ah-**cheh**-voh-lay

REPAIRS

These handy lines can apply to various repairs, whether you tackle them yourself or go to a shop.

This is broken.	Questo è rotto. **kweh**-stoh eh **roh**-toh
Can I borrow...?	Posso prendere in prestito...? **poh**-soh **prehn**-deh-ray een **preh**-stee-toh
Do you have...?	Avete...? ah-**veh**-tay
screwdriver (Phillips / straight edge)	cacciavite (a stella / a taglio) kah-chah-**vee**-tay (ah **steh**-lah / ah **tahl**-yoh)

pliers	tenaglie tehn-**ahl**-yay
wrench	chiave inglese kee-**ah**-vay een-**gleh**-zay
hammer	martello mar-**teh**-loh
scissors	forbici **for**-bee-chee
needle	ago per cucire **ah**-goh pehr koo-**chee**-ray
thread	filo per cucire **fee**-loh pehr koo-**chee**-ray
string	spago **spah**-goh
duct tape	nastro adesivo **nah**-stroh ah-deh-**zee**-voh
Can you fix it?	Lo può riparare? loh pwoh ree-pah-**rah**-ray
Just do the essentials.	Faccia solamente le cose essenziali. **fah**-chah soh-lah-**mehn**-tay lay **koh**-zay eh-sehnt-see-**ah**-lee
How much?	Quanto costa? **kwahn**-toh **koh**-stah
When will it be ready?	Quando sarà pronta? **kwahn**-doh sah-**rah** **prohn**-tah
I need it by ____.	Ne ho bisogno entro ____. nay oh bee-**zohn**-yoh **ehn**-troh ____
Without it, I'm lost.	Senza sono perso. **sehnt**-sah **soh**-noh **pehr**-soh

LAUNDRY

Laundry Locator

Where is a...?	Dov'è una...? doh-**veh** **oo**-nah
...full-service laundry	...lavanderia lah-vahn-deh-**ree**-ah
...self-service laundry	...lavanderia self-service lah-vahn-deh-**ree**-ah sehlf-**sehr**-vees
Do you offer laundry service? (ask hotelier)	Avete un servizio lavanderia? ah-**veh**-tay oon sehr-**veet**-see-oh lah-vahn-deh-**ree**-ah

How much?	Quanto costa? **kwahn**-toh **koh**-stah
When does this open / close?	A che ora apre / chiude? ah kay **oh**-rah **ah**-pray / kee-**oo**-day

Full-Service Laundry

At some launderettes, you can pay extra to have the attendant wash, dry, and fold your clothes. Be sure to clearly communicate the time you will pick it up.

full-service laundry	lavanderia lah-vahn-deh-**ree**-ah
Same-day service?	Servizio in giornata? sehr-**veet**-see-oh een jor-**nah**-tah
By when do I need to drop off my clothes?	Quando devo portare qui i miei vestiti? **kwahn**-doh **deh**-voh por-**tah**-ray kwee ee mee-**eh**-ee veh-**stee**-tee
When will my clothes be ready?	Quando saranno pronti i miei vestiti? **kwahn**-doh sah-**rah**-noh **prohn**-tee ee mee-**eh**-ee veh-**stee**-tee
Could I get them sooner?	Li posso ritirare prima? lee **poh**-soh ree-tee-**rah**-ray **pree**-mah
Do you...?	Li...? lee
...dry them	...asciugate ah-shoo-**gah**-tay
...fold them	...piegate pee-eh-**gah**-tay
...iron them	...stirate stee-**rah**-tay
Please don't dry this.	Questo non va asciugato per favore. **kweh**-stoh nohn vah ah-shoo-**gah**-toh pehr fah-**voh**-ray
I'll come back...	Torno... **tor**-noh
...later today.	...oggi più tardi. **oh**-jee pew **tar**-dee
...tomorrow.	...domani. doh-**mah**-nee
...at ____ o'clock.	...alle ____. **ah**-lay ____

This isn't mine.	Questo non è mio. **kweh**-stoh nohn eh **mee**-oh
I'm missing a ___.	Manca un / una ___. **mahn**-kah oon / **oo**-nah ___

For a list of clothes and colors, see pages 262 and 265.

Self-Service Laundry

self-service laundry	lavanderia self-service lah-vahn-deh-**ree**-ah sehlf-**sehr**-vees
washer / dryer	lavatrice / asciugatrice lah-vah-**tree**-chay / ah-shoo-gah-**tree**-chay
soap	sapone sah-**poh**-nay
detergent	detersivo da bucato deh-tehr-**see**-voh dah boo-**kah**-toh
softener	ammorbidente ah-mor-bee-**dehn**-tay
stain remover	smacchiatore zmah-kee-ah-**toh**-ray
money	soldi / denaro **sohl**-dee / deh-**nah**-roh
token	gettone jeh-**toh**-nay
Help me, please.	Mi aiuti, per favore. mee ah-**yoo**-tee pehr fah-**voh**-ray
Where do I pay?	Dove pago? **doh**-vay **pah**-goh
I need change.	Ho bisogno di moneta. oh bee-**zohn**-yoh dee moh-**neh**-tah
How does this work?	Come funziona? **koh**-may foont-see-**oh**-nah
Where is the soap?	Dov'è il sapone? doh-**veh** eel sah-**poh**-nay
Where do I put the soap?	Dove va il sapone? **doh**-vay vah eel sah-**poh**-nay
This isn't working.	Questo non funziona. **kweh**-stoh nohn foont-see-**oh**-nah
How do I start this?	Come si avvia? **koh**-may see ah-**vee**-ah

How long will it take?	Quanto ci vuole? **kwahn**-toh chee **vwoh**-lay
Are these yours?	Sono suoi questi? **soh**-noh **swoh**-ee **kweh**-stee
This stinks.	Questo puzza. **kweh**-stoh **pood**-zah
Smells...	C'è odore... cheh oh-**doh**-ray
...like springtime.	...del profumo di primavera. dehl proh-**foo**-moh dee pree-mah-**veh**-rah
...like a locker room.	...di uno spogliatoio. dee **oo**-noh spohl-yah-**toh**-yoh
...like cheese.	...di formaggio. dee for-**mah**-joh
Hey there, what's spinning?	Salve, come gira? **sahl**-vay **koh**-may **jee**-rah

Don't begin a load too soon before closing time—or you might get evicted with a damp pile of partly washed laundry. Look for a sign telling you the last time you're allowed to start a load, such as ***ultimo lavaggio alle 20:00*** (last load at 8 p.m.).

Laundry Instructions Decoder

Many launderettes are unstaffed. Every launderette has clearly posted instructions, but they're not always in English. Use this decoder to figure things out.

instruzioni	instructions
lavatrice	washer
vestiti	clothes
caricare	load
lavare / asciugare	wash / dry
sapone / detersivo	soap / detergent
ammorbidente	softener
candeggina	bleach
liquido / in polvere	liquid / powder
vaschetta (per il detersivo)	reservoir (for adding soap)
a vostro rischio	at your own risk
caricare / inserire	insert (clothes) / insert (money)

moneta / gettone	coin / token
importo esatto	exact change required
no dà resto	no change given
aprire / chiudere oblò	open / close door
pulsante premere	press button
selezionare / conferma	choose / enter
inizio / programma	start / program
bianchi / colorati	whites / colors
delicati	delicates
caldo / tiepido / freddo	hot / warm / cold
in funzione	in use
prelavaggio / lavaggio	pre-wash / main wash cycle
centrifuga / risciacquo	spin / rinse cycle
asciugatrice	dryer
per ____ minuti di asciugatura	per ____ minutes of drying
scaricare	empty / remove
terminato	finished

Wash Temperatures

When choosing your wash cycle, you might see a series of numbers, such as:

45° / 90° / 55 m	whites
45° / 60° / 50 m	colors
45° / 45° / 40 m	permanent press / mixed
– / 30° / 30 m	warm
– / 17° / 25 m	cold / delicates

The first two numbers are the temperatures in Celsius for the pre-wash cycle and the main-wash cycle; the third number shows how many minutes the load takes. (For a rough conversion from Celsius to Fahrenheit, double the number and add 30.)

You'll likely buy drying time in small units (5- or 10-minute increments) rather than a full cycle. The choice of temperatures are ***basso*** (low and slow), ***medio*** (medium), and ***alto*** (high).

PERSONAL CARE AND HEALTH

This chapter will help keep you supplied with toiletries and guide you in getting treatment if you're not feeling well. Along with words for ailments, body parts, and medications, you'll find sections on eye and ear care, dental needs, reproductive health, women, babies, allergies, mental health, disabilities, and various medical conditions. For medical emergencies, see page 288 in the Help! chapter.

PERSONAL CARE

aftershave lotion lozione dopobarba
loht-see-**oh**-nay doh-poh-**bar**-bah

antiperspirant antitraspirante
ahn-tee-trah-spee-**rahn**-tay

breath mints mentine per l'alito
mehn-**tee**-nay pehr **lah**-lee-toh

cologne colonia koh-**loh**-nee-ah

comb pettine peh-**tee**-nay

conditioner balsamo bahl-**sah**-moh

dental floss filo interdentale
fee-loh een-tehr-dehn-**tah**-lay

deodorant deodorante deh-oh-doh-**rahn**-tay

face cleanser latte detergente
lah-tay deh-tehr-**jehn**-tay

facial tissue fazzoletto di carta
fahd-zoh-**leh**-toh dee **kar**-tah

fluoride rinse colluttorio al fluoro
koh-loo-**toh**-ree-oh ahl floo-**oh**-roh

hair dryer phon fohn

hairbrush spazzola per capelli
spahd-**zoh**-lah pehr kah-**peh**-lee

hand lotion crema per le mani
kreh-mah pehr lay **mah**-nee

hand sanitizer igienizzante per le mani
ee-jehn-eed-**zahn**-tay pehr lay **mah**-nee

lip balm	burro di cacao **boo**-roh dee kah-**kah**-oh
lip gloss	lucidalabbra loo-chee-dah-**lah**-brah
lipstick	rossetto roh-**seh**-toh
makeup	trucco **troo**-koh
mirror	specchio **speh**-kee-oh
moisturizer (with sunblock)	crema idratante (con protezione solare) **kreh**-mah ee-drah-**tahn**-tay (kohn proh-teht-see-**oh**-nay soh-**lah**-ray)
mouthwash	colluttorio koh-loo-**toh**-ree-oh
nail clippers	tagliaunghie tahl-yah-**oon**-gee-ay (hard "g")
nail file	limetta per unghie lee-**meh**-tah pehr **oon**-gee-ay (hard "g")
nail polish	smalto per le unghie **zmahl**-toh pehr lay **oon**-gee-ay (hard "g")
nail polish remover	solvente per le unghie sohl-**vehn**-tay pehr lay **oon**-gee-ay (hard "g")
perfume	profumo proh-**foo**-moh
Q-tips (cotton swabs)	cotton fioc **koh**-tohn fee-**ohk**
razor	rasoio rah-**zoh**-yoh
sanitary pads	assorbenti igienici ah-sor-**behn**-tee ee-**jehn**-ee-chee
scissors	forbici **for**-bee-chee
shampoo	shampoo **shahm**-poo
shaving cream	crema da barba **kreh**-mah dah **bar**-bah
soap	sapone sah-**poh**-nay
sunscreen	protezione solare proh-teht-see-**oh**-nay soh-**lah**-ray
suntan lotion	crema solare **kreh**-mah soh-**lah**-ray
tampons	assorbenti interni ah-sor-**behn**-tee een-**tehr**-nee
tissues	fazzoletti di carta fahd-zoh-**leh**-tee dee **kar**-tah

toilet paper	carta igienica **kar**-tah ee-**jehn**-ee-kah
toothbrush	spazzolino da denti spahd-zoh-**lee**-noh dah **dehn**-tee
toothpaste	dentifricio dehn-tee-**free**-choh
tweezers	pinzette peent-**seh**-tay

HEALTH

Throughout Europe, people with simple ailments go first to the pharmacist, who can diagnose and prescribe remedies. Pharmacists are usually friendly and speak English. If necessary, the pharmacist will send you to a doctor or a clinic.

Getting Help

Where is a...?	Dov'è...? doh-**veh**
...pharmacy (open 24 hours)	...una farmacia (aperta ventiquattro ore) **oo**-nah far-mah-**chee**-ah (ah-**pehr**-tah vehn-tee-**kwah**-troh **oh**-ray)
...clinic	...una clinica **oo**-nah **klee**-nee-kah
...hospital	...un ospedale oon oh-speh-**dah**-lay
I am sick.	Sto male. stoh **mah**-lay
He / She is sick.	Lui / Lei sta male. **loo**-ee / **leh**-ee stah **mah**-lay
I / We need a doctor...	Ho / Abbiamo bisogno di un dottore... oh / ah-bee-**ah**-moh bee-**zohn**-yoh dee oon doh-**toh**-ray
...who speaks English.	...che parli inglese. kay **par**-lee een-**gleh**-zay
Please call a doctor.	Per favore, chiami un dottore. pehr fah-**voh**-ray kee-**ah**-mee oon doh-**toh**-ray
Could a doctor come here?	Puo venire qua un dottore? pwoh veh-**nee**-ray kwah oon doh-**toh**-ray

Key Phrases: Health

I am sick.	Sto male. stoh **mah**-lay
I need a doctor (who speaks English).	Ho bisogno di un dottore (che parli inglese). oh bee-**zohn**-yoh dee oon doh-**toh**-ray (kay **par**-lee een-**gleh**-zay)
pain	dolore doh-**loh**-ray
It hurts here.	Fa male qui. fah **mah**-lay kwee
medicine	farmaco **far**-mah-koh
Where is a pharmacy?	Dov'è una farmacia? doh-**veh oo**-nah far-mah-**chee**-ah

It's urgent.	È urgente. eh oor-**jehn**-tay
ambulance	ambulanza ahm-boo-**lahnt**-sah
health insurance	assicurazione medica ah-see-koo-raht-see-**oh**-nay **meh**-dee-kah
Receipt, please.	La ricevuta, per favore. lah ree-cheh-**voo**-tah pehr fah-**voh**-ray

Ailments

I have...	Ho... oh
He / She has...	Lui / Lei ha... **loo**-ee / **leh**-ee ah
I need medicine for...	Mi serve un farmaco per... mee **sehr**-vay oon **far**-mah-koh pehr
bee sting	una puntura d'ape **oo**-nah poon-**too**-rah **dah**-pay
bites from...	puncture di... poonk-**too**-ray dee
...bedbugs	...cimici **chee**-mee-chee
...a dog	...un cane oon **kah**-nay

...mosquitoes	...zanzare	zahnt-**sah**-ray
...a spider	...un ragno	oon **rahn**-yoh
...a tick	...una zecca	**oo**-nah **zeh**-kah
blisters	le vesciche	lay **veh**-shee-kay
body odor	puzzo	**pood**-zoh
burn	una bruciatura	**oo**-nah broo-chah-**too**-rah
chapped lips	le labbra secche	lay **lah**-brah **seh**-kay
chest pains	un dolore al petto	oon doh-**loh**-ray ahl **peh**-toh
chills	i brividi	ee bree-**vee**-dee
cold	un raffreddore	oon rah-freh-**doh**-ray
congestion	una congestione	**oo**-nah kohn-jeh-stee-**oh**-nay
constipation	la stitichezza	lah stee-tee-**kehd**-zah
cough	la tosse	lah **toh**-say
cramps...	i crampi...	ee **krahm**-pee
...menstrual	...mestruali	meh-stroo-**ah**-lee
...muscle	...muscolari	moo-skoh-**lah**-ree
...stomach	...allo stomaco	**ah**-loh **stoh**-mah-koh
diarrhea	la diarrea	lah dee-ah-**reh**-ah
dizziness	i capogiri	ee kah-poh-**jee**-ree
earache	il mal d'orecchi	eel mahl doh-**reh**-kee
eczema	un eczema	oon ehk-**zeh**-mah
fever	la febbre	lah **feh**-bray
flu	l'influenza	leen-floo-**ehnt**-sah
food poisoning	l'avvelenamento da cibo	lah-veh-leh-nah-**mehn**-toh dah **chee**-boh
gas	l'aria nello stomaco	**lah**-ree-ah **neh**-loh **stoh**-mah-koh
hay fever	il raffreddore da fieno	eel rah-freh-**doh**-ray dah fee-**eh**-noh

headache	il mal di testa eel mahl dee **teh**-stah
heartburn	il bruciore di stomaco eel broo-**choh**-ray dee **stoh**-mah-koh
hemorrhoids	le emorroidi lay eh-moh-roh-**ee**-dee
hot flashes	le vampate di calore lay vahm-**pah**-tay dee kah-**loh**-ray
indigestion	un'indigestione oon-een-dee-jeh-stee-**oh**-nay
infection	un'infezione oon-een-feht-see-**oh**-nay
inflammation	un'infiammazione oon-een-fee-ah-maht-see-**oh**-nay
insomnia	l'insonnia leen-**soh**-nee-ah
lice	i pidocchi ee pee-**doh**-kee
lightheadedness	i capogiri ee kah-poh-**jee**-ree
migraine	l'emicrania leh-mee-**krah**-nee-ah
motion sickness (car)	il mal di macchina eel mahl dee **mah**-kee-nah
motion sickness (sea)	il mal di mare eel mahl dee **mah**-ray
nausea	la nausea lah **now**-zee-ah
numbness	l'intorpidimento leen-tor-pee-dee-**mehn**-toh
pain	il dolore eel doh-**loh**-ray
pimples	i foruncoli ee for-oon-**koh**-lee
pneumonia	la broncopolmonite lah brohn-koh-pohl-moh-**nee**-tay
pus	il pus eel poos
rash	l'irritazione della pelle lee-ree-taht-see-**oh**-nay **deh**-lah **peh**-lay
sinus problems	la sinusite lah see-noo-**zee**-tay
sneezing	gli starnuti lee star-**noo**-tee
sore throat	il mal di gola eel mahl dee **goh**-lah
splinter	una scheggia **oo**-nah **skeh**-jah

stomachache	il mal di stomaco eel mahl dee **stoh**-mah-koh
(bad) sunburn	una (brutta) scottatura solare **oo**-nah (**broo**-tah) skoh-tah-**too**-rah soh-**lah**-ray
swelling	un gonfiore oon gohn-fee-**oh**-ray
tendonitis	la tendinite lah tehn-dee-**nee**-tay
toothache	il mal di denti eel mahl dee **dehn**-tee
urinary tract infection	un'infezione urinaria oon-een-feht-see-**oh**-nay oo-ree-**nah**-ree-ah
urination (frequent / painful)	un'urinazione (frequente / dolorosa) oon-oo-ree-naht-see-**oh**-nay (freh-**kwehn**-tay / doh-loh-**roh**-zah)
vomiting	il vomito eel **voh**-mee-toh
wart	una verruca **oo**-nah veh-**roo**-kah
I'm going bald.	Perdo i capelli. **pehr**-doh ee kah-**peh**-lee

For major illnesses, see "Medical Conditions" on page 327.

It Hurts

pain	dolore doh-**loh**-ray
painful	doloroso doh-loh-**roh**-zoh
hurts	fa male fah **mah**-lay
It hurts here.	Fa male qui. fah **mah**-lay kwee
My ____ hurts. (body parts listed next)	Mi fa male il / la ____. mee fah **mah**-lay eel / lah ____
aching	dolorante doh-loh-**rahn**-tay
bleeding	sanguinare sahn-gwee-**nah**-ray
blocked	bloccato bloh-**kah**-toh
broken	rotto **roh**-toh
bruised	contuso kohn-**too**-zoh
chafing	irritazione ee-ree-taht-see-**oh**-nay
cracked	incrinato een-kree-**nah**-toh

fractured	fratturato frah-too-**rah**-toh
infected	infetto een-**feh**-toh
inflamed	infiammato een-fee-ah-**mah**-toh
punctured (rusty nail)	punto (chiodo arruginito) **poon**-toh (kee-**oh**-doh ah-roo-jee-**nee**-toh)
scraped	sbucciato zboo-**chah**-toh
sore	dolorante doh-loh-**rahn**-tay
sprained	distorsione dee-stor-see-**oh**-nay
swollen	gonfio **gohn**-fee-oh
weak	debole **deh**-boh-lay
diagnosis	diagnosi dee-**ahn**-yoh-zee
What can I do?	Cosa posso fare? **koh**-zah **poh**-soh **fah**-ray
Is it serious?	È grave? eh **grah**-vay
Is it contagious?	È contagioso? eh kohn-tah-**joh**-zoh

Body Parts

ankle	caviglia kah-**veel**-yah
appendix	appendice ah-pehn-**dee**-chay
arm	braccio **brah**-choh
back	schiena skee-**eh**-nah
bladder	vescica **veh**-shee-kah
blood	sangue **sahn**-gway
body	corpo **kor**-poh
bone	osso **oh**-soh
bowel movement	movimento intestinale moh-vee-**mehn**-toh een-teh-stee-**nah**-lay
brain	cervello chehr-**veh**-loh
breast	seno **seh**-noh
chest	petto **peh**-toh
ear	orecchio oh-**reh**-kee-oh

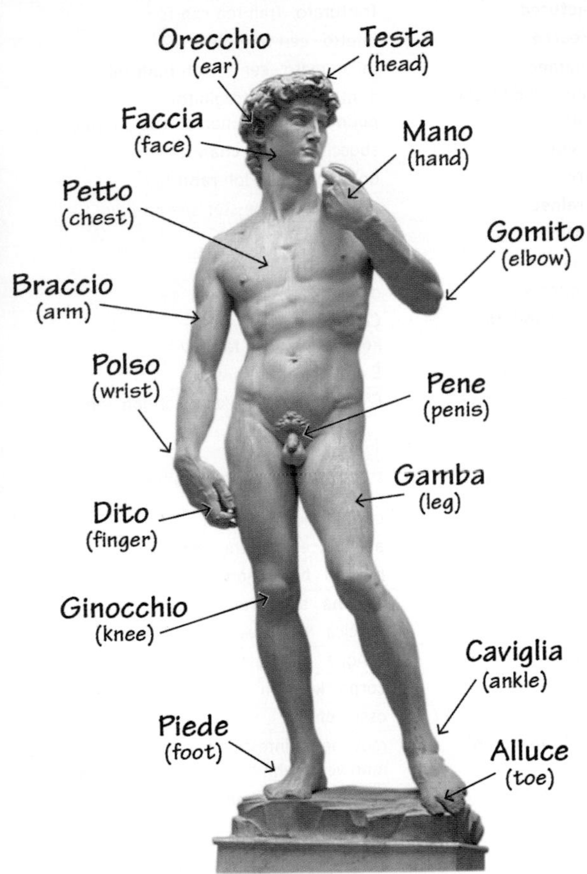
Orecchio
(ear)
Testa
(head)
Faccia
(face)
Mano
(hand)
Petto
(chest)
Gomito
(elbow)
Braccio
(arm)
Polso
(wrist)
Pene
(penis)
Gamba
(leg)
Dito
(finger)
Ginocchio
(knee)
Caviglia
(ankle)
Piede
(foot)
Alluce
(toe)

elbow	gomito **goh**-mee-toh
eye	occhio **oh**-kee-oh
face	faccia / viso **fah**-chah / **vee**-zoh
finger	dito **dee**-toh
fingernail	unghia **oon**-gee-ah (hard "g")
foot	piede pee-**eh**-day
hand	mano **mah**-noh
head	testa **teh**-stah
heart	cuore **kwoh**-ray
hip	anca **ahn**-kah
kidney	rene **reh**-nay
knee	ginocchio jee-**noh**-kee-oh
leg	gamba **gahm**-bah
lips	labbra **lah**-brah
liver	fegato feh-**gah**-toh
lung	polmone pohl-**moh**-nay
mouth	bocca **boh**-kah
muscles	muscoli **moo**-skoh-lee
neck	collo **koh**-loh
nose	naso **nah**-zoh
ovary	ovaia oh-**vah**-yah
penis	pene **peh**-nay
poop	pupu **poo**-poo
shoulder	spalla **spah**-lah
skin	pelle **peh**-lay
stomach	stomaco **stoh**-mah-koh
teeth	denti **dehn**-tee
testicles	testicoli teh-**stee**-koh-lee
throat	gola **goh**-lah
toe	alluce ah-**loo**-chay
toenail	unghia del piede **oon**-gee-ah (hard "g") dehl pee-**eh**-day

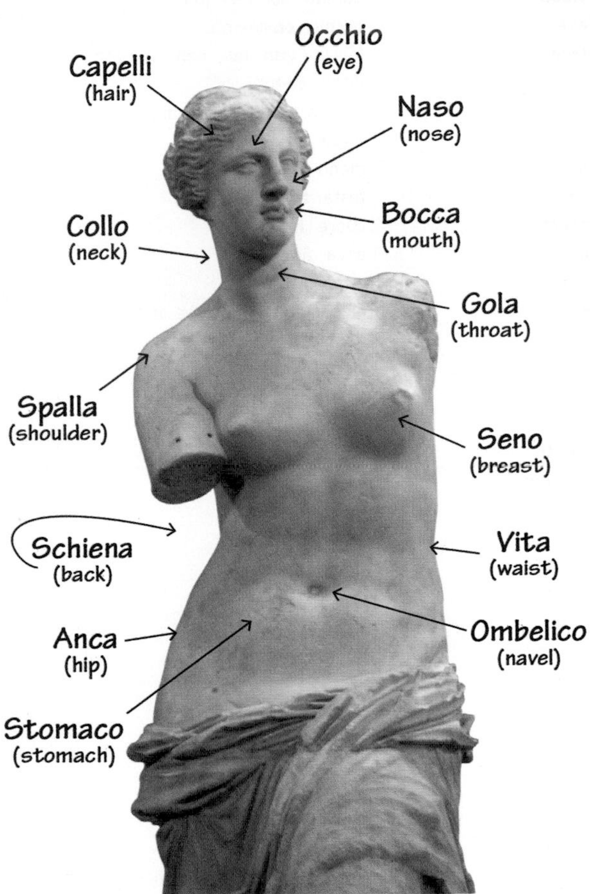
Capelli
(hair)
Occhio
(eye)
Naso
(nose)
Bocca
(mouth)
Collo
(neck)
Gola
(throat)
Spalla
(shoulder)
Seno
(breast)
Schiena
(back)
Vita
(waist)
Anca
(hip)
Ombelico
(navel)
Stomaco
(stomach)

tongue	lingua **leen**-gwah
urine	urina oo-**ree**-nah
uterus	utero **oo**-teh-roh
vagina	vagina vah-**jee**-nah
waist	vita **vee**-tah
wrist	polso **pohl**-soh
right / left	destro[a] / sinistro[a] **deh**-stroh / see-**nee**-stroh

First-Aid Kit and Medications

American name-brand medications are rare in Europe, but you'll find equally good local equivalents. Rather than looking for Sudafed, ask for a ***decongestionante*** (decongestant). Instead of Nyquil, request a ***farmaco per il raffreddore*** (cold medicine). For prescription drugs, ask your doctor for the generic name (for example, atorvastatin instead of Lipitor), which is more likely to be understood internationally. If using a European thermometer, see page 437 for help with temperature conversions.

medicine	farmaco **far**-mah-koh
pill	pillola pee-**loh**-lah
prescription	ricetta ree-**cheh**-tah
pharmacy	farmacia far-mah-**chee**-ah
24-hour pharmacy	farmacia aperta ventiquattro ore far-mah-**chee**-ah ah-**pehr**-tah vehn-tee-**kwah**-troh **oh**-ray
adult diapers (like Depends)	pannoloni pah-noh-**loh**-nee
antacid	antiacido ahn-tee-ah-**chee**-doh
anti-anxiety medicine	farmaco ansiolitico **far**-mah-koh ahn-see-oh-**lee**-tee-koh
antibiotic	antibiotici ahn-tee-bee-**oh**-tee-chee

antihistamine (like Benadryl)	antistaminico ahn-tee-stah-**mee**-nee-koh
aspirin	aspirina ah-spee-**ree**-nah
non-aspirin substitute (like Tylenol)	Saridon **sah**-ree-dohn
bandage	benda **behn**-dah
Band-Aids	cerotti cheh-**roh**-tee
cold medicine	farmaco per il raffreddore **far**-mah-koh pehr eel rah-freh-**doh**-ray
cough drops	caramelle per la tosse kah-rah-**meh**-lay pehr lah **toh**-say
decongestant (like Sudafed)	decongestionante deh-kohn-jeh-stee-oh-**nahn**-tay
diarrhea medicine	farmaco per la diarrea **far**-mah-koh pehr lah dee-ah-**reh**-ah
disinfectant	disinfettante dee-zeen-feh-**tahn**-tay
first-aid cream	pomata antistaminica poh-**mah**-tah ahn-tee-stah-**mee**-nee-kah
gauze / tape	garza / nastro **gart**-sah / **nah**-stroh
hemorrhoid medicine	farmaco per le emorroidi **far**-mah-koh pehr lay eh-moh-roh-**ee**-dee
hydrogen peroxide	acqua ossigenata **ah**-kwah oh-see-jeh-**nah**-tah
ibuprofen (like Advil)	ibuprofene ee-boo-proh-**feh**-nay
inhaler	inalatore een-ah-lah-**toh**-ray
insulin	insulina een-soo-**lee**-nah
itch reliever	pomata antiprurito poh-**mah**-tah ahn-tee-**proo**-ree-toh
laxative	lassativo lah-sah-**tee**-voh
moleskin (for blisters)	feltro / moleskin **fehl**-troh / "moleskin"
mosquito repellant	repellente per zanzare reh-peh-**lehn**-tay pehr zahnt-**sah**-ray

painkiller	analgesico ah-nahl-**jeh**-zee-koh
stomachache medicine	farmaco per il mal di stomaco **far**-mah-koh pehr eel mahl dee **stoh**-mah-koh
support bandage	fascia di sostegno **fah**-shah dee soh-**stehn**-yoh
syringe	siringa see-**reen**-gah
tetanus shot	antitetanica ahn-tee-teh-**tah**-nee-kah
thermometer	termometro tehr-moh-**meh**-troh
Vaseline	vaselina vah-zeh-**lee**-nah
vitamins	vitamine vee-tah-**mee**-nay
Does it sting?	Fa punture? fah poon-**too**-ray
Take one pill every ____ hours for ____ days.	Prenda una pillola ogni ____ ore per ____ giorni. **prehn**-dah **oo**-nah pee-**loh**-lah **ohn**-yee ____ **oh**-ray pehr ____ **jor**-nee

SPECIFIC NEEDS

The Eyes Have It

optician	ottico **oh**-tee-koh
eye / eyes	occhio / occhi **oh**-kee-oh / **oh**-kee
eye drops (for inflammation)	collirio koh-**lee**-ree-oh
artificial tears	lacrime artificiali **lah**-kree-may ar-tee-fee-chee-**ah**-lee
glasses	occhiali oh-kee-**ah**-lee
sunglasses	occhiali da sole oh-kee-**ah**-lee dah **soh**-lay
reading glasses	occhiali da lettura oh-kee-**ah**-lee dah leh-**too**-rah
glasses case	custodia per occhiali koo-**stoh**-dee-ah pehr oh-kee-**ah**-lee

(broken) lens	lenti (rotte) **lehn**-tee (**roh**-tay)
to repair	riparare ree-pah-**rah**-ray
replacement	sostituire soh-stee-**twee**-ray
prescription	ricetta ree-**cheh**-tah
contact lenses...	lenti a contatto... **lehn**-tee ah kohn-**tah**-toh
...soft	...morbide **mor**-bee-day
...hard	...dure **doo**-ray
all-purpose solution	liquido unico per lenti a contatto **lee**-kwee-doh **oo**-nee-koh pehr **lehn**-tee ah kohn-**tah**-toh
contact lens case	porta lenti a contatto **por**-tah **lehn**-tee ah kohn-**tah**-toh
I don't see well.	Non vedo bene. nohn **veh**-doh **beh**-nay
nearsighted	miope mee-**oh**-pay
farsighted	presbite prehs-**bee**-tay
20 / 20 vision	visione perfetto vee-zee-**oh**-nay pehr-**feh**-toh

All Ears

ear / ears	orecchio / orecchie oh-**reh**-kee-oh / oh-**reh**-kee-ay
right / left	destro / sinistro **deh**-stroh / see-**nee**-stroh
earache	mal d'orecchi mahl doh-**reh**-kee
ear infection	otite oh-**tee**-tay
ear wax (removal)	cerume (eliminare) cheh-**roo**-may (eh-lee-mee-**nah**-ray)
I don't hear well.	Non sento bene. non **sehn**-toh **beh**-nay
hearing aid	apparecchio acustico ah-pah-**reh**-kee-oh ah-**koo**-stee-koh
batteries	batterie bah-teh-**ree**-ay

Tooth Trouble

dentist	dentista dehn-**tee**-stah
tooth / teeth	dente / denti **dehn**-tay / **dehn**-tee
toothache	mal di denti mahl dee **dehn**-tee
braces	apparecchio ah-pah-**reh**-kee-oh
crown	capsula kahp-**soo**-lah
dentures	dentiera dehn-tee-**eh**-rah
filling	otturazione oh-too-raht-see-**oh**-nay
gums	gengive jehn-**jee**-vay
broken / cracked	rotto **roh**-toh
The filling / The tooth fell out.	È caduta l'otturazione / il dente. eh kah-**doo**-tah loh-too-raht-see-**oh**-nay / eel **dehn**-tay
Ouch! It hurts!	Ahi! Fa male! **ah**-ee / fah **mah**-lay

Dental products (such as dental floss) appear in the "Personal Care" list on page 306.

On Intimate Terms

personal lubricant (like KY Jelly)	lubrificante intimo loo-bree-fee-**kahn**-tay **een**-tee-moh
contraceptives	contraccettivi kohn-**trah**-cheh-tee-vee
condoms	preservativi preh-**zehr**-vah-tee-vee
birth-control pills	pillole anticoncezionali pee-**loh**-lay ahn-tee-kohn-cheht-see-oh-**nah**-lee
morning-after pill	pillola del giorno dopo pee-**loh**-lah dehl **jor**-noh **doh**-poh
herpes (inactive)	herpes (non attivo) **ehr**-pays (nohn ah-**tee**-voh)
HIV / AIDS	HIV / AIDS **ah**-kah-ee-vee / **ah**-eeds
STD (sexually transmitted disease)	MST (malattia sessualmente trasmissibile) **ehm**-ay-**ehs**-ay-tee (mah-lah-**tee**-ah seh-soo-ahl-**mehn**-tay trahs-mee-**see**-bee-lay)

For Women

menstruation / period	le mestruazioni lay meh-stroo-aht-see-**oh**-nee
tampons	assorbenti interni ah-sor-**behn**-tee een-**tehr**-nee
sanitary pads	assorbenti igienici ah-sor-**behn**-tee ee-**jehn**-ee-chee
I need medicine for...	Mi serve un farmaco per... mee **sehr**-vay oon **far**-mah-koh pehr
...menstrual cramps.	...i crampi mestruali. ee **krahm**-pee meh-stroo-**ah**-lee
...a yeast infection.	...un'infezione da candida. oon-een-feht-see-**oh**-nay dah **kahn**-dee-dah
...a urinary tract infection.	...un'infezione urinaria. oon-een-feht-see-**oh**-nay oo-ree-**nah**-ree-ah
I'd like to see...	Vorrei vedere... voh-**reh**-ee veh-**deh**-ray
...a female doctor.	...una dottoressa. **oo**-nah doh-toh-**reh**-sah
...a female gynecologist.	...una ginecologa. **oo**-nah jee-neh-**koh**-loh-gah
I've missed a period.	Ho saltato il ciclo mestruale. oh sahl-**tah**-toh eel **chee**-kloh meh-stroo-**ah**-lay
pregnancy test	test di gravidanza tehst dee grah-vee-**dahnt**-sah
ultrasound	ecografia eh-koh-grah-**fee**-ah
I am / She is... pregnant.	Sono / È incinta... **soh**-noh / eh een-**cheen**-tah
... ____ weeks / months	...di ____ settimane / mesi. dee ____ seh-tee-**mah**-nay / **meh**-zee

miscarriage	aborto spontaneo ah-**bor**-toh spohn-**tah**-neh-oh
abortion	aborto ah-**bor**-toh
menopause	menopausa meh-noh-**pow**-zah

For Babies

baby	neonato neh-oh-**nah**-toh
baby food	omogeneizzati oh-moh-jeh-nayd-**zah**-tee
backpack to carry baby	zaino per portare i neonati **zī**-noh pehr por-**tah**-ray ee neh-oh-**nah**-tee
bib	bavaglino bah-vahl-**yee**-noh
booster seat	seggiolino per neonati seh-joh-**lee**-noh pehr neh-oh-**nah**-tee
bottle	biberon **bee**-beh-rohn
breastfeeding	allattamento al seno ah-lah-tah-**mehn**-toh ahl **seh**-noh
Where can I breastfeed?	Dove posso allattare? **doh**-vay **poh**-soh ah-lah-**tah**-ray
car seat	seggiolino per la macchina seh-joh-**lee**-noh pehr lah **mah**-kee-nah
crib	culla **koo**-lah
diapers	pannolini pah-noh-**lee**-nee
diaper ointment	olio per neonati **oh**-lee-oh pehr neh-oh-**nah**-tee
diaper wipes	salviettine per neonati sahl-vee-eh-**tee**-nay pehr neh-oh-**nah**-tee
formula	latte in polvere per neonati **lah**-tay een **pohl**-veh-ray pehr neh-oh-**nah**-tee
high chair	seggiolone seh-joh-**loh**-nay

medication for...	farmaco per... **far**-mah-koh pehr
...diaper rash	...le dermatite da pannolino lay dehr-mah-**tee**-tay dah pah-noh-**lee**-noh
...ear infection	...l'otite loh-**tee**-tay
...teething	...la dentizione lah dehn-teet-see-**oh**-nay
nipple	capezzolo kah-pehd-**zoh**-loh
pacifier	ciuccio **choo**-choh
playpen	box bohks
stroller	passeggino pah-seh-**jee**-noh
Is it safe for children?	È sicuro per i bambini? eh see-**koo**-roh pehr ee bahm-**bee**-nee
He / She is ___ months / years old.	Lui / Lei ha ___ mesi / anni. **loo**-ee / **leh**-ee ah ___ **meh**-zee / **ahn**-nee
Will you refrigerate this?	Può metterlo in frigo? pwoh **meh**-tehr-loh een **free**-goh
Will you warm... for a baby?	Può riscaldare... per un neonato? pwoh ree-skahl-**dah**-ray... pehr oon neh-oh-**nah**-toh
...this	...questo **kweh**-stoh
...some water	...un po' d'acqua oon poh **dah**-kwah
...some milk	...un po' di latte oon poh dee **lah**-tay
Not too hot, please.	Non troppo caldo, per favore. nohn **troh**-poh **kahl**-doh pehr fah-**voh**-ray

Allergies

If you need to explain which specific food you're allergic to, look it up in this book's Menu Decoder, starting on page 187.

I am...	Sono... **soh**-noh
He / She is...	Lui / Lei è... **loo**-ee / **leh**-ee eh

...allergic to...	...allergico[a] a... ah-**lehr**-jee-koh ah
...gluten / wheat.	...glutine / frumento. gloo-**tee**-nay / froo-**mehn**-toh
...dairy products.	...latticini. lah-tee-**chee**-nee
...nuts.	...noci. **noh**-chee
...penicillin.	...pennicillina. peh-nee-chee-**lee**-nah
...pet fur.	...pelo di animali domestici. **peh**-loh dee ah-nee-**mah**-lee doh-**meh**-stee-chee
...pollen.	...polline. poh-**lee**-nay
...shellfish.	...crostacei. kroh-**stah**-cheh-ee
...sulfa.	...ai sulfamidici. ī sool-fah-**mee**-dee-chee
epipen	epipen (epinefrina) **eh**-pee-pehn (eh-pee-neh-**free**-nah)

Mental Health

anxiety	ansia **ahn**-see-ah
bipolar disorder	disturbo bipolare dee-**stoor**-boh bee-poh-**lah**-ray
confusion	confusione kohn-foo-zee-**oh**-nay
depression	depressione deh-preh-see-**oh**-nay
panic attacks	attacchi di panico ah-**tah**-kee dee **pah**-nee-koh
I feel suicidal.	Penso al suicidio. **pehn**-soh ahl swee-**chee**-dee-oh
I need...	Ho bisogno di... oh bee-**zohn**-yoh dee
...medicine to calm down.	...un farmaco per calmarmi. oon **far**-mah-koh pehr kahl-**mar**-mee
...to call home.	...chiamare casa. kee-ah-**mah**-ray **kah**-zah

...a psychologist.	...uno psicologo. **oo**-noh see-**koh**-loh-goh
...a psychiatrist.	...uno psichiatra. **oo**-noh see-kee-**ah**-trah

Disabilities

cane	bastone bah-**stoh**-nay
disabled	disabile dee-**zah**-bee-lay
elevator	ascensore ah-shehn-**soh**-ray
ramp	rampa **rahm**-pah
stairs	scale **skah**-lay
walker	deambulatore deh-ahm-boo-lah-**toh**-ray
wheelchair	sedia a rotelle **seh**-dee-ah ah roh-**teh**-lay
I am disabled.	Sono disabile. **soh**-noh dee-**zah**-bee-lay
He / She is disabled.	Lui / Lei è disabile. **loo**-ee / **leh**-ee eh dee-**zah**-bee-lay
Stairs are difficult / impossible.	Le scale sono difficili / impossibili. lay **skah**-lay **soh**-noh dee-**fee**-chee-lee / eem-poh-**see**-bee-lee
Do you have a fully adapted entrance / room?	Avete un ingresso per disabili / stanza attrezzata per disabili? ah-**veh**-tay oon een-**greh**-soh pehr dee-**zah**-bee-lee / **stahnt**-sah ah-trehd-**zah**-tah pehr dee-**zah**-bee-lee
Do you have an elevator?	Avete un ascensore? ah-**veh**-tay oon ah-shehn-**soh**-ray

MEDICAL CONDITIONS

If you have a condition that's not listed here, find out the Italian word and keep it handy.

I have...	Ho... oh
He / She has...	Lui / Lei ha... **loo**-ee / **leh**-ee ah
Alzheimer's disease	Alzheimers "Alzheimers"
arthritis	l'artrite lar-**tree**-tay
asthma	l'asma **lahs**-mah
cancer	il cancro eel **kahn**-kroh
cancer of the ____ (body parts listed earlier)	cancro al / alla ____ **kahn**-kroh ahl / **ah**-lah ____
leukemia	leucemia leh-oo-cheh-**mee**-ah
lymphoma	linfoma leen-**foh**-mah
I have been in remission for ____ months / years.	Sono in remissione da ____ mesi / anni. **soh**-noh een reh-mee-see-**oh**-nay dah ____ **meh**-zee / **ahn**-nee
chronic pain	dolore cronico doh-**loh**-ray **kroh**-nee-koh
diabetes	il diabete eel dee-ah-**beh**-tay
epilepsy	l'epilessia leh-pee-**leh**-see-ah
heart attack	infarto een-**far**-toh
heart condition	disturbi cardiaci dee-**stoor**-bee kar-dee-**ah**-chee
heart disease	malato di cuore mah-**lah**-toh dee **kwoh**-ray
I have a pacemaker.	Ho un pacemaker. oh oon "pacemaker"
high blood pressure	la pressione alta lah preh-see-**oh**-nay **ahl**-tah
high cholesterol	colesterolo alto koh-leh-steh-**roh**-loh **ahl**-toh
incontinence	incontinenza een-kohn-tee-**nehnt**-sah

multiple sclerosis	sclerosi multipla skleh-**roh**-zee **mool**-tee-plah
stroke	ictus **eek**-toos
Aging sucks.	Che schifo invecchiare. kay **skee**-foh een-veh-kee-**ah**-ray

CHATTING

When it comes time to connect with locals, these phrases can help you strike up a conversation, talk to children, chat about the weather, or ignite an Italian romance.

SMALL TALK

Introductions

My name is ____.	Mi chiamo ____. mee kee-**ah**-moh ____
What's your name?	Come si chiama? **koh**-may see kee-**ah**-mah
Pleased to meet you.	Piacere. pee-ah-**cheh**-ray
This is ____.	Le presento ____. lay preh-**zehn**-toh ____
How are you?	Come sta? **koh**-may stah
Very well, thanks.	Molto bene, grazie. **mohl**-toh **beh**-nay **graht**-see-ay

Key Phrases: Chatting

My name is ____.	Mi chiamo ____. mee kee-**ah**-moh ____
What's your name?	Come si chiama? **koh**-may see kee-**ah**-mah
Where are you from?	Di dove È? dee **doh**-vay eh
I'm from ____.	Sono di ____. (city) / Vengo da ____. (country) **soh**-noh dee ____ / **vehn**-goh dah ____
I like ____.	Mi piace ____. mee pee-**ah**-chay ____
Do you like ____?	Le piace ____? lay pee-**ah**-chay ____
I'm going to ____.	Vado a ____. **vah**-doh ah ____
Where are you going? (sing / pl)	Dove va? / Dove andate? **doh**-vay vah / **doh**-vay ahn-**dah**-tay
Happy travels!	Buon viaggio! bwohn vee-**ah**-joh

May I sit here?	Posso sedermi qui? **poh**-soh seh-**dehr**-mee kwee
May we sit here?	Possiamo sederci qui? poh-see-**ah**-moh seh-**dehr**-chee kwee
Where are you from?	Di dove È? dee **doh**-vay eh
What...?	Da che...? dah kay
...city	...città chee-**tah**
...country	...paese pah-**eh**-zay
...planet	...pianeta pee-ah-**neh**-tah
I'm from...	Vengo... **vehn**-goh
...America.	...dall'America. dahl-ah-**meh**-ree-kah
...Canada.	...dal Canada. dahl **kah**-nah-dah
I'm from ____. (city)	Sono di ____. **soh**-noh dee ____
Where are you going? (sing / pl)	Dove va? / Dove andate? **doh**-vay vah / **doh**-vay ahn-**dah**-tay
I'm going to ____.	Vado a ____. **vah**-doh ah ____
We're going to ____.	Andiamo a ____. ahn-dee-**ah**-moh ah ____

Nothing More than Feelings

I am / You are...	Sono / È... **soh**-noh / eh
He / She is...	Lui / Lei è... **loo**-ee / **leh**-ee eh
...happy.	...felice. feh-**lee**-chay
...sad.	...triste. **tree**-stay
...tired.	...stanco[a]. **stahn**-koh
...angry.	...arrabbiato[a]. ah-rah-bee-**ah**-toh
...jealous.	...geloso[a]. jeh-**loh**-soh
...lucky.	...fortunato[a]. for-too-**nah**-toh
I am...	Ho... oh
He / She is...	Lui / Lei ha... **loo**-ee / **leh**-ee ah
...hungry.	...fame. **fah**-may

...thirsty.	...sete. **seh**-tay
...too warm.	...troppo caldo. **troh**-poh **kahl**-doh
...cold.	...freddo. **freh**-doh
...homesick.	...nostalgia di casa. noh-stahl-**jee**-ah dee **kah**-zah
He / She is frustrated.	Lui / Lei si sente frustrato[a]. **loo**-ee / **leh**-ee see **sehn**-tay froo-**strah**-toh
I can't wait.	Non vedo l'ora. nohn **veh**-doh **loh**-rah

Who's Who

He is my / She is my...	Lui è mio / Lei è mia... **loo**-ee eh **mee**-oh / **leh**-ee eh **mee**-ah
friend (m / f)	amico / amica ah-**mee**-koh / ah-**mee**-kah
boyfriend / girlfriend	ragazzo / ragazza rah-**gahd**-zoh / rah-**gahd**-zah
husband / wife	marito / moglie mah-**ree**-toh / **mohl**-yay
son / daughter	figlio / figlia **feel**-yoh / **feel**-yah
brother / sister	fratello / sorella frah-**teh**-loh / soh-**reh**-lah
father / mother	padre / madre **pah**-dray / **mah**-dray
uncle / aunt	zio / zia **tsee**-oh / **tsee**-ah
nephew / niece	nipote nee-**poh**-tay
cousin (m / f)	cugino / cugina koo-**jee**-noh / koo-**jee**-nah
grandfather / grandmother	nonno / nonna **noh**-noh / **noh**-nah
grandchild	nipote nee-**poh**-tay
great-____	bis-____ bees-____

Italians use the same word—***nipote***—to mean a nephew, niece, or grandchild (boy or girl).

Family Matters

Are you...?	È...? eh
I am / We are...	Sono / Siamo... **soh**-noh / see-**ah**-moh
...married (sing / pl)	...sposato[a] / sposati spoh-**zah**-toh / spoh-**zah**-tee
...engaged (sing / pl)	...fidanzato[a] / fidanzati fee-dahnt-**sah**-toh / fee-dahnt-**sah**-tee
...friends	...amici ah-**mee**-chee
...a couple	...una coppia **oo**-nah **koh**-pee-ah
Do you have...?	Ha...? ah
I have / We have...	Ho / Abbiamo... oh / ah-bee-**ah**-moh
...children	...figli **feel**-yee
...grandchildren	...nipoti nee-**poh**-tee
...photos	...foto **foh**-toh
boy / girl	ragazzo / ragazza rah-**gahd**-zoh / rah-**gahd**-zah
How many boys and girls?	Quanti maschi e femmine? **kwahn**-tee **mah**-skee ay **feh**-mee-nay
Beautiful boy!	Che bel bambino! kay behl bahm-**bee**-noh
Beautiful girl!	Che bella bambina! kay **beh**-lah bahm-**bee**-nah
Beautiful children!	Che bei bambini! kay **beh**-ee bahm-**bee**-nee
How old is your child?	Quanti anni ha il suo bambino? **kwahn**-tee **ahn**-nee ah eel **soo**-oh bahm-**bee**-noh
age / ages	età eh-**tah**
grown-up children	figli grandi **feel**-yee **grahn**-dee

Chatting with Children

What's your name?	Come ti chiami? **koh**-may tee kee-**ah**-mee
My name is ____.	Mi chiamo ____. mee kee-**ah**-moh ____
How old are you?	Quanti anni hai? **kwahn**-tee **ahn**-nee ī
How old am I?	Quanti anni ho? **kwahn**-tee **ahn**-nee oh
I'm ____ years old.	Ho ____ anni. oh ____ **ahn**-nee
Do you have brothers and sisters?	Hai fratelli e sorelle? ī frah-**teh**-lee ay soh-**reh**-lay
Do you like school?	Ti piace la scuola? tee pee-**ah**-chay lah **skwoh**-lah
What are you studying?	Che cosa stai studiando? kay **koh**-zah stī stoo-dee-**ahn**-doh
What's your favorite subject?	Qual'è la tua materia preferita? kwah-**leh** lah **too**-ah mah-**teh**-ree-ah preh-feh-**ree**-tah
Will you teach me / us some Italian words?	Mi / Ci insegni delle parole in italiano? mee / chee een-**sehn**-yee **deh**-lay pah-**roh**-lay een ee-tah-lee-**ah**-noh
Do you have pets?	Hai animali domestici? ī ah-nee-**mah**-lee doh-**meh**-stee-chee
I have / We have a...	Ho / Abbiamo un... oh / ah-bee-**ah**-moh oon
...cat / dog / fish / bird.	...gatto / cane / pesce / uccello. **gah**-toh / **kah**-nay / **peh**-shay / oo-**cheh**-loh
Gimme five.	Dammi il cinque. **dah**-mee eel **cheen**-kway

Linguistically speaking, a ***bambino*** becomes a ***ragazzo*** at about age 10.

Work

What is your job?	Che lavoro fa? kay lah-**voh**-roh fah
Do you like your work?	Le piace il suo lavoro? lay pee-**ah**-chay eel **soo**-oh lah-**voh**-roh
I am...	Sono... **soh**-noh
...retired.	...in pensione. een pehn-see-**oh**-nay
...unemployed.	...disoccupato[a]. dee-zoh-koo-**pah**-toh
...a student. (m / f)	...uno studente / una studentessa. **oo**-noh stoo-**dehn**-tay / **oo**-nah stoo-dehn-**teh**-sah
...a professional traveler.	...turista di professione. too-**ree**-stah dee proh-feh-see-**oh**-nay
I'm studying to work in...	Studio per lavorare... **stoo**-dee-oh pehr lah-voh-**rah**-ray
I work in...	Lavoro... lah-**voh**-roh
I used to work in...	Lavoravo... lah-voh-**rah**-voh
I want a job in...	Vorrei un lavoro... voh-**reh**-ee oon lah-**voh**-roh
accounting	nella contabilità **neh**-lah kohn-tah-bee-lee-**tah**
the arts	nel campo artistico nehl **kahm**-poh ar-**tee**-stee-koh
banking	nel settore bancario nehl seh-**toh**-ray bahn-**kah**-ree-oh
business	in un'azienda een oon-aht-see-**ehn**-dah
construction	nell'edilizia neh-leh-dee-**leet**-see-ah
engineering	nell'ingegneria neh-leen-jehn-yeh-**ree**-ah
a factory	in una fabbrica een **oo**-nah **fah**-bree-kah
government	nel governo nehl goh-**vehr**-noh
information technology	nel campo informatico nehl **kahm**-poh een-for-**mah**-tee-koh
journalism	nel giornalismo nehl jor-nah-**leez**-moh

the legal profession	nel campo legale nehl **kahm**-poh leh-**gah**-lay
the medical field	nel campo medico nehl **kahm**-poh **meh**-dee-koh
the military	sono nell'esercito **soh**-noh neh-leh-**zehr**-chee-toh
public relations	nelle relazioni pubbliche **neh**-lay reh-laht-see-**oh**-nee **poo**-blee-kay
a restaurant	in un ristorante een oon ree-stoh-**rahn**-tay
science	nel campo scientifico nehl **kahm**-poh shehn-**tee**-fee-koh
social services	nell'assistenza sociale neh-lah-see-**stehnt**-sah soh-**chah**-lay
a store	in un negozio een oon neh-**goht**-see-oh
teaching	come insegnante **koh**-may een-sehn-**yahn**-tay
the travel industry	nel settore turistico nehl seht-**toh**-ray too-**ree**-stee-koh

If you've been chatting with someone who's working, you can bid farewell by saying ***Buon lavoro!*** (Be happy in your work!).

Travel Talk

I am / Are you...?	Sono / È...? **soh**-noh / eh
...on vacation	...in vacanza een vah-**kahnt**-sah
...on business	...qui per lavoro kwee pehr lah-**voh**-roh
How long have you been traveling?	Da quanto tempo è in viaggio? dah **kwahn**-toh **tehm**-poh eh een vee-**ah**-joh
days / weeks	giorni / settimane **jor**-nee / seh-tee-**mah**-nay
months / years	mesi / anni **meh**-zee / **ahn**-nee
When are you going home?	Quando ritorna a casa? **kwahn**-doh ree-**tor**-nah ah **kah**-zah

This is my / our first time in ___.	Questa è la mia / nostra prima volta in ___. **kweh**-stah eh lah **mee**-ah / **noh**-strah **pree**-mah **vohl**-tah een ___
It's (not) a tourist trap.	(Non) è una trappola per turisti. (nohn) eh **oo**-nah **trah**-poh-lah pehr too-**ree**-stee
This is paradise.	Questo è il paradiso. **kweh**-stoh eh eel pah-rah-**dee**-zoh
This is a wonderful country.	Questo è un paese meraviglioso. **kweh**-stoh eh oon pah-**eh**-zay meh-rah-veel-**yoh**-zoh
The Italians are friendly / rude.	Gli italiani sono amichevoli / maleducati. lee ee-tah-lee-**ah**-nee **soh**-noh ah-mee-**keh**-voh-lee / mah-leh-doo-**kah**-tee
What is your favorite...?	Qual'è il tuo... preferito? kwah-**leh** eel **too**-oh... preh-feh-**ree**-toh
...country	...paese pah-**eh**-zay
...place	...posto **poh**-stoh
What's your favorite city?	Qual'è la tua città preferita? kwah-**leh** lah **too**-ah chee-**tah** preh-feh-**ree**-tah
My favorite is ___. (m / f)	Il mio / La mia preferito[a] è ___. eel **mee**-oh / lah **mee**-ah preh-feh-**ree**-toh eh ___
I've traveled / We've traveled to ___.	Sono stato[a] / Siamo stati[e] a ___. **soh**-noh **stah**-toh / see-**ah**-moh **stah**-tee ah ___
Next I'll go / we'll go to ___.	Poi andrò / andremo a ___. **poh**-ee ahn-**droh** / ahn-**dreh**-moh ah ___
I'd like / We'd like...	Vorrei / Vorremmo... voh-**reh**-ee / voh-**reh**-moh
...to go to ___.	...andare a ___. ahn-**dah**-ray ah ___
...to return to ___.	...tornare a ___. tor-**nah**-ray ah ___

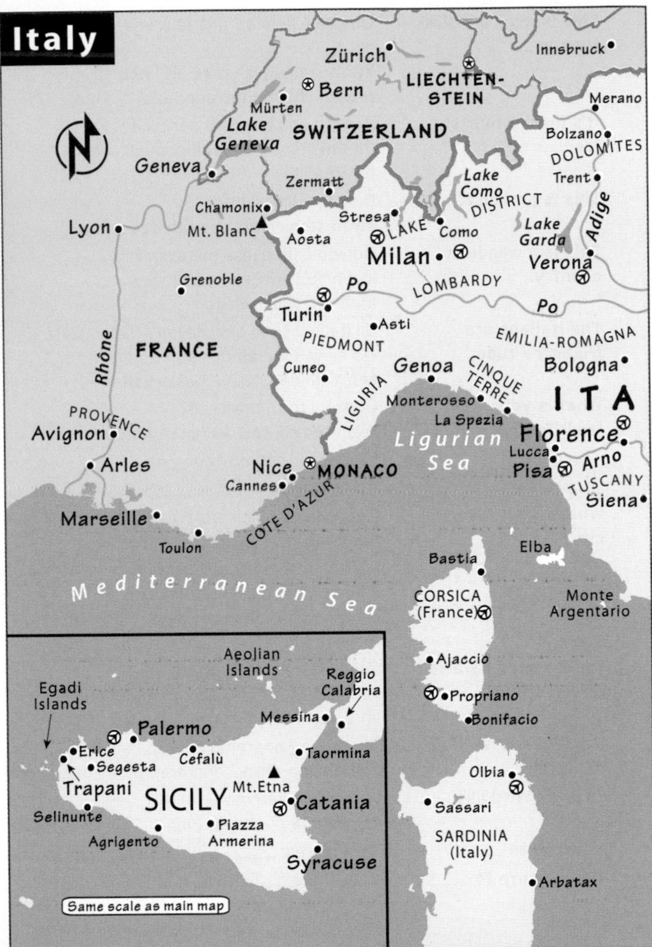
Italy
Zürich
Bern
LIECHTENSTEIN
Innsbruck
Merano
Mürten
Lake Geneva
SWITZERLAND
Bolzano
DOLOMITES
Geneva
Zermatt
Lake Como
DISTRICT
Trent
Chamonix
Mt. Blanc
Stresa
LAKE
Como
Lake Garda
Adige
Lyon
Aosta
Milan
Verona
Grenoble
Po
LOMBARDY
Turin
Po
Asti
PIEDMONT
EMILIA-ROMAGNA
Rhône
FRANCE
Cuneo
Genoa
CINQUE TERRE
Bologna
LIGURIA
Monterosso
ITA
PROVENCE
La Spezia
Avignon
Ligurian Sea
Florence
Lucca
Arles
Nice
MONACO
Pisa
Arno
Cannes
TUSCANY
Siena
Marseille
COTE D'AZUR
Toulon
Elba
Bastia
Mediterranean Sea
CORSICA (France)
Monte Argentario
Ajaccio
Propriano
Bonifacio
Aeolian Islands
Reggio Calabria
Egadi Islands
Messina
Palermo
Erice
Cefalù
Taormina
Segesta
Trapani
Mt.Etna
SICILY
Catania
Selinunte
Piazza Armerina
Agrigento
Syracuse
Same scale as main map
Olbia
Sassari
SARDINIA (Italy)
Arbatax

AUSTRIA
Graz
Lienz
HUNGARY
Pécs
Danube
Lake Bled
Ljubljana
FRIULI
Udine
SLOVENIA
Zagreb
SERBIA
VENETO
Trieste
CROATIA
Padua
Venice
ISTRIA
Ferrara
BOSNIA & HERZOGOVINA
Ravenna
Zadar
Sarajevo
Rimini
L Y
SAN MARINO
Urbino
Split
Mostar
LE MARCHE
Ancona
Loreto
Cortona
Hvar
MONTE-NEGRO
Perugia
Assisi
Adriatic Sea
DALMATIAN COAST
Dubrovnik
UMBRIA
Orvieto
Kotor
Tiber
ABRUZZO
Pescara
Gargano Peninsula
LAZIO
50 Kilometers
50 Miles
MOLISE
Vieste
Rome
Isernia
Foggia
Anzio
Bari
CAMPANIA
PUGLIA
Formia
Alberobello
Mt. Vesuvius
BASILICATA
Naples
Brindisi
Pompeii
Potenza
Matera
Sorrento
Lecce
Capri
AMALFI COAST
Paestum
Tyrrhenian Sea
CALABRIA
Ionian Sea
To Sicily (See Detail Map)
Cosenza

Europe
200 Kilometers
200 Miles
Bergen
SCOTLAND
Belfast
Edinburgh
N. IRE.
North Sea
Galway
Dublin
York
ENGLAND
IRELAND
Dingle Peninsula
WALES
Cardiff
NETH.
Amsterdam
London
Bath
Bruges
Brussels
BELG.
Mont St-Michel
NORMANDY
LUX.
Paris
ALSACE
Atlantic Ocean
BRITTANY
LOIRE
Colmar
FRANCE
SWITZ.
Chamonix
DORDOGNE
Lyon
PROVENCE
Santiago de Compostela
San Sebastián
Monaco
Arles
Carcassonne
Nice
Andorra
Porto
Salamanca
PORTUGAL
Barcelona
Nazaré
Madrid
Lisbon
Toledo
SPAIN
Córdoba
Sevilla
Granada
Mediterranean
ALGARVE
ANDALUCÍA
Algiers
Tangier
Gibraltar (UK)
ALGERIA
MOROCCO

FINLAND
Helsinki
Turku
NORWAY
Oslo
SWEDEN
Stockholm
Tallinn
ESTONIA
Baltic Sea
RUSSIA
LATVIA
Riga
To Moscow →
DENMARK
Copenhagen
LITHUANIA
RUSS.
Vilnius
Minsk
Gdansk
Hamburg
POLAND
BELARUS
Berlin
Warsaw
GERMANY
Kiev
RHINE VALLEY
Prague
Kraków
Frankfurt
CZECH REP.
UKRAINE
SLOVAK.
Munich
BAVARIA
Vienna
Brat.
MOL.
Salzburg
Budapest
Bern
TIROL
AUST.
HUNG.
ROMANIA
DOLOMITES
SLOV.
Milan
CROATIA
Belgrade
Bucharest
Black Sea
CINQUE TERRE
Venice
Zag.
BOSNIA-HERZ.
Sara.
SERBIA
Florence
Mostar
Sofia
TUSCANY
Dubrovnik
SAN MARINO
MONT.
KOS.
BULGARIA
CORSICA (FRANCE)
Istanbul
Rome
Adriatic Sea
MAC.
ITALY
ALB.
Naples
SARDINIA (ITALY)
TURKEY
AMALFI COAST
GREECE
CORFU
Athens
Sea
SICILY
PELOPONNESE
TUNISIA
CRETE

My / Our vacation is ____ days long.	La mia / La nostra vacanza dura ____ giorni. lah **mee**-ah / lah **noh**-strah vah-**kahnt**-sah **doo**-rah ____ **jor**-nee
Travel is enlightening.	Viaggiare apre la mente. vee-ah-**jah**-ray **ah**-pray lah **mehn**-tay
I wish all (American) politicians traveled.	Vorrei che tutti i politici (americani) viaggiassero. voh-**reh**-ee kay **too**-tee ee poh-**lee**-tee-chee (ah-meh-ree-**kah**-nee) vee-ah-**jah**-seh-roh
Happy travels!	Buon viaggio! bwohn vee-**ah**-joh
Keep on travelin'! (sing / pl)	Continua / Continuate a viaggiare! kohn-**tee**-noo-ah / kohn-tee-noo-**ah**-tay ah vee-ah-**jah**-ray

Staying in Touch

What is your...?	Qual'è il tuo...? kwah-**leh** eel **too**-oh
Here is my...	Ecco il mio... **eh**-koh eel **mee**-oh
...email address	...indirizzo email een-dee-**reed**-zoh "email"
...street address	...indirizzo een-dee-**reed**-zoh
...phone number	...numero di telefono **noo**-meh-roh dee teh-**leh**-foh-noh
I am / Are you on Facebook?	Sono / Sei su Facebook? **soh**-noh / **seh**-ee soo "Facebook"

Weather

Is it going to rain...?	Pioverà...? pee-oh-veh-**rah**
What will the weather be like...?	Come sarà il tempo...? **koh**-may sah-**rah** eel **tehm**-poh

...today	...oggi **oh**-jee
...tomorrow	...domani doh-**mah**-nee
cloudy	nuvoloso noo-voh-**loh**-zoh
cold	freddo **freh**-doh
cool	fresco **freh**-skoh
foggy	nebbioso neh-bee-**oh**-zoh
hot / warm	caldo **kahl**-doh
icy	ghiacciato gee-ah-**chah**-toh (hard "g")
muggy	umido **oo**-mee-doh
rainy	piovoso pee-oh-**voh**-zoh
snow	neve **neh**-vay
stormy	perturbato pehr-toor-**bah**-toh
sunny	bello **beh**-loh
windy	ventoso vehn-**toh**-zoh
Like today?	Come oggi? **koh**-may **oh**-jee
Should I bring a jacket / an umbrella?	Devo portare una giacca / un ombrello? **deh**-voh por-**tah**-ray **oo**-nah **jah**-kah / oon ohm-**breh**-loh
A rainbow!	Un arcobaleno! oon ar-koh-bah-**leh**-noh

To figure out temperature conversions, see page 437.

Thanks a Million

Thank you very much.	Molte grazie. **mohl**-tay **graht**-see-ay
A thousand thanks.	Grazie mille. **graht**-see-ay **mee**-lay
This is great fun.	È un vero divertimento. eh oon **veh**-roh dee-vehr-tee-**mehn**-toh
You are...	Lei è... **leh**-ee eh
...kind.	...gentile. jehn-**tee**-lay
...helpful.	...di aiuto. dee ah-**yoo**-toh

...wonderful.	...meraviglioso[a]. meh-rah-veel-**yoh**-zoh
...generous.	...generoso[a]. jeh-neh-**roh**-zoh
You've been a great help.	Lei è di grande aiuto. **leh**-ee eh dee **grahn**-day ah-**yoo**-toh
I'll remember you...	Mi ricorderò di lei... mee ree-kor-deh-**roh** dee **leh**-ee
...always.	...sempre. **sehm**-pray
...till Tuesday.	...fino a martedì. **fee**-noh ah mar-teh-**dee**

Responses for All Occasions

I / We like that.	Mi / Ci piace. mee / chee pee-**ah**-chay
I / We like you.	Lei mi / ci piace. **leh**-ee mee / chee pee-**ah**-chay
I trust you.	Mi fido di lei. mee **fee**-doh dee **leh**-ee
I will miss you.	Mi mancherà. mee mahn-keh-**rah**
Great!	Ottimo! **oh**-tee-moh
Fantastic!	Fantastico! fahn-**tah**-stee-koh
What a nice place.	Che bel posto. kay behl **poh**-stoh
Perfect.	Perfetto. pehr-**feh**-toh
Funny.	Divertente. dee-vehr-**tehn**-tay
Interesting.	Interessante. een-teh-reh-**sahn**-tay
I understand.	Capisco. kah-**pees**-koh
Why not?	Perché no? pehr-**keh** noh
Really?	Davvero? dah-**veh**-roh
Wow!	Wow! wow
Congratulations!	Congratulazioni! kohn-grah-too-laht-see-**oh**-nee
Well done!	Bravo[a]! **brah**-voh
You're welcome.	Prego. **preh**-goh

Bless you! (after sneeze)	Salute! sah-**loo**-tay
What a pity.	Che peccato. kay peh-**kah**-toh
That's life.	È la vita! eh lah **vee**-tah
No problem.	Non c'è problema. nohn cheh proh-**bleh**-mah
OK.	Va bene. vah **beh**-nay
I'll be right back.	Torno subito. **tor**-noh **soo**-bee-toh
I hope so.	Spero di sì. **speh**-roh dee see
I hope not.	Spero di no. **speh**-roh dee noh
This is the good life!	Questa sì che è vita! **kweh**-stah see kay eh **vee**-tah
I feel like a pope! (happy)	Sto come un papa! stoh **koh**-may oon **pah**-pah
Have a good day!	Buona giornata! **bwoh**-nah jor-**nah**-tah
Good luck!	Buona fortuna! **bwoh**-nah for-**too**-nah
Let's go!	Andiamo! ahn-dee-**ah**-moh

Favorite Things

What is your favorite...?	Qual'è il tuo... preferito? kwah-**leh** eel **too**-oh... preh-feh-**ree**-toh
My favorite... is ____.	Il mio... preferito è ____. eel **mee**-oh... preh-feh-**ree**-toh eh ____
art	genere d'arte **jeh**-neh-ray **dar**-tay
book	libro **lee**-broh
food	cibo **chee**-boh
hobby	passatempo pah-sah-**tehm**-poh
ice cream	gelato jeh-**lah**-toh
movie	film feelm
music	genere di musica **jeh**-neh-ray dee **moo**-zee-kah

TV show	programma televisivo proh-**grah**-mah teh-leh-vee-**zee**-voh
vice	vizio **veet**-see-oh
video game	videogioco vee-deh-oh-**joh**-koh
sport	sport sport
What's your favorite team?	Qual'è il tua squadra preferita? kwah-**leh** eel **too**-ah **skwah**-drah preh-feh-**ree**-tah
Who is your favorite...?	Chi è il tuo... preferito? kee eh eel **too**-oh... preh-feh-**ree**-toh
...actor	...attore ah-**toh**-ray
...singer	...cantante kahn-**tahn**-tay
...artist	...artista ar-**tee**-stah
...author	...autore ow-**toh**-ray
...director	...regista reh-**jee**-stah
...athlete	...atleta aht-**leh**-tah

For sports words, see page 246.

GRUNTS AND CURSES, SMOKES AND TOKES

Conversing With Animals

rooster / cock-a-doodle-doo	gallo / chicchirichì **gah**-loh / kee-kee-ree-**kee**
bird / tweet tweet	uccello / cip cip oo-**cheh**-loh / cheep cheep
cat / meow	gatto / miao **gah**-toh / **mee**-ow
dog / bark bark	cane / bau bau **kah**-nay / bow bow
duck / quack quack	anatra / quac quac **ah**-nah-trah / kwahk kwahk
cow / moo	mucca / muu **moo**-kah / moo
pig / oink oink	maiale / oinc oinc mī-**yah**-lay / oynk oynk

Profanity

People make animal noises, too. These words will help you understand what the more colorful locals are saying.

Go to hell!	Vai al diavolo! vī ahl dee-**ah**-voh-loh
Damn it.	Dannazione. dah-naht-see-**oh**-nay
This sucks.	Che schifo. kay **skee**-foh
Fuck.	Cazzo. **kahd**-zoh
Fuck off.	Vaffanculo. vah-fahn-**koo**-loh
Shit.	Merda. **mehr**-dah
Bullshit.	Balle. **bah**-lay
Go take a shit.	Va'a cagare. **vah**-ah kah-**gah**-ray
You are a...	Sei un... **seh**-ee oon
Don't be a...	Non essere un... nohn **eh**-seh-ray oon
...asshole.	...stronzo. **strohnt**-soh
...bastard.	...bastardo. bah-**star**-doh
...imbecile.	...imbecille. eem-beh-**chee**-lay
...stupid.	...stupido. **stoo**-pee-doh

Sweet Curses

My goodness.	Mamma mia. **mah**-mah **mee**-ah
Good heavens.	Santo cielo. **sahn**-toh **chay**-loh
Oh, my gosh.	Oddio. oh-**dee**-oh
Shoot.	Cavolo. **kah**-voh-loh
Darn it!	Accidenti! ah-chee-**dehn**-tee
Too bad.	Peccato. peh-**kah**-toh

Smokes and Tokes

Do you smoke?	Fuma? **foo**-mah
Do you smoke pot?	Fuma marijuana? **foo**-mah mah-ree-**wah**-nah
I (don't) smoke.	(Non) fumo. (nohn) **foo**-moh
We (don't) smoke.	(Non) fumiamo. (nohn) foo-mee-**ah**-moh
I don't have any.	Non ne ho. nohn nay oh
lighter	accendino ah-chehn-**dee**-noh
cigarettes	sigarette see-gah-**reh**-tay
cigar	sigaro see-**gah**-roh
marijuana	marijuana mah-ree-**wah**-nah
hash	hashish hah-**sheesh**
joint	canna **kah**-nah
stoned	fumato / fatto foo-**mah**-toh / **fah**-toh
Wow!	Wow! wow

AN ITALIAN ROMANCE

Words of Love

I / me / you / we	io / mi / ti / noi **ee**-oh / mee / tee / **noh**-ee
love	amore ah-**moh**-ray
kiss	bacio **bah**-choh
hug	abbraccio ah-**brah**-choh
to flirt	flirtare fleer-**tah**-ray
to cuddle	coccolare koh-koh-**lah**-ray
to go out	uscire oo-**shee**-ray
to make love	fare l'amore **fah**-ray lah-**moh**-ray
single	single **seen**-glay
married	sposato[a] spoh-**zah**-toh

engaged	fidanzato[a] fee-dahnt-**sah**-toh
anniversary	anniversario ah-nee-vehr-**sah**-ree-oh
faithful	fedele feh-**deh**-lay
sexy	sensuale sehn-soo-**ah**-lay
cozy	accogliente ah-kohl-**yehn**-tay
romantic	romantico roh-**mahn**-tee-koh
darling / baby	tesoro teh-**zoh**-roh
honey bunch	dolce come il miele **dohl**-chay **koh**-may eel mee-**eh**-lay
cupcake	pasticcino pah-stee-**chee**-noh
sugar pie	zuccherino tsoo-keh-**ree**-noh
pussy cat	gattino[a] gah-**tee**-noh

Ah, Amore

For words related to birth control and safe sex, see page 321.

What's the matter?	Qual'è il problema? kwah-**leh** eel proh-**bleh**-mah
Nothing.	Niente. nee-**ehn**-tay
I am / Are you...?	Sono / È...? **soh**-noh / eh
...single	...single **seen**-glay
...straight	...etero **eh**-teh-roh
...gay	...gay gay
...bisexual	...bisessuale bee-seh-**swah**-lay
...undecided	...indeciso[a] een-deh-**chee**-zoh
...prudish	...pudico[a] poo-**dee**-koh
I have...	Ho... oh
Do you have...?	Ha...? ah
...a boyfriend	...un ragazzo oon rah-**gahd**-zoh
...a girlfriend	...una ragazza **oo**-nah rah-**gahd**-zah

We are on our honeymoon.	Siamo in luna di miele. see-**ah**-moh een **loo**-nah dee mee-**eh**-lay
I'm married (but...).	Sono sposato[a] (ma...). **soh**-noh spoh-**zah**-toh (mah)
I'm not married.	Non sono sposato[a]. nohn **soh**-noh spoh-**zah**-toh
I'm adventurous.	Sono avventuroso. **soh**-noh ah-vehn-too-**roh**-zoh
I'm lonely (tonight).	Sono solo[a] (stasera). **soh**-noh **soh**-loh (stah-**seh**-rah)
I'm rich and single.	Sono ricco[a] e single. **soh**-noh **ree**-koh ay **seen**-glay
Do you mind if I sit here?	Le dispiace se mi siedo qui? lay dee-spee-**ah**-chay say mee see-**eh**-doh kwee
Would you like a drink?	Vuole qualcosa da bere? **vwoh**-lay kwahl-**koh**-zah dah **beh**-ray
Will you go out with me?	Vuole uscire con me? **vwoh**-lay oo-**shee**-ray kohn may
Would you like to go out tonight for...?	Vuole uscire stasera per...? **vwoh**-lay oo-**shee**-ray stah-**seh**-rah pehr
...a walk	...una passeggiata **oo**-nah pah-seh-**jah**-tah
...dinner	...cena **cheh**-nah
...a drink	...qualcosa da bere kwahl-**koh**-zah dah **beh**-ray
Where can we go dancing?	Dove andiamo a ballare? **doh**-vay ahn-dee-**ah**-moh ah bah-**lah**-ray
Do you want to dance?	Vuole ballare? **vwoh**-lay bah-**lah**-ray
Again?	Di nuovo? dee **nwoh**-voh
Let's party!	Divertiamoci! dee-vehr-tee-**ah**-moh-chee
Let's just be friends.	Solo amici. **soh**-loh ah-**mee**-chee

I have only safe sex.	Faccio solo sesso sicuro. **fah**-choh **soh**-loh **seh**-soh see-**koo**-roh
Can I take you home?	Posso accompagnarti a casa? **poh**-soh ah-kohm-pahn-**yar**-tee ah **kah**-zah
Kiss me.	Baciami. **bah**-chee-ah-mee
May I kiss you?	Posso baciarti? **poh**-soh bah-**char**-tee
Can I see you again?	Ti posso rivedere? tee **poh**-soh ree-veh-**deh**-ray
Your place or mine?	A casa tua o a casa mia? ah **kah**-zah **too**-ah oh ah **kah**-zah **mee**-ah
You are my most beautiful souvenir.	Sei il mio più bello ricordo. **seh**-ee eel **mee**-oh pew **beh**-loh ree-**kor**-doh
Oh my God!	Oh mio Dio! oh **mee**-oh **dee**-oh
I love you.	Ti amo. tee **ah**-moh
Darling, will you marry me?	Cara, mi vuoi sposare? **kah**-rah mee **vwoh**-ee spoh-**zah**-ray

DICTIONARY

ITALIAN / ENGLISH

A

a to; at
a bordo aboard
abbastanza enough
abbigliamento, boutique di clothing boutique
abbraccio hug
abbronzarsi to sunbathe; to tan
abbronzatura suntan
abitudine habit
aborto abortion
aborto spontaneo miscarriage
abusare to abuse
accanto a next to
accappatoio bathrobe
accendere to light; to turn on (device)
accendino lighter (n)
accessibile con la sedia a rotelle wheelchair-accessible
accesso access; entrance
accesso all' Internet Internet access
accettare to accept
accontentare to please; to make happy
accorgersi to realize
acerbo unripe; sour
acqua water
acqua del rubinetto tap water
acqua minerale mineral water
acqua non potabile undrinkable water
acqua potabile drinkable water
acquario aquarium
adattatore elettrico electrical adapter
addormentato asleep
adesso now
adolescente adolescent; teenager
adulto adult
aeroplano airplane
aeroporto airport
affamato hungry
affare deal (good value); bargain; business
affascinante charming
affettare to slice
affittare to rent
agenzia di viaggi travel agency
aggiustare to fix
aggressivo aggressive
agnello lamb
agnostico agnostic
ago needle
agosto August
agriturismo farm with sleeping accommodations
aiutare to help
aiuto help
aiuto, di helpful
ala wing
alba sunrise
albergo hotel
albergo a conduzione familiare family-run hotel
albergo storico historic hotel
albero tree
alcool alcohol

Italian Dictionary Rules

Here are a few tips for using this dictionary:

- Remember that all Italian nouns have a grammatical **gender** (masculine or feminine). Even inanimate objects are assigned a gender. In general, words ending in ***o*** relate to males or masculine words, while those ending in ***a*** relate to females or feminine words—though there are many exceptions. Because casual visitors aren't expected to get this perfect—and because it's often possible to guess correctly—I haven't listed the gender for each noun.
- To make nouns ending in ***o*** plural, change the last letter to ***i*** (one ***treno,*** two ***treni***). To make nouns ending in ***a*** plural, change the last letter to ***e*** (one ***piazza,*** two ***piazze***).
- **Adjectives** match their nouns. For simplicity, I've listed all adjectives with the masculine ending, often ***o.*** To change a word to feminine, just swap the ***o*** for an ***a.*** (A handsome man is ***bello,*** while an attractive woman is ***bella.***) Adjectives ending in ***e*** don't change with the gender (either a man or a woman can be ***felice,*** happy). Adjectives should also match whether the noun is singular or plural: Happy men are ***signori felici.***
- Verbs are listed in their infinitive form (usually ending in ***are, ere,*** or ***ire***). This loosely translates to the English form "to ____" (for example, ***parlare*** is "to talk"). To use a verb correctly in a sentence, you'll have to conjugate it (for example, if ***parlare*** is "to talk," then ***parlo*** means "I talk"). For examples of conjugated verbs, see page 427.
- Most food terms are not included in the Dictionary but rather in my Menu Decoder, starting on page 187.

alimentari grocery store
aliscafo hydrofoil
alito breath
all'aria aperta outdoors
allattamento al seno breastfeeding
allattare to nurse; to breastfeed
allergia allergy
allergico allergic
alt stop (command)
altare altar
alterare to alter; to modify
alto tall; high
altro other
altro, un another
amante lover
amare to love
amaro bitter
ambasciata embassy
ambiente environment; space; setting
ambulanza ambulance
amicizia friendship
amico friend
amore love
analgesico painkiller
anatra duck
anca hip (n)
ancora more; again
andare to go
andata one-way (ticket)
andata e ritorno round-trip
anello ring
angolo corner
angolo cottura kitchenette ("corner for cooking")
animale animal
animale domestico pet
anniversario anniversary
anno year
annullare to cancel
annuncio announcement
ansia anxiety
antenato ancestor
antiacido antacid
antibiotico antibiotic
antichità antiques (furniture)
antico ancient
antipasto appetizer
antiquariato antiques
anziano senior; old; elderly
aperto open (adj)
appartamento apartment
appendere to hang
appendiabiti coat hanger
appropriato appropriate
appuntamento appointment
aprile April
aprire to open; to unlock
apriscatola can opener
arancia orange (fruit)
arancione orange (color)
architetto architect
architettura architecture
arcobaleno rainbow
area per campeggio campsite
area Wi-Fi Wi-Fi hotspot
argento silver
aria air; gas (stomach)
aria condizionata air-conditioned
armadietto locker
armadio closet
aroma aroma; scent

arrabbiato angry; mad
arrivare to arrive
arrivederci goodbye
arrivo arrival
arrivo orario arrival time
arte art; craft
artificiale artificial
artigianato handicraft
artista artist
artrite arthritis
ascensore elevator
asciugacapelli hair dryer
asciugamano towel
asciugare to dry
asciugatrice dryer
asciutto dry
ascoltare to listen
asino donkey
asma asthma
aspettare to wait
aspirina aspirin
aspro sour
assaggiare to taste
assegno check (money)
assetato thirsty
assicurato insured
assicurazione insurance
assicurazione medica health insurance
assolato sunny
assonnato sleepy
assorbente igienico sanitary pad
assorbente interno tampon
astratto abstract
ateo atheist
atleta athlete
attenzione caution
attraente handsome
attraversare to go through; to cross (a street)
attraverso through
audioguida audioguide
autista driver
autobus bus (city)
automatico automatic
autore author
autoritratto self-portrait
autorizzare to authorize
autostop hitchhiking
autostrada highway
autotraghetto car ferry
autunno fall; autumn
avere to have
avere bisogno di to need
avere fretta to hurry
avere mal di to have an ache
avvelenamento da cibo food poisoning
avventuroso adventurous
avvocato lawyer

B

Babbo Natale Santa Claus
bacio kiss
baffi moustache
bagaglio luggage
bagaglio a mano carry-on luggage
bagnato wet
bagno bathroom; restroom; bath
balcone balcony
ballare to dance
balsamo conditioner (hair)

bambino child
bambola doll
banca bank
bancomat cash machine; ATM
banconota bill (money)
bandiera flag
bar bar; coffee shop
barba beard
barbiere barber; barber shop
barca boat
barca a remi rowboat
basket basketball
Bassi, Paesi Netherlands
basso low
batteria battery
batteria per orologio watch battery
battito cardiaco pulse
bavaglino bib
Belgio Belgium
bello beautiful; nice
belvedere viewpoint
benda bandage
bene fine; good; well
benvenuto welcome
benzina gasoline
benzinaio gas station
bere to drink
berretto cap
bevanda drink
bianchetto whitener; white-out
bianco white
Bibbia Bible
biblioteca library
bicchiere glass (cup)
bicicletta bicycle
bidone per i rifiuti trashcan (outdoors)
biglietto ticket; note (message)
biglietto da visita business card
binario platform; track (train)
biondo blond
birra beer
bisogno need (n)
bisogno di, avere to need
blando bland
bloccato locked (mobile phone)
block notes notepad
blu blue
bocca mouth
boccaglio snorkel
bollire to boil
bollito boiled
bollitore kettle
bomba bomb
borotalco talcum powder
borsa purse
borseggiatore pickpocket
bottiglia bottle
bottone button
boutique di abbigliamento clothing boutique
box playpen; one-car garage
barca a vela sailboat
braccialetto bracelet
braccio arm
brillante bright
brivido shiver (from cold); shudder (from fear) (n)
broncopolmonite pneumonia
bronzo bronze
bruciatura burn (from fire)
bruciore di stomaco heartburn

brutto ugly
buco hole
bugia lie (n)
bulbo bulb
buongiorno good day
buono good
burro butter
burro di cacao lip salve; lip balm
bus navetta shuttle bus
busta envelope; bag (plastic, paper)
busta di plastica plastic bag
busta di plastica sigillabile Ziploc bag

C

cabina telefonica phone booth
cacciavite screwdriver
cadere to fall
caffè coffee; coffee shop
cagnaccio mean dog
calcio soccer
calcolo renale kidney stone
caldo hot (temperature)
calendario calendar
calmo calm
calorie calorie
calzini socks
cambiare to change; to transfer; to exchange
cambio change; exchange
camera room
camera da letto bedroom
camerata dormitory
camere disponibili / camere libere vacancy (hotel)
cameriera waitress
cameriere waiter
camicetta blouse
camicia shirt
camminare to walk
campagna countryside
campana bell
campeggio camping
camper RV
campionato championship
campo field
canadese Canadian
canale canal
cancellare to delete; to erase
candela candle; spark plug
cane dog
canna joint (marijuana)
cannuccia straw (drinking)
canoa canoe
cantante singer
cantare to sing
cantina cellar
canzone song
capelli hair
capire to understand
capitano captain
capo boss
capogiro dizziness
capolavoro masterpiece
capotreno train conductor
cappella chapel
cappello hat
cappotto coat
caraffa carafe
caramella candy
caramelle per la tosse cough drops
carica batterie battery charger

carino pretty; cute
carne meat
caro expensive
carrello bagagli luggage cart
carro attrezzi tow truck
carta paper
carta di credito credit card
carta di debito debit card
carta igienica toilet paper
carta ricaricabile debit card
carta SIM SIM card
carta telefonica telephone card
carte cards (deck)
cartina card; map
cartoleria office supplies store
cartolina postcard
casa house
casalingo homemade
cascata waterfall
casco helmet
caseficio cheese shop
cassa speaker (audio); cash register
cassetta postale mailbox
cassiere cashier
castello castle
catena chain
cattedrale cathedral
cattivo bad
cattolico Catholic
cavaliere knight
cavallo horse
cavatappi corkscrew
caviglia ankle
cavo cable (cord)
cena dinner
cento hundred
centralinista operator; receptionist
centro center; downtown
centro commerciale shopping mall
centro benessere spa
ceramica ceramic
cercare to look for; to search
cerchio circle (shape)
ceretta wax (hair removal)
cerotto Band-Aid
cestino basket
cestino per i rifiuti trashcan (indoors)
che cosa what
che peccato it's a pity
check-in bagagli baggage check
chi who
chiamare to call
chiaro clear; light; pale
chiave key
chiedere to ask for
chiesa church
chilometraggio mileage (in kilometers)
chilometro kilometer
chiocciola "at" symbol (@)
chiostro cloister
chitarra guitar
chiudere to close
chiudere a chiave to lock
chiuso closed
chiusura lampo zipper
ciabatte slippers
ciabatte da piscina flip-flops
ciao hello; goodbye (informal)
cibo food

cielo sky; heaven
cimice bedbug
cinema movie theater
cinghia del ventilatore fan belt
cinque five
cintura belt
cioccolato chocolate
cipria face powder
città city; town
ciuccio pacifier
classe class
classe, prima first class
classe, seconda second class
classico classical
clinica medical clinic
coda tail; line (queue)
codice postale zip code
codice segreto PIN code
cognome last name
coincidenza connection (train)
colazione breakfast
collana necklace
collant nylons (panty hose)
collina hill
collirio eye drops
collo neck
collocare to place; to set (put something down)
colluttorio mouthwash
colore color
colpevole guilty
coltello knife
combattere to fight
combattimento di galli cockfight
come how
cominciare to begin
commercialista accountant
commissione errand
compagno companion; partner (relationship)
compleanno birthday
completo no vacancy
complicato complicated
comprare to buy
comune common
con with
concerto concert
conchiglia shell
condurre to lead
conducente conductor; driver
conferma confirmation
confermare to confirm
confortevole comfortable
congestione congestion (sinus)
congratulazioni congratulations
coniglio rabbit
connettere to connect
conoscenza knowledge
conservatore conservative (n)
consorte spouse
contadino farmer
contagioso contagious
contante cash
contare to count
contento happy
continuare to continue
conto bill (payment)
contraccettivo contraceptive
contraccezione birth control
contrazione contraction (pregnancy)
controllare to control

C

conveniente affordable; appropriate
coperta blanket
coperto cover charge
copia copy (n)
copiare to copy; to mimic; to duplicate
copisteria photocopy shop
coprifuoco curfew
coprire to cover
corda rope
corda stendipanni clothesline
coro choir
corpo body
corrente current (water)
correre to run
corridoio aisle; hallway
corriera long-distance bus
corruzione corruption
corto short
cosa thing
cosa, che what
coscia thigh
costa coast
costare to cost
costo cost
costruire to build
costruzione construction
costume da bagno swimsuit
cotone cotton
cotto cooked
cotton fioc Q-tip (cotton swab)
crampi cramps
cravatta tie (clothing)
credere (in) to believe (in)
crema da barba shaving cream
crema idratante moisturizer
crema solare suntan lotion
crema per le mani hand lotion
cripta crypt
cristiano Christian
croce cross
crostacei shellfish
crudo raw
cuccetta berth (train)
cucchiaio spoon
cucina kitchen
cucinare to cook
cucire to sew
cuffie headphones
cugino cousin
culla crib (for baby)
cuoco chef; cook
cuore heart
cupola dome
cura treatment (medical)
curare to treat (medical)
cuscino pillow

D

d'accordo agree; OK
da from; since
da qualche parte somewhere
dal vivo live (music)
dare to give
dare prurito to be itchy
data date; day
data di scadenza expiration date
davanti front
decaffeinato decaffeinated; decaf
decongestionante decongestant
delicato delicate
delizioso delicious

democrazia democracy
dente tooth
denti teeth
denti, mal di toothache
dentifricio toothpaste
dentista dentist
dentizione teething (baby)
dentro inside
deodorante deodorant
deposito deposit
depressione depression
dermatite da pannolino diaper rash
derubato robbed
desiderare to wish; to require
destinazione destination
destra right (direction)
detersivo da bucato laundry detergent
deviazione detour (n)
di of
di aiuto helpful
di sopra upstairs
diabete diabetes
diabetico diabetic
diamante diamond
diarrea diarrhea
dicembre December
dichiarare to declare (customs)
dieci ten
dietro behind
difficile difficult
digitare to type
dimenticare to forget
Dio God
dipingere to paint
dire to say; to tell
diretto direct
direttore manager
direzione direction
dirupo cliff
disabile disabled; handicapped
disastro disaster
discesa, in downhill
discoteca nightclub
discriminazione discrimination
discutere to discuss
disinfettante disinfectant
disoccupato unemployed
disperato desperate
dispiace, mi sorry
disponibile available
distanza distance
disturbare to disturb
disturbi cardiaci heart condition
dito finger
dito del piede toe
divertire to amuse; to entertain
divertente funny
divertimento fun; entertainment
divertirsi to enjoy; to have fun
dividere to share; to split
divorziato divorced
dizionario dictionary
doccia shower
documento file (computer)
dogana customs
dolce sweet; dessert; pastry
dolorante sore
dolore pain; ache
dolore al petto chest pains
dolori mestruali menstrual cramps
domanda question

domandare to ask
domani tomorrow
domenica Sunday
donna woman
donne women
dopo after
dopobarba aftershave
dopodomani day after tomorrow
doppio double
dormire to sleep
dottore doctor
dove where
dozzina dozen
dritto straight
dubitare to doubt
due two
due volte twice
duro hard

E

e and
è is
ebreo Jewish
eccellente excellent
eccetto except
economico cheap; economical
edicola newsstand
edificio building
efficace effective
elenco telefonico telephone book
emergenza emergency
emicrania migraine
emorroidi hemorrhoids
enoteca wine shop; wine bar
entrambi both
entrare to enter
entrata entry
epatite hepatitis
epilessia epilepsy
equitazione horse riding
erba grass
erbe medicinali herb (medicine)
errore mistake
esaminare to examine
esattamente exactly
esatto exact
esaurito sold out
esausto exhausted
escursione hike (n)
escursionismo hiking
esempio example
esperienza experience (n)
espressione expression
espresso express (fast)
est east
estate summer
età age
Europa Europe

F

fa male it hurts
fabbrica factory
faccia face
facciata facade
facile easy
falso false
famiglia family
familiare familiar
famoso famous
fantastico fantastic
fard blush (makeup)
fare to make

fare fumo smoking (engine, stove, etc.)
fare la spesa to shop (for groceries)
fare le valigie to pack
fare pratica to practice
fare shopping to go shopping
fare sport to exercise
fare una gita to go on a day trip
fare un'escursione to hike
farmacia pharmacy; drug store
farmaco per la diarrea diarrhea medicine
faro headlight
fascia di sostegno support bandage
fatto made; done; stoned
fatto a mano handmade
fattoria farm
favore favor (n)
fazzoletto di carta facial tissue
febbraio February
febbre fever
feci stool (fecal matter)
felicità happiness
feltro moleskin; felt (fabric)
femmina female
ferire to hurt; to injure
ferirsi to hurt oneself
ferito hurt (adj)
fermare to stop
fermata stop (train, bus)
ferramenta hardware store
ferrovia railway
festa party; festival
festeggiare to celebrate
fetta slice (thick; e.g., cake, bread)
fettina slice (thin; e.g., cold cuts)
fiammifero match; matchstick
fidanzata girlfriend
fidanzato boyfriend
figlia daughter
figlio son
fila line; row; queue
film movie
filo string
filo interdentale dental floss
finale final
finalmente finally
fine end
fine settimana weekend
finestra window
finire to finish
finito over; finished
fiore flower
firma signature
fiume river
flirtare to flirt
fodera per occhiali glasses case
folla crowd
fondo bottom
fondotinta foundation (makeup)
fontana fountain
football soccer
football americano American football
footing jogging
forbici scissors
forchetta fork
foresta forest
formaggio cheese
formica ant

forno oven
forse maybe
forte strong; loud
fortuna luck
fortunato lucky
fossato moat
foto photo
fotocopia photocopy
foto-ottica camera shop
Francia France
francobolli stamps
frangia bangs (hair)
fratello brother
freccia turn signal
freddo cold (adj) ; chill (temperature) (n)
freno brake
frequenza frequency
fresco fresh; cool
fretta, avere to hurry
frizzante fizzy
frontiera border
frumento wheat
frutta fruit
frutti di mare seafood
fumare to smoke; smoking (cigarettes)
fumato stoned
fumatore smoker (person)
fumo smoke
funerale funeral
fuochi d'artificio fireworks
fuoco fire
fuori outside
fusibile fuse
futuro future

G

galleria gallery; tunnel
galleria d'arte art gallery
gamba leg
garantito guaranteed
garanzia guarantee (n)
garza gauze
gas gas (vapor)
gatto cat
gelato ice cream
geloso jealous
gemello twin
generoso generous
gengiva gum (mouth)
genitore parent
gennaio January
gentile kind (courteous)
genuino genuine
Germania Germany
gestire to manage (oversee)
gettone token (n)
ghiaccio ice
già already
giacca jacket
giallo yellow
giardinaggio gardening
giardino garden
gilè vest
ginecologo gynecologist
ginnastica gymnastics
ginocchio knee
giocare to play (sports, games)
giocatore player (sports); athlete
giocattolo toy
giochi, parco playground
gioco game
gioielli jewelry

gioiellieria jewelry shop
giornalaio newsstand
giornale newspaper
giornaliero daily
giorno day
giorno festivo holiday
giorno, buon good day (hello)
giovane young; youth
giovedì Thursday
gioventù, ostello della youth hostel
giro tour (n)
gita, fare una to go on a day trip
giù down
giubbotto jacket
giudicare to judge
giugno June
giusto fair; just; right; correct
globalizzazione globalization
glutei buttocks
glutine gluten
gola throat; gorge
gola, mal di sore throat
gomito elbow
gomma tire
gomma da cancellare eraser
gomma da masticare chewing gum
gomma a terra flat tire
gommone raft
gonfiore swelling
gonna skirt
Gotico Gothic
governante ruler
governo government
graffetta paper clip
grammatica grammar
Gran Bretagna Great Britain
grande big
grande magazzino department store
grassi fat (n)
grasso fat (adj); greasy
gratis free (no cost)
gravidanza pregnancy
grazie thanks
Grecia Greece
grigio gray
grotta cave
gruppo group
gruppo musicale band (musical)
guaio trouble
guanti gloves
guardando browsing
guardare to look at; to watch
guerra war
guida guide; guidebook
guidare to drive; to guide
guidato, visita guided tour
gusto flavor; taste (n)

H

handicappato handicapped

I

i loro their
ibuprofene ibuprofen
idea idea
ideale ideal
idiota idiot
ieri yesterday
igienico hygienic
ignorare to ignore
il loro their

il migliore best
il tuo your
il vostro your
illegale illegal
illuminare to light up; to illuminate
imbarazzante embarrassing
imbarcare to board (transportation)
imbarco boarding (transportation)
immangiabile inedible
immediatamente immediately
immigrazione immigration
immondizia trash; garbage
imparare to learn
impermeabile raincoat
importante important
importato imported
importo amount
Impressionista Impressionist
improvvisamente suddenly
in in; into; by (car, train, etc.)
in coda back (of train)
in discesa downhill
in nessun posto nowhere
in orario on time
in pensione retired
in ritardo late (train, bus)
in salita uphill
incartare to wrap
incastrato stuck
incidente accident
incinta pregnant
includere to include
incluso included
incomprensione misunderstanding
incontrare to meet
incredibile incredible
incrocio intersection
indicare to point
indigestione indigestion
indipendente independent
indirizzo address
indirizzo di posta elettronica / indirizzo email email address
indossare to wear
industria industry
infastidire to bother
infermiera nurse
infezione infection
infezione urinaria urinary tract infection
infiammazione inflammation
influenza flu
informare to inform
informazioni information
infortunato injured
ingegnere engineer
Inghilterra England
inglese English
ingoiare to swallow
ingresso entrance
iniziare to start
inizio beginning; start
innocente innocent
inquinamento pollution
insalata salad
insegnante teacher
insegnare to teach
insetto insect
insieme together

insolazione sunstroke
insulto insult (n)
intelligente intelligent
intendere to intend
interessante interesting
internazionale international
intestino intestine
intimo underwear
intollerante ai latticini lactose intolerant
intorno around (go around)
intrattenimento entertainment
invece instead
inverno winter
investigazione investigation
invitare to invite
invito invitation
iodio iodine
Irlanda Ireland
irritazione della pelle rash
islamico Islamic
isola island
isolato block (city)
ispezionare to inspect
istante instant
istruzione education; instruction
Italia Italy
itinerario route

L

là there
la loro their
la tua your
labbro lip
laccio delle scarpe shoelace
ladro thief
lago lake
lampada lamp
lampadina lightbulb
lana wool
larghezza width
largo loose; wide
lasciare to let; to allow
lasciare la stanza to check out (hotel)
lassativo laxative
lato side
latte milk
latte detergente face cleanser
latte in polvere per neonati baby formula
latticino dairy product
lattina can (n)
lavanderia launderette
lavandino sink
lavare to wash
lavare a mano to hand wash
lavatrice washer
lavorare to work
lavoro work; occupation
le loro their
le vostre your
legale legal
legare to tie
leggere to read
legno wood
lei she; you (formal)
lente a contatto contact lens
lento slow
lenzuolo sheet
lesbica lesbian
lesione injury
lettera letter
lettino cot

letto bed
letto a castello bunk bed
letto, camera da bedroom
letto, matrimoniale double bed
letto, singolo single bed
letto, vagone sleeper car (train)
liberale liberal (n)
liberare to release; to free; to liberate
libere, camere vacancy (hotel)
libero vacant
libreria book shop
libro book
limetta per unghie nail file
limite di peso weight limit
limite di velocità speed limit
linea line (transportation; e.g., bus line)
linea aerea airline
linea bassa underscore (_)
lingua language; tongue (mouth)
lino linen
liquidazione sale
liquido liquid
liquido della trasmissione transmission fluid
lista list
litro liter
locale local; bar; club; pub
locale notturno nightclub
locanda di campagna country inn
lontano far
loro they
lotta fight (n)
lozione anti-zanzare insect repellant
luce light (n)
luce posteriore taillight
luglio July
lui he
luna moon
luna di miele honeymoon
lunedì Monday
lunghezza length
lungo long
lungomare waterfront
luogo place; site
lussuoso luxurious

M

macchina car; machine
macchina fotografica camera
madre mother
maggio May
maglietta T-shirt
maglione sweater
magro skinny
mai never
maiale pig; pork
mal d'orecchi earache
mal di, avere to have an ache
mal di denti toothache
mal di gola sore throat
mal di macchina motion sickness (car, etc.)
mal di mare seasickness
mal di stomaco stomachache
mal di testa headache
malato sick
malattia disease; illness
maleducato rude
mancia tip (gratuity)
mangiare to eat

maniche sleeves
manico handle (n)
manifestazione demonstration (public)
mano hand
mano, bagaglio a carry-on luggage
manzo beef
mappa per escursioni hiking map
marca brand
marcia gear; march (n)
marcio rotten
mare sea
marito husband
marmo marble (material)
marrone brown
martedì Tuesday
martello hammer
marzo March
mascella jaw
maschio male
massaggio massage
massimo maximum
materiale material
matita pencil; eyeliner
matrimonio wedding; marriage
mattina morning
matto crazy
maturo ripe
meccanico mechanic
medicina medicine
medicina per il raffreddore cold medicine
medicinale drug (medicine)
medio medium
meglio better
mela apple
meno minus
meno, più o approximately
mente mind (brain)
menù menu
mercato market
mercato dei fiori flower market
mercato delle pulci flea market
mercoledì Wednesday
mese month
messa church service; Mass
messaggio message
mestruazioni menstruation; period (woman's)
metà half
metallo metal
metodo method
metropolitana subway
mettere giù to place; to set (put something down)
mettersi in fila to line up
mezza porzione half portion (food)
mezzanotte midnight
mezzo middle
mezzogiorno noon
mi dispiace sorry
mi gira la testa dizzy; lightheaded ("my head is spinning")
mi scusi excuse me
mia my; mine
mie / miei mine
migliore, il best
militare military
mille thousand
minerale, acqua mineral water

minestra soup
minimo minimum
minuto minute
mio my; mine
miope nearsighted
mischiare to mix
mischiato mixed
misto mix (n)
mobili furniture
moda fashion
moderno modern
modulo form (document)
moglie wife
molletta per bucato clothespin
molti many
molto much; very
momento moment
monastero monastery
mondo world
moneta coin
monovolume van
montagna mountain
monumento monument
morbido soft
morire to die
morso bite (n)
morto dead
moschea mosque
mostra exhibit; exhibition
mostrare to show
motocicletta motorcycle
motorino motor scooter
mucca cow
mulino a vento windmill
multa fine; penalty
mura wall (barrier; e.g., city wall)
mura fortificate fortified wall
murales mural
muro wall (room)
muscolo muscle
museo museum
musica music
musicista musician
musulmano Muslim
mutande men's underwear
mutandine women's underwear

N

nascosto hidden
naso nose
nastro adesivo tape (adhesive)
Natale Christmas
natura nature
naturale natural
nave ship
nave da crociera cruise ship
nazionale national
nazionali domestic
nazionalità nationality
ne... ne... neither... nor...
nebbia fog
necessario necessary
negozio shop; store
negozio di antiquariato antique shop
negozio di abbigliamento clothing shop
negozio di cellulari mobile-phone shop
negozio di dolciumi sweets shop
negozio di giocattoli toy store
negozio di souvenir souvenir shop
negozio di vini wine shop

neonato baby; infant
nero black
nervoso nervous
nessuno no one
nessuno dei due neither
neve snow
niente nothing
nipote grandchild; nephew; niece
no no
noce nut (food)
noi we; us
noioso boring
nome name
non not
non è corretto incorrect
nonna grandmother
nonno grandfather
nord north
normale normal; regular
nostalgico homesick
notizie news
notte night
nove nine
novembre November
nubile single (female)
nudo naked
numero number
numero telefonico telephone number
numero verde toll-free number
nuotare to swim
nuovo new
nutrire to feed
nuvoloso cloudy
nylon nylon (material)

O

o or
obliterare to validate
occhi eyes
occhiali eyeglasses
occhiali da lettura reading glasses
occhiali da sole sunglasses
occhio eye
occupato occupied; busy
oceano ocean
odiare to hate
odore smell (odor); herb (cooking)
offerta offer (n)
offrire to offer
oggi today
ogni each; every
Olimpiadi Olympics
olio oil
olio per neonati diaper ointment
ombra shade (n)
ombrello umbrella
ombretto eye shadow
omogeneizzati baby food
omosessuale gay
onda wave (water)
onesto honest
operazione operation (medical)
opinione opinion
opportunità opportunity
ora hour; time (clock time)
orario timetable; schedule
orario, arrivo arrival time
orario, check-in check-in time
orario d'apertura opening hours
orario, in on time

orario, partenza departure time
ordinare to order
ordine order (layout; restaurant)
orecchi, mal d' earache
orecchini earrings
orecchio ear
organo organ
originale original
oro gold
orologio clock; watch
orribile horrible
ospedale hospital
ospite guest
ostello hostel
ostello della gioventù youth hostel
ottenere to get
ottico optician
ottimista optimistic
ottimo great
otto eight
ottobre October
ottone brass
ovest west
ovunque anywhere

P

pacco package
pace peace
padre father
padrone owner
paese country town; village
paese antico old town
paese in collina hill town
Paesi Bassi Netherlands
Paesi Scandinavi Scandinavia
pagare to pay
pagina page
paio pair
palazzo palace
palla ball
pane bread
panificio bakery
panino sandwich
panna cream; whipped cream
pannolino diaper
panoramico scenic
pantaloncini shorts
pantaloni pants
pantofole slippers
papà dad
paradiso heaven; paradise
parcheggiare to park
parcheggio parking lot
parco park (garden)
parco giochi playground
parete wall (room)
parlare to talk
parola word
parrucchiere beauty salon; hair salon
partecipare to attend (an event)
partenza departure
partenza orario departure time
partire to leave
partita game (sports)
Pasqua Easter
passaporto passport
passato past
passeggero passenger
passeggino stroller (for baby)
passo di montagna mountain pass
pasticceria pastry shop

pasticcino pastry
pastiglia per la gola lozenge
pastiglia per la tosse cough drops
pasto meal
pattinaggio skating
pattini a rotelle roller skates
pausa break (rest)
pavimento floor (ground)
peccato, che it's a pity
pedaggio toll
pedalò paddleboat
pedone pedestrian
peggio worse
peggiore worst
pelle skin; leather
pelletteria leather shop
peltro pewter
pene penis
penna pen
pensare to think
pensione, in retired
pepe pepper (spice)
per for
per favore please
percentuale percent
perché why (question); because (answer)
percorso route
perdere to lose; to miss (bus, train, etc.)
perfetto perfect
pericolo danger
pericoloso dangerous
periodo period (of time)
permanente permanent
permesso allowed
permettere to allow
perso lost; missing
persona person
pesante heavy
pescare to fish
pesce fish
peso weight
peso, limite di weight limit
pessimista pessimistic
pettine comb
petto chest
pezzo piece
phon hair dryer
piacere to like
piangere to cry
piano floor; story (building)
pianta plant
pianura plain (n)
piatto plate; dish
piatto, primo course, first
piatto, secondo course, second
piazza square (town)
piccante hot (spicy)
picchetto della tenda tent peg
piccolo small
pidocchi lice
piede foot
piede d'atleta athlete's foot
pietra rock
pigiama pajamas
pigro lazy
pillola pill
pillola anticoncezionale birth control pill
pinacoteca painting gallery
pinzatrice stapler
pinzette pliers; tweezers

P

pioggia rain
piovere to rain
piscina swimming pool
pisolino nap
pistola gun
più more
più o meno approximately
più tardi later; afterward
pizzo lace
plastica plastic
po', un some
poco few; a bit
poco cotto undercooked
politica policy
politico political; politician
polizia police
pollame poultry
pollice thumb
pollo chicken
polmoni lungs
polso wrist
polvere dust; powder
poliestere polyester
pomata antiprurito itch reliever
pomata antistaminica first-aid cream
pomeriggio afternoon
pompa pump (n)
ponte bridge
popolare popular
porcellana porcelain
porta door
portacenere ashtray
portafoglio wallet
portar via take out (food)
portare to carry; to bring
portatile laptop
porto harbor
Portogallo Portugal
porzione portion
possedere to own
possibile possible
possibilità chance; possibility
posta mail
posta elettronica email
posto seat; place; space (room)
posto a conduzione familiare family-run place
potabile, acqua drinkable water
potente powerful
potere can (v)
povero poor
pranzo lunch
pratico practical
preferire to prefer
preferito favorite
prefisso area code
prendere to take; to catch
prendere in prestito to borrow
prenotare to book (reserve, purchase)
prenotazione reservation
preoccupare to worry
presa (di corrente) electrical outlet
presbite farsighted
prescrizione prescription
preservativo condom
presidente president
pressione alta high blood pressure
prestare to lend
presto early
prete priest

previsioni del tempo weather forecast
prezioso precious
prezzo price
prima before
prima classe first class
primavera spring (season)
primo first
primo soccorso first aid
principale main
principe prince
principessa princess
principio principle
privato private
privo di sensi unconscious; passed out
problema problem
prodotto product
produrre to produce
professione profession
profugo refugee
profumo perfume
proibito prohibited
prolungare to prolong; to extend (time)
promessa promise
promettere to promise
pronto ready
pronto soccorso emergency room
pronuncia pronunciation
prosciutto cotto boiled ham
prosperare to prosper
prossimo next
prostituta prostitute
proteggere to protect
protestante Protestant (adj)
protestare to complain
protezione solare sunscreen
provare to try (attempt)
prudente careful
prurito itch
pubblico public
pudico prudish
pulce flea
pulire to clean; to wipe
pulito clean (adj)
pullman long-distance bus
pulpito pulpit
punto point (reason; dot)
punto panoramico viewpoint
puntuale punctual
puntura di insetto bug bite
pupu poop
puttana bitch (n)
puzza stink; stench
puzzare to stink

Q

quaderno notebook
quadro painting
qualcosa something
qualcuno anyone
qualsiasi cosa whatever (anything)
qualità quality
quando when
quanti how many
quantità quantity
quanto costa how much ($)
quarto quarter (¼)
quattro four
quello that (thing)
qui here

R

raccomandare to recommend
raccordo anulare ring road
racommandazione recommendation
radere to shave
radiatore radiator
radicale radical (adj, n)
radiografia X-ray
raffreddore cold (n)
raffreddore da fieno hay fever
ragazza girl; girlfriend
ragazzo boy; boyfriend
ragionevole sensible
ragno spider
rame copper
rasoio razor
razzismo racism
re king
recente recent
reclamo complaint
regalo gift
reggiseno bra
regina queen
regola rule (n)
religione religion
reliquia relic
Repubblica Ceca Czech Republic
resistente sturdy
respirare to breathe
restauro restoration
restituire to return (something)
rete network (technology)
retto rectum
ricaricare to recharge
ricco rich
ricetta prescription; recipe
ricevere to receive
ricevuta receipt
ricordare to remember; to remind
ridere to laugh
riempire to fill; to refill
rifiuti trash; garbage
rifiuti, bidone per i trashcan (outdoors)
rifiuti, cestino per i trashcan (indoors)
rilassamento relaxation
rimborso refund
Rinascimento Renaissance
riparare to repair
riposare to relax; to rest
risolvere to resolve
rispetto respect
rispondere to answer
risposta answer
ristorante restaurant
ristorante, vagone dining car (train)
ritardo delay
ritirare to pull back; to withdraw
ritirarsi to shrink
ritiro bagagli baggage claim
ritornare to return (go back)
ritorno return (n)
ritratto portrait
rivista magazine
Romanico Romanesque
Romantico Romantic
romantico romantic
rosa pink
rossetto lipstick
rosso red

rotaie railway track
rotonda roundabout
rotto broken
rovine ruins
rubato stolen
rubinetto faucet
rubinetto, acqua del tap water
rumoroso noisy
ruota wheel
ruscello stream
russare to snore

S

sabato Saturday
sacchetto bag
sacchetto di plastica plastic bag
sacco a pelo sleeping bag
sacro holy
saggio wise
sala room (hall; e.g., sitting room)
sala colazione breakfast room (hotel)
sala d'aspetto / sala di attesa waiting room
saldi sale
sale salt
salita, in uphill
salone hall (big room)
salsiccia sausage
saltare to jump
salumeria delicatessen
salute health
Salute! Cheers!
salvare to save
salvietta napkin
salviettine per neonati diaper wipes
sandali sandals
sandali infradito thongs
sangue blood
sanguinare to bleed
sano healthy
santo saint
sapere to know
sapone soap
saporito tasty
Saridon non-aspirin substitute
scadenza expiration (validity)
scala ladder
scaldare to heat
scaldato toasted; heated
scale stairs
scalo transfer; layover
scandaloso scandalous
Scandinavi, Paesi Scandinavia
scapolo single (male)
scarafaggio cockroach
scaricare to download
scarpe shoes
scarpe da ginnastica sneakers
scarpe da tennis tennis shoes
scarpe, laccio delle shoelace
scatola box
scheggia splinter
schermo screen
scherzo joke
schiena back
sci skiing
sci acquatico waterskiing
sciare to ski
sciarpa scarf
scienza science

scienziato scientist
sciopero strike (stop work)
sciroppo per la tosse cough syrup
scivoloso slippery
scodella bowl
sconto discount
scorretto incorrect; unfair
scorso last (previous; e.g., last week)
scotch tape (adhesive)
scottatura da sole sunburn
scrivania desk
scrivere to write
scultore sculptor
scultura sculpture
scuola school
scuro dark
scuse apology
scusi, mi excuse me
se if
secchio bucket
secco dry (adj)
secolo century
seconda classe second class
secondo piatto main course (food)
sedere butt
sedersi to sit
sedia chair
sedia a rotelle wheelchair
sedia a rotelle, accessibile con la wheelchair-accessible
seggiolino per la macchina car seat (baby)
seggiolino per neonati booster seat
seggiolone highchair
segno sign
segrete dungeon
segreto secret
seguire to follow
sei six
selvaggio wild
semaforo stoplight
sembrare to seem
seminterrato basement
semplice simple; plain
sempre always; anytime
seno breast
senso unico one-way (street)
sentiero trail
sentire to feel (touch); to hear
sentire la mancanza to miss (long for)
sentire un odore to smell (detect by smell)
senza without
senza piombo unleaded
separato separate (adj)
sera evening
serbatoio gas tank
serio serious
serratura lock (n)
servire to serve
servizio service; restroom; toilet
sesso sex (intercourse; gender)
seta silk
sette seven
settembre September
settimana week
settimana, fine weekend
sfortunatamente unfortunately
sfortunato unfortunate

si yes
sicuro safe
sigaretta cigarette
Signora Mrs.
signore gentleman (sing); ladies (pl)
Signore Mr.
Signorina Miss
silenzio silence
simile similar
sinagoga synagogue
sinistra left (direction)
sintetico synthetic
sinusite sinus problem
sito Internet website
slip panties; women's underwear
smalto per unghie nail polish
snowboard snowboarding
soccorso, primo first aid
soccorso, pronto emergency room
socio member; business partner
soffrire to suffer
sognare to dream
sogno dream
soldato soldier
soldi money
sole sun; sunshine
sole, occhiali da sunglasses
sole, scottatura da sunburn
sollevare to lift
solo only; alone
soluzione solution (answer)
soluzione salina solution (contacts)
solvente per le unghie nail polish remover
sopra above; over
sopra, di upstairs
sopracciglio eyebrow
soprannome nickname
sorella sister
sorpresa surprise
sorriso smile
sostanzioso filling; nourishing; substantial
sottile thin
sotto under; below
sottosopra upside-down
sottotitolo subtitle
sottoveste slip (undergarment)
sovrappeso overweight
Spagna Spain
spalla shoulder
spaventato afraid
spazzola brush
spazzolino da denti toothbrush
specchio mirror
speciale special
specialità specialty
specialmente especially
spedire to send; to mail; to ship
spegnere to turn off (device)
spendere to spend
speranza hope
sperare to hope
spesa, fare la to shop (for groceries)
spesso thick
spettacolo show (performance)
spezia spice (seasoning)
spiaggia beach
spiegare to explain
spiegazione explanation

spilla pin; brooch
spilla da balia safety pin
spingere to push
sporco dirty
sportello service desk
sposato married
spostare to move (change position)
sprecare to waste
spuntare to trim
spuntatina trim (hair)
spuntino snack
squadra team
stabilire to set (schedule)
stagione season
stampare to print
stanco tired
stanotte tonight
stanza room
stare bene to fit (clothes); to look nice; to be well (health)
starnuto sneeze
Stati Uniti United States
stato state
stazione station
stazione degli autobus bus station
stazione della metropolitana subway station
stazione ferroviaria train station
stella star (in sky)
stesso same
stile style
stitichezza constipation
stivali boots
stoffa cloth
stomaco stomach
stomaco, mal di stomachache
storia history; story (tale)
strada street; road
straniero foreign
strano strange; odd
stretto tight; narrow
studente student
stupido stupid
stupro rape (n)
stuzzicadenti toothpick
su on; up
sua hers; his
subito soon
succhiotto pacifier
succo juice
sud south
sudare to sweat
sue hers; his
suo hers; his
suocera mother-in-law
suoi hers; his
suonare to play (music)
superalcolico hard liquor
supermercato supermarket
supplemento supplement
sveglia alarm clock
svegliare to wake up
svenuto unconscious
Svizzera Switzerland

T

tablet tablet computer
tacchino turkey (meat)
taglia size
tagliare to cut
tagliaunghie nail clippers

taglio cut
taglio di capelli haircut
tappeto carpet; rug
tappi per le orecchie earplugs
tappo cork; sink stopper
tardi late
tardi, più later; afterward
tariffa fee
tasca pocket
tassametro taxi meter
tastiera keyboard
tatuaggio tattoo
tavola table
tavola calda fast food
tavola da surf surfboard
tavolo desk
tazza cup
tè tea
teatro theater; play (performance)
telefono telephone
telefono cellulare mobile phone
televisione television
temere to fear
temperatura temperature
tempo weather; time (general term; period of time)
tempo, previsioni del weather forecast
temporale storm
temporaneo temporary
tenda tent; curtain
tendinite tendinitis
tenere to keep; to hold
tenero tender
tergicristallo windshield wiper
terminal terminal (n)
terminare to run out of
termini per la cancellazione della prenotazione cancellation policy
termometro thermometer
terra ground; land; earth; soil
terrazzo terrace
terremoto earthquake
terrorista terrorist
tesoro treasury
tessera membership card (hostel)
test di gravidanza pregnancy test
testa head
testa, mal di headache
testare to test
testicolo testicle
tetto roof
tiepido lukewarm
timbrare to validate
timido shy
tirare to pull; to throw
toccare to touch
togliere to remove
toilette toilet
tonno tuna
torcia flashlight
torre tower
tosse cough (n)
tossire to cough
totale total
tra between
tradizionale traditional
tradizione tradition
tradurre to translate
traffico traffic

traghetto ferry
tramonto sunset
tranquillo quiet; tranquil
trattamento viso facial (n)
trattino hyphen (-)
tre three
treno train
treno notturno overnight train
treppiede tripod
triangolo triangle
triste sad
troppo too
troppo cotto overcooked
trovare to find
trucco makeup
tu you (informal)
Turchia Turkey
turista tourist
tutto everything
tutto esaurito sold out

U

ubriaco drunk
uccello bird
uccidere to kill
udire to hear
ufficiale official
ufficio office
ufficio oggetti smarriti lost and found
uguale equal
ultima offerta last offer
ultimo last (final)
umano human (n)
umido muggy; humid
un altro another
un po' some
una volta once
unghia fingernail
unico, senso one-way (street)
Unione Europea European Union (EU)
università university
uno one
uomini men
uomo man
uovo egg
uretra urethra
urgente urgent
urina urine
usare to use
uscita exit
uscita d'emergenza emergency exit
utero uterus

V

vacanza vacation
vagone train car
vagone letto sleeper car (train)
vagone ristorante dining car (train)
valido valid
valigia suitcase
valle valley
valore value (worth)
vampate di calore hot flashes
vasca da bagno bathtub
vaselina Vaseline
vaso vase
vecchio old
vedere to see
vedova widow
vedovo widower

vegetariano vegetarian
vela sailing
velluto velvet
veloce fast; quick
velocità speed
vendere to sell
vendita sale
venerdì Friday
venire to come
ventilatore fan (machine)
vento wind
ventoso windy
verde green
verdura vegetable
verità truth
verme worm
verruca wart
vescica bladder; blister
vestaglia robe
vestiti clothes
vestito dress (n)
vetro glass (material)
via aerea air mail
viaggi, agenzia di travel agency
viaggiare to travel
viaggiatore traveler
viaggio trip (n)
vicino near
videogioco video game
video registratore video recorder
vietato forbidden
vietato fumare non-smoking
vigili del fuoco fire department
vigneto vineyard
villaggio village
vino wine
vino bianco white wine
vino rosso red wine
viola purple
violenza violence
violenza carnale rape (n)
viscido creep; slimy
visita visit (n)
visita, biglietto da business card
visita guidata guided tour
visitare to visit
viso face
viso, trattamento facial (n)
vista view
vita life; waist
vitamina vitamin
vivere to live
vivo live; alive
voce voice
volare to fly
volere to want
volo flight
volta, una once
volte, due twice
vomitare to vomit
vostri / vostro yours
vuoto empty

Z

zainetto backpack
zaino rucksack
zanzara mosquito
zecca tick (insect)
zia aunt
zio uncle
zucchero sugar
zuppa soup

ENGLISH / ITALIAN

A

aboard a bordo
abortion aborto
above sopra
abstract astratto
abuse (v) abusare
accept accettare
access (n) accesso; ingresso (entrance)
accident incidente
accountant commercialista
ache (n) dolore
(to have an) ache avere mal di
adapter, electrical adattatore elettrico
adolescent adolescente
address indirizzo
address, email indirizzo email; indirizzo di posta elettronica
adult adulto
adventurous avventuroso
affordable conveniente
afraid spaventato
Africa Africa
after dopo
afternoon pomeriggio
aftershave dopobarba
afterward più tardi
again ancora
age età
aggressive aggressivo
agnostic agnostico
agree d'accordo
AIDS AIDS
air aria
air mail via aerea
air-conditioned aria condizionata
airline linea aerea
airplane aeroplano
airport aeroporto
aisle corridoio
alarm clock sveglia
alcohol alcool
alive vivo
allergic allergico
allergy allergia
allow lasciare; permettere
allowed permesso
alone solo
already già
altar altare
alter alterare
always sempre
ambulance ambulanza
America America
amount importo
amuse divertire
ancestor antenato
ancient antico
and e
angry arrabbiato
animal animale
ankle caviglia
anniversary anniversario
announcement annuncio
another un altro
answer (n) risposta
answer (v) rispondere
ant formica

antacid antiacido
antibiotic antibiotico
antiques antiquariato; antichità (furniture)
antique shop negozio di antiquariato
anxiety ansia
anyone qualcuno
anything qualcosa
anytime sempre; in qualunque momento
anywhere ovunque
apartment appartamento
apology scuse
appetizer antipasto
apple mela
appointment appuntamento
appropriate appropriato
approximately più o meno
April aprile
aquarium acquario
architect architetto
architecture architettura
area code prefisso
arm braccio
aroma aroma
around (go around) intorno
arrival arrivo
arrive arrivare
art arte
art gallery galleria d'arte
Art Nouveau Art Nouveau
arthritis artrite
artificial artificiale
artist artista
ashtray portacenere
ask domandare
ask for chiedere
asleep addormentato
aspirin aspirina
asthma asma
at a
"at" symbol (@) chiocciola
atheist ateo
athlete atleta; giocatore
athlete's foot piede d'atleta
ATM bancomat
attempt provare
attend (an event) partecipare
attractive bello
audioguide audioguida
August agosto
aunt zia
Austria Austria
author autore
authorize autorizzare
automatic automatico
autumn autunno
available disponibile

B

baby neonato
baby booster seat seggiolino per neonati
baby car seat seggiolino pe la macchina
baby food omogeneizzati
baby formula latte in polvere per neonati
babysitter babysitter
babysitting service servizio di babysitter
back schiena
back (of train) in coda

B

backpack zainetto
bad cattivo
bag sacchetto; busta
bag (handbag) borsa
bag, plastic sacchetto di plastica; busta di plastica
bag, Ziploc busta di plastica sigillabile
baggage bagaglio
baggage check check-in bagagli
baggage claim ritiro bagagli
bakery panificio
balcony balcone
ball palla
banana banana
band (musical) gruppo musicale
bandage benda
bandage, support fascia di sostegno
Band-Aid cerotto
bangs (hair) frangia
bank banca
bar bar; locale
barber / barber shop barbiere
bargain (n) affare
baseball baseball
basement seminterrato
basket cestino
basketball basket
bastard bastardo
bath bagno
bathrobe accappatoio
bathroom bagno
bathtub vasca da bagno
battery batteria
battery charger carica batterie
battery, watch batteria per orologio
beach spiaggia
beach, nude spiaggia nudista
beard barba
beautiful bello
beauty salon parrucchiere
because perché
bed letto
bed, bunk letto a castello
bed, double matrimoniale letto
bed, single singolo letto
bedbug cimice
bedroom camera da letto
bedsheet lenzuolo
beef manzo
beer birra
before prima
begin cominciare
beginning inizio
behind dietro
Belgium Belgio
believe (in) credere (in)
bell campana
below sotto
belt cintura
berth (train) cuccetta
best il migliore
better meglio
between tra
bib bavaglino
Bible Bibbia
bicycle bicicletta
big grande
bill (payment) conto
bill (money) banconota
bird uccello

birth control contraccezione
birth control pill pillola anticoncezionale
birthday compleanno
bitch (n) puttana
bite (n) morso
bitter amaro
black nero
bladder vescica
bland blando
blanket coperta
bleed sanguinare
blister (n) vescica
block (city) isolato
blond biondo
blood sangue
blood pressure, high pressione alta
blouse camicetta
blue blu
blush (makeup) fard
board (transportation) imbarcare
boarding (transportation) imbarco
boat barca
body corpo
boil bollire
boiled bollito
bomb bomba
book (n) libro
book (reserve, purchase) prenotare
book shop libreria
book, telephone elenco telefonico
booster seat (for child) seggiolino per neonati
boots stivali
border frontiera
boring noioso
borrow prendere in prestito
boss capo
both entrambi
bother infastidire
bottle bottiglia
bottom fondo
boutique, clothing boutique di abbigliamento
bowl scodella
box scatola
boy ragazzo
boyfriend ragazzo; fidanzato
bra reggiseno
bracelet braccialetto
brake freno
brass ottone
bread pane
break (rest) pausa
breakdown guasto
breakfast colazione
breakfast room (hotel) sala colazione
breast seno
breastfeed allattare
breastfeeding allattamento al seno
breath alito
breathe respirare
bridge ponte
briefs (men's underwear) mutande
bright brillante

bring portare
Britain Gran Bretagna
broken rotto
bronze bronzo
brooch spilla
brother fratello
brown marrone
browsing guardando
brush (n) spazzola
bucket secchio
bug insetto
bug bite puntura di insetto
bug repellant lozione anti-zanzare
build costruire
building edificio
bulb, light lampadina
bunk bed letto a castello
burn (from fire) (n) bruciatura
burn (from sun) (n) scottatura
bus autobus
bus station stazione degli autobus
bus stop fermata
bus, city autobus
bus, long-distance pullman; corriera
business affare
business card biglietto da visita
business partner socio
busy occupato
butt sedere
butter burro
buttocks glutei
button bottone
buy comprare
by (train, car, etc.) in

C

cable (cord) cavo
calendar calendario
calm calmo
calorie calorie
camera macchina fotografica
camera shop foto-ottica
camper camper
camping campeggio
campsite area per campeggio
can (n) lattina
can (v) potere
can opener apriscatola
Canada Canada
Canadian canadese
canal canale
cancel annullare
cancellation policy termini per la cancellazione della prenotazione
candle candela
candy caramella
canoe canoa
cap berretto
captain capitano
car macchina
car (train) vagone
car ferry autotraghetto
car seat (for baby) seggiolino per la macchina
car, dining (train) vagone ristorante
car, sleeper (train) vagone letto
carafe caraffa
card cartina
card, telephone carta telefonica
cards (deck) carte

careful prudente
carpet tappeto
carry portare
carry-on luggage bagaglio a mano
cash contante
cash machine bancomat
cash register cassa
cashier cassiere
castle castello
cat gatto
catch (v) prendere
cathedral cattedrale
Catholic cattolico
caution attenzione
cave grotta
celebrate festeggiare
cell phone telefono cellulare
cell-phone shop negozio di cellulari
cellar cantina
center centro
century secolo
ceramic ceramica
chain (n) catena
chair sedia
championship campionato
chance possibilità
change (n) cambio
change (v) cambiare
chapel cappella
charge (cost) (v) costare
charger, battery carica batterie
charming affascinante
cheap economico
check (money) (n) assegno
check-in (hotel) (n) check-in
check-in time orario check-in
check out (hotel) (v) lasciare la stanza
Cheers! Salute!
cheese formaggio
cheese shop caseficio
chef chef; cuoco
chest petto
chest pains dolore al petto
chewing gum gomma da masticare
chicken pollo
child bambino
children bambini
chill (temperature) freddo
Chinese cinese
chocolate cioccolato
choir coro
Christian cristiano
Christmas Natale
church chiesa
church service messa
cigarette sigaretta
cinema cinema
circle (shape) cerchio
city città
class classe
class, first prima classe
class, second seconda classe
classical classico
clean (adj) pulito
clean (v) pulire
clear (adj) chiaro
cliff dirupo
clinic, medical clinica
clock orologio
clock, alarm sveglia

cloister chiostro
close (v) chiudere
closed chiuso
closet armadio
cloth stoffa
clothes vestiti
clothespin molletta per bucato
clothesline corda stendipanni
clothing boutique boutique di abbigliamento
cloudy nuvoloso
club (for entertainment) locale
coast (n) costa
coat cappotto
coat hanger appendiabiti
cockfight combattimento di galli
cockroach scarafaggio
coffee caffè
coffee shop bar; caffè
coin moneta
cold (adj) freddo
cold (n) raffreddore
cold medicine medicina per il raffreddore
color colore
comb pettine
come venire
comfortable confortevole
common comune
compact disc compact disc
companion compagno
complain protestare
complaint reclamo
complete (adj) completo
complicated complicato
computer computer
concert concerto
conditioner (hair) balsamo
condom preservativo
conductor capotreno; conducente
confirm confermare
confirmation conferma
congestion (sinus) congestione
congratulations congratulazioni
connect connettere
connection (train) coincidenza
conservative (n) conservatore
constipation stitichezza
construction costruzione
contact lens lente a contatto
contagious contagioso
continue continuare
contraceptive contraccettivo
contraction (pregnancy) contrazione
control (v) controllare
cook (n) cuoco
cook (v) cucinare
cooked cotto
cool fresco
copper rame
copy (n) copia
copy (v) copiare
copy shop copisteria
cork tappo
corkscrew cavatappi
corner angolo
correct giusto
corridor corridoio
corruption corruzione
cost (n) costo
cost (v) costare
cot lettino

cotton cotone
cotton swab (Q-tip) cotton fioc
cough (n) tosse
cough (v) tossire
cough drops caramelle per la tosse; pastiglia per la tosse
cough syrup sciroppo per la tosse
count (v) contare
country paese
country inn locanda di campagna
countryside campagna
course, first primo piatto
course, second secondo piatto
cousin cugino
cover (v) coprire
cover charge coperto
cow mucca
cozy confortevole
craft arte
cramps crampi
cramps, menstrual dolori mestruali
crazy matto
cream panna
cream, first-aid pomata antistaminica
credit card carta di credito
creep (slimy) viscido
crib (for baby) culla
cross (n) croce
cross (e.g., the street) (v) attraversare
crowd (n) folla
cruise ship nave da crociera
cry piangere
crypt cripta
cup tazza
curfew coprifuoco
curtain tenda
customs dogana
cut (n) taglio
cut (v) tagliare; affettare
cute carino
Czech Republic Repubblica Ceca

D

dad papà
daily giornaliero
dairy product latticino
dance (v) ballare
danger pericolo
dangerous pericoloso
dark scuro
dash (-) trattino
date (day) data
date (v) uscire
daughter figlia
day giorno
day after tomorrow dopodomani
(to go on a) day trip fare una gita
dead morto
deal (good value) affare
debit card carta di debito; carta ricaricabile
decaffeinated / decaf decaffeinato
December dicembre
declare (customs) dichiarare
decongestant decongestionante
delay (n) ritardo
delete cancellare

delicate delicato
delicatessen salumeria
delicious delizioso
democracy democrazia
demonstration (public) manifestazione
dental floss filo interdentale
dentist dentista
deodorant deodorante
depart partire
department store grande magazzino
departure partenza
departure time partenza orario
deposit (n) deposito
depression depressione
desk (furniture) scrivania
desk (service) sportello
desperate disperato
dessert dolce
destination destinazione
detergent detersivo da bucato
detour (n) deviazione
diabetes diabete
diabetic diabetico
diamond diamante
diaper pannolino
diaper ointment olio per neonati
diaper rash dermatite da pannolino
diaper wipes salviettine per neonati
diarrhea diarrea
diarrhea medicine farmaco per la diarrea
dictionary dizionario
die morire
difficult difficile
dining car (train) vagone ristorante
dinner cena
direct diretto
direction direzione
dirty sporco
disabled disabile
disaster disastro
discount (n) sconto
discrimination discriminazione
discuss discutere
disease malattia
dish piatto
disinfectant disinfettante
distance distanza
disturb disturbare
divorced divorziato
dizziness capogiro
dizzy mi gira la testa ("my head is spinning")
do fare
doctor dottore
dog cane
dog, mean cagnaccio
doll bambola
dome cupola
domestic nazionali
done fatto
donkey asino
door porta
dormitory camerata
dot (computer) punto
double doppio
doubt (v) dubitare
down giù
downhill in discesa

download scaricare
downtown centro
dozen dozzina
dream (n) sogno
dream (v) sognare
dress vestito
drink (n) bevanda
drink (v) bere
drive (v) guidare
driver autista
drug (medicine) medicinale
drug store farmacia
drunk ubriaco
dry (adj) secco; asciutto
dry (v) asciugare
dryer asciugatrice
duck (n) anatra
duct tape nastro adesivo
dungeon segrete
duplicate (v) copiare
dust (n) polvere
duty free duty free

E

each ogni
ear orecchio
earache mal d'orecchi
earbuds auricolari
early presto
earplugs tappi per le orecchie
earrings orecchini
earth terra
earthquake terremoto
east est
Easter Pasqua
easy facile
eat mangiare
economical economico
eczema eczema
education istruzione
effective efficace
egg uovo
eight otto
elbow gomito
elderly anziano
electrical adapter adattatore elettrico
electrical outlet presa; presa di corrente
elevator ascensore
email posta elettronica
email address indirizzo email; indirizzo di posta elettronica
embarrassing imbarazzante
embassy ambasciata
emergency emergenza
emergency exit uscita d'emergenza
emergency room pronto soccorso
empty vuoto
end fine
engine motore
engineer ingegnere
England Inghilterra
English inglese
enjoy divertirsi
enough abbastanza
enter entrare
entertain divertire
entertainment intrattenimento
entrance ingresso; accesso
entrance (road) entrata
entry entrata

envelope busta
environment (nature) ambiente
epilepsy epilessia
equal uguale
erase cancellare
eraser gomma da cancellare
errand commissione
especially specialmente
Europe Europa
European Union (EU) Unione Europea
evening sera
every ogni
everything tutto
everywhere ovunque
exact esatto
exactly esattamente
examine esaminare
example esempio
excellent eccellente
except eccetto
exchange (n) cambio
exchange (v) cambiare
excuse me mi scusi
exercise (v) fare sport
exhausted esausto
exhibit / exhibition mostra
exit uscita
exit, emergency uscita d'emergenza
expensive caro
experience (n) esperienza
expiration (validity) scadenza
expiration date data di scadenza
explain spiegare
explanation spiegazione
express (fast) espresso
expression espressione
extend (time) prolungare
extension numero interno
extra extra
eye occhio
eye drops collirio; gocce per gli occhi
eye shadow ombretto
eyebrow sopracciglio
eyeglasses occhiali
eyeliner matita; eyeliner
eyes occhi

F

facade facciata
face faccia; viso
face cleanser latte detergente
face powder cipria
facial (n) trattamento viso
facial tissue fazzoletto di carta
factory fabbrica
fair (just) giusto
fall (autumn) autunno
fall (v) cadere
false falso
familiar familiare
family famiglia
family-run place posto a conduzione familiare
famous famoso
fan (machine) ventilatore
fan belt cinghia del ventilatore
fantastic fantastico
far lontano
farm fattoria
farm (with sleeping accommodations) agriturismo

farmer contadino
farsighted presbite
fashion moda
fast veloce
fast food tavola calda
fat (adj) grasso
fat (n) grassi
father padre
faucet rubinetto
favor (n) favore
favorite preferito
fax fax
fear (v) temere
February febbraio
fee tariffa
feed nutrire
feel (touch) sentire
felt (fabric) feltro
female femmina
ferry traghetto
ferry, car autotraghetto
festival festival; festa
fever febbre
few poco
field campo
fight (n) lotta
fight (v) combattere
file (computer) documento; file
fill (v) riempire
filling (adj) sostanzioso
final finale
finally finalmente
find trovare
fine (good) bene
fine (penalty) multa
finger dito
fingernail unghia
finish (v) finire
fire fuoco
fire department vigili del fuoco
fireworks fuochi d'artificio
first primo
first aid primo soccorso
first class prima classe
first-aid cream pomata antistaminica
fish (n) pesce
fish (v) pescare
fit (clothes) (v) stare bene
five cinque
fix (v) aggiustare
fizzy frizzante
flag bandiera
flash (camera) flash
flash drive flash drive
flashlight torcia
flavor (n) gusto
flea pulce
flea market mercato delle pulci
flight volo
flip-flops ciabatte da piscina
flirt (v) flirtare
floor (building) piano
floor (ground) pavimento
floss, dental filo interdentale
flower fiore
flower market mercato dei fiori
flu influenza
fly (v) volare
fog nebbia
follow seguire
food cibo
food poisoning avvelenamento da cibo

foot piede
football (soccer) football; calcio
football, American football americano
for per
forbidden vietato
foreign straniero
forest foresta
forget dimenticare
fork forchetta
form (document) modulo
formula (for baby) latte in polvere per neonati
foundation (makeup) fondotinta
fountain fontana
four quattro
fragile fragile
France Francia
free (no cost) gratis
free (liberate) liberare
frequency frequenza
fresh fresco
Friday venerdì
friend amico
friendship amicizia
Frisbee frisbee
from da
front davanti
fruit frutta
fun (n) divertimento
(to have) fun divertirsi
funeral funerale
funny divertente
furniture mobili
fuse fusibile
future futuro

G

gallery galleria
game gioco
game (sports) partita
garage garage
garbage rifiuti; immondizia
garbage can (indoors / outdoors) cestino / bidone per i rifiuti
garden giardino
gardening giardinaggio
gas (fuel) benzina
gas (stomach) aria
gas (vapor) gas
gas station benzinaio
gas tank serbatoio
gasoline benzina
gauze garza
gay omosessuale; gay
gear marcia
gender sesso
generous generoso
gentleman signore
genuine genuino
Germany Germania
get ottenere
gift regalo
girl ragazza
girlfriend ragazza; fidanzata
give dare
glass (cup) bicchiere
glass (material) vetro
glasses (eye) occhiali
glasses case fodera per occhiali
globalization globalizzazione
gloves guanti
gluten glutine

go andare
go back (return) ritornare
go through attraversare
God Dio
gold oro
golf golf
good buono
good day buongiorno
goodbye arrivederci; ciao (informal)
gorge (n) gola
Gothic Gotico
government governo
grammar grammatica
grandchild nipote
grandchildren nipoti
grandfather nonno
grandmother nonna
grass erba
gray grigio
greasy grasso
great ottimo
Great Britain Gran Bretagna
Greece Grecia
green verde
grocery store alimentari
ground (earth) terra
group (n) gruppo
guarantee (n) garanzia
guaranteed garantito
guest ospite
guide (n) guida
guide (v) guidare
guidebook guida
guided tour visita guidata
guilty colpevole
guitar chitarra
gum (chewing) gomma da masticare
gum (mouth) gengiva
gun pistola
gymnastics ginnastica
gynecologist ginecologo

H

habit abitudine
hair capelli
hair dryer asciugacapelli; phon
hair salon parrucchiere
haircut taglio di capelli
half metà
half portion (food) mezza porzione
hall (big room) salone
hall (hallway) corridoio
ham, boiled prosciutto cotto
hammer (n) martello
hand mano
hand lotion crema per le mani
hand sanitizer igienizzante per le mani
handbag borsa
handicapped disabile; handicappato
handicrafts artigianato
handle (n) manico
handmade fatto a mano
handsome attraente
hand wash lavare a mano
hang appendere
happiness felicità
happy contento
harbor porto
hard duro

hardware store ferramenta
hash (drug) hashish
hat cappello
hate (v) odiare
have avere
hay fever raffreddore da fieno
he lui
head testa
headache mal di testa
headlight faro
headphones cuffie
health salute
health insurance assicurazione medica
healthy sano
hear udire; sentire
heart cuore
heart condition disturbi cardiaci
heartburn bruciore di stomaco
heat (n) calore
heat (v) scaldare
heated scaldato
heaven paradiso
heavy pesante
hello ciao
helmet casco
help (n) aiuto
help (v) aiutare
helpful di aiuto
hemorrhoids emorroidi
hepatitis epatite
herb (cooking) odore
herb (medicine) erbe medicinali
here qui
hers suo; sua; suoi; sue
hi ciao
hidden nascosto
high alto
high blood pressure pressione alta
highchair seggiolone
high-speed train treno ad alta velocità
highway autostrada
hike (n) escursione
hike (v) fare un'escursione
hiking escursionismo
hiking map mappa per escursioni
hill collina
hill town paese in collina
hip (body part) anca
his suo; sua; suoi; sue
history storia
hitchhiking autostop
hobby hobby
hockey hockey
hold tenere
hole buco
holiday giorno festivo
holy sacro
home page home page
homemade casalingo
homesick nostalgico
honest onesto
honeymoon luna di miele
hope (n) speranza
hope (v) sperare
horrible orribile
horse cavallo
horse riding equitazione
hospital ospedale
hostel ostello
hot (temperature) caldo

hot (spicy) piccante
hot flashes vampate di calore
hotel hotel; albergo
hotel, family-run albergo a conduzione familiare; hotel a conduzione familiare
hotel, historic albergo storico
hour ora
house casa
how come
how many quanti
how much ($) quanto costa
hug (n) abbraccio
human umano
humid umido
hundred cento
hungry affamato
hurry (v) avere fretta
hurt (adj) ferito
hurt (v) ferire
hurt oneself (v) ferirsi
(it) hurts fa male
husband marito
hydrofoil aliscafo
hyphen (-) trattino

I

I io
ibuprofen ibuprofene
ice ghiaccio
ice cream gelato
idea idea
ideal ideale
idiot idiota
if se
ignore ignorare
ill malato
illegal illegale
illness malattia
immediately immediatamente
immigration immigrazione
important importante
imported importato
impossible impossibile
Impressionist Impressionista
in in
include includere
included incluso
incorrect non è corretto; scorretto
incredible incredibile
independent indipendente
indigestion indigestione
industry industria
inedible immangiabile
infant neonato
infection infezione
infection, urinary tract infezione urinaria
inflammation infiammazione
inform informare
information informazioni
injure ferire
injured infortunato
injury lesione
inn, country locanda di campagna
innocent innocente
insect insetto
insect repellant lozione anti-zanzare
inside dentro
inspect ispezionare
instant istante

instead invece
instruction istruzione
insult (n) insulto
insurance assicurazione
insurance, health assicurazione medica
insured assicurato
intelligent intelligente
intend intendere
interesting interessante
international internazionale
Internet Internet
Internet access accesso all' Internet
intersection incrocio
intestines intestino
into in
investigation investigazione
invitation invito
invite invitare
iodine iodio
Ireland Irlanda
is è
Islamic islamico
island isola
Italy Italia
itch (n) prurito
itch reliever pomata antiprurito
(to be) itchy dare prurito

J

jacket giubbotto; giacca
January gennaio
jaw mascella
jealous geloso
jeans jeans
jewelry gioielli
jewelry shop gioiellieria
Jewish ebreo
job lavoro
jogging footing
joint (marijuana) canna
joke (n) scherzo
journey viaggio
judge (v) giudicare
juice succo
July luglio
jump saltare
June giugno

K

kayak kayak
keep tenere
kettle bollitore
key chiave
keyboard tastiera
kidney stone calcolo renale
kill uccidere
kilogram kilogrammo
kilometer chilometro
kind (courteous) gentile
king re
kiss bacio
kitchen cucina
kitchenette cucina; angolo cottura ("corner for cooking")
knee ginocchio
knife coltello
knight cavaliere
know sapere
knowledge conoscenza

L

lace pizzo
lactose intolerant intollerante ai latticini
ladder scala
ladies signore
lady signora
lake lago
lamb agnello
lamp lampada
land (earth, soil) terra
language lingua
laptop portatile
large grande
last (final) ultimo
last (previous; e.g., last week) scorso
last name cognome
late tardi
late (train, bus) in ritardo
later più tardi
laugh (v) ridere
launderette lavanderia
laundry soap detersivo da bucato
lawyer avvocato
laxative lassativo
layover scalo
lazy pigro
lead (v) condurre
learn imparare
leather pelle
leather shop pelletteria
leave partire
left (direction) sinistra
leg gamba
legal legale
lend prestare
length lunghezza
lenses, contact lenti a contatto
lesbian lesbica
let (allow) lasciare; permettere
letter lettera
liberal (n) liberale
liberate liberare
library biblioteca
lice pidocchi
lie (n) bugia
life vita
lift (v) sollevare
light (adj) chiaro
light (n) luce
light (v) accendere
light up (illuminate) illuminare
lightbulb lampadina
lighter (n) accendino
lightheaded mi gira la testa ("my head is spinning")
like (v) piacere
line (queue) fila; coda
line (thin rope) filo
line (transportation; e.g., bus line) linea
line up (stand in line) mettersi in fila
linen lino
lip labbro
lip balm / lip salve burro di cacao
lipstick rossetto
liquid liquido
list (n) lista
listen ascoltare
liter litro

little (adj) piccolo
live (animal) (adj) vivo
live (music) (adj) dal vivo
live (v) vivere
local locale
lock (n) serratura
lock (v) chiudere a chiave
locked (mobile phone) bloccato
locker armadietto
long lungo
look / look at guardare
look for cercare
loose largo
lose perdere
lost perso
lost and found ufficio oggetti smarriti
lotion, hand crema per le mani
loud forte
love (n) amore
love (v) amare
lover amante
low basso
lozenge pastiglia per la gola
luck fortuna
lucky fortunato
luggage bagaglio
luggage cart carrello bagagli
luggage, carry-on bagaglio a mano
lukewarm tiepido
lunch pranzo
lungs polmoni
luxurious lussuoso

M

machine macchina
macho macho
mad (angry) arrabbiato
magazine rivista
mail (n) posta
mail (v) spedire
mailbox cassetta postale
main principale
main course (food) secondo piatto
make (v) fare
makeup trucco
male maschio
mall (shopping) centro commerciale
man uomo
manage (oversee) gestire
manager direttore
manicure manicure
many molti
map cartina
marble (material) marmo
march (n) marcia
March marzo
marijuana marijuana
market mercato
market, flea mercato delle pulci
market, flower mercato dei fiori
market, open-air mercato
marriage matrimonio
married sposato
mascara mascara
Mass messa
massage massaggio
masterpiece capolavoro
match (sports) partita
match / matchstick fiammifero
material materiale

maximum massimo
May maggio
maybe forse
me me
meal pasto
meat carne
mechanic meccanico
media media
medical clinic clinica
medicine medicina
medicine for a cold medicina per il raffreddore
medicine, non-aspirin substitute Saridon
medieval medievale
medium medio
meet (v) incontrare
member socio
membership card (hostel) tessera
memory card memory card
men uomini
menstrual cramps dolori mestruali
menstruation mestruazioni
menu menù
message messaggio
metal metallo
meter, taxi tassametro
method metodo
middle mezzo
midnight mezzanotte
migraine emicrania
mileage (in kilometers) chilometraggio
military militare
milk latte
mind (brain) mente
mine mio; mia; miei; mie
mineral water acqua minerale
minimum minimo
minus meno
minute minuto
mirror specchio
miscarriage aborto spontaneo
Miss Signorina
miss (long for) sentire la mancanza
miss (bus, train, etc.) perdere
missing (lost) perso
mistake errore
misunderstanding incomprensione
mix (n) misto
mix (v) mischiare
mixed mischiato
moat fossato
mobile phone telefono cellulare
mobile-phone shop negozio di cellulari
modern moderno
modify alterare
moisturizer crema idratante
moleskin feltro; moleskin
moment momento
monastery monastero
Monday lunedì
money soldi
month mese
monument monumento
moon luna
more ancora
morning mattina
mosque moschea

mosquito zanzara
mother madre
mother-in-law suocera
motion sickness mal di macchina (car, etc.); mal di mare (sea)
motor scooter motorino
motorcycle motocicletta
mountain montagna
mountain bike mountain bike
mountain pass passo di montagna
moustache baffi
mouth bocca
mouthwash colluttorio
move (change position) spostare
movie film
movie theater cinema
Mr. Signore
Mrs. Signora
much molto
muggy umido
mural murale
muscle muscolo
museum museo
music musica
musician musicista
Muslim (adj) musulmano
my mio; mia

N

nail (finger) unghia
nail clippers tagliaunghie
nail file limetta per unghie
nail polish smalto per unghie
nail polish remover solvente per le unghie
naked nudo
name nome
name, last cognome
nap (n) pisolino
napkin salvietta
narrow stretto
national nazionale
nationality nazionalità
natural naturale
nature natura
nausea nausea
near vicino
nearsighted miope
necessary necessario
neck collo
necklace collana
necktie cravatta
need (n) bisogno
need (v) avere bisogno di
needle ago
neither nessuno dei due
neither... nor... ne... ne...
Neoclassical Neoclassico
nephew nipote
nervous nervoso
Netherlands Paesi Bassi
network (technology) rete
never mai
new nuovo
news notizie
newspaper giornale
newsstand edicola; giornalaio
next prossimo
next to accanto a
nice bello

nickname soprannome
niece nipote
night notte
nightclub locale notturno; discoteca
nightgown camicia da notte
nine nove
no no
no one nessuno
no vacancy completo
noisy rumoroso
non-aspirin substitute Saridon
non-smoking vietato fumare
noon mezzogiorno
normal normale
north nord
nose naso
not non
note (message) biglietto
notebook quaderno
notepad block notes
nothing niente
November novembre
now adesso
nowhere in nessun posto
nude nudo
number numero
numbness intorpidimento
nurse (n) infermiera
nurse (breastfeed) allattare
nut (food) noce
nylon (material) nylon
nylons (panty hose) collant

O

occupation lavoro
occupied occupato
ocean oceano
October ottobre
odor odore
of di
offer (n) offerta
offer (v) offrire
offer, last ultima offerta
office ufficio
office supplies store cartoleria
official ufficiale
oil (n) olio
OK d'accordo
old vecchio
old (elderly) anziano
old town paese antico
Olympics Olimpiadi
on su
on time in orario
once una volta
one uno
one-way (street) senso unico
one-way (ticket) andata
only solo
open (adj) aperto
open (v) aprire
open-air market mercato
opening hours orario d'apertura
opera opera
operation (medical) operazione
operator centralinista
opinion opinione
opportunity opportunità
optician ottico
optimistic ottimista
or o
orange (color) arancione
orange (fruit) arancia

order (layout; restaurant) (n) ordine
order (v) ordinare
organ organo
original originale
other altro
outdoors all'aria aperta
outlet, electrical (plug) presa
outside fuori
oven forno
over (above) sopra
over (finished) finito
overcooked troppo cotto
overnight train treno notturno
overweight sovrappeso
own (v) possedere
owner padrone

P

pacifier succhiotto; ciuccio
pack (v) fare le valigie
package pacco
pad, sanitary assorbente igienico
paddleboat pedalò
page pagina
pail secchio
pain dolore
painkiller analgesico
pains, chest dolore al petto
paint (v) dipingere
painting quadro
painting gallery pinacoteca
pair paio
pajamas pigiama
palace palazzo
panties (women's underwear) mutandine; slip
pants pantaloni
paper carta
paper clip graffetta
paradise paradiso
parents genitori
park (n) parco
park (v) parcheggiare
parking lot parcheggio
partner (business) socio
partner (relationship) compagno
party (celebration) festa
party (group) gruppo
passenger passeggero
passport passaporto
past passato
pastry pasticcino; dolce
pastry shop pasticceria
pay pagare
peace pace
pedestrian pedone
pedicure pedicure
pen penna
pencil matita
penis pene
people persone
pepper (spice) pepe
percent percentuale
perfect (adj) perfetto
perfume profumo
period (of time) periodo
period (woman's) mestruazioni
permanent permanente
person persona
pessimistic pessimista

pet (n) animale domestico
pewter peltro
pharmacy farmacia
phone telefono
phone booth cabina telefonica
phone, mobile telefono cellulare
photo foto
photocopy fotocopia
photocopy shop copisteria
pickpocket borseggiatore
picnic picnic
piece pezzo
pig maiale
pill pillola
pillow cuscino
pill, birth control pillola anticoncezionale
pin (n) spilla
PIN code codice segreto
pink rosa
pity, it's a che peccato
place (position) posto
place (site) luogo
place (v) collocare
plain (adj) semplice
plain (n) pianura
plane aeroplano
plant pianta
plastic plastica
plastic bag sacchetto di plastica; busta di plastica
plate piatto
platform (train) binario
play (performance) teatro
play (music) (v) suonare
play (sports, games) (v) giocare
player (sports) giocatore
playground parco giochi
playpen box
please per favore
please (v) accontentare
pliers pinze
plug (outlet) spina
pneumonia broncopolmonite
pocket tasca
point (reason; dot) punto
point (v) indicare
police polizia
policy politica
political politico
politician politico
pollution inquinamento
polyester poliestere
poop pupu
poor povero
popular popolare
porcelain porcellana
pork maiale
portion porzione
portrait ritratto
Portugal Portogallo
possibility possibilità
possible possibile
possibly forse
postcard cartolina
poster poster
poultry pollame
powder polvere
power (n) potere
powerful potente
practical pratico
practice (v) fare pratica
precious prezioso
prefer preferire

P

pregnancy gravidanza
pregnancy test test di gravidanza
pregnant incinta
Preparation H Preparazione H
prescription ricetta; prescrizione
present (gift) regalo
president presidente
pretty carino
price prezzo
priest prete
prince principe
princess principessa
principle principio
print stampare
private privato
problem problema
produce (v) produrre
product prodotto
profession professione
prohibited proibito
prolong prolungare
promise (n) promessa
promise (v) promettere
pronunciation pronuncia
prosper prosperare
prostitute prostituta
protect proteggere
Protestant (adj) protestante
prudish pudico
pub locale; pub
public pubblico
pull tirare
pull back ritirare
pulpit pulpito
pulse battito cardiaco
pump (n) pompa
punctual puntuale
purple viola
purse borsa
push spingere

Q

Q-tip (cotton swab) cotton fioc
quad-band quad-band
quality qualità
quantity quantità
quarter (¼) quarto
queen regina
question (n) domanda
quick veloce
quickly velocemente
quiet tranquillo

R

RV camper
rabbit coniglio
racism razzismo
radiator radiatore
radical (adj, n) radicale
radio radio
raft gommone
railway ferrovia
rain (n) pioggia
rain (v) piovere
rainbow arcobaleno
raincoat impermeabile
rape (n) stupro; violenza carnale
rash irritazione della pelle
rash, diaper dermatite da pannolino
raw crudo
razor rasoio
read leggere

reading glasses occhiali da lettura
ready pronto
realize accorgersi
receipt ricevuta
receive ricevere
recent recente
receptionist centralinista
recharge ricaricare
recipe ricetta
recommend raccomandare
recommendation racommandazione
rectum retto
red rosso
refill (v) riempire
refugee profugo
refund (n) rimborso
regular normale
relax riposare
relaxation rilassamento
release liberare
relic reliquia
religion religione
remember ricordare
remind ricordare
remove togliere
Renaissance Rinascimento
rent affittare
repair (v) riparare
require (demand) pretendere
require (need) desiderare
reservation prenotazione
reserve prenotare
resolve risolvere
respect (n) rispetto
rest (v) riposare
restaurant ristorante
restoration restauro
restroom servizio; toilette; bagno
retired in pensione
return (go back) ritornare
return (something) restituire
rich ricco
right (correct) giusto
right (direction) destra
ring anello
ring road raccordo anulare
ripe maturo
river fiume
road strada
robe vestaglia; accappatoio
robbed derubato
rock pietra
roller skates pattini a rotelle
rollerblades rollerblades
Romanesque Romanico
Romantic Romantico
romantic romantico
roof tetto
room camera; stanza
room (hall; e.g., sitting room) sala
rope corda
rotten marcio
round-trip andata e ritorno
roundabout rotonda
route (n) itinerario; percorso
row (n) fila
rowboat barca a remi
rucksack zaino
rude maleducato
rug tappeto
ruins rovine

rule (n) regola
ruler governante
run correre
run out of terminare
Russia Russia

S

sad triste
safe sicuro
safety pin spilla da balia
sailboat barca a vela
sailing vela
saint santo
salad insalata
sale liquidazione; vendita; saldi
salt sale
same stesso
sandals sandali
sandwich panino
sanitary pad assorbente igienico
Santa Claus Babbo Natale
Saturday sabato
sausage salsiccia
save salvare
say dire
scandalous scandaloso
Scandinavia Paesi Scandinavi
scarf sciarpa
scenic panoramico
scent aroma
schedule (timetable) orario
school scuola
science scienza
scientist scienziato
scissors forbici
scotch tape nastro adesivo
screen (n) schermo
screwdriver cacciavite
sculptor scultore
sculpture scultura
sea mare
seafood frutti di mare
search (v) cercare
seasickness mal di mare
season (n) stagione
seat posto
second class seconda classe
secret segreto
see vedere
seem sembrare
self-portrait autoritratto
self-service self-service
sell vendere
send spedire
senior anziano
sensible ragionevole
separate (adj) separato
September settembre
serious serio
serve servire
server (restaurant) cameriere
service servizio
service desk sportello
service, church messa
set (schedule) (v) stabilire
set (put something down) (v) mettere giù; collocare
setting ambiente
seven sette
sew cucire
sex (intercourse; gender) sesso
sexy sexy
shade (n) ombra
shampoo shampoo

share (v) dividere
shave (v) radere
shaving cream crema da barba
she lei
sheet lenzuolo
shell conchiglia
shellfish crostacei
ship (n) nave
ship (v) spedire
shirt camicia
shiver (from cold) (n) brivido
shoelace laccio delle scarpe
shoes scarpe
shoes, tennis scarpe da tennis
shop (n) negozio
shop (v) fare shopping
shop (for groceries) (v) fare la spesa
shop, antique negozio di antiquariato
shop, barber barbiere
shop, camera foto-ottica
shop, cheese caseficio
shop, clothing negozio di abbigliamento
shop, coffee bar; caffè
shop, jewelry gioiellieria
shop, leather pelletteria
shop, mobile-phone negozio di cellulari
shop, pastry pasticceria
shop, photocopy copisteria
shop, souvenir negozio di souvenir
shop, sweets pasticceria; negozio di dolciumi
shop, wine negozio di vini; enoteca
(to go) shopping fare shopping
shopping mall centro commerciale
short corto
shorts pantaloncini
shoulder spalla
show (performance) spettacolo
show (v) mostrare
shower (n) doccia
shrink ritirarsi
shuttle bus bus navetta
shy timido
sick malato
side lato
sign segno
signature firma
silence silenzio
silk seta
silver argento
SIM card SIM card; carta SIM
similar simile
simple semplice
since da
sing cantare
singer cantante
single single; nubile (f); scapolo (m)
sink lavandino
sink stopper tappo
sinus problem sinusite
sir signore
sister sorella
sit sedersi
site luogo
six sei

size taglia
skating pattinaggio
ski (v) sciare
skiing sci
skin pelle
skinny magro
skirt (n) gonna
sky cielo
sleep (v) dormire
sleeper car (train) vagone letto
sleeping bag sacco a pelo
sleepy assonnato
sleeves maniche
slice (thick; e.g., cake and bread) fetta
slice (thin; e.g., coldcuts) fettina
slice (v) affettare; tagliare
slip (undergarment) sottoveste
slippers ciabatte; pantofole
slippery scivoloso
slow lento
small piccolo
smartphone smartphone
smell (odor) (n) odore
smell (stink, stench) (n) puzza
smell (detect by smell) (v) sentire un odore
smile (n) sorriso
smoke (n) fumo
smoke (v) fumare
smoker (person) fumatore
smoking (cigarettes) fumare
smoking (engine, stove, etc) fare fumo
snack (n) spuntino
sneakers scarpe da ginnastica
sneeze (n) starnuto
snore russare
snorkel boccaglio
snow (n) neve
snowboarding snowboard
soap sapone
soap, laundry detersivo da bucato
soccer calcio; football
socks calzini
soft morbido
soil (earth) terra
sold out tutto esaurito
soldier soldato
solution (answer) soluzione
solution (contacts) soluzione salina
some un po'
someone qualcuno
something qualcosa
somewhere da qualche parte
son figlio
song canzone
soon subito
sore dolorante
sore throat mal di gola
sorry mi dispiace
soup zuppa; minestra
sour aspro; acerbo
south sud
souvenir shop negozio di souvenir
soy soia
spa centro benessere
space (room) posto
Spain Spagna
spark plug candela

speak parlare
speaker (audio) cassa
special speciale
specialty specialità
speed velocità
speed limit limite di velocità
spend spendere
spice (seasoning) spezia
spider ragno
splinter scheggia
split dividere
spoon cucchiaio
sport sport
spouse consorte
spring (season) primavera
square (shape) quadrato
square (town) piazza
stairs scale
stamps francobolli
stapler pinzatrice
star (in sky) stella
start (n) inizio
start (v) iniziare; cominciare
state stato
station stazione
stench puzza
stiff drink superalcolico
stink (n) puzza
stink (v) puzzare
stolen rubato
stomach stomaco
stomachache mal di stomaco
stoned fumato; fatto
stool (fecal matter) feci
stop (command) alt
stop (train, bus) (n) fermata
stop (v) fermare
stoplight semaforo
stopper, sink tappo
store negozio
store, clothing negozio di abbigliamento
store, department grande magazzino
store, drug farmacia
store, hardware ferramenta
store, jewelry gioiellieria
store, mobile-phone negozio di cellulari
store, office supplies cartoleria
store, souvenir negozio di souvenir
store, toy negozio di giocattoli
storm temporale
story (building) piano
story (tale) storia
straight dritto
strange (odd) strano
straw (drinking) cannuccia
stream ruscello
street strada
strike (stop work) sciopero
string filo
stroller (for baby) passeggino
strong forte
stuck incastrato
student studente
stupid stupido
sturdy resistente
style stile
substantial sostanzioso
subtitle sottotitolo
subway metropolitana
subway entrance entrata

subway exit uscita
subway map cartina
subway station stazione della metropolitana
subway stop fermata
suddenly improvvisamente
suffer soffrire
sugar zucchero
suitcase valigia
summer estate
sun sole
sunbathe abbronzarsi
sunburn scottatura da sole
Sunday domenica
sunglasses occhiali da sole
sunny assolato
sunrise alba
sunscreen protezione solare
sunset tramonto
sunshine sole
sunstroke insolazione
suntan abbronzatura
suntan lotion crema solare
supermarket supermercato
supplement supplemento
surfboard tavola da surf
surfer surfer
surprise (n) sorpresa
swallow ingoiare
sweat (v) sudare
sweater maglione
sweet dolce
sweets shop pasticceria; negozio di dolciumi
swelling gonfiore
swim nuotare
swim trunks costume da bagno
swimming pool piscina
swimsuit costume da bagno
Switzerland Svizzera
synagogue sinagoga
synthetic sintetico

T

table tavola
tablet computer tablet
tail coda
taillight luce posteriore
take prendere
take out (food) portar via
talcum powder borotalco
talk parlare
tall alto
tampon assorbente interno
tan (v) abbronzarsi
tank, gas serbatoio
tape (adhesive) nastro adesivo; scotch
taste (n) gusto
taste (v) assaggiare
tasty saporito
tattoo tatuaggio
tax tassa
taxi taxi
taxi meter tassametro
tea tè
teach (v) insegnare
teacher insegnante
team squadra
teenager adolescente
teeth denti
teething (baby) dentizione
telefonare to phone
telephone telefono

telephone card carta telefonica
telephone number numero telefonico
television televisione
tell dire
temperature temperatura
temporary temporaneo
ten dieci
tender tenero
tendinitis tendinite
tennis tennis
tennis shoes scarpe da tennis
tent tenda
tent peg picchetto della tenda
terminal (n) terminal
terrace terrazzo
terrible terribile
terrorist terrorista
test (v) testare
testicle testicolo
thanks grazie
that (thing) quello
theater teatro
their i loro; il loro; la loro; le loro
then poi
there là
thermometer termometro
they loro
thick spesso
thief ladro
thigh coscia
thin sottile
thing cosa
think pensare
thirsty assetato
thongs sandali infradito
thousand mille
thread filo
three tre
throat gola
throat, sore mal di gola
through attraverso
throw tirare
thumb pollice
Thursday giovedì
tick (insect) zecca
ticket biglietto
tie (clothing) cravatta
tie (v) legare
tight stretto
time (clock time) ora
time (general term; period of time) tempo
time, arrival arrivo orario
time, check-in check-in orario
time, departure partenza orario
time, on in orario
timetable orario
tip (gratuity) mancia
tire (n) gomma
tire, flat gomma a terra
tired stanco
tissue, facial fazzoletto di carta
to a
toasted scaldato
today oggi
toe dito del piede
together insieme
toilet toilette; servizio; bagno
toilet paper carta igienica
token (n) gettone
toll pedaggio
toll-free number numero verde
tomorrow domani

tongue (mouth) lingua
tonight stanotte
too troppo
tooth dente
toothache mal di denti
toothbrush spazzolino da denti
toothpaste dentifricio
toothpick stuzzicadenti
total totale
touch toccare
tour (n) giro
tour, guided visita guidata
tourist turista
tow truck carro attrezzi
towel asciugamano
tower torre
town città; paese
toy giocattolo
toy store negozio di giocattoli
track (train) binario
tradition tradizione
traditional tradizionale
traffic traffico
trail (n) sentiero
train treno
train car vagone
train station stazione ferroviaria
train, high-speed treno ad alta velocità
tranquil tranquillo
transfer (n) transfer; scalo
transfer (v) cambiare
translate tradurre
transmission fluid liquido della trasmissione
trash rifiuti; immondizia
trashcan (indoors) cestino per i rifiuti
trashcan (outdoors) bidone per i rifiuti
travel (n) viaggiare
travel agency agenzia di viaggi
traveler viaggiatore
treasury tesoro
treat (medical) (v) curare
treatment (medical) cura
tree albero
triangle triangolo
tri-band tri-band
trim (hair) (n) spuntatina
trim (v) spuntare
trip (n) viaggio
tripod treppiede
trouble guaio
truth verità
try (attempt) provare
T-shirt maglietta
Tuesday martedì
tuna tonno
tunnel galleria
turkey (meat) tacchino
Turkey Turchia
turn off (device) spegnere
turn on (device) accendere
turn signal freccia
tweezers pinzette
twice due volte
twin gemello
two due
type (v) digitare

U

ugly brutto

umbrella ombrello
uncle zio
unconscious svenuto; privo di sensi
under sotto
undercooked poco cotto
underscore (_) linea bassa
understand capire
underwear intimo
underwear (men) mutande
underwear (women) mutandine
undrinkable water acqua non potabile
unemployed disoccupato
unfair scorretto
unfortunate sfortunato
unfortunately sfortunatamente
United States Stati Uniti
university università
unleaded senza piombo
unlock (door) aprire
unlock (mobile phone) sbloccare
unripe acerbo
until fino
up su
uphill in salita
upside-down sottosopra
upstairs di sopra
urethra uretra
urgent urgente
urinary tract infection infezione urinaria
urine urina
us noi
use (v) usare
uterus utero

V

vacancy (hotel) camere libere; camere disponibili
vacancy, no completo
vacant libero
vacation vacanza
vagina vagina
valid valido
validate timbrare
valley valle
value (worth) valore
van monovolume
vase vaso
Vaseline vaselina
vegetable verdura
vegetarian vegetariano
velvet velluto
very molto
vest gilè
video video
video camera video camera
video game videogioco
video recorder video registratore
view vista
viewpoint punto panoramico; belvedere
village villaggio; paese
vineyard vigneto
violence violenza
virus virus
visit (n) visita
visit (v) visitare
vitamin vitamina
voice voce
vomit (v) vomitare

W

waist vita
wait aspettare
waiter cameriere
waiting room sala di attesa; sala d'aspetto
waitress cameriera
wake up svegliare
walk (v) camminare
wall (barrier; e.g., city wall) mura
wall (room) parete; muro
wall, fortified mura fortificate
wallet portafoglio
want volere
war guerra
warm caldo
wart verruca
wash lavare
wash (by hand) lavare a mano
washer lavatrice
waste (v) sprecare
watch (clock) orologio
watch (v) guardare
watch battery batteria per orologio
water acqua
water, drinkable acqua potabile
water, tap acqua del rubinetto
water, undrinkable acqua non potabile
waterfall cascata
waterfront lungomare
waterskiing sci acquatico
wave (water) onda
wax (hair removal) ceretta
we noi
wear (v) indossare
weather tempo
weather forecast previsioni del tempo
webcam webcam
website sito Internet
wedding matrimonio
Wednesday mercoledì
week settimana
weekend weekend; fine settimana
weight peso
weight limit limite di peso
welcome benvenuto
well (well-being, manner) bene
(to be) well (health) stare bene
west ovest
wet bagnato
what che cosa
whatever (anything) qualsiasi cosa
wheat frumento
wheel ruota
wheelchair sedia a rotelle
wheelchair-accessible accessibile con la sedia a rotelle
when quando
where dove
whipped cream panna
white bianco
whitener / white-out bianchetto
who chi
why perché
wide largo
widow vedova
widower vedovo
width larghezza

wife moglie
Wi-Fi Wi-Fi
Wi-Fi hotspot area Wi-Fi
wild selvaggio
wind vento
windmill mulino a vento
window finestra
windshield wiper tergicristallo
windsurfing windsurf
windy ventoso
wine vino
wine shop negozio di vini
wine, red vino rosso
wine, white vino bianco
wing ala
winter inverno
wipe (v) pulire
wiper, windshield tergicristallo
wireless wireless
wise saggio
wish (v) desiderare
with con
withdraw ritirare
without senza
woman donna
women donne
wood legno
wool lana
word parola
work (n) lavoro
work (v) lavorare
world mondo
worm verme
worry (v) preoccupare
worse peggio
worst peggiore
wrap incartare
wrist polso
write scrivere

X

X-ray radiografia

Y

year anno
yellow giallo
yes si
yesterday ieri
yoga yoga
yogurt yogurt
you (formal) Lei
you (informal) tu
young giovane
your il tuo; il vostro; la tua; le vostre
yours tuo; tuoi; vostro; vostri
youth giovane
youth hostel ostello della gioventù

Z

zero zero
zip code codice postale
Ziploc bag busta di plastica sigillabile
zipper chiusura lampo
zoo zoo

TIPS FOR HURDLING THE LANGUAGE BARRIER

A fear of the language barrier keeps many people (read: English speakers) out of Europe, but the "barrier" is getting smaller every day. English has arrived as Europe's second language, but you'll win the respect of locals by starting conversations in Italian—ask ***Parla inglese?*** (Do you speak English?). And if you need help speaking Italian, remember that you're surrounded by expert tutors.

Creative Communication

Speak slowly, clearly, and with carefully chosen words. When speaking English, choose easy words and clearly pronounce each syllable (fried po-ta-toes). Avoid contractions. Be patient—speaking louder and tossing in a few extra words doesn't help.

Keep your messages grunt-simple. Make single nouns work as entire sentences. A one-word question ("Photo?") is just as effective as something grammatically correct ("May I take your picture, sir?"). Things go even easier if you include the local "please" (for instance, "Toilet, ***per favore?***").

Can the slang. Someone who learned English in a classroom will be stumped by American expressions such as "sort of like," "pretty bad," or "Howzit goin'?"

Risk looking goofy. Butcher the language if you must, but communicate. I'll never forget the postal clerk who flapped her arms and asked, "Tweet, tweet, tweet?" I answered with a nod, and she gave me the airmail stamps I needed.

Be melodramatic. Exaggerate the native accent. The locals won't be insulted; they'll be impressed. English spoken with an over-the-top sexy Italian accent makes more sense to the Italian ear.

A notepad works wonders. Written words and numbers are much easier to understand than their mispronounced counterparts. Bring a notepad. To repeatedly communicate something difficult or important (such as medical instructions, "I'm a strict vegetarian," etc.), write it in the local language.

Assume you understand and go with your gut. Treat most problems as multiple-choice questions, make an educated guess at the meaning, and proceed confidently. I'm correct about 80 percent of the time—and even when I'm wrong, I usually never know it. I only blow it about 10 percent of the time. My trip becomes easier—and occasionally much more interesting.

Italian Gestures

Body language is an important part of communicating in Italy, especially hand gestures. Here are a few common gestures and their meanings:

Hand purse: Straighten the fingers and thumb of one hand, bringing them all together making an upward point about a foot in front of your face. Your hand can be held still or moved a little up and down at the wrist. This is a common and very Italian gesture for a query. It is used to say "What do you want?" or "What are you doing?" or "What is it?" or "What's new?" It can also be used as an insult to say "You fool."

Cheek screw: Make a fist, stick out your forefinger, and (without piercing the skin) screw it into your cheek. The cheek screw is used widely in Italy to mean good, lovely, beautiful. Many Italians also use it to mean clever.

Eyelid pull: Place your extended forefinger below the center of your eye and pull the skin downward. It means "Be alert, that guy is clever."

Forearm jerk: Clench your right fist and jerk your forearm up as you slap your right bicep with your left palm. This is a rude, phallic gesture that men throughout southern Europe often use the way many Americans give someone the finger. This jumbo version of "flipping the bird" says "I'm superior."

Chin flick: Tilt your head back slightly and flick the back of your fingers forward in an arc from under your chin. In Italy this means "I'm not interested, you bore me," or "You bother me." In southern Italy it can mean "No."

Beckoning and waving: To beckon someone in southern Europe, you wave your palm down; to summon someone in northern Europe you bring your palm up. While most people greet each other by waving with their palm out, you'll find many Italians wave "at themselves" as infants do, with their palm toward their face. ***Ciao-ciao.***

International Words

As our world shrinks, more and more words leap their linguistic boundaries and become international. Sensitive travelers choose words most likely to be universally understood ("auto" instead of "car"; "holiday" for "vacation"; "kaput" for "broken"; "photo" for "picture"). They also internationalize their pronunciation: "University," if you play around with its sound (oo-nee-vehr-see-tay), can be understood anywhere.

Here are a few internationally understood words. Remember, cut out the Yankee accent and give each word a pan-European sound ("autoboooos," "Engleesh").

Hello
No
Stop
Kaput
Ciao
Bye-bye
OK
Mañana
Pardon
Rock 'n' roll
Mamma mia
No problem
Super
Sex / Sexy
Oh la la
Moment
Bon voyage
Restaurant
Bank
Hotel
Post (office)
Camping
Auto
Autobus
Taxi
Tourist
Beer
Coke / Coca-Cola
Tea
Coffee
Vino
Chocolate
Picnic
Self-service
Yankee / Americano
Amigo
Toilet
Police
English
Telephone
Photo
Photocopy
Computer
Sport
Internet
Central
Information
University
Passport
Holiday (vacation)
Gratis (free)
America's favorite four-letter words

Italian Verbs

These conjugated verbs will help you construct a caveman sentence in a pinch.

TO GO	ANDARE	ahn-**dah**-ray
I go	io vado	**ee**-oh **vah**-doh
you go (formal)	Lei va	**leh**-ee vah
you go (informal)	tu vai	too **vah**-ee
he / she goes	lui / lei va	**loo**-ee / **leh**-ee vah
we go	noi andiamo	**noh**-ee ahn-dee-**ah**-moh
you go (pl. formal)	voi andate	**voh**-ee ahn-**dah**-tay
they go	loro vanno	**loh**-roh **vah**-noh
TO BE	**ESSERE**	**eh**-seh-ray
I am	io sono	**ee**-oh **soh**-noh
you are (formal)	Lei è	**leh**-ee eh
you are (informal)	tu sei	too **seh**-ee
he / she is	lui / lei è	**loo**-ee / **leh**-ee eh
we are	noi siamo	**noh**-ee see-**ah**-moh
you are (pl. formal)	voi siete	**voh**-ee see-**eh**-tay
they are	loro sono	**loh**-roh **soh**-noh
TO DO	**FARE**	**fah**-ray
I do	io faccio	**ee**-oh **fah**-choh
you do (formal)	Lei fa	**leh**-ee fah
you do (informal)	tu fai	too **fah**-ee
he / she does	lui / lei fa	**loo**-ee / **leh**-ee fah
we do	noi facciamo	**noh**-ee fah-chee-**ah**-moh
you do (pl. formal)	voi fate	**voh**-ee **fah**-tay
they do	loro fanno	**loh**-roh **fah**-noh

TO HAVE	AVERE	ah-**veh**-ray
I have	io ho	**ee**-oh oh
you have (formal)	Lei ha	**leh**-ee ah
you have (informal)	tu hai	too **ah**-ee
he / she has	lui / lei ha	**loo**-ee / **leh**-ee ah
we have	noi abbiamo	**noh**-ee ah-bee-**ah**-moh
you have (pl. formal)	voi avete	**voh**-ee ah-**veh**-tay
they have	loro hanno	**loh**-roh **ahn**-noh

TO SEE	VEDERE	veh-**deh**-ray
I see	io vedo	**ee**-oh **veh**-doh
you see (formal)	Lei vede	**leh**-ee **veh**-day
you see (informal)	tu vedi	too **veh**-dee
he / she sees	lui / lei vede	**loo**-ee / **leh**-ee **veh**-day
we see	noi vediamo	**noh**-ee veh-dee-**ah**-moh
you see (pl. formal)	voi vedete	**voh**-ee veh-**day**-tay
they see	loro vedono	**loh**-roh veh-**doh**-noh

TO SPEAK	PARLARE	par-**lah**-ray
I speak	io parlo	**ee**-oh **par**-loh
you speak (formal)	Lei parla	**leh**-ee **par**-lah
you speak (informal)	tu parli	too **par**-lee
he / she speaks	lui / lei parla	**loo**-ee / **leh**-ee **par**-lah
we speak	noi parliamo	**noh**-ee par-lee-**ah**-moh
you speak (pl. formal)	voi parlate	**voh**-ee par-**lah**-tay
they speak	loro parlano	**loh**-roh par-**lah**-noh

TO LIKE	PIACERE	pee-ah-**cheh**-ray
I like	mi piace	mee pee-**ah**-chay
you like (formal)	Le piace	lay pee-**ah**-chay
you like (informal)	ti piace	tee pee-**ah**-chay
he / she likes	gli / le piace	lee / lay pee-**ah**-chay
we like	ci piace	chee pee-**ah**-chay
you like (pl. formal)	vi piace	vee pee-**ah**-chay
they like	gli piace	lee pee-**ah**-chay
WOULD LIKE		
I would like	io vorrei	**ee**-oh voh-**reh**-ee
you'd like (formal)	Lei vorrebbe	**leh**-ee voh-**reh**-bay
you'd like (informal)	tu vorresti	too voh-**reh**-stee
he / she would like	lui / lei vorrebbe	**loo**-ee / **leh**-ee voh-**reh**-bay
we'd like	noi vorremmo	**noh**-ee voh-**reh**-moh
you'd like (pl. formal)	voi vorreste	**voh**-ee voh-**reh**-stay
they'd like	loro vorrebbero	**loh**-roh voh-**reh**-beh-roh

TO MAKE	FARE	**fah**-ray
I make	io faccio	**ee**-oh **fah**-choh
you make (formal)	Lei fa	**leh**-ee fah
you make (informal)	tu fai	too **fah**-ee
he / she makes	lui / lei fa	**loo**-ee / **leh**-ee fah
we make	noi facciamo	**noh**-ee fah-chee-**ah**-moh
you make (pl. formal)	voi fate	**voh**-ee **fah**-tay
they make	loro fanno	**loh**-roh **fah**-noh

TO NEED	AVERE BISOGNO DI	ah-**veh**-ray bee-**zohn**-yoh dee
I need	io ho bisogno di	**ee**-oh oh bee-**zohn**-yoh dee
you need (formal)	Lei ha bisogno di	**leh**-ee ah bee-**zohn**-yoh dee
you need (informal)	tu hai bisogno di	too **ah**-ee bee-**zohn**-yoh dee
he / she needs	lui / lei ha bisogno di	**loo**-ee / **leh**-ee ah bee-**zohn**-yoh dee
we need	noi abbiamo bisogno di	**noh**-ee ah-bee-**ah**-moh bee-**zohn**-yoh dee
you need (pl. formal)	voi avete bisogno di	**voh**-ee ah-**veh**-tay bee-**zohn**-yoh dee
they need	loro hanno bisogno di	**loh**-roh **ahn**-noh bee-**zohn**-yoh dee

Italian Tongue Twisters

Tongue twisters are a great way to practice a language and break the ice with locals. Here are a few Italian tongue twisters (called ***scioglilingue,*** or "tongue melters") that are sure to challenge you—and amuse your hosts:

Trentatrè trentini arrivarono a Trento tutti e trentatrè trottorellando.	Thirty-three people from Trent arrived in Trent, all thirty-three trotting.
Chi fù quel barbaro barbuto che barbaramente sbarbò la barba ai barbari barbuti di Barbarossa?	Who was that bearded barbarian who brutally shaved the beard of the bearded barbarians of Barbarossa?

Sopra la panca la capra canta, sotto la panca la capra crepa.	On the bench the goat sings, under the bench the goat dies.
Tigre contro tigre.	Tiger against tiger.

English Tongue Twisters

After your Italian friends have laughed at you, let them try these tongue twisters in English.

If neither he sells seashells, nor she sells seashells, who shall sell seashells? Shall seashells be sold?	Se ne lui ne lei vende conchiglie chi vende conchiglie? Saranno vendute le conchiglie?
Peter Piper picked a peck of pickled peppers.	Pietro Piper ha colto una misura di due galloni di peperoni sottaceto.
Rugged rubber baby buggy bumpers.	Forte paraurti di gomma di carrozzelle.
The sixth sick sheik's sixth sheep's sick.	La sesta pecora del sesto sciecco ammalato è ammalata.
Red bug's blood and black bug's blood.	Il sangue del insetto rosso e il sangue del insetto nero.
Soldiers' shoulders.	Le spalle dei soldati.
Thieves seize skis.	I ladri afferano gli sci.
I'm a pleasant mother pheasant plucker. I pluck mother pheasants. I'm the most pleasant mother pheasant plucker that ever plucked a mother pheasant.	Io sono uno[a] spennatore / trice di fagiani femmine piacevole. Io spenno fagiani femmine. Sono il / la più piacevole spennatore / trice di fagiani femmine che abbia mai spennato un fagiano femmina.

APPENDIX

LET'S TALK TELEPHONES

Smart travelers use the telephone to reserve or reconfirm rooms, get tourist information, reserve restaurants, confirm tour times, and phone home.

Dialing Within Italy

Italy has a direct-dial phone system (without area codes). That means all phone numbers can be dialed direct throughout the country. For example, the number of one of my recommended hotels in Florence is 055-289-592. That's exactly what you dial, whether you're calling it from across the street or across the country.

Italy's landlines start with 0, and mobile lines start with 3. The country's toll-free lines begin with 80. These 80 numbers—called *freephone* or *numero verde* (green number)—can be dialed free from any phone without using a phone card. Any Italian phone number that starts with 8 but isn't followed by a 0 is a toll call.

Italian phone numbers vary in length; a hotel can have, say, an eight-digit phone number and a nine-digit fax number.

For more information, see www.ricksteves.com/phoning.

Dialing Internationally

If you want to make an international call, follow these steps:

• Dial the international access code (00 if you're calling from Europe, 011 from the US or Canada). If you're dialing from a mobile phone, you can replace the international access code with +, which works regardless of where you're calling from. (On many mobile phones, you can insert a + by pressing and holding the 0 key.)

• Dial the country code ***(prefisso per il paese)*** of the country you're calling (for example, 39 for Italy, or 1 for the US or Canada; see the chart on the next page).

• If the country you're calling uses area codes, dial the area code ***(prefisso),*** then dial the local number, keeping in mind that you may need to drop the initial zero of the phone number. If the country you're calling *doesn't* use area codes (like Italy), just dial the local number (and for Italy, you include the initial zero of the local number).

Calling from the US to Italy: Dial 011 (the US international access code), 39 (Italy's country code), then the Italian phone number. For example, if you're calling the Florence hotel cited earlier, you'd dial 011-39-055-289-592.

Calling from any European country to the US: To call my office in Edmonds, Washington, from anywhere in Europe, I dial 00 (Europe's international access code), 1 (the US country code), 425 (Edmonds' area code), and 771-8303.

European Country Codes	
Austria	43
Belgium	32
Bosnia-Herzegovina	387
Croatia	385
Czech Republic	420
Denmark	45
Estonia	372
Finland	358
France	33
Germany	49
Gibraltar	350
Great Britain	44
Greece	30
Hungary	36
Iceland	354
Ireland & N. Ireland	353 / 44
Italy	39
Latvia	371
Montenegro	382
Morocco	212
Netherlands	31
Norway	47
Poland	48
Portugal	351
Russia	7
Slovakia	421
Slovenia	386
Spain	34
Sweden	46
Switzerland	41
Turkey	90

Embassies

US Embassy: 24-hour emergency line—tel. 06-46741, non-emergency—tel. 06-4674-2420; Via Vittorio Veneto 121, Rome, http://italy.usembassy.gov.

Canadian Embassy: Tel. 06-854-442-911; Via Zara 30, Rome, www.italy.gc.ca

NUMBERS AND STUMBLERS

- Europeans write a few of their numbers differently than we do. 1= 1, 4= 4, 7= 7.
- In Europe, dates appear as day/month/year.
- Commas are decimal points and decimals are commas. A dollar and a half is 1,50, one thousand is 1.000, and there are 5.280 feet in a mile.
- When counting with your fingers, start with your thumb. If you hold up only your first finger to request one item, you'll probably get two.
- What Americans call the second floor of a building is the first floor in Europe.
- On escalators and moving sidewalks, Europeans keep the left "lane" open for passing. Keep to the right.

Metric Conversions

A kilogram is 2.2 pounds, and l liter is about a quart, or almost four to a gallon. A kilometer is six-tenths of a mile. I figure kilometers to miles by cutting the kilometers in half and adding back 10 percent of the original (120 km: 60 + 12 = 72 miles, 300 km: 150 + 30 = 180 miles).

Temperature Conversion

For a rough conversion from Celsius to Fahrenheit, double the number and add 30. For weather, remember that 28°C is 82°F—perfect. For health, 37°C is just right.

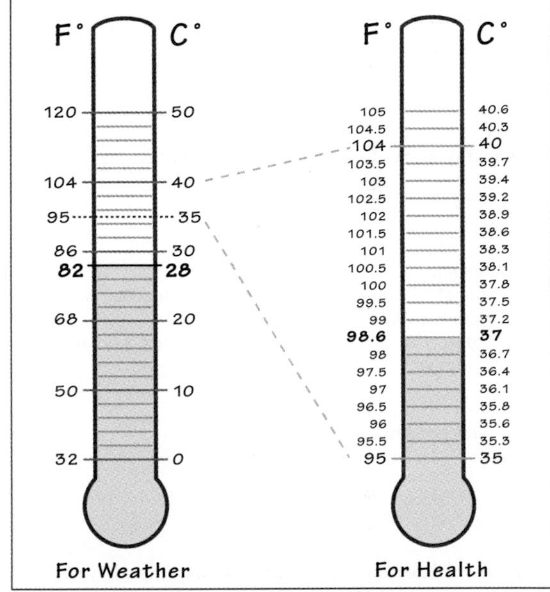

FILLING OUT FORMS

Signore	Mr.
Signora	Mrs.
Signorina	Miss
nome	first name
cognome	last name
indirizzo / domicilio	address
strada	street
città	city
stato	state
paese	country
nazionalità	nationality
origine / destinazione	origin / destination
età	age
data di nascita	date of birth
luogo di nascita	place of birth
sesso	sex
maschio / femmina	male / female
sposato / sposata (also coniugato / coniugata)	married man / married woman
scapolo / nubile	single man / single woman
divorziato / vedovo	divorced / widowed
professione	profession
adulto	adult
bambino / ragazzo / ragazza	child / boy / girl
bambini	children
famiglia	family
firma	signature
data	date

When filling out dates, do it European-style: day/month/year.

TEAR-OUT CHEAT SHEETS

Basics

Tear out this sheet of Italian survival phrases and keep it in your pocket to use in case you're caught without your phrase book.

Good day.	Buongiorno. bwohn-**jor**-noh
Mr.	Signore seen-**yoh**-ray
Mrs.	Signora seen-**yoh**-rah
Miss	Signorina seen-yoh-**ree**-nah
Do you speak English?	Parla inglese? **par**-lah een-**gleh**-zay
Yes. / No.	Si. / No. see / noh
I don't speak Italian.	Non parlo l'italiano. nohn **par**-loh lee-tah-lee-**ah**-noh
I'm sorry.	Mi dispiace. mee dee-spee-**ah**-chay
Please.	Per favore. pehr fah-**voh**-ray
Thank you.	Grazie. **graht**-see-ay
You're welcome.	Prego. **preh**-goh
Excuse me. (to get attention)	Mi scusi. mee **skoo**-zee
Excuse me. (to pass)	Permesso. pehr-**meh**-soh
It's not a problem.	Non c'è problema. nohn cheh proh-**bleh**-mah
Good.	Bene. **beh**-nay
Goodbye.	Arrivederci. ah-ree-veh-**dehr**-chee
How much (does it cost)?	Quanto (costa)? **kwahn**-toh (**koh**-stah)
Write it for me?	Me lo scrive? may loh **skree**-vay
euro (€)	euro eh-**oo**-roh
zero	zero **zeh**-roh
one / two	uno / due **oo**-noh / **doo**-ay
three / four	tre / quattro tray / **kwah**-troh

five / six	cinque / sei **cheen**-kway / **seh**-ee
seven / eight	sette / otto **seh**-tay / **oh**-toh
nine / ten	nove / dieci **noh**-vay / dee-**eh**-chee
Can you help me?	Può aiutarmi? pwoh ah-yoo-**tar**-mee
I'd like / We'd like...	Vorrei / Vorremmo... voh-**reh**-ee / voh-**reh**-moh
...that.	...quello. **kweh**-loh
...a ticket.	...un biglietto. oon beel-**yeh**-toh
...the bill.	...il conto. eel **kohn**-toh
Where is a cash machine?	Dov'è un bancomat? doh-**veh** oon **bahn**-koh-maht
Where is the toilet?	Dov'è la toilette? doh-**veh** lah twah-**leh**-tay
men	uomini / signori **woh**-mee-nee / seen-**yoh**-ree
women	donne / signore **doh**-nay / seen-**yoh**-ray
Is it free?	È gratis? eh **grah**-tees
Is it included?	È incluso? eh een-**kloo**-zoh
Is it possible?	È possibile? eh poh-**see**-bee-lay
entrance / exit	entrata / uscita ehn-**trah**-tah / oo-**shee**-tah
What time does this open / close?	A che ora apre / chiude? ah kay **oh**-rah **ah**-pray / kee-**oo**-day
now / soon / later	adesso / presto / più tardi ah-**deh**-soh / **preh**-stoh / pew **tar**-dee
today / tomorrow	oggi / domani **oh**-jee / doh-**mah**-nee
Sunday	domenica doh-**meh**-nee-kah
Monday	lunedì loo-neh-**dee**
Tuesday	martedì mar-teh-**dee**
Wednesday	mercoledì mehr-koh-leh-**dee**
Thursday	giovedì joh-veh-**dee**
Friday	venerdì veh-nehr-**dee**
Saturday	sabato **sah**-bah-toh

Restaurants

I'd like / We'd like...	Vorrei / Vorremmo... voh-**reh**-ee / voh-**reh**-moh
...to reserve...	...prenotare... preh-noh-**tah**-ray
...a table for one / two.	...un tavolo per uno / due. oon **tah**-voh-loh pehr **oo**-noh / **doo**-ay
Is this table free?	È libero questo tavolo? eh **lee**-beh-roh **kweh**-stoh **tah**-voh-loh
How long is the wait?	Quanto c'è da aspettare? **kwahn**-toh cheh dah ah-speh-**tah**-ray
The menu (in English), please.	Il menù (in inglese), per favore. eel meh-**noo** (een een-**gleh**-zay) pehr fah-**voh**-ray
breakfast	colazione koh-laht-see-**oh**-nay
lunch	pranzo **prahnt**-soh
dinner	cena **cheh**-nah
service (not) included	servizio (non) incluso sehr-**veet**-see-oh (nohn) een-**kloo**-zoh
cover charge	coperto koh-**pehr**-toh
to go	da portar via dah por-**tar vee**-ah
with / without	con / senza kohn / **sehnt**-sah
and / or	e / o ay / oh
fixed-price menu	menù fisso meh-**noo fee**-soh
daily specials	piatti del giorno pee-**ah**-tee dehl **jor**-noh
specialty of the house	specialità della casa speh-chah-lee-**tah deh**-lah **kah**-zah
What do you recommend?	Che cosa raccomanda? kay **koh**-zah rah-koh-**mahn**-dah
appetizers	antipasti ahn-tee-**pah**-stee
first course(s) (pasta, soup)	primo piatto / primi **pree**-moh pee-**ah**-toh / **pree**-mee
main course(s) (meat, fish)	secondo piatto / secondi seh-**kohn**-doh pee-**ah**-toh / seh **kohn**-dee

bread	pane **pah**-nay
cheese	formaggio for-**mah**-joh
sandwich	panino pah-**nee**-noh
soup	zuppa **tsoo**-pah
salad	insalata een-sah-**lah**-tah
meat	carni **kar**-nee
chicken	pollo **poh**-loh
fish	pesce **peh**-shay
seafood	frutti di mare **froo**-tee dee **mah**-ray
vegetables	verdure vehr-**doo**-ray
fruit	frutta **froo**-tah
dessert	dolce **dohl**-chay
mineral water	acqua minerale **ah**-kwah mee-neh-**rah**-lay
tap water	acqua del rubinetto **ah**-kwah dehl roo-bee-**neh**-toh
milk	latte **lah**-tay
coffee / tea	caffè / tè kah-**feh** / teh
wine	vino **vee**-noh
red / white	rosso / bianco **roh**-soh / bee-**ahn**-koh
glass / bottle	bicchiere / bottiglia bee-kee-**eh**-ray / boh-**teel**-yah
beer	birra **bee**-rah
Cheers!	Cin cin! cheen cheen
More. / Another.	Di più. / Un altro. dee pew / oon **ahl**-troh
The same.	Lo stesso. loh **steh**-soh
Finished.	Finito. fee-**nee**-toh
The bill, please.	Il conto, per favore. eel **kohn**-toh pehr fah-**voh**-ray
Do you accept credit cards?	Accettate carte di credito? ah-cheh-**tah**-tay **kar**-tay dee **kreh**-dee-toh
tip	mancia **mahn**-chah
Delicious!	Delizioso! deh-leet-see-**oh**-zoh

The perfect complement to your phrase book

Travel with Rick Steves' candid, up-to-date advice on the best places to eat and sleep, the must-see sights, getting off the beaten path—and getting the most out of every day and every dollar while you're in Europe.

Start your trip at

Our website enhances this book and turns

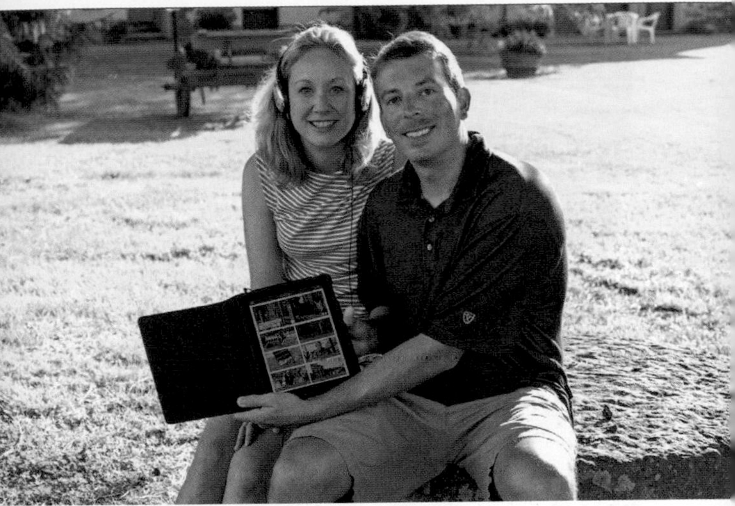

Explore Europe

At ricksteves.com you can browse through thousands of articles, videos, photos and radio interviews, plus find a wealth of money-saving travel tips for planning your dream trip. And with our mobile-friendly website, you can easily access all this great travel information anywhere you go.

TV Shows

Preview the places you'll visit by watching entire half-hour episodes of Rick Steves' Europe (choose from all 100 shows) on-demand, for free.

ricksteves.com

your travel dreams into affordable reality

Radio Interviews

Enjoy ready access to Rick's vast library of radio interviews covering travel tips and cultural insights that relate specifically to your Europe travel plans.

Travel Forums

Learn, ask, share! Our online community of savvy travelers is a great resource for first-time travelers to Europe, as well as seasoned pros.

Travel News

Subscribe to our free Travel News e-newsletter, and get monthly updates from Rick on what's happening in Europe.

Classroom Europe

Check out our free resource for educators with 300+ short video clips from the Rick Steves' Europe TV show.

Audio Europe™

Rick Steves AUDIO EUROPE

Rick's Free Travel App

Get your FREE **Rick Steves Audio Europe**™ app to enjoy...

- Dozens of self-guided tours of Europe's top museums, sights and historic walks
- Hundreds of tracks filled with cultural insights and sightseeing tips from Rick's radio interviews
- All organized into handy geographic playlists
- For Apple and Android

With Rick whispering in your ear, Europe gets even better.

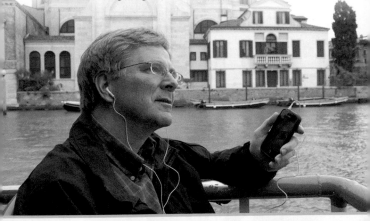

Find out more at ricksteves.com

Pack Light and Right

Gear up for your next adventure at ricksteves.com

Light Luggage

Pack light and right with Rick Steves' affordable, custom-designed rolling carry-on bags, backpacks, day packs and shoulder bags.

Accessories

From packing cubes to moneybelts and beyond, Rick has personally selected the travel goodies that will help your trip go smoother.

Shop at ricksteves.com

Rick Steves has

Experience maximum Europe

Rick Steves Tours

A Rick Steves tour takes you to Europe's most interesting places with great guides and small groups of 28 or less. We follow Rick's favorite itineraries, ride in comfy buses, stay in family-run hotels, and bring you intimately close to the Europe you've traveled so far to see. Most importantly, we take away the logistical headaches so you can focus on the fun.

great tours, too!

with minimum stress

Join the fun

This year we'll take thousands of free-spirited travelers—nearly half of them repeat customers—along with us on four dozen different itineraries, from Ireland to Italy to Istanbul. Is a Rick Steves tour the right fit for your travel dreams? Find out at ricksteves.com, where you can also request Rick's latest tour catalog.

Europe is best experienced with happy travel partners. We hope you can join us.

See our itineraries at ricksteves.com

A Guide for Every Trip

COMPREHENSIVE GUIDES

City, country, and regional guides printed on Bible-thin paper. Packed with detailed coverage for a multi-week trip exploring iconic sights and more

Amsterdam & the Netherlands
Barcelona
Belgium: Bruges, Brussels, Antwerp & Ghent
Berlin
Budapest
Croatia & Slovenia
Eastern Europe
England
Florence & Tuscany
France
Germany
Great Britain
Greece: Athens & the Peloponnese
Iceland
Ireland
Istanbul
Italy
London
Paris
Portugal
Prague & the Czech Republic
Provence & the French Riviera
Rome
Scandinavia
Scotland
Sicily
Spain
Switzerland
Venice
Vienna, Salzburg & Tirol

POCKET GUIDES

Compact guides for shorter city trips

Amsterdam
Athens
Barcelona
Florence
Italy's Cinque Terre
London
Munich & Salzburg
Paris
Prague
Rome
Venice
Vienna

BEST OF GUIDES

Full-color guides in an easy-to-scan format, focusing on top sights and experiences in popular destinations

Best of England
Best of Europe
Best of France
Best of Germany
Best of Ireland
Best of Italy
Best of Scotland
Best of Spain

CRUISE PORTS GUIDES

Reference for cruise ports of call

Mediterranean Cruise Ports
Scandinavian & Northern European Cruise Ports

TRAVEL SKILLS & CULTURE

Greater information and insight

Europe 101: History and Art for the Traveler
Europe Through the Back Door: the Travel Skills Handbook
European Christmas
European Easter
European Festivals
Postcards from Europe
Travel as a Political Act

PHRASE BOOKS & DICTIONARIES

French
French, Italian & German
German
Italian
Portuguese
Spanish

PLANNING MAPS

Britain, Ireland & London
Europe
France & Paris
Germany, Austria & Switzerland
Iceland
Ireland
Italy
Spain & Portugal

Also available: Snapshot Guides featuring focused single-destination coverage

Avalon Travel
Hachette Book Group
1700 Fourth Street, Berkeley, CA 94710

Text © 2019 by Rick Steves' Europe, Inc. All rights reserved.
Maps © 2019 by Rick Steves' Europe, Inc. All rights reserved.

Printed in China by RR Donnelley.

Eighth Edition.
First printing September 2019.

ISBN 978-1-64171-196-8

For the latest on Rick's talks, guidebooks, tours, public television series, and public radio show, contact Rick Steves' Europe, 130 Fourth Avenue North, Edmonds, WA 98020, 425/771-8303, www.ricksteves.com, rick@ricksteves.com.

Hachette Book Group supports the right to free expression and the value of copyright. The purpose of copyright is to encourage writers and artists to produce the creative works that enrich our culture. The scanning, uploading, and distribution of this book without permission is a theft of the author's intellectual property. If you would like permission to use material from the book (other than for review purposes), please contact permissions@hbgusa.com. Thank you for your support of the author's rights.

The publisher is not responsible for websites (or their content) that are not owned by the publisher.

Avalon Travel
Hachette Book Group
1700 Fourth Street, Berkeley, CA 94710

Text © 2019 by Rick Steves' Europe, Inc. All rights reserved.
Maps © 2019 by Rick Steves' Europe, Inc. All rights reserved.

Printed in China by RR Donnelley.

Eighth Edition.
First printing September 2019.

ISBN: 978-1-64171-196-8

For the latest on Rick's talks, guidebooks, tours, public television series, and public radio show, contact Rick Steves' Europe, 130 Fourth Avenue North, Edmonds, WA 98020, 425/771-8303, www.ricksteves.com, rick@ricksteves.com.

Hachette Book Group supports the right to free expression and the value of copyright. The purpose of copyright is to encourage writers and artists to produce the creative works that enrich our culture. The scanning, uploading, and distribution of this book without permission is a theft of the author's intellectual property. If you would like permission to use material from the book (other than for review purposes), please contact permissions@hbgusa.com. Thank you for your support of the author's rights.

The publisher is not responsible for websites (or their content) that are not owned by the publisher.

Let's Keep on Travelin'

Your trip doesn't need to end.

Follow Rick on social media!

Rick Steves' Europe
Managing Editor: Jennifer Madison Davis
Assistant Managing Editor: Cathy Lu
Special Publications Manager: Risa Laib
Editors: Glenn Eriksen, Tom Griffin, Suzanne Kotz, Rosie Leutzinger, Jessica Shaw, Carrie Shepherd
Editorial & Production Assistant: Megan Simms
Translation: Francesca Caruso, Heidi Van Sewell
Lead Researcher: Cameron Hewitt **Research Assistance:** Tommaso Fuzier Cayla, Julie Coen, Luca Martilli, Paola Migliorini, Kelly Raye
Graphic Content Director: Sandra Hundacker
Maps & Graphics: David C. Hoerlein, Lauren Mills, Mary Rostad
Digital Asset Coordinator: Orin Dubrow

Avalon Travel
Senior Editor and Series Manager: Madhu Prasher
Editors: Jamie Andrade, Sierra Machado
Proofreader: Kelly Lydick
Cover Design: Kimberly Glyder Design
Interior Design: McGuire Barber Design
Production: Christine DeLorenzo
Maps & Graphics: Kat Bennett, Mike Morgenfeld

Photography: Dominic Arizona Bonuccelli, Rick Steves
Front Cover Photo © PK-Photos/Getty Images
Title page © gail221/istockphoto.com

Although every effort was made to ensure that the information was correct at the time of going to press, the author and publisher do not assume and hereby disclaim any liability to any party for any loss or damage caused by errors, omissions, overcooked pasta, or any potential travel disruption due to labor or financial difficulty, whether such errors or omissions result from negligence, accident, or any other cause.